Risk Management and Analysis

VOLUME 1: MEASURING AND MODELLING FINANCIAL RISK

OTHER TITLES IN THE WILEY SERIES IN FINANCIAL ENGINEERING

INTEREST-RATE OPTION MODELS, Second Edition
Riccardo Rebonato

STRUCTURED SECURITIES FOR INVESTMENT PROFESSIONALS
John C. Braddock

MANAGING CREDIT RISK
John B. Caouette

MANAGING DERIVATIVE RISK
Lillian Chew

DYNAMIC HEDGING
Nassim Taleb

DERIVATIVES FOR DECISION MAKERS
George Crawford and Bidyut Sen

Risk Management and Analysis

VOLUME 1: MEASURING AND MODELLING FINANCIAL RISK

Edited by Carol Alexander

JOHN WILEY & SONS

Chichester • New York • Weinheim • Brisbane • Singapore • Toronto

#39122685

Other Wiley Editorial Offices

John Wiley & Sons, Inc., 605 Third Avenue,
New York, NY 10158-0012, USA

WILEY-VCH Verlag GmbH, Pappelallee 3,
D-69469 Weinheim, Germany

Jacaranda Wiley Ltd, 33 Park Road, Milton,
Queensland 4064, Australia

John Wiley & Sons (Canada) Ltd, 22 Worcester Road,
Rexdale, Ontario M9W 1L1, Canada

John Wiley & Sons (Asia) Pte Ltd, 2 Clementi Loop #02-01,
Jin Xing Distripark, Singapore 129809

Library of Congress Cataloging-in-Publication Data

Risk management and analysis. Volume 1: Measuring and modelling financial risk / edited by Carol Alexander.
p.   cm. — (Wiley series in financial engineering)
Includes bibliographical references and index.
ISBN 0-471-97957-0 (alk. paper)
1. Financial futures.   2. Risk management.   3. Bank capital.
I. Alexander, Carol.   II. Series.
HG6024.3.R57   1998
332.64'5 — dc21   98-24147
CIP

British Library Cataloguing in Publication Data

A catalogue record for this book is available from the British Library

ISBN 0 471 97957 0

Typeset in 10/12pt Times by Laser Words, Madras, India
Printed and bound in Great Britain by Biddles Ltd, Guildford and King's Lynn.
This book is printed on acid-free paper responsibly manufactured from sustainable forestation,
for which at least two trees are planted for each one used.

Contents

List of Contributors   xi

About the Contributors   xiii

Preface   xix

Foreword   xxi

1 The New 1998 Regulatory Framework for Capital Adequacy: "Standardized Approach" versus "Internal Models", Michel Crouhy, Dan Galai, and Robert Mark   **1**

1.1   Introduction   1

1.2   The 1988 BIS Accord: The "Accord"   2

     1.2.1   The Assets to Capital Multiple   3

     1.2.2   The Risk-Weighted Amount Used to Compute the Cooke Ratio   3

     1.2.3   Calculation of the Credit Equivalent for Off-Balance-Sheet Exposures   4

     1.2.4   Netting of Derivatives Positions   6

     1.2.5   Capital and the Cooke Ratio   6

1.3   The 1995 BIS Market Risk proposal: The "1996 Amendment"   7

     1.3.1   Issues Regarding the Adoption of the Internal Models Approach   9

     1.3.2   Qualitative Requirements   9

     1.3.3   Quantitative and Modelling Requirements   10

     1.3.4   Specific Risk   12

     1.3.5   New Capital Requirements   14

     1.3.6   Back Testing   15

     1.3.7   Stress Testing   16

1.4   The Standardized Approach   17

     1.4.1   Interest Rate Risk   17

     1.4.2   Equity Risk   23

	1.4.3	Foreign Exchange Risk, Including Gold Price Risk	23
	1.4.4	Commodities Risk	24
1.5		The Pros and Cons of the Standardized Approach and the Internal Models: A New Proposal — The "Pre-Commitment Approach"	25
1.6		Comparisons of the Capital Charges for Various Portfolios According to the Standardized and the Internal Models Approaches	27
1.7		Endnotes	34
1.8		References	36

2 A Survey of Risk Measurement Theory and Practice, Stan Beckers **39**

2.1		Introduction	39
2.2		The Basics	40
	2.2.1	Markowitz and the Principle of Diversification	40
	2.2.2	Sharpe and the Distinction Between Systematic and Residual Risk	41
2.3		Multiple Factor Models	44
	2.3.1	Fundamental Factor Models	45
	2.3.2	Macroeconomic Factor Models	47
	2.3.3	Statistical Models	47
	2.3.4	A Comparison	48
2.4		Absolute Versus Relative Risk	48
	2.4.1	The Role of the Benchmark	48
	2.4.2	The Notion of Tracking Error	50
	2.4.3	Concluding Remarks	52
2.5		International Portfolio Diversification	53
	2.5.1	Integration versus Segmentation	53
	2.5.2	The Problem of Currency Risk	55
	2.5.3	Concluding Remarks	57
2.6		Conclusion	57
2.7		Endnotes	58
2.8		References	60

3 Value at Risk, Thomas C. Wilson **61**

3.1		Introduction	61
3.2		Uses of VaR	62
	3.2.1	Why Can VaR Have an Impact?	62
	3.2.2	Where is VaR *Unlikely* to Have Impact?	64
	3.2.3	Preconditions for a VaR Impact: More Than Numbers	65
	3.2.4	Three Preconditions for a VaR Impact	66
3.3		Calculating Market VaR	69
	3.3.1	Measurement Issues	69
	3.3.2	Internal Models	78
	3.3.3	"Linear" Methods	78
	3.3.4	Non-Linear Methods	85
3.4		Calculating Credit VaR	103
	3.4.1	Measurement Issues	103
	3.4.2	Comparison of Different Methods	118

3.5	Acknowledgements	121
3.6	Endnotes	121
3.7	References	123

4 Volatility and Correlation: Measurement, Models and Applications, Carol Alexander **125**

4.1	Introduction	125
4.2	Moving Averages	127
	4.2.1 "Historic Methods"	127
	4.2.2 Exponentially Weighted Moving Averages	129
	4.2.3 Volatility Term Structures in Moving Average Models: The Square Root of Time Rule	132
4.3	GARCH Models in Finance	133
	4.3.1 Introduction	133
	4.3.2 A Survey of GARCH Volatility Models	136
	4.3.3 GARCH Volatility Term Structure Forecasts	140
	4.3.4 Estimating GARCH Models: Methods and Results	141
	4.3.5 Choosing the Data Period and the Appropriate GARCH Model	144
	4.3.6 Multivariate GARCH	145
	4.3.7 Generating Large GARCH Covariance Matrices: Orthogonal GARCH	147
4.4	"Implied" Volatility and Correlation	148
	4.4.1 Black–Scholes Implied Volatility	149
	4.4.2 Implied Correlation	150
4.5	A Short Survey of Applications to Measuring Market Risk	151
	4.5.1 Factor Models	151
	4.5.2 Capital Allocation	152
	4.5.3 Option Pricing and Hedging	154
	4.5.4 Value-at-Risk Models	155
4.6	Special Issues and New Directions	158
	4.6.1 Evaluating Volatility and Correlation Forecasts	158
	4.6.2 Modelling "Fat-Tailed" Distributions	159
	4.6.3 Downside Risk and Expected Maximum Loss	161
	4.6.4 Cointegration	162
4.7	Conclusion	165
4.8	Acknowledgements	165
4.9	Endnotes	166
4.10	References	168

5 Simulation for Option Pricing and Risk Management, Mark Broadie and Paul Glasserman **173**

5.1	Introduction	173
5.2	Underlying Processes	173
5.3	Generating Paths	176
	5.3.1 Random Number Generation	176
	5.3.2 Random Variables and Vectors	177

	5.3.3	Basic Path Generation	180
	5.3.4	Computing Payoffs	182
5.4	Improved Path Generation and Estimation		183
	5.4.1	Antithetics	183
	5.4.2	Stratification	186
	5.4.3	Matching the Underlying	189
	5.4.4	Control Variates	192
5.5	Quasi Monte Carlo		196
5.6	Estimating Value at Risk		202
	5.6.1	Covariance Solution	203
	5.6.2	Historical Simulation	204
	5.6.3	Monte Carlo Simulation with Full Revaluation	204
	5.6.4	Monte Carlo Simulation with Interpolation	204
5.7	Endnotes		205
5.8	References		206

6   An Introduction to the Technology of Risk, Nigel Webb   **209**
6.1	Introduction		209
6.2	Functional Requirements		209
	6.2.1	The Front Office Requirement	210
	6.2.2	The Middle Office Requirement	212
	6.2.3	The Back Office Requirement	214
	6.2.4	Key Design Considerations	215
	6.2.5	A Final Note on Organizational Structure	215
6.3	Designing Risk Systems		215
	6.3.1	The Risk Management System	216
	6.3.2	Risk Control Systems	216
6.4	The Risk Technology Industry		221
	6.4.1	The Two Types of Software Vendor	221
	6.4.2	The Way Forward for the Technology Vendors	222

**7   Mark-to-Future™: A Consistent Firm-Wide Paradigm for Measuring
Risk and Return, Ron S. Dembo**   **225**
7.1	Introduction	225
7.2	A Paradigm for Measuring Risk	226
7.3	Mark-to-Future™	229
7.4	Regret: An Ideal Measure of Risk	231
7.5	Accounting for the Upside	233
7.6	Risk-Adjusted Valuation	233
7.7	Trading-Off Risk and Return	234
7.8	Conclusion	235
7.9	Notes	236
7.10	References	236

8   Credit Risk, Robert Jarrow and Stuart Turnbull   **237**
| 8.1 | Introduction | 237 |
| 8.2 | Pricing Credit Risky Bonds | 237 |

	8.2.1	Lattice of Default-free Interest Rates	238
	8.2.2	Risky Debt	239
	8.2.3	Credit Risky Debt	240
8.3	Pricing Options on Credit Risky Bonds		245
8.4	Pricing Vulnerable Derivatives		248
	8.4.1	Formalization	249
	8.4.2	Example	251
8.5	Credit Default Swap		251
8.6	Summary		253
8.7	Endnotes		254
8.8	References		254

9 Credit Enhancement, Lee Wakeman **255**

9.1	Introduction		255
9.2	The Basic Credit Model		256
9.3	Credit Exposure Modifiers		256
	9.3.1	Modelling Credit Exposure	256
	9.3.2	Collateral Arrangements	259
	9.3.3	Recouponing	260
	9.3.4	Netting	261
9.4	Default Modifiers		262
	9.4.1	Credit Guarantees	265
	9.4.2	Credit Triggers	265
9.5	Mutual Termination Options		266
9.6	Recovery Rates		267
9.7	Examples		268
9.8	Implementation		271
	9.8.1	Legal Considerations	271
	9.8.2	Economic Considerations	271
9.9	Conclusion		272
	9.9.1	Incentives for Marketers	273
	9.9.2	Role of the Credit Officer	274
9.10	Endnotes/References		274

Index   **277**

List of Contributors

CAROL ALEXANDER
University of Sussex, Brighton, UK

STAN BECKERS
Barra International, London, UK

MARK BROADIE
Graduate School of Business, Columbia University, New York, USA

MICHEL CROUHY
Canadian Imperial Bank of Commerce, Toronto, Canada

RON DEMBO
Algorithmics Inc., Toronto, Canada

DAN GALAI
Hebrew University, Jerusalem, Israel

PAUL GLASSERMAN
Graduate School of Business, Columbia University, New York, USA

ROBERT JARROW
Johnson Graduate School of Management, Cornell University, New York, USA

ROBERT MARK
Canadian Imperial Bank of Commerce, Toronto, Canada

STUART TURNBULL
Queen's University, Kingston, Canada

LEE WAKEMAN
Darien, Connecticut, USA

NIGEL WEBB
Greenwich NatWest, London, UK

THOMAS C. WILSON
McKinsey & Company, New York, USA

About the Contributors

CAROL ALEXANDER

Carol Alexander obtained her Ph.D. in Algebraic Number Theory, and then worked at the Gemente Universiteit in Amsterdam and at UBS Phillips and Drew in London before joining the Mathematics faculty of the University of Sussex in 1985. She holds a B.Sc. in Mathematics with Experimental Psychology and an M.Sc. in Econometrics and Mathematical Economics from the London School of Economics. Since 1990 she has been consulting, training, speaking at conferences, writing books and articles and developing software in the areas of risk management and investment analysis. In 1996 she became the academic director of Algorithmics Inc. and in 1998 she eventually left the academic world to join Nikko Global Holdings as Director and Head of Market Risk Modelling. However, she retains a visiting fellowship at the University of Sussex.

STAN BECKERS

Stan Beckers received his Ph.D. in Finance from the University of California, Berkeley. He is President of BARRA International, Ltd. Stan started BARRA's international operations in London in November 1982 after having worked as a consultant to BARRA for four years. Since 1997 he has been in charge of BARRA's Institutional Analytics Division. Previously, Stan was Senior Economist at Chase Econometric Associates in Philadelphia. He has published articles on a wide range of international investment topics and frequently speaks at financial industry practitioner forums. Stan is currently a professor of Finance at the K.U. Leuven (Belgium), and at various times Stan has taught at the University of California, the European Institute for Advanced Studies in Management (Brussels), London's City University Business School and the Free University of Amsterdam (The Netherlands).

MARK BROADIE

Mark Broadie is a professor at the Graduate School of Business at Columbia University. He received a B.S. from Cornell University and Ph.D. from Stanford University. His research focuses on problems in risk management, the pricing of derivative securities and portfolio optimization. Professor Broadie is an associate editor of *Management Science, Mathematical Finance* and a founding co-editor of the *Journal of Computational Finance*.

He has done extensive consulting for financial firms and previously he was a vice president at Lehman Brothers in their fixed-income research group.

MICHEL CROUHY

Dr Michel Crouhy is Senior Vice President, Global Analytics, Market Risk Management Division, at the Canadian Imperial Bank of Commerce (CIBC). His responsibilities include the approval of all pricing models used in trading and for P&L calculation, the development of risk management methodologies as well as the implementation of the VaR model of market risk and credit risk, the implementation of the financial rates database for the bank and the production of statistical and econometric studies related to risk management and model calibration. Prior to his current position at CIBC, Michel Crouhy was Professor of Finance at the HEC School of Management where he was also Director of M.S. HEC in International Finance. He has been a visiting professor at the Wharton School and at UCLA. Dr Crouhy holds a Ph.D. from the Wharton School and is a graduate from Ecole National des Ponts et Chaussées, France. He has published extensively in academic journals across the areas of banking, options and financial markets, and is editor of the collection *Banque & Bourse* at Presses Universitaires de France. He is also associate editor of *The Journal of Derivatives*, the *Journal of Banking and Finance*, and *Financial Engineering and the Japanese Markets*. He is a board member of the European Institute for Advanced Studies in Management (AIMS), Brussels. He has also served as a consultant to major financial institutions in Europe and in the United States in the areas of quantitative portfolio management, risk management, valuation and hedging of derivative products, forecasting volatility term structure and correlations.

RON DEMBO

Dr Ron S. Dembo is President and Chief Executive Officer of Algorithmics Inc., a leading provider of innovative enterprise-wide financial risk management software, which he founded in 1989. For the past nine years, Algorithmics has pioneered financial risk management solutions with an impressive array of products. Before founding Algorithmics, Dr Dembo created and managed a group at Goldman Sachs responsible for fixed income optimization modelling. Prior to that, he had a distinguished academic career and served on the faculties of several universities. From 1976 to 1986, he served as an assistant and associate professor of Operations Research in Computer Science at Yale University and as a visiting professor for Operations Research at the Massachusetts Institute of Technology. Dr Dembo has written and published over 50 technical papers on Finance and Mathematical Optimization and holds two trademark patents for Portfolio Replication. Currently, he is an adjunct professor for Operations Research at the University of Toronto. He is also the founder of *NetExposure*, the electronic journal of financial risk. His latest book on risk, *Seeing Tomorrow*, which he co-authored with Andrew Freeman, explains how to apply risk management to everyday life and business decisions. Dr Dembo holds several degrees, including a B.Sc. in Engineering from the University of Witwatersrand, Johannesburg (1969), an M.Sc. in Chemical Engineering from the Technion-Israel Institute of Technology (1972), and a Ph.D. in Operations Research from the University of Waterloo, Ontario (1975). He also received a Diploma in French Civilization and Language from the Sorbonne University in 1972.

DAN GALAI

Dan Galai is the Abe Gray Professor of Finance and Business Administration at the Hebrew University School of Business Administration in Jerusalem. He was a visiting professor of Finance at INSEAD and has also taught at the University of California, Los Angeles, and the University of Chicago. Dr Galai holds a Ph.D. from the Univeristy of Chicago and undergraduate and graduate degrees from the Hebrew University. He has served as a consultant for the Chicago Board of Options Exchange and the American Stock Exchange as well as for major banks. He has published numerous articles in leading business and finance journals, on options, financial assets and corporate finance, and was a winner of the First Annual Pomeranze Prize for excellence in options research presented by CBOE. Dr Galai is a principal in SIMGA P.C.M., which is engaged in portfolio management and corporate finance.

PAUL GLASSERMAN

Paul Glasserman is a professor in the Columbia University Graduate School of Business. He earned an A.B. in Mathematics from Princeton University in 1984 and a Ph.D. in Applied Mathematics from Harvard University in 1988. From 1988 to 1991 he was with Bell Laboratories, and in 1991 he joined the Columbia faculty. His research focuses on computational methods for the pricing and hedging of derivative securities and for risk management, particularly the development of efficient Monte Carlo methods. Professor Glasserman is a recipient of a National Young Investigator Award from the US National Science Foundation, of the Erlang Prize in Applied Probability, and of the Outstanding Simulation Publication Award of the Institute for Management Science.

ROBERT JARROW

Robert Jarrow is the Ronald P. and Susan E. Lynch Professor of Investment Management at the Johnson Graduate School of Management, Cornell University. He is also a managing director and Director of Research at Kamakura Corporation. He is the 1997 IAFE/SunGard Financial Engineer of the year. He is a graduate of Duke University, Dartmouth College and the Massachusetts Institute of Technology. Professor Jarrow is renowned for his pioneering work on the Heath–Jarrow–Morton model for pricing interest rate derivatives. His current research interests include the pricing of exotic interest rate options and credit derivatives as well as investment management theory. His publications include four books: *Options Pricing; Finance Theory; Modelling Fixed Income Securities and Interest Rate Options* and *Derivative Securities*, as well as over 65 publications in leading finance and economics journals. Professor Jarrow is currently co-editor of *Mathematical Finance* and an associate editor of: *The Journal of Financial and Quantitative Analysis; The Review of Derivatives Research; Journal of Fixed Income; The Financial Review; The Journal of Derivatives*; and *The Review of Futures Markets*. He is also an advisory editor for *Financial Engineering and the Japanese Markets*.

ROBERT MARK

Dr Robert M. Mark is an executive vice president at the Canadian Imperial Bank of Commerce (CIBC). His responsibilities at CIBC encompass corporate treasury and risk management functions. This is a CIBC-wide group that has global responsibility to cover all market trading related credit and operating risks for the wholesale and retail banks as well as for its subsidiaries. His corporate treasury responsibilities include actively managing the gap created by imbalances between interest rate repricings on assets and liabilities. His responsibilities also include managing the Risk MIS Analytics, Capital Attribution and Risk Advisory Units. Dr Mark works in partnership with CIBC managers and ensures that all risks are accurately measured, controlled and managed. He also approves credits and serves on the Senior Credit Committee of the bank. He was also appointed to the Board of CIBC Mortgage Corporation. Prior to his current position at CIBC, he was the partner in charge of the Financial Risk Management Consulting Practice at Cooper & Lybrand (C&L). The Risk Management Practice at C&L advised clients on market and credit risk management issues and was directed toward financial institutions and multinational corporations. This speciality area also co-ordinated the delivery of the firm's accounting, tax, control and litigation services to provide clients with integrated and comprehensive risk management solutions and opportunities. Prior to his position at C&L, he was a managing director in the Asia, Europe and Capital Markets Group (AECM) at Chemical Bank. His responsibilities within AECM encompassed risk management, asset/liability management, research (quantitative analysis, strategic planning and analytic systems). He served on the Senior Credit Committee of the bank. Before he joined Chemical Bank, he was a senior officer at Marine Bank/Hong Kong Shanghai Bank Group (HKSB), where he headed the technical analysis trading group within the capital markets sector. He earned his Ph.D. with a dissertation in options pricing from New York University's Graduate School of Engineering and Science, graduating first in his class. He subsequently received an Advanced Professional Certificate (APC) in accounting from NYU's Stern Graduate School of Business. He was also appointed Chairperson of the National Asset/Liability Management Association (NALMA), and an adjunct professor at NYU's Stern Graduate School of Business.

STUART TURNBULL

Stuart M. Turnbull is Bank of Montreal Professor of Banking and Finance, Queen's University (Canada), and a Research Fellow, Institute for Policy Analysis (Toronto). He is a graduate of the Imperial College of Science and Technology (London) and the University of British Columbia. He is the author of *Option Valuation*, and (with Robert A. Jarrow) *Derivative Securities*. He has published over 30 articles in major finance and economics journals, and in law and economics journals, as well as many articles in practitioner journals. His current research interests include the pricing of credit derivatives, exotic options, risk management and asset pricing theory. Professor Turnbull is an associate editor of *Mathematical Finance*, and the *Journal of Financial Engineering*, and has served as an associate editor for the *Journal of Finance*.

LEE WAKEMAN

Lee Macdonald Wakeman is currently a partner at Risk Analysis & Control Ltd, specializing in market and credit risk management. His previous positions include President of TMG Financial Products, Global Head of Trading at Sakura Global Capital, Managing Director in the Treasury Group at Continental Bank, and Head of Interest Rate Arbitrage at Chemical Bank. Prior to joining Citicorp as Head of Risk Management at CIBL, London, he was an associate professor of finance at the University of Rochester and a visiting professor at UCLA. He holds a BA from Cambridge University and a Ph.D. from MIT.

NIGEL WEBB

Nigel Webb is a Managing Director and Global Chief Operating Officer of Greenwich NatWest (GNW). In this role he is responsible for IT and operations across the institution. He joined GNW from Arthur Andersen in early 1998, where he was a partner in the firm's Financial Markets Division. During his time at Arthur Andersen, Nigel was responsible for consulting on, and implementing, numerous firm-wide risk management systems in Europe, North America and Asia. Nigel's career opened with the now legendary Drexel Burnham Lambert, where he was involved in the design and implementation of Bond trading systems. Subsequent career moves have seen him in a variety of roles, both business- and IT-orientated, with such institutions as Bankers Trust, Nomura International, and Digital Equipment Corporation. Nigel holds an Economics degree from the London School of Economics (LSE), and is married with a baby daughter.

THOMAS C. WILSON

Thomas C. Wilson is a partner in the New York office of McKinsey & Company, an international management consulting firm, and leads the firm's Global Risk Management Practice. Since joining the firm in 1990, he has worked almost exclusively with financial institutions, helping them better to create value from their risk intermediation, absorption and advisory businesses by focusing their risk/reward strategy, optimizing their structure and management processes and improving their information systems. During this time, he has been active with clients in the United States, Europe and the Far East and has published several articles on risk and performance measurement and management issues. Prior to joining McKinsey & Company, he worked at the Union Bank of Switzerland in Zurich as a trader and risk manager in their swaps department. He earned a Ph.D. in International Finance from Stanford University and a B.Sc. in Business Administration with an emphasis on Finance from the University of California at Berkeley.

Preface

In the two years since John Wiley published *The Handbook of Risk Management and Analysis*, interest in the management, modelling and control of financial risks has grown enormously. New geographical markets have emerged as more countries develop derivatives markets and place less restrictions on foreign trade. New products such as credit derivatives and exotic instruments for hedging market risk are being established very rapidly. Financial products such as loans, which, traditionally, have been on the banking book only, are now being structured and transformed into tradable instruments.

Currently, experience is of a revolution in risk management to become more quantitative in its approach to all risks. The new, more constraining, regulatory environment has prompted the rapid development of new methods for measuring and modelling financial risk. Financial institutions are setting new standards for risk control that require better pricing models and more stringent validation of all trading models. And recent changes in the rules for calculating risk capital charges have promoted the development of new risk systems, from data management to the internal models for measuring market and credit risk capital.

My initial intention in editing this work was to produce a second edition of the *Handbook*. But the subject has developed and expanded so much that only about one third of the original book remains. To reflect the division mentioned above, the new book, *Risk Management and Analysis*, is published in two volumes: Volume 1: *Measuring and Modelling Financial Risk* and Volume 2: *New Markets and Products*.

Measuring and Modelling Financial Risk has been structured in four parts: the first three chapters survey standard approaches to measuring and modelling financial risk from the risk manager perspective. Chapters 4 and 5 are aimed primarily at quantitative risk analysts whose job it is to put the systems in place. Chapters 6 and 7 discuss important issues in IT and systems design, and the last two chapters cover pricing and risk management of credit risky products.

The book begins with a review of the new regulatory framework for assessing market risk capital. The first chapter, by Michel Crouhy, Dan Galai and Robert Mark, contains a detailed review of the standardized approach, the 1988 BIS Accord, the 1996 Amendment and a new proposal for 'pre-commitment' to capital charges. An informative comparison of the capital charges for various portfolios according to the standardized and the internal models approaches demonstrates that many financial institutions without internal models could be heavily penalized. The second chapter, by Stan Beckers, is reproduced from the original work with minor changes. His survey of risk measurement theory and practice begins with an overview of the basics of risk–return analysis, and factor models for modelling risk in large portfolios of traded securities. A discussion of the importance of developing new methods for benchmarking risk, portfolio diversification and managing currency risks concludes the chapter. Chapter 3, by Tom Wilson, introduces Value at Risk (VaR), its risk management applications and methods for calculating market and credit risk capital charges with internal VaR models. More than half of the 60 pages concentrate on market VaR: the measurement issues and a review of standard modelling procedures.

The fourth chapter presents a comprehensive overview of volatility and correlation. Carol Alexander reviews the advantages and limitations of standard statistical methods for estimating and forecasting volatility and correlation, and presents a detailed account of the important issues for applying GARCH models to financial data. Applications to financial markets include factor modelling, capital allocation, option pricing and hedging and VaR models, and the chapter concludes with a discussion of some new directions such as modelling non-normal distributions and cointegration. The next chapter, by Mark Broadie and Paul Glasserman, surveys the use of simulation for option pricing and risk management. It begins with a detailed account of standard simulation methodologies, suggesting various methods for improving speed and accuracy. The final part of the chapter reviews the application of simulation to estimating VaR.

As more markets and products are developed, new risk systems for modelling the risk taken by large financial institutions on a firm-wide level must be implemented. Nigel Webb discusses the functional requirements of such systems in the sixth chapter, assessing the problems facing the risk technology industry for the efficient design of risk management and risk control systems. Ron Dembo presents new paradigms for measuring risk and return, with forward-looking scenario analysis, in Chapter 7. Marking both portfolio and benchmark to market at a future risk horizon, applying appropriate measures of risk, and trading-off risk and return are explained in a concise, but complete, account of some of the important issues facing risk management today.

The next chapter on pricing credit risk, by Robert Jarrow and Stuart Turnbull, is reproduced from *The Handbook of Risk Management and Analysis*. Their classic work on pricing credit risky securities using a lattice of default-free interest rates is explained in full, with examples and extensions to vulnerable derivatives. The last chapter on credit enhancement techniques, by Lee Wakeman, also appeared in the original book. It covers default modifiers, such as guarantees and triggers, as well as standard credit exposure modification techniques (collateral arrangement, recouping, netting) and a discussion of legal and economic considerations.

All the authors are acknowledged experts in their field and have been availed upon to find time to write for this book because of their excellent expository skills. I present it with much gratitude to John and Celia Hall for their excellent project management, and with great appreciation for the authors, since they have so little time. My hope is that it may provide some help to the financial risk community in performing the important tasks they currently face.

Carol Alexander

Foreword

Russian bonds falling into an abyss; stock market prices in South East Asia more than halved in less than a month; Latin America on the verge of being sucked into a spiral of devaluations; even the mighty Dow–Jones losing more than 12% in a week on fears about the political future of the American President; rumours of a major US bank filing for protection under Chapter 11 — these are some of today's financial risks.

How much is a particular financial institution exposed to these market risks and through exposures to counterparties? Has it a comprehensive system of limits and controls? Has it qualified personnel with proper authorities, accurate, speedy and robust information systems and adequate capital resources? These are fundamental questions for risk management. On the answers rest the survival chances of the firm.

In what started as a second edition of the well-received *Handbook of Risk Management and Analysis*, Carol Alexander has taken up the challenge of the increasing complexity of today's markets by selecting additional material to cover new aspects of risk modelling and new products, hence the present two-volume edition. As before, the authors are well known not only for their mastery of the subject matter but also for their expository skills. Sound theories and tried methods are explained; new markets and products are clearly described. This is essential reading for the growing community of quantitatively minded risk managers.

Financial risk measurement is based on a two-step process: first, measure the current value of a business; that is, the difference between the values at which assets could be sold and liabilities could be bought (at least in theory); secondly, estimate by how much this current, or so-called mark-to-market value could fluctuate over time as a function of varying market factors and operational changes. The variations are weighted with probabilities to reflect their likelihood.

In practice, this process is fraught with difficulties. Vast areas of business are not valued for fear of relying on model-based values for illiquid products (for example, loans). Many theoretical valuations fall short of taking into account all expected costs such as expected losses because of counterparty risks. Too often, obsolete accounting standards or bizarre tax incentives still obscure or bias the valuation process.

When measuring potential variations over time, the desire of regulators to impose prudential standards has led to simplistic and largely arbitrary rules (as in the case of large exposures measurements) or benchmarks of limited significance (as in the case of Value at Risk (VaR) measurements). Thus, enormous investments in personnel, data bases and calculation tools are being made to obtain results that may satisfy regulators but are otherwise of limited operational value. Indeed, they may at worst give a false sense of security and divert attention from critical issues.

Financial risk management aims to balance risks and returns in accordance with a stated risk management policy, from tactical dynamic hedging decisions to strategic capital allocation decisions. Few institutions have a firm-wide risk policy expressed as a trade-off between risks and returns; perhaps because returns are even more difficult to predict than risks; perhaps because delegation of authority and control is easier when subject to a set of absolute limits; or perhaps because senior management think that the degree of risk-taking should be left to the initiative of individuals. It may also be, however, that these beliefs are remnants of times past and that a modicum of reflection would reveal the advantages of risk management systems based on a pricing of risks.

Such issues and many more have been addressed in these two volumes. General results and state of the art solutions are given, but without pretence to be either comprehensive or final answers. This second edition is a valuable analysis of today's issues but the risk management revolution that started some 12 years ago in the financial markets has still a long way to run. I would not be surprised if a third edition in three volumes became necessary soon.

Jacques Pézier

General Manager
Crédit Agricole Lazard Financial Products Bank

—————— 1 ——————
The New 1998 Regulatory Framework for Capital Adequacy: "Standardized Approach" versus "Internal Models"

MICHEL CROUHY, DAN GALAI, AND ROBERT MARK*

1.1 INTRODUCTION

Why is there a need to impose regulatory capital on commercial banks, and not on other institutions? Simply because banks are different. They collect deposits and play a key role in the payment system. Deposits are insured, but still governments always act as a guarantor for commercial banks, and as a lender of last resort. Capital plays the role of a buffer against unanticipated losses, and in some way participates in the privatization of the burden that would otherwise be born by the government in case of a bank failure. In addition, fixed-rate deposit insurance creates, by itself, the need for capital regulation because of the moral hazard and adverse selection problems that it generates. Under current regulation, insured banks have an incentive to take more risk, since fixed-rate deposit insurance is like a put option sold by the government to banks at a fixed premium, independent of the riskiness of their assets. This option increases in value when the bank's assets become riskier.[1] Moreover, as deposits are insured, there is no incentive for depositors to cautiously select their bank. Instead, depositors may be tempted to look for the highest deposit rates, without paying enough attention to banks' creditworthiness.

Prior to the implementation in 1992 of the 1988 Basle Accord, capital regulation consisted only of uniform minimum capital standards that were applied to banks, regardless of their risk profiles, and ignoring off-balance-sheet positions. For the first time, the 1988 Basle Accord (or the BIS Accord as we will refer to it) established international minimum capital guidelines that linked banks' capital requirements to their credit

* Sanjiv Talwar deserves a special acknowledgement for his comments, suggestions, improvements and the countless discussions we have had on this subject while implementing our internal models at CIBC. The authors are very appreciative for the constructive comments of the two referees and the editor, Carol Alexander.

Risk Management and Analysis. Vol. 1: Measuring and Modelling Financial Risk.
Edited by Carol Alexander   © 1998 John Wiley & Sons Ltd

exposures, but only to credit exposures. More recently, the 1996 Amendment extended the initial Accord to include risk-based capital requirements for market risks in the bank trading accounts.[2]

This chapter presents the new Bank for International Settlements (BIS) framework to assess regulatory capital for banks, which came into force in January 1998. Banks will be required to satisfy three capital adequacy standards: first, a maximum assets to capital multiple of 20; second, an 8 per cent minimum ratio of eligible capital to risk-weighted assets;[3] and third, a minimum capital charge to compensate for market risk of traded instruments on and off balance sheet. In addition to these capital adequacy requirements, BIS has set limits on concentration risks. Large risks that exceed 10 per cent of the bank's capital must be reported, and positions which are greater than 25 per cent of the bank's capital are forbidden.[4] The new BIS proposal, which supplements the old risk-based capital standards, now incorporates market risk. It also officially consecrates VaR as the proper methodology to assess market risk exposure.

Section 1.2 of this chapter discusses the initial 1988 BIS Accord. Then, in Section 1.3, we turn to the new 1995 market risk proposal which became mandatory in January 1998, and which is known as the 1996 Amendment. The regulators have given the opportunity to the banks to develop their own internal models to assess market risks. However, the effective acceptance of these models by the supervisory agencies is subject to minimum requirements that banks should meet in the first place. Banks should establish a strong and independent risk management infrastructure, with sound risk management practices; the models should properly capture all market risks, linear and non-linear as well as specific risk for debt and equity instruments. Institutions whose internal models are not satisfactory in the eyes of the regulators, will not have any other choice than to use the standardized approach proposed by the Basle Committee. Rough-cut calculations show that substantial capital savings can be realized when using the internal models instead of the standardized approach. In Section 1.4 we give a detailed presentation of the standardized approach. In Section 1.5 we discuss the inherent weaknesses of both models and present an alternative, the "pre-commitment approach", which would require a bank to pre-commit itself to a maximum loss exposure for its trading account over a fixed subsequent period.

Finally, in Section 1.6 we compare the capital charges, using both the standardized and the internal approaches, for various portfolios. We show that there is considerable capital savings to be expected for banks that adopt the internal models approach. It is expected that for very large and diversified portfolios the capital savings will be quite substantial. The difference in capital charge between the two approaches is so considerable that those banks that will be subject to the standardized approach may find themselves at such a competitive disadvantage that, in order to survive, there will be no alternative than to put in place the necessary infrastructure to satisfy to the internal models prerequisites.

1.2 THE 1988 BIS ACCORD: THE "ACCORD"

The risk-based capital adequacy standards rely on principles which are laid out in the *International Convergence of Capital Measurement and Capital Standards* document, published in July 1988 (cf. Basle (1988)), and referred to in what follows as the "Accord". This Accord was initially developed by the Basle Committee on Banking Supervision, and later endorsed by the central bank governors of the Group of Ten (G-10) countries.[5] The proposed approach is quite simple, and somewhat arbitrary, and has been subject to many criticisms. This Accord should be viewed as a first step in establishing a level playing field for banks across member countries. It defined two minimum standards for meeting acceptable capital adequacy requirements: (i) an assets to capital multiple and (ii) a risk-based capital ratio. The first standard is an overall measure of a bank's capital adequacy. The second measure focuses on the credit risk associated with specific on- and off-balance-sheet asset categories. This second measure is a solvency ratio, known as the Cooke ratio, and is defined as the ratio of capital to risk-weighted on-balance-sheet assets plus off-balance-sheet exposures, where the weights are assigned on the basis of counterparty credit risk.

The scope of the Accord is limited since it does not address various complex issues related to capital adequacy, like portfolio effects and netting. Indeed, credit risk is partially offset by diversification across issuers, industries, and geographical locations. When there are netting agreements in place, the net exposure may be small because the amount lent is matched by the amount borrowed.[6] It also completely ignores capital adequacy for the marketable securities in the trading book. For example, government holdings were excluded from the capital calculations. In recognition of these drawbacks, the Basle Committee amended the Accord in 1996. The new proposal is discussed in Section 1.3.

We now review the main features of the Accord on credit risk as it stands today after several modifications.

1.2.1 The Assets to Capital Multiple

A simple test for determining the overall adequacy of a financial institution's capital is the assets to capital multiple. This test calculates the multiple by dividing the bank's total assets, including specified off-balance-sheet items, by its total capital. The off-balance-sheet items included in this test are direct credit substitutes (including letters of credit and guarantees), transaction-related contingencies, trade-related contingencies, and sale and repurchase agreements. All of these items are included at their notional principal amount.

At present, the maximum multiple allowed is 20. In general this test does not set the capital requirements. However, it is possible that a bank with large off-balance-sheet activities may trigger this multiple as the minimum requirement.

1.2.2 The Risk-Weighted Amount Used to Compute the Cooke Ratio

In determining the Cooke ratio it is necessary to consider both the on-balance-sheet as well as specific off-balance-sheet items. On-balance-sheet items have risk weightings from 0 per cent for cash and OECD government securities, to 100 per cent for corporate bonds and others. Off-balance-sheet items are first expressed as a credit equivalent, see Section 1.2.3, and then are appropriately risk weighted by counterparty. The risk-weighted amount is then the sum of the following two components: (i) the risk-weighted assets for on-balance-sheet instruments and (ii) the risk-weighted credit equivalent for off-balance-sheet items. Table 1.1 gives the risk capital weights (WA) by asset categories, and Table 1.2 shows the weights that apply to credit equivalents by type of counterparty (WCE).

$$\text{Risk-weighted amount} = \sum \text{assets} * WA + \sum \text{credit equivalent} * WCE$$

Table 1.1 Risk capital weights by broad on-balance-sheet asset category (WA)

Risk Weights (%)	Asset Category
0	Cash and gold bullion, claims on OECD governments like Treasury bonds, insured residential mortgages.
20	Claims on OECD banks and OECD public sector entities like securities issued by US Government agencies, claims on municipalities.
50	Uninsured residential mortgages.
100	All other claims like corporate bonds and less developed country debt, claims on non-OECD banks, equity, real estate, premises, plant and equipment.

Table 1.2 Risk capital weights for off-balance-sheet credit equivalents by type of counterparty (WCE)

Risk Weights (%)	Type of Counterparty
0	OECD governments
20	OECD banks and public sector entities
50	Corporate and other counterparties

There is an apparent inconsistency between Table 1.1 and Table 1.2 where the risk weights for corporates related to off-balance-sheet instruments is half what is required for on-balance-sheet assets. BIS's rationale for this asymmetry is the better quality of the corporates that participate in the market for off-balance-sheet products. There was a time when only the most financially sophisticated corporations entered the world of derivatives; however, this is no longer the case. Evidence of this has been documented by the media in such cases as Procter and Gamble, and Gibson Greeting Cards to name only two.

1.2.3 Calculation of the Credit Equivalent for Off-Balance-Sheet Exposures

(i) The Case of Non-Derivative Exposures

In this case a conversion factor applies, because the notional amount of these instruments is not always representative of the true credit risk being assumed; its value is set by the regulators between 0 and 1, depending on the nature of the instrument (cf. Table 1.3). The resulting credit equivalent is then treated exactly as on-balance-sheet instruments.

Table 1.3 Credit conversion factors for non-derivative off-balance-sheet exposures

Conversion Factor (%)	Off-Balance-Sheet Exposure
100	Direct credit substitutes, bankers' acceptances, standby letters of credit, sale and repurchase agreements, forward purchase of assets.
50	Transaction-related contingencies like performance bonds, revolving underwriting facilities (RUFs) and note issuance facilities (NIFs).
20	Short-term self liquidating trade related contingencies like letters of credit.
0	Commitments with an original maturity of one year or less.

(ii) The Case of Derivative Positions Like Forwards, Swaps, and Options

The Accord recognizes that the credit risk exposure of long dated financial derivatives fluctuates in value, and estimates this exposure both in terms of the current marked-to-market value, plus a simple measure of the projected future risk exposure.

Calculation of the BIS risk-weighted amount for derivatives proceeds in two steps, as shown in Figure 1.1. The first step involves computing a credit equivalent amount, which is the sum of the current replacement cost when it is positive (and zero otherwise), and an add-on amount that approximates future replacement costs.

The current replacement value of a derivative is its marked-to-market or liquidation value, only when it is positive. Indeed, when it is negative the institution is not exposed to default risk because the counterparty goes bust, and therefore the replacement cost is set to zero.

The add-on amount is computed by multiplying the notional amount of the transaction by the BIS required add-on factor, as shown in Table 1.4. Here, five categories of underlying are considered, i.e. interest rate, exchange rate and gold, equity, precious metals except gold, and other commodities. The add-on factor differs quite substantially from one category to the other, although the rationale for such differences is not always clear.

Interest rate contracts include single currency interest rate swaps, basis swaps, forward rate agreements and products with similar characteristics, interest rate futures, and interest rate options purchased. Exchange rate contracts include gold contracts that are treated the same way as exchange rate contracts, cross-currency swaps, cross-currency interest rate swaps, outright forward foreign exchange contracts, and currency options purchased.

Step 1: Credit-equivalent amount

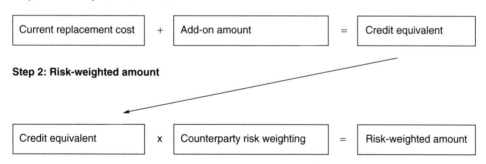

Step 2: Risk-weighted amount

Figure 1.1   Calculating BIS risk-weighted amounts for derivative products

Table 1.4   Add-on factors by type of underlying and maturity

Residual Maturity	Interest Rate (%)	Exchange Rate and Gold (%)	Equity (%)	Precious Metals Except Gold (%)	Other Commodities (%)
One year or less	0.0	1.0	6.0	7.0	10.0
Over one year to five years	0.5	5.0	8.0	7.0	12.0
Over five years	1.5	7.5	10.0	8.0	15.0

Equity contracts based on individual stocks as well as equity indices, precious metals contracts (except for gold), and contracts on other commodities, like energy products, agricultural commodities, base metals (aluminium, copper and zinc), include forwards, swaps, purchased options.

For example, a $100 million 5-year interest rate swap would have an add-on amount of $0.5 million, i.e. 0.5 per cent × $100 million, where 0.5 per cent is the add-on factor given in Table 1.4 for this instrument.

The credit equivalent amount can be interpreted as an on-balance-sheet amount for regulatory purposes. Unfortunately, the BIS approach fails to distinguish between the credit risk of plain vanilla swaps and that of more volatile structures, such as the well publicized highly levered swaps, e.g. the Banker's Trust's $200 million 5-year leveraged interest rate swap with Procter & Gamble.

The second step in the BIS calculation consists of calculating the regulatory capital related to the credit risk exposure. It is simply derived by multiplying the credit equivalent amount by a counterparty risk weighting factor as given in Table 1.2. The result of this calculation is the final risk-weighted amount.

1.2.4 Netting of Derivatives Positions

In 1995 the initial BIS agreement was modified to allow banks to reduce their credit equivalent when bilateral netting agreements are in place. According to some surveys, netting reduces the banks' gross replacement value by half on average. The new BIS formula for add-on amounts is now:

$$\text{add-on amount} = \text{notional} * \text{add-on factor} * (40 \text{ per cent} + 60 \text{ per cent} * NPR)$$

The add-on factors are the same as in Table 1.4. NPR denotes the net replacement ratio which is the net replacement cost when positive, or zero otherwise, divided by the gross replacement cost calculated as before, without taking netting into account, i.e. the sum of the positive replacement cost for the transactions covered by the netting agreement. Note that the new BIS formula does not allow for complete offsetting, even if netting agreements are in place. It is tempting to believe that the rationale favouring a minimum add-on amount stems from the legal risks associated with the possibility of the courts finding netting agreements unenforceable in certain jurisdictions, and even if the netting agreements are upheld, the delay in reaching a settlement can negate any possible benefit that may have resulted had the netting agreement been enforced immediately. However, this reasoning is not valid. The leading global financial institutions negotiated with the BIS to allow for netting and showed that a seasoned portfolio had a stable ratio of net to gross marked-to-market. It was argued that 100 per cent of this ratio should be allowed. The BIS did not agree that the ratio was stable in the long run and therefore imposed the 40 per cent minimum. Thus, the formula in fact demonstrates a discounted benefit for the effects of netting.

These calculations are done by counterparty; then the counterparty risk weight applies to derive the risk-weighted amount. Table 1.5 illustrates the calculations on a simple example.

1.2.5 Capital and the Cooke Ratio

Banks are required to maintain a capital amount of at least 8 per cent of the total risk-weighted assets calculated as shown in the previous section. Capital, as defined by the Cooke ratio, is broader than equity capital. It consists of three components:

Table 1.5 Illustration of the calculation of the add-on and risk-weighted amounts with netting

Risk capital weight (Table 1.2)		Counterparty A 20%			Counterparty B 50%		
	Add-on factor	Notional Amount	Marked-to-Market Value	Add-on Amount 1988	Notional Amount	Marked-to-Market Value	Add-on Amount 1988
Transaction 1	0.5%	1000	400	5	700	−100	3.5
Transaction 2	1.5%	500	−200	7.5	1000	200	15
Transaction 3	5%	1000	−100	50	500	−200	25
Add-on amount 1988−A1988				62.5			43.5
Gross replacement cost (GR)			400			200	
Net replacement cost (NR)			100			0(*)	
NPR(= NR/GR)			0.25			0	
Add-on amount 1995−A1995			34.375			17.4	
Credit equivalent			134.375			17.4	
Risk-weighted amount			26.875			8.7	

A1995 = A1988(0.4 + 0.6 NPR).
Credit equivalent = NR + A1995.
*Note that the "negative" replacement cost for counterparty B cannot be used to offset the positive replacement costs of counterparty A. This is why it is set to zero.

Tier 1, or core capital, which includes common stockholder's equity, non-cumulative perpetual preferred stock, and minority equity interests in consolidated subsidiaries, less goodwill and other deductions.

Tier 2, or supplementary capital, which includes hybrid capital instruments, like cumulative perpetual preferred shares and qualifying 99-year debentures which are essentially permanent in nature and have certain characteristics of both equity and debt; limited life instruments, like subordinated debt with an original average maturity of at least five years.

In the 1996 Amendment to the original BIS Accord, a third tier of capital has been added only to meet market risk requirements.

Tier 3, or sub-supplementary capital, which consists of short-term subordinated debt with an original maturity of at least two years. It must be unsecured and fully paid up. It is also subject to lock-in clauses that prevent the issuer from repaying the debt before maturity, or even at maturity should the issuer's capital ratio become less than 8 per cent after repayment. In Section 1.3.5 we review in some depth how tier 3 capital can be allocated against market risk for the trading book.[7]

According to the original Accord, tier 1 and tier 2 capital should represent at least 8 per cent of the risk-weighted assets, as a protection against credit risk. At least 50 per cent must be covered by tier 1 capital.

1.3 THE 1995 BIS MARKET RISK PROPOSAL: THE "1996 AMENDMENT"

In April 1995 the Basle Committee issued a consultative proposal to amend the Accord. It now requires financial institutions to measure and hold capital to cover their exposure to "market risk" associated with debt and equity positions located in the trading book, and foreign exchange and commodity positions in both the trading and banking books.[8] These positions should include all financial instruments which are marked-to-market, whether they are plain vanilla products like bonds or stocks, or complex derivative instruments like options, swaps, or credit derivatives. Marking financial instruments to market must be done for both accounting and management purposes.

The most significant risk for the non-trading activities of financial institutions is credit risk associated with default.[9] The Accord treated all instruments equivalently, whether in the trading or non-trading book. The 1995 BIS market risk proposal has introduced the requirement of measuring market risk in addition to credit risk. The initial Accord still applies *in extenso* to the non-trading items both on balance sheet and off balance sheet. Market risk must now be measured for both on- and off-balance-sheet traded instruments. However, on-balance-sheet assets are subject to market risk capital charge only, while off-balance-sheet derivatives, like swaps and options, are subject to both market risk and credit risk capital charges. The bank's overall capital requirement will be the sum of:

- credit risk capital charge, as proposed in the initial Accord and presented in Section 1.2, which applies to all positions in the trading and banking books, as well as over-the-counter (OTC) derivatives and off-balance-sheet commitments, but excluding debt and equity traded securities in the trading book, and all positions in commodities and foreign exchange;

- market risk capital charge for the instruments of the trading book on, as well as off balance sheet.[10]

According to BIS, market risk encompasses both "general market risk" and "specific risk". General market risk refers to changes in the market value of on-balance-sheet assets and liabilities, and off-balance-sheet instruments, resulting from broad market movements, such as changes in the level of interest rates, equity prices, exchange rates, and commodity prices. Specific risk refers to changes in the market value of individual positions due to factors other than broad market movements like liquidity, exceptional events, and credit quality.

This proposal was adopted by the US regulatory agencies in July 1995, and became mandatory to all financial institutions with a significant trading activity, as of 1 January 1998.[11] The final version of the proposal will be referred to in what follows as the "1996 Amendment".

The complexity of correctly assessing market risk exposure, especially for derivative products, has been recognized by the authorities. Flexibility in the modelling of the many components of market risk is thus allowed. The most sophisticated institutions that already have an independent risk management division in place, with sound risk management practices, will have the choice between their own "internal Value at Risk (VaR) model", referred to as the *internal models approach*, and the "standard model" proposed by BIS, referred to as the *standardized approach*, to determine market risk related regulatory capital.

The new capital requirement related to market risks should largely be offset by the fact that the capital charge calculated under the 1988 Accord to cover credit risk will no longer need to be held for on-balance-sheet securities in the trading portfolio. The capital charge for general market risks and specific risks should be, on aggregate, much smaller than the credit risk capital charge for large trading books. Then, banks adopting the internal models approach should realize substantial capital savings, probably of the order of 20 per cent–50 per cent, depending on the size of their trading operations, and the type of instruments they trade.

While the regulators are not too specific about the modelling requirements and the choice of the relevant risk factors, banks will have to satisfy some minimum qualitative and quantitative requirements before they can envisage adopting the internal model approach.

We first review the issues and the minimum requirements that apply to the internal model approach, and then present in the next section the standardized approach.

1.3.1 Issues Regarding the Adoption of the Internal Models Approach

The regulators accept that institutions will use different assumptions and modelling techniques simply because trading financial products relies on proprietary expertise both in trading and modelling markets. Modelling market risk is thus an issue, and will stay an issue since it is inherent to the trading of derivatives. Indeed, the ability of a trading institution to stay profitable relies in part on the skill of its financial engineers and traders to build the appropriate pricing and hedging models. State of the art modelling provides institutions with a unique competitive edge. These models are kept relatively secret, although most of them are based on published papers in academic journals. However, the implementation and calibration of these models require a lot of ingenuity, strong numerical and computer skills, a good understanding of the products and the markets. Very few "bar tenders" are able to produce this elaborate cocktail. The same proprietary models are used in risk management to derive risk exposures, like deltas, gammas, vegas, and other "Greeks". However, the wrong model may lead to large trading losses as has been reported in the financial press. It can also lead to a poor assessment of market risk exposure. Financial institutions learn the hard way how to correct the limitations of their models. Recently, in the *Wall Street Journal* (28 March 1997) it was reported that Bank of Tokyo–Mitsubishi had to write off $83 million on its US interest rate derivatives book because of the use of the wrong interest rate pricing model which led to systematic overvaluation of the position.

The regulator recognizes this unique feature of investment banking activity and requires institutions to scale up their VaR number derived from their internal model by a factor of three, referred to in what follows as the *multiplier*. This multiplier should be viewed as an insurance against model risk, imperfect assessment of specific risks, and other operational risks, although, as we discuss later in the chapter the application of such a multiplier has been widely criticized. Another view on this multiplier is a safety factor against "non-normal" market moves.

1.3.2 Qualitative Requirements

Before an institution can expect to be eligible to use its own internal model to assess regulatory capital related to market risk, it should have sound risk management practices already in place. The institution should have a strong risk management group which is independent from the business units it monitors, and which reports directly to the senior executive management of the institution.[12]

The internal models should not be used only for calculating regulatory capital; it should be fully integrated in the daily risk management of the institution. In addition, the regulator requires that systematic backtesting and stress testing be conducted on a regular basis, in order to test the robustness of the internal model to various market conditions and crises. Improvements should be implemented in the case when the model fails to pass the tests, e.g. when backtesting exhibits too many days where the trading losses are greater than VaR.

Implementing a VaR model is a massive and intensive system endeavour. The aim is to build a truly integrated, global, real-time system which records all positions centrally in a data warehouse, and map them to the risk factors tracked by the VaR model. Part of the challenge of implementing such a system is a need to have in place controls to ensure that the model inputs, and therefore the risk measures, are reliable and accurate:

- A formal vetting system is needed to approve the models, their modifications, assumptions, and calibration.
- Model parameters should be estimated independently of the trading desks to avoid the temptation by the traders to "fudge" volatility numbers and other key parameters to make their position smaller.
- The financial rates and prices that feed the risk management system should come from sources independent of the front office, and be located in a financial database independently controlled by risk management.

1.3.3 Quantitative and Modelling Requirements

The internal model approach should capture the materiality of all market risks of the trading positions. Although each institution has some discretion in the choice of the risk factors, these risk factors should be selected with great care to guarantee the robustness of the VaR model. Oversimplification and failure to select the right risk factors inherent in the trading positions may have serious consequences because the VaR model may miss components of basis risk, curve risk, or spread risk. These shortcomings should be revealed when backtesting the model, and may lead to penalties in the form of a multiplier greater than three.

Market risk can be broken down into four categories: interest rate risk, equity risk, exchange rate risk, and commodity price risk as follows.

1. Interest rate risk applies only to the trading book. The base yield curve in each currency (government curve or swap curve) should be modelled with a minimum of six risk points. The other relevant yield curves, i.e. corporate curves and provincial curves for Canada, are defined with regard to the base curve by the addition of a spread (positive or negative). The model should also incorporate separate risk factors to capture spread risk.

2. Equity price risk should incorporate risk factors corresponding to each of the equity markets in which the trading book holds significant positions. At a minimum, there should be a risk factor designed to capture market-wide movements in equity prices, e.g. the broad market index in each national equity market to assess both market risk and idiosyncratic risk, according to the Capital Asset Pricing Model (CAPM). The most extensive approach would have risk factors corresponding to each asset.

3. Exchange rate risk should include risk factors corresponding to the individual currencies in which the trading and banking books have positions.

4. Commodity price risk should incorporate risk factors corresponding to each of the commodity markets in which the trading and banking books have significant positions. The model should account for variations in the convenience yield.[13] It should also encompass directional risk to capture exposure from changes in spot prices, forward gap and interest rate risk to capture exposure to changes in forward prices arising from maturity mismatches, and basis risk to capture the exposure to changes in price relationship between similar commodities, as for energy products which are defined relative to West Texas Intermediate (WTI) crude oil.

The 1996 Amendment requires VaR to be derived at the 99 per cent (one-tailed) confidence level, with a 10-day horizon, i.e. with 10-day movements in rates and prices. However, in the initial phase of implementation of the internal model, the BIS allows the 10-day VaR to be proxied by multiplying the one day VaR by the square root of 10, i.e. 3.16.[14]

The effective daily regulatory capital requirement corresponds to the maximum of the previous day's VaR, and the average of daily VaRs over the preceding 60 business days, scaled up by the multiplier k, which normally should be equal to 3 (see Table 1.7):[15]

$$\text{Market risk capital charge } (t) = \max\{\text{VaR}_{t-1}, k\overline{\text{VaR}}\} \tag{1}$$

with

$$\overline{\text{VaR}} = \frac{1}{60} \sum_{i=t-1}^{t-60} \text{VaR}_i.$$

As we discussed in Section 1.3.1, this arbitrary multiplicative factor of 3 is adopted to compensate for model errors, and imperfect assessment of specific risks and operational risks. This multiplicative factor can be increased, up to 4, by the regulators if the models do not meet backtesting requirements (see Section 1.3.6).

Institutions are allowed to take into account correlations among risk categories. Volatilities and correlations should be estimated based on past historical data with a minimum history of 250 days,[16] i.e. approximately one year. Market parameters should be updated at least once every three months, or more frequently if market conditions warrant. If empirical correlations between risk categories are unavailable, then the aggregate VaR is calculated as the simple arithmetic sum of the VaR for each block, i.e. equity, interest rate, FX and commodities. In that case, the aggregate VaR does not benefit from the risk reduction that results from diversification across risk classes.

The internal model should capture not only linear risks, known as delta risks, but also non-linear risks, like convexity risk (gamma) and volatility risk (vega) inherent in options positions. The choice of the method is left to the institution, whether it chooses to implement full Monte Carlo simulation or other pseudo-analytic methods based on the Greeks.

Banks which will not be able to meet all the requirements for the internal models will be allowed to use a combination of standard models and internal models, although they are expected to move towards an all internal models framework. Each risk category, however, must be measured according to only one approach. If a combination of approaches is used, then the total capital charge is determined by a simple arithmetic sum, without accounting for a possible correlation effect between risk categories.

1.3.4 Specific Risk

According to the 1996 Amendment institutions are required to hold capital in support of specific risk associated with debt and equity positions in the trading books. In return, no more credit capital charge is allocated to them. In other words, specific risk is just a substitute for credit risk for traded on-balance-sheet products.

Derivative instruments will have specific risk capital charge when the underlying is subject to specific risk. Thus, there will be no specific risk charge on interest rate and currency swaps, forward rate agreements (FRAs), forward FX contracts, interest rate futures, and futures on an interest rate index. However, when not traded on an exchange, i.e. when they are traded over-the-counter (OTC), these instruments have counterparty risk and they will be charged a capital amount to cover their credit risk exposure according to rules of the 1988 Accord.

Specific risk relates to the risk that the price of an individual debt or equity security moves by more or less than what is expected from general market movements, due to specific credit and/or liquidity events related to individual issuers. The capital charge for specific risk can be determined either using the internal models, still scaled up by a multiplier of 4, or the standardized approach.

Under the standardized approach, specific risk charges vary across debt and equity instruments, with individual equities receiving 8 per cent charges, while those held in well-diversified and liquid portfolios being charged 4 per cent. Major stock indices are subject to 2 per cent charges, but certain arbitrage positions have lower requirements. For bonds, specific risk charges vary between 0 per cent and 8 per cent depending on the issuer and the maturity of the instrument, but no diversification is recognized.[17]

The new 1998 regulatory framework views specific risk, and consequently credit risk, as an outgrowth of market risk. As such it should be modelled with assumptions that are consistent with the market risk model. This is a significant improvement with respect to the 1988 Accord, where credit risk capital charge was calculated according to somewhat arbitrary ratios which did not correctly account for the specificity of the instrument.[18]

At CIBC, the internal model for bonds captures both spread risk, and credit risk which comes from the event of default as well as credit migration, whether it is an upgrade or a downgrade. An approach like CreditMetrics® proposed by J.P. Morgan (1997) is a good candidate for the internal model related to specific risk for bonds.

For equities, the approach is different since market risk, measured by the volatility of stock returns, already captures both general market risk and specific risk. Market risk and default risk for stocks are already fully accounted for in the current spot price. The problem is now to break down the total risk for a stock into general market risk and specific risk. For this purpose we rely on the statistical properties of a single index model, known also as the market model.[19] The basic idea is that the rate of return on any stock i is related to some common index I by a linear equation of the form

$$R_i = \alpha_i + \beta_i I + u_i \tag{2}$$

where

R_i is the rate of return on stock i,

α_i is the constant component of the return of stock i,

I is the value of the index,

β_i is a measure of the average change in R_i as a result of a given change in the index I,

u_i is a deviation of the actual observed return from the regression line $\alpha_i + \beta_i R_i$, i.e. the error term which is assumed to be normally distributed $N(0, \sigma_{u_i})$.

The index I generally used for this model is the rate of return on the market portfolio, which we denote R_m. The crucial assumption is that for every pair of stocks (i, j) the error terms are uncorrelated, i.e. $\text{Cov}(u_i, u_j) = 0$. The error term is also assumed to be uncorrelated with the market portfolio, i.e. $\text{Cov}(u_i, R_m) = 0$. The parameters of (2) are estimated in practice by using the *ex post* historical rates of return, and running a time series regression. It follows that

$$\beta_i = \frac{\text{Cov}(R_i, R_m)}{\text{Var}(R_m)}$$

Taking the variance of both sides of equation (2) we obtain

$$\sigma_i^2 = \beta_i^2 \sigma_m^2 + \sigma_{u_i}^2$$

The total risk of a security as measured by its variance can be divided into two components:

(i) $\beta_i^2 \sigma_m^2$ — systematic risk, or general market risk, which is non-diversifiable and associated with market fluctuations; and

(ii) $\sigma_{u_i}^2$ — idiosyncratic risk, or specific risk, which can be eliminated through diversification.

Given a stock, or a portfolio, whose price is denoted S_i, the general market risk (GMR) of the position is, according to the market model:

$$\text{GMR}_i = S_i \times \beta_i \times \sigma_m$$

and its specific risk (SR) is

$$\text{SR}_i = S_i \sigma_u = S_i \sqrt{\sigma_i^2 - \beta_i^2 \sigma_m^2}$$

These risks can be easily aggregated. For a portfolio, with a total value of P, composed of n securities S_i, $i = 1, \ldots, n$, the general market risk for the portfolio is

$$\text{GMR}_P = \sum_{i=1}^{n} S_i \beta_i \sigma_m = P \sum_{i=1}^{m} \frac{S_i}{P} \beta_i \sigma_m$$

$$= P \beta_P \sigma_m$$

where

$$\beta_P = \sum_{i=1}^{m} \frac{S_i}{P} \beta_i$$

represents the beta of the portfolio P, which is the weighted average of the betas of the individual stocks, with the individual weight $x_i = S_i/P$ being the proportion of stock i in the portfolio.

Under the assumption that the error terms are uncorrelated, the specific risk for the portfolio is simply

$$\text{SR}_P = P \sqrt{\sum_{i=1}^{n} x_i^2 \sigma_{u_i}^2}$$

1.3.5 New Capital Requirements

Under the 1996 Amendment, banks will now be allowed to add a new category of capital–tier 3 capital–which mainly consists of short-term subordinated debt subject to certain conditions, as described in Section 1.2.5, but only to meet on a daily basis market risk capital requirement as defined in (1).

Banks should first allocate tier 1 and tier 2 capital to meet credit risk capital requirements according to the 1988 Accord, so that together they represent 8 per cent of the risk-weighted assets, adjusted for the positions that are no longer subject to the 1988 credit risk rules, i.e. the traded instruments on balance sheet like bonds and equities which are already subject to specific risk.

Then, the bank should satisfy a second ratio of eligible capital to the risk-weighted asset equivalent. The risk-weighted asset equivalent is simply the sum of the risk-weighted on-balance-sheet assets, the risk-weighted off-balance-sheet items, and 12.5 times the market risk capital charge, where 12.5 is the reciprocal of the minimum capital ratio of 8 per cent.

Eligible capital is the sum of first, the whole bank's tier 1 capital; secondly, all of its tier 2 capital under the limit imposed by the 1988 Accord, i.e. tier 2 capital may not exceed 50 per cent of tier 1 capital; and thirdly, some of its tier 3 capital. Banks will be entitled to use tier 3 capital solely to satisfy market risk capital charge, but under some limiting conditions. The market risk capital charge should be met with tier 3 capital, and additional tier 1 and tier 2 capital not allocated to credit risk. Tier 1 capital should constitute the most substantial portion of the bank's capital, with the final rule imposing that:

- at least 50 per cent of a bank's qualifying capital must be tier 1 capital, with term subordinated debt not exceeding 50 per cent of tier 1 capital, and
- the sum of tier 2 and tier 3 capital allocated for market risk must not exceed 250 per cent of tier 1 capital allocated for market risk, i.e. 28.57 per cent of market risk capital charge should be met with tier 1 capital.[20]

The following example illustrates the calculation of the capital ratio.

Suppose the bank has:

- risk-weighted assets that amount to 7500, and
- a market risk capital charge of 350.

The bank capital is assumed to be constituted of tier 1 capital for 700, tier 2 capital for 100, and tier 3 capital for 600.

Does the bank meet the BIS capital ratio requirements?

Table 1.6 shows a possible allocation of capital. Because after allocating tier 1 and tier 2 capital to credit risk, there remains 200 of unused tier 1 capital available to support market risk, the maximum eligible tier 3 capital is only 500 according to the 250 per cent rule. After the full allocation for credit risk there remains 250 of tier 3 capital that is still unused, but eligible, and 100 unused tier 3 capital, but not eligible. In this example the capital ratio is greater than the minimum of 8 per cent, because we added 100 unused tier 1 capital in the numerator of the capital ratio.

Table 1.6 Calculation of the capital ratio under the 1996 Amendment

Risk-Weighted Assets		Minimum Capital Charge (8%)	Available Capital		Minimum Capital for Meeting Requirement		Eligible Capital (Excluding Unused Tier 3)		Unused but Eligible Tier 3		Unused but Not Eligible Tier 3	
Credit risk	7500	600	tier 1	700	tier 1	500	tier 1	700				
			tier 2	100	tier 2	100	tier 2	100				
Market risk	4375	350	tier 3	600	tier 1	100	tier 3	250	tier 3	250	tier 3	100
(i.e. 350 × 12.5)					tier 3	250						
Total	11 875	950		1400		950		1050		250		100

Capital ratio: 1050/11 875 = 8.8%
Excess tier 3 Capital ratio: 250/11 875 = 2.1%

1.3.6 Backtesting

The backtests must compare daily VaR measures calibrated to a one-day movement in rates and prices and a 99 per cent (one-tailed) confidence level, against two measures of the profit and loss (P&L):

- the actual net trading P&L for the next day, and
- the theoretical P&L that would have occurred had the position at the close of the previous day been carried forward to the next day.[21]

Assuming that the risk factors are correctly modelled and that markets behave accordingly, we expect, on average, the absolute value of actual P&L to be greater than the VaR only 5 days over the last 250 days.[22]

Backtesting should be performed daily.[23] In addition, institutions must identify the number of times when its net trading losses, if any, for a particular day exceed the corresponding daily VaR. This BIS multiplicative factor can become higher than three if the number of exceptions during the previous 250 days is greater than five, and can rise up to four if the number of exceptions reaches ten or more during the period, as shown in Table 1.7.

However, there is some doubt about how seriously this rule will be enforced since exceptions to the rule are already envisaged when abnormal situations occur, e.g. a market crash, a major political event, or a natural disaster. In addition, the regulators should

Table 1.7 Multiplier based on the number of exceptions in backtesting

Number of Exceptions	Multiplier
4 or fewer	3.00
5	3.40
6	3.50
7	3.65
8	3.75
9	3.85
10 or more	4.00

acknowledge that all the financial institutions, including the regulators, are learning by doing. It may thus not be appropriate to penalize an institution by applying a higher multiplier if the institution reacts quickly, and subsequently implements improvements to its VaR model after it has recognized its weaknesses.

The ISDA/LIBA Joint Models Task Force (see ISDA (1996)) has criticized the non-discriminatory imposition of this scaling factor of three, and simply suggests the repeal of this rule. Although it recognizes the benefits associated with backtesting in assessing the accuracy of the internal model, it considers the multiplier of three as an unfair penalty on banks which are already sophisticated in the design of their risk management system, and the modelling of general as well as specific risks. Instead they should be rewarded.[24] Backtesting is a powerful process to validate the predictive power of a VaR model, without requiring the use of a benchmark model. It is a self-assessment mechanism which allows a bank to check the validity of its internal model on an ongoing basis, and challenges its key assumptions whenever the bank's actual trading results become inconsistent with the VaR numbers. It provides a natural incentive framework to continuously improve and refine the risk modelling techniques.

The regulators should develop the right incentives for banks to implement best practices, and only banks that fail to take the appropriate actions should be applied a scaling factor greater than one. An arbitrary high scaling factor may even provide perverse incentives to abandon initiatives to implement prudent modifications of the internal model.

1.3.7 Stress Testing

In developing the VaR model many assumptions have to be made to make it practical. In particular, most market parameters are set to match normal market conditions. It should be noted that this is somewhat contradictory with the concept of maximum loss at the 99 per cent confidence level. How robust is the VaR model? How sensitive are the VaR numbers to key assumptions? These are questions that stress testing aims to address.

Stress testing is a process which consists of generating market "extreme scenarios", although plausible, for which key assumptions in the VaR model may be violated. Stress testing should assess the impact on VaR of the breakdown of some, otherwise stable, relationships, like relative prices, correlations, and volatilities. Stress testing should also investigate some causal relationships between market factors, between market and credit risks, and other exceptional relationships which may be triggered by abnormal events, i.e. low probability events.

The debt crisis of the 1980s reminds us that the distinction between general market risk, specific risk, and credit risk is indeed important to bear in mind, although we cannot ignore the potential impact of a sudden change in market risk on credit risk exposure. In the 1970s commercial banks involved in lending to Latin American countries innovated by proposing "syndicated Eurodollar loans" denominated in US dollars, therefore without currency exposure for the US banks, payable on a floating-rate basis, thus without interest rate risk, and were made to governments that were thought initially free from any credit risk exposure. After US interest rates skyrocketed in the early 1980s, countries like Mexico and Brazil went into default and were unable, or unwilling, to stand by their commitments.

Other scenarios that require simulations are the oil shocks of the 1970s, recent crises like the October 1987 and October 1989 market crashes, the ERM crises of 1992 and 1993, credit spreads widening, and the fall in the bond markets in May 1994 consecutive to the Fed tightening.[25] For Canada we would also include a yes scenario to the next Quebec referendum. These stress scenarios should simulate large price movements, combined with a sharp reduction in market liquidity for several consecutive days, and a dramatic change in instantaneous volatilities and correlations. In a period of market anomalies, it is the correlation structure that breaks down with correlations tending to the extremes, either $+1$ or -1.

Obviously, the impact of these stress tests will vary greatly depending on the bank's positions in the markets affected by the simulated crises. Accordingly, additional stress scenarios may be run to reflect specific concentration risk in one geographic region or in one market. In some ways, stress testing allows the bank to derive some kind of confidence interval on its VaR numbers.

1.4 THE STANDARDIZED APPROACH

The standardized model uses a "building block" type of approach where the capital charge for each risk category, i.e. interest rate, equity, foreign exchange and commodities, is first determined separately. Then, the four measures are simply added together to obtain the global capital charge related to market risk. In this section we present, and illustrate with simple examples, the main thrust of the method for the four risk categories.

1.4.1 Interest Rate Risk

The model encompasses all fixed-rate and floating-rate debt securities, zero-coupon instruments, interest rate derivatives, and hybrid products like convertible bonds, although they are treated like debt securities only when they trade like debt securities, i.e. when their price is below par, and are treated like equities otherwise. Simple interest rate derivatives like futures and forward contracts, including FRAs and swaps, are treated like a combination of short and long positions in debt contracts. Options are treated separately and will be covered later in this section.

The interest risk capital charge is the sum of two components calculated separately, one related to "specific risk", which applies to the net holdings for each instrument, the other related to "general market risk", where long and short positions in different securities or derivatives can be partially offset.

(i) Specific Risk

The capital charge for specific risk is designed to protect the bank against an adverse price movement in the price of an individual security due to idiosyncratic factors related to the individual issuer. Offsetting is thus restricted to matched positions in the identical issue, including derivatives. The capital charge applies whether it is a net long, or net short position. Even if the issuer is the same, but there are differences in maturity, coupon rates, call features, etc., no offsetting is allowed since a change in the credit quality of the issuer may have a different effect on the market value of each instrument.

Table 1.8 shows the specific risk charge for various types of debt positions. The weighting factors apply to the market value of the debt instruments, and not their notional amount.

Government debt includes all forms of debt instruments issued by OECD central governments, as well as non-OECD central governments, provided some conditions are satisfied. The qualifying category includes debt securities issued by OECD public sector entities, regulated securities firms of the G-10 countries plus Switzerland and Luxembourg, and other rated investment grade bonds. The other category receives the same specific risk capital charge as a private sector borrower under the credit risk requirements of the 1988 Accord, i.e. 8 per cent.

A specific risk charge also applies to derivative contracts in the trading book only when the underlying is subject to specific risk. For example, an interest rate swap based on LIBOR will not be subject to specific risk charge, while an option on a corporate bonds will. All over-the-counter derivative contracts are subject to counterparty credit risk charge according to guidelines of the 1988 Accord, even where a specific risk charge is required.

(ii) General Market Risk

Capital requirements for general market risk are designed to capture the risk of loss arising from changes in market interest rates. Banks have the choice between two methods, the "maturity" method and the "duration" method. The duration method is just a variant of the maturity method.[26]

The maturity method uses a "maturity ladder", i.e. a series of "maturity bands" that are divided into "maturity zones" according to the rule given in Table 1.9. These maturity bands and zones are chosen to take into account differences in price sensitivities and interest rate volatilities across different maturities. A separate maturity ladder must be constructed for each currency in which the bank has a significant trading position. No offsetting is allowed among maturity ladders of different currencies. As illustrated in the previous section, the disallowance of offsetting between currencies greatly impacts financial institutions that trade in one currency and hedge in another currency owing to the high correlation between them. For instance, if one did a swap in US dollars and performed an exactly offsetting swap in Canadian dollars, then the institution should be exposed to some FX risk and to cross-currency basis risk. The BIS methodology will impose an onerous amount of capital for this trade and its hedge, while this institution is only exposed to little residual risk.

The first step in the maturity ladder method consists of allocating the marked-to-market value of the positions to each maturity band. Fixed rate instruments are allocated according

Table 1.8   Specific risk charge factor for net debt positions

Debt Category	Remaining Maturity	Capital Charge (%)
Government	N/A	0.00
Qualifying	6 months or less	0.25
	6 to 24 months*	1.00
	over 2 years	1.60
Other	N/A	8.00

*For Canada, OSFI has set the horizon of the second bucket to 12 months instead of 24.

Table 1.9   Maturity bands and risk weights

Zone	Coupon 3% or More	Coupon Less Than 3%	Risk Weights (Sensitivities)	Assumed Changes in Yield (in Percentage Points)
1	1 month or less	1 month or less	0.00%	1.00
	1–3 months	1–3 months	0.20%	1.00
	3–6 months	3–6 months	0.40%	1.00
	6–12 months	6–12 months	0.70%	1.00
2	1–2 years	1.0–1.9 years	1.25%	0.90
	2–3 years	1.9–2.8 years	1.75%	0.80
	3–4 years	2.8–3.6 years	2.25%	0.75
3	4–5 years	3.6–4.3 years	2.75%	0.75
	5–7 years	4.3–5.7 years	3.25%	0.70
	7–10 years	5.7–7.3 years	3.75%	0.65
	10–15 years	7.3–9.3 years	4.50%	0.60
	15–20 years	9.3–10.6 years	5.25%	0.60
	over 20 years	10.6–12 years	6.00%	0.60
		12–20 years	8.00%	0.60
		over 20 years	12.50%	0.60

to the residual term to maturity, and floating-rate instruments according to the residual term to the next repricing date.

Derivatives, like forwards, futures and swaps, should be converted into long and short positions in the underlying positions. Options are treated separately (see below). For example, a long one-year forward contract on a two-year bond is equivalent to a short position in the 6–12 month maturity band for an amount equal to the discounted value of the forward price of the bond, and a long position in the 1–2 year maturity band for the same market value. For swaps, the paying side is treated as a short position and the receiving side as a long position on the relevant underlying instruments.

Offsetting is only allowed for matched positions in identical instruments with exactly the same issuer.

In the second step the positions in each maturity band are risk weighted according to the sensitivities given in Table 1.9. The third step consists of calculating capital requirements for general market risk according to the following principles:

1. Vertical disallowance to account for basis risk. In each maturity band the matched weighted position is imposed a capital charge of 10 per cent. Then, only the unmatched positions in each maturity band is considered in the rest.

2. Horizontal disallowance to account for the risk related to twists in the yield curve. The matched weighted positions in each zone (zones 1, 2 and 3, respectively), between adjacent zones (between zones 1 and 2, then between zones 2 and 3), and between the two extreme zones (between zones 1 and 3) are allocated a capital charge given in Table 1.10. Again, only the unmatched positions at each step are considered in the remaining calculations.

3. To account for the risk associated with a parallel shift in the yield curve, the residual unmatched weighted positions are given a capital charge of 100 per cent.

Table 1.10   Horizontal disallowances

Zones	Time Band	Within the Zone (%)	Between Adjacent Zones (%)	Between Zones 1 and 3 (%)
1	1 month or less			
	1–3 months	40		
	3–6 months			
	6–12 months		40	
2	1–3 years			
	2–3 years	30		100
	3–4 years			
3	4–5 years		40	
	5–7 years			
	7–10 years			
	10–15 years	30		
	15–20 years			
	over 20 years			

The following portfolio is analysed in order to illustrate the standardized approach for general market risk.

Portfolio:
   A. Qualifying bond with a $13.33 million market value, a residual maturity of 8 years, and a coupon of 8 per cent.
   B. Government bond with a market value of $75 million, a residual maturity of 2 months and a coupon of 7 per cent.
   C. Interest rate swap at par-value, i.e. with a zero net market value, with a notional amount of $150 million, where the bank receives floating and pays fixed, with the next fixing in 9 months, and a residual life of 8 years.
   D. Long position in interest rate futures contract with 6 months delivery date, for which the underlying instrument is a government bond with a 3.5 year maturity and a market value of $50 million.

The example presented in Table 1.11 shows the allocation process to each maturity band, and the calculation of the capital charge for general market risk. Note that there is vertical disallowance only in zone 3 for the 7–10 year time band. There is no horizontal disallowance within zones 2 and 3, since there is no offsetting positions between time bands within each of these two zones. However, there is horizontal disallowance within zone 1, and between zones 1 and 3. The short risk-weighted position in the 3–6 month time band partially offsets the long positions in the adjacent time bands in zone 1. Then, after vertical disallowance in the 7–10 year time band for $0.5 million, the net unmatched position in zone 3 becomes net short $5.125 million. Given the net long position for $1.125 million in zone 2 there is partial offsetting for this amount between zones 2 and 3, which leaves a net unmatched position of 0 in zone 2 and of net short $4 million in zone 3. After horizontal disallowance in zone 1, the net unmatched position becomes net long $1 million in this zone. Finally, there is partial offsetting for $1 million between zones 1 and 3, which leaves an overall net unmatched position of $3 million.

Table 1.11 Illustration of the calculation of the capital charge to cover general market risk for interest rate instruments (except options)

Time band	Zone 1 (months)				Zone 2 (years)						Zone 3 (years)				
Coupon >3%	0–1	1–3	3–6	6–12	1–2	2–3	3–4	4–5	5–7	7–10	10–15	15–20	>20		
Coupon <3%					1–1.9	1.9–2.8	2.8–3.6	3.6–4.3	4.3–5.7	5.7–7.3	7.3–9.3	9.3–10.6	10.6–12	12–20	>20
Positions															
A		+75 Gov.													
B										+13.33 Qual.					
C			−50 Fut.				+50 Fut.								
D				+150 Swap						−150 Swap					
Weight (%)	0.00	0.20	0.40	0.70	1.25	1.75	2.25	2.75	3.25	3.75	4.50	5.25	6.00	8.00	12.5
Position × Weight		+0.15	−0.20	+1.05			+1.125			+0.5 / −5.625					
Vertical Disallowance										$0.5 \times 10\% = 0.05$					

Horizontal Disallowance 1: ← $0.20 \times 40\% = 0.08$ →

Horizontal Disallowance 2: $1.125 \times 40\% = 0.45$

Horizontal Disallowance 3: $1.0 \times 100\% = 1.0$

The total capital charge is (in $ million):

for the vertical disallowance (basis risk)	$0.050
for the horizontal disallowance in zone 1 (curve risk)	$0.080
for the horizontal disallowance between adjacent zones (curve risk)	$0.450
for the horizontal disallowance between zones 1 and 3 (steepening of the curve risk)	$1.000
for the overall net open position (parallel shift risk)	$3.000
Total	**$4.580**

(iii) Treatment of Options

There are three different approaches. The "simplified approach" applies to banks that only buy options, while the "delta-plus method" or the "scenario approach" should be used by banks that also write options.

Simplified approach.   Table 1.12 shows the capital charge according to the simplified approach. As an example, suppose the bank is long 100 shares currently valued at $10, and has a put on this quantity of shares with a strike price of $11. The capital charge would be:

$+$1000 * 16\%$ (8% for specific risk plus 8% for general market risk) $= 160

$-$the amount the option is in the money, i.e. ($11 - $10) * 100$ $= 100

Total $60

Delta-plus approach.   For the purpose of capital charge calculation related to general market risk, the option is first considered as its delta equivalent in the underlying instrument, which is then allocated into the time band corresponding to the maturity of the option (cf. example in Table 1.11).

Then, two additional capital charges are added. The first one adjusts the capital charge for gamma risk or convexity risk, i.e.

$$\text{gamma capital charge} = \tfrac{1}{2}\text{gamma} * \Delta V^2$$

Table 1.12   Capital charge for options according to the simplified approach

Position	Treatment
Long cash and long put or Short cash and long call	The capital charge is the market value of the underlying security multiplied by the sum of specific and general market risk charges for the underlying, less the amount the option is in the money (if any), bounded at zero.
Long call or Long put	The capital charge will be the lesser of: (i) the market value of the underlying security multiplied by the sum of specific and general market risk charges for the underlying, or (ii) the market value of the option.

It is simply the second-order term in the Taylor expansion of the option price formula, where ΔV denotes the change in the value of the underlying. For interest rate products it is calculated according to the assumed changes in yield in the maturity band, as given in Table 1.9. For equities and foreign exchange and gold the price change is taken as 8 per cent, while for commodities it is taken as 15 per cent.

The second capital charge compensates for vega risk, i.e.

$$\text{vega capital charge} = \text{vega} * 0.25*$$

where vega is the sensitivity of the option price to one unit of volatility, σ.

This vega term is the absolute value of the impact of a 25 per cent increase or decrease in volatility.

Scenario matrix approach.   The scenario matrix approach adopts as capital charge the worst loss for all the scenarios generated by a grid which allows for a combination of possible values of the underlying price, the volatility, and the cost of carry, with the range of values to be considered being the same as for the delta-plus approach.

1.4.2 Equity Risk

General market risk charge is 8 per cent of each net position. Capital charge for specific risk is 8 per cent, unless the portfolio is both liquid and well diversified, in which case the charge is 4 per cent.

Equity derivatives are treated in the same way as interest rate derivatives. While there is no specific charge when the underlying is a government security or a market rate like Libor, for well-diversified broad market indices there is a specific risk charge of 2 per cent of the underlying market value.

The example given in Table 1.13 illustrates the delta-plus approach. Note that the gamma adjustment is based on an 8 per cent move in the stock price. If the underlying were a commodity, then the gamma adjustment would be based on a 15 per cent move, and the delta-equivalent would have been allocated to the time band corresponding to the maturity of the option (see Table 1.15)

1.4.3 Foreign Exchange Risk, Including Gold Price Risk

There are two steps in the calculation of the capital charge. First, the exposure in each currency is measured, and second, the net long and net short exposures in all currencies

Table 1.13   Delta-plus approach for an equity option

Consider a short position in a European one-year call option on a stock with a striking price of $490. The underlying spot price is $500, the risk-free rate is 8 per cent per annum, and the annualized volatility is 20 per cent. The option value is $65.48, with a delta and gamma of −0.721 and −0.0034, respectively, corresponding to a $1 change in the underlying price; its vega is 1.68 associated with a change in volatility of 1 percentage point.

The three components of the capital charge are:

delta equivalent: $500 * 0.721 * 8% =	$28.84
gamma adjustment: $\frac{1}{2} * 0.0034 * (\$500 * 8\%)^2 =$	$ 2.72
vega adjustment: $1.68 * (25\% * 20) =$	$ 8.40
Total	**$39.96**

Table 1.14   Shorthand approach to capital charge for foreign exchange and gold risk

Assume the net positions in each currency, expressed in the reporting currency, i.e. $, are as follows:

	Long			Short	
Yen	DM	GBP	FFR	US$	Gold
+50	+100	+150	−20	−180	−35
	+300			−200	−35

Capital charge = 8% ∗ 300 + 8% ∗ 35 = $26.80

are translated into an overall capital charge according to a rule called the "shorthand method".

The measurement of the exposures is straightforward. It consists of the net spot position, the net forward position,[27] the delta-equivalent for options as discussed above, accrued interest and expenses, and other future income and expenses that are already fully hedged.

The capital charge is the absolute value of 8 per cent of the greater of the net open long positions and the net open short positions in all currencies, plus 8 per cent of the absolute value of the net open position in gold plus the gamma and vega adjustments for options. The example in Table 1.14 illustrates the application of the rule.

1.4.4 Commodities Risk

Commodities are broadly defined as physical products which can be traded on an organized market, like agricultural products, oil, gas, electricity, and precious metals (except gold which is treated as a foreign currency). Commodities' risks are often more complex to measure than for other financial instruments because markets are less liquid, prices are affected by seasonal patterns in supply and demand, and inventories play a critical role in the determination of the equilibrium price.

The main components of market risk are:

- outright price risk, i.e. the risk of price movements in the spot prices;
- basis risk, i.e. the risk of a movement in the price differential between different related commodity prices, as it is inherent for energy products whose prices are quoted as a spread over a benchmark index;
- interest rate risk, i.e. the risk of a change in the cost of carry;
- time spread risk, or forward gap risk, i.e. the risk of movements in the forward commodity prices for other reasons than a change in interest rates; the shape of the forward curve is a function of supply and demand in the short run, and fundamental factors in the longer run;
- options risk, i.e. delta, gamma and vega risk as already discussed for other classes of products.

The standardized model for commodities is somewhat similar to the maturity ladder approach for interest rate products, the idea being to design a simple framework which captures directional, curve risk as well as time spread risk.

Table 1.15 Maturity ladder approach for commodities

Time Band	Spread Capital Charge (%)	Position	Capital Charge
0–1 month	1.5	—	
1–3 months	1.5	—	
3–6 months	1.5	long $600 short $1000	matched position: $600 × 3% = $18 $400 carried forward two time bands: $400 × 2 × 0.6% = $4.8
6–12 months	1.5	—	
1–2 years	1.5	long $500	matched position: $400 × 3% = $12 $100 carried forward one time band: $100 × 0.6 = $0.6
2–3 years	1.5	short $300	matched position: $100 × 3% = $3
over 3 years	1.5	—	
			net unmatched position: $200 × 15% = $30
			Total **$68.4**

First, positions are converted at current spot rates into the reporting currency, and located into the relevant time band. Forwards, futures, and swaps are decomposed as a combination of long and short positions as for interest rate products. The delta equivalent of options is placed in the time band corresponding to the maturity of the option.

To capture spread risk and some of the forward gap risk the matched position in a time band is allocated a capital charge of 3 per cent. The unmatched position is carried forward into the nearest available time band at a cost of 0.6 per cent per time band. For example, if it is moved forward two time bands it is charged $2 * 0.6$ per cent $= 1.2$ per cent. At the end of the process, the net unmatched position is given a capital charge of 15 per cent.

The example given in Table 1.15 illustrates the principle of the maturity ladder for commodities.

1.5 THE PROS AND CONS OF THE STANDARDIZED APPROACH AND THE INTERNAL MODELS: A NEW PROPOSAL — THE "PRE-COMMITMENT APPROACH"

The standardized approach has been criticized for the reason that it applies the same capital charge to vastly different financial instruments, e.g. to plain vanilla swaps and highly levered transactions. It also fails to account for portfolio effects for both credit risk and market risk.

The internal models approach obviously remedies many of these criticisms, and is an attempt to improve the accuracy of the standardized approach. However, some regulators question the banks' ability to properly capture the key risks imbedded in their portfolios, i.e. directional, spread, curve, volatility, liquidity risks, and are still sceptical about the capacity of many banks to correctly model these risk factors (see Kupiec and O'Brien (1995a, 1995c, 1995d, 1996)). Even if banks have the knowledge to develop the analytics, do they have the resources to implement the right infrastructure, especially the transactions database and the financial rates database, without which the best VaR software is as useful as a Ferrari on a sandy trail in the middle of the Sahara Desert? The proper infrastructure is key to success in risk management. Regulators bought an insurance policy by imposing safety factors like the multiplier of three to translate VaR into capital charge, and a multiplier of four for the capital charge related to specific risk. These conservative measures are not a panacea, since they may discourage the most sophisticated banks from improving their internal model, at least for regulatory capital purposes, and they may also induce a distorted allocation of capital.

Rating institutions like Standard & Poors have also expressed their concern that the new 1998 regulatory framework may substantially reduce the amount of regulatory capital, since for on-balance-sheet traded products like bonds and stocks, the expensive credit risk capital charge according to the initial 1988 Accord will be replaced by the less onerous capital charge associated with specific risk. The net effect, as we discussed earlier, should be an average net capital savings of 20 per cent–50 per cent for the largest trading banks. Standard & Poors (1996) argue that market risks in a trading operation are largely overshadowed by other risks that are difficult to quantify, such as operating risks related to employee fraud and systems failure, legal risk related to the potential for lawsuits from frustrated clients, reputation risk, liquidity risk, and operating leverage. For example, Bankers Trust lost $200 million on legal settlements when its regulatory capital, according to the internal models approach, would have been $285 million at the end of 1995. Apparently, it is not enough to be considered a credible counterparty by rating institutions.

In recognition of the weaknesses inherent in both the standardized approach and the internal models, two senior economists at the Board of Governors of the Federal Reserve Board, P. Kupiec and J. O'Brien, have proposed an alternative approach, the so-called "Pre-commitment Approach" (PCA) (see Kupiec and O'Brien (1995b, 1995c, 1995d, 1996)).[28] The PCA would require a bank to pre-commit to a maximum loss exposure for its trading account positions over a fixed subsequent period. This maximum loss pre-commitment would be the bank's market risk capital charge. Should the bank incur trading losses that exceed its capital commitment, it would be subject to penalties. Violation of the limit would also bring public scrutiny to the bank, which also would provide a further feedback mechanism for sound management.

Under the PCA, the bank's maximum loss pre-commitment can reflect the bank's internal assessment of risks, including formal model estimates as well as management's subjective judgements. The PCA approach is an interesting initiative since it aims to replace regulatory capital requirements based on *ex ante* estimates of the bank's risks, with a capital charge that is set endogenously through the optimal resolution of an incentive contract between the bank and its regulators. Indeed, it can be shown that the PCA takes the form of a put option written on the bank's assets and issued to the regulators. The value of this liability for the bank increases with the penalty rate, set by the regulator, and the riskiness of the bank's assets, while it decreases with the striking price of the put, i.e. the pre-commitment level. When the bank increases the risk of its assets it increases the value of its pre-commitment liability, which is more or less than offset by the increase in the value of the fixed-rate deposit insurance. The optimal design of the incentive contract becomes bank specific and should be such that the bank finds itself the right trade-off between the riskiness of its trading book and the level of pre-committed capital with the objective of maximizing the shareholder value and of minimizing the exposure of the deposit insurance institution (see Kupiec and O'Brien (1997)).

The PCA has been criticized by Gumerlock (1996) who uses a metaphor comparing the PCA to speed limits and fines for reckless driving, while he compares the internal models approach to inspections to guarantee that vehicles are roadworthy at all speeds and on all types of roads and weather conditions.

The issue debated here is that risk management consists of more than internal models. They are only one important element of risk measurement. In practice, risk managers should rely on their experience, judgement and controls, and not just on formulas to translate models' results into actual capital. Pre-commitment attempts to take these multiple factors into account.

1.6 COMPARISONS OF THE CAPITAL CHARGES FOR VARIOUS PORTFOLIOS ACCORDING TO THE STANDARDIZED AND THE INTERNAL MODELS APPROACHES

The standardized approach will in general produce a much larger capital charge than any reasonable VaR-based model. At CIBC we have compared the capital charges attributed to general market risk, on actual positions over a six-month period. The capital savings, i.e. the reduction in capital charge realized by adopting our internal model instead of the standardized approach, varies between a low of 60 per cent to a high of 85 per cent. The capital savings is higher when the portfolio is highly diversified across maturities and across countries, and when the portfolio is relatively well hedged in a VaR sense, i.e. its VaR exposure is small. The multiplier of three makes the capital charge according to the internal model quite sensitive to the market risk exposure.

To gain a better understanding of the extent of the capital charge differences between the standardized method and CIBC's internal method, four basic portfolios and a relatively well diversified cross-currency portfolio were investigated. The portfolio contents are given in Table 1.16. The cross-currency portfolio has products in both Canadian and US dollars covering a wide range of maturities. These portfolios are limited to linear interest rate products. All bonds are considered to be government issue to avoid the calculation of a specific risk capital charge. The following examples all concentrate only on general market risk.

To illustrate the differences between the two methods in capturing the portfolio effects, we consider portfolios with short and long positions, first in a single currency, and then in two different currencies, namely the US and the Canadian dollars. The interest rate curves that we used to perform the computations are given in Table 1.17 and correspond to market data as of 5 April 1997.

The first portfolio is simply a plain vanilla swap where the bank receives the fixed rate, the counterparty being a corporate. The internal model is a simple VaR model where the risk factors are the zero-coupon rates for the maturities shown in Table 1.17. The changes in those rates are supposed to follow a multivariate-normal distribution with the volatilities given in Table 1.18 for the US swap curve.[29] The VaR for this swap is US$927 000, while the sum of the VaR for each risk point on the curve is US$962 549. The changes in the

Table 1.16 Portfolios of fixed income instruments

Portfolios

1	US$ 100 million 10-year swap, receive fixed against three-month Libor. Counterparty is a corporate
2	Portfolio 1 + US$ 100 million 5-year swap, pay fixed against three-month Libor. Counterparty is a corporate
3	• long a US$ 100 million 10-year government bond with a 6.50% semi-annual coupon • US$ 100 million 10-year swap, pay fixed against three-month Libor. Counterparty is a corporate
4	• US$ 100 million 10-year swap, pay fixed against three-month Libor. Counterparty is a corporate • 140 million Canadian dollar 10-year swap, receive fixed against three-month Libor. Counterparty is a corporate
5	**Canadian dollars** • long 100 million three-month T-bill • long 75 million 8% government bond maturing in 20 years • long 25 million 8% government bond maturing in three years • short 25 million 8% government bond maturing in 12 years • 100 million 5-year swap, receive fixed against three-month Libor • 100 million 20-year swap, pay fixed against three-month Libor **US dollars** • short 300 million three-month T-bill • long 100 million six-month T-bill • short 200 million nine-month T-bill • long 100 million 6.5% government bond maturing in four years • long 200 million 6.7% government bond maturing in five years • long 100 million 7% government bond maturing in 12 years • 100 million two year swap, pay fixed against three-month Libor • 100 million 10-year swap, pay fixed against three-month Libor • 100 million 20-year swap, pay fixed against three-month Libor

rates being highly correlated the risk reduction due to the portfolio effect is relatively modest, i.e. 3.7 per cent in this example. The application of the standardized approach for general market risk, already presented in Section 1.4.1, is shown in Table 1.19a. It produces a capital charge of US$3 750 000. The capital charges calculated according to the standardized and the internal model approaches is shown in Table 1.20. For this 10-year swap, the adoption of the internal model does not allow any capital saving to be realized, but on the contrary generates a capital surcharge of 132 per cent.

There is also a capital surcharge of 103 per cent for the second portfolio which consists of a long and short position in two plain vanilla swaps of different maturities, but in the same currency, the US dollar. The bank receives fixed on the 10-year swap, and pays fixed on the five-year swap. Since there is partial offsetting of cash flows up to five years, the portfolio effect is expected to be more substantial than for the first portfolio. Table 1.18 shows the details of the derivation of the VaR number. The standardized approach for general market risk is detailed in Table 1.19b, and shows a capital charge of US$1 845 000, with US$1 million related to parallel shift in the yield curve, and US$845 000 to compensate for curve risk. In this case the cash flows are not well distributed among the various buckets. As a consequence, there is little capital charge for basis risk and curve risk among the different zones of the interest rate curve.

Table 1.17 Interest rate curves: zero-coupon curves with continuously compounded rates (5 April 1997)

Term	United States (US dollars)		Canada (Canadian dollars)	
	Treasuries (%)	Swaps (%)	Treasuries (%)	Swaps (%)
On	5.31	3.04	3.00	3.00
1 month	5.32	5.50	2.92	3.10
2 months	5.31	5.55	3.05	3.18
3 months	5.39	5.56	3.15	3.25
6 months	5.44	5.62	3.46	4.70
9 months	5.45	5.70	3.75	5.09
1 year	5.46	5.79	3.89	5.34
1.25 years	5.73	5.88	4.28	5.50
1.5 years	5.94	5.96	4.57	5.64
1.75 years	6.12	6.03	4.92	5.75
2 years	6.24	6.10	5.17	5.85
3 years	6.41	6.41	5.72	6.59
4 years	6.47	6.56	6.06	6.62
5 years	6.54	6.66	6.27	6.58
7 years	6.56	6.66	6.55	7.13
10 years	6.61	6.66	6.96	7.73

From these zero-coupon swap curves we can derive the following:
- 10-year US dollar (Canadian dollar) swap rates = 6.70% (7.55%).
- 5-year US dollar (Canadian dollar) swap rates = 6.68%(6.59%).
- First US dollar (Canadian dollar) floating three-month rate = 5.59% (3.15%).

Table 1.18 Internal model for Portfolios 1 and 2

Term	DV01 (US dollars)		Volatility (bp)	VaR/risk point (US dollars)	
	Portfolio 1	Portfolio 2	(σ)	Portfolio 1	Portfolio 2
3 months	(2459)		3.59	20 588	
6 months	28		3.35	215	
9 months	123		3.46	988	
1 year	162		3.58	1350	
1.25 years	195		3.95	1794	
1.5 years	230		4.33	2319	
1.75 years	264		4.70	2894	
2 years	746	2	5.08	8824	27
3 years	1681	5	5.29	20 742	63
4 years	2092	6	5.50	26 808	81
5 years	3579	(34 320)	5.50	45 897	440 110
7 years	7308	7308	5.63	95 878	95 878
10 years	58 138	58 128	5.42	734 252	734 252

Notes:
- DV01 denotes the sensitivity of the position to a decrease of 1 bp in the corresponding zero-coupon rate, and is expressed in currency units.
- σ denotes the daily volatility of the zero-coupon rate and is expressed in bp.
- VaR/risk point denotes the VaR for the corresponding zero-coupon rate, at the 99% confidence level (one-tailed) and for a one-day horizon, i.e. 2.33 σ |DV01|, assuming that interest rate changes are normally distributed.

	Portfolio 1 (US dollars)	Portfolio 2 (US dollars)
(1) Sum of the VaR/risk point	= 962 549	= 1 270 411
(2) VaR	= 927 000	= 407 532
Portfolio effect: (1) − (2)	= 35 549	= 862 879

Table 1.19(a) Standardized approach for general market risk: Portfolio 1

Time band	Zone 1 (months)				Zone 2 (years)			Zone 3 (years)							
Coupon >3%	0–1	1–3	3–6	6–12	1–2	2–3	3–4	4–5	5–7	7–10	10–15	15–20	>20		
Coupon <3%					1–1.9	1.9–2.8	2.8–3.6	3.6–4.3	4.3–5.7	5.7–7.3	7.3–9.3	9.3–10.6	10.6–12	12–20	>20
US dollar 10 yr swap fixed receiver		(100)								100					
Weight (%)	0.00	0.20	0.40	0.70	1.25	1.75	2.25	2.75	3.25	3.75	4.50	5.25	6.00	8.00	12.5
Position × weight long										3.75					
short		(0.20)													
Vertical Disallowance															

Horizontal Disallowance 1: ←—— 0 × 40% = 0 ——→   ←—— 0 × 30% = 0 ——→   ←—— 0 × 30% = 0 ——→

Horizontal Disallowance 2: ←—— 0 × 40% = 0 ——→   ←—— 0 × 40% = 0 ——→

Horizontal Disallowance 3: ←———— 0.2 × 100% = 0.2 ————→

Overall Net Position: ←———— 3.55 × 100% = 3.55 ————→

Total Capital Charge for General Market Risk = 3.75

Table 1.19(b) Standardized approach for general market risk: Portfolio 2

	Zone 1 (months)				Zone 2 (years)						Zone 3 (years)				
Time band															
Coupon >3%	0–1	1–3	3–6	6–12	1–2	2–3	3–4	4–5	5–7	7–10	10–15	15–20	>20		
Coupon <3%					1–1.9	1.9–2.8	2.8–3.6	3.6–4.3	4.3–5.7	5.7–7.3	7.3–9.3	9.3–10.6	10.6–12	12–20	>20
Positions															
A		(100)								100					
B		100						(100)							
Weight (%)	0.00	0.20	0.40	0.70	1.25	1.75	2.25	2.75	3.25	3.75	4.50	5.25	6.00	8.00	12.5
Position × weight															
long		0.20								3.75					
short		(0.20)						(2.75)							
Vertical Disallowance		0.20 × 10% = 0.02													

Horizontal Disallowance 1: ←— 0 × 40% = 0 —→ (Zone 1); ←— 0 × 30% = 0 —→ (Zone 2); ←— 2.75 × 30% = 0.825 —→ (Zone 3)

Horizontal Disallowance 2: ←— 0 × 40% = 0 —→ (Zone 1–2); ←— 0 × 40% = 0 —→ (Zone 2–3)

Horizontal Disallowance 3: ←— 0 × 100% = 0 —→

Overall Net Position: ←— 1 × 100% = 1 —→

Total Capital Charge for General Market Risk = 1.845

A: US$ 100 million 10-year swap, receive fixed against three-month Libor (counterparty is a corporate).
B: US$ 100 million five-year swap, pay fixed against three-month Libor (counterparty is a corporate).

Table 1.20   Standardized versus internal models: Capital charge for Portfolios 1 and 2

	Portfolio 1	Portfolio 2
Internal model		
(1) VaR	= US$927 000	US$407 532
(2) general market risk: $3 \times \text{VaR} \times \sqrt{10}$	= US$8 794 294	US$3 866 188
(3) counterparty risk*	= US$60 000	US$120 000
(1988 Accord)		
Capital charge: (2) + (3)	= US$8 854 294	US$3 986 188
Standardized Approach		
(4) general market risk	= US$3 750 000	US$1 845 000
(cf. Table 1.19)		
(5) counterparty risk*	= US$60 000	US$120 000
(1988 Accord)		
Capital charge: (4) + (5)	= US$3 810 000	US$1 965 000
Capital addition**	= 132%	103%

*Details for the calculation of the capital charge for counterparty risk:
- replacement cost = 0 (at-the-money swap)
- add-on (cf. Table 1.4) = US$100 million $\times$ 1.5% = US$1 500 000
- risk-weighted amount (cf. Table 1.2) = US$1 500 000 $\times$ 50% = US$750 000
- capital charge = US$750 000 $\times$ 8% = US$60 000

**Capital addition (saving) is the addition (saving) of capital realized by the bank by adopting the internal models instead of the standardized approach.

Table 1.21   Standardized versus internal models: Capital charge for Portfolios 3 and 4

	Portfolio 3	Portfolio 4
Internal Model		
(1) VaR	= US$19 068	970 330 Canadian dollars
(2) general market risk: $3 \times \text{VaR} \times \sqrt{10}$	= US$180 898	9 205 390 Canadian dollars
(3) counterparty risk (swap)	= US$60 000	166 800 Canadian dollars***
(1988 Accord)		
Capital charge: (2) + (3)	= US$240 898	9 372 190 Canadian dollars
Standardized Approach		
(4) general market risk*	= US$575 000*	10 425 000 Canadian dollars**
(5) counterparty risk	= US$60 000	166 800 Canadian dollars
(1988 Accord)		
Capital charge: (4) + (5)	= US$635 000	10 591 800 Canadian dollars
Capital saving	= 62%	11.5%

*The derivation is left to the reader. The capital charge is made of US$375 000 for basis risk and US$200 000 for the overall net outright position. Obviously, for this portfolio the standardized approach appears to be excessively onerous, while the VaR is small as the portfolio is relatively hedged.
**According to the standardized approach the Canadian dollar swap has a capital charge of 5 250 000 Canadian dollars while it is US$3 750 000 for the US swap, i.e. 5 175 000 Canadian dollars.
***The capital charge for the US swap is US$60 000, i.e. 82 800 Canadian dollars assuming an exchange rate of US$1 = 1.38 Canadian dollars. The capital charge for the Canadian dollar swap is 84 000 Canadian dollars.

Table 1.22   Internal model for Portfolio 4

Term	Canadian Dollar Swap			US Dollar Swap		
	DV01 (Canadian dollars)	Volatility (bp) (σ)	VaR (Canadian dollars)	DV01 (US$)	Volatility (bp) (σ)	VaR (US$)
On	0	10.40	0	0	30.23	0
1 month	0	4.63	0	0	6.30	0
2 months	(161)	4.07	1523	0	3.91	0
3 months	(3300)	5.09	39 150	2459	3.59	20 588
6 months	131	6.67	2042	(28)	3.35	215
9 months	196	7.16	3264	(123)	3.46	988
1 year	250	7.64	4446	(162)	3.58	1350
1.25 years	307	8.11	5796	(195)	3.95	1794
1.5 years	362	8.58	7230	(230)	4.33	2319
1.75 years	433	9.05	9124	(264)	4.70	2894
2 years	1152	9.51	25 541	(746)	5.08	8824
3 years	2614	9.13	55 584	(1681)	5.29	20 742
4 years	3253	8.63	65 407	(2092)	5.50	26 808
5 years	5551	8.14	105 280	(3579)	5.50	45 897
7 years	11 049	7.55	194 397	(7308)	5.63	95 878
10 years	73 161	7.00	1 193 291	(58 138)	5.42	734 252
15 years	0	6.39	0	0	5.44	0
20 years	0	6.07	0	0	5.07	0
30 years	0	5.79	0	0	5.18	0

Exchange rate US$ 1	=	1.38 Canadian dollars
VaR US dollar swap	=	1 279 000 Canadian dollars
VaR Canadian dollar swap	=	1 626 000 Canadian dollars
VaR Portfolio 4	=	970 330 Canadian dollars

Table 1.23   Standardized versus internal models for Portfolio 5 capital charges for general market risk

Internal Model		
VaR for the Canadian dollar position		408 350 Canadian dollars
VaR for the US dollar position		425 660 Canadian dollars
VaR for Portfolio 5		662 610 Canadian dollars
Capital charge $3 \times$ VaR $\times \sqrt{10}$	=	6 286 078 Canadian dollars
Standardized Approach		
Canadian dollar position		3 570 000 Canadian dollars
US dollar position		9 239 100 Canadian dollars
Total	=	12 809 100 Canadian dollars
Capital savings	=	51%

The third portfolio consists of a long government bond position which is hedged by a swap of the same tenor, 10 years in our example, and in the same currency. The capital saving is substantial–62 per cent as shown in Table 1.21. In that case the position is relatively well hedged in a VaR sense, since its VaR exposure is only US$19 068. The internal model benefits, with its multiplier of three from this situation.

The fourth portfolio is constituted of two 10-year swaps, a long and a short position, but in two different currencies, the US dollar and the Canadian dollar. In this instance the capital saving is 11.5 per cent. The calculations are detailed in Tables 1.21 and 1.22. For this portfolio the internal model benefits from the diversification across two different currencies. The standardized approach treats each currency independently, adding the capital charges without any benefit from diversification and hedging across the two countries.

Finally, Portfolio 5 (Table 1.23) shows the full benefit of the internal model when the position is well diversified across maturities and countries. We obtain a capital savings of 51 per cent, which is comparable with the actual savings that we expect to achieve.

1.7 ENDNOTES

1. See Merton (1977) and Crouhy and Galai (1986, 1991).
2. It should be noted that both the Bank of England and SFA in the United Kingdom have had models based on market risk capital charges for many years under the Amsterdam Accord.
3. The precise definition of these capital ratios under the 1988 Accord and the new 1996 Amendment are discussed in Sections 1.2.1 – 1.2.2 and 1.3.5, respectively.
4. Ironically, had these rules been effective in 1994, Barings could not have built these huge futures positions on the SIMEX and OSE, and its failure could have been avoided. Indeed, when Barings collapsed in February 1995, Barings' exposures on the SIMEX and OSE were 40 per cent and 73 per cent of its capital, respectively (cf. Rawnsley (1975)).
5. The G-10 is composed of Belgium, Canada, France, Germany, Italy, Japan, the Netherlands, Sweden, the United Kingdom, and the United States. On the Basle Committee sit senior officials of the central banks and supervisory authorities from the G-10 as well as Switzerland and Luxembourg. The Accord was fully implemented in 1993 in the 12 ratifying countries. This Accord is also known as the BIS requirements since the Basle Committee meets four times a year, usually in Basle, Switzerland, under the patronage of the Bank for International Settlements (BIS). BIS is used in the text as a generic term to represent indifferently the Basle Committee and the regulatory authorities which supervise the banks in the member countries.
6. Netting is, *de facto*, in effect in many derivatives transactions, like interest rate swaps, where only interest payments are exchanged and not the principal amounts.
7. Tier 3 capital, however, cannot support capital requirements from the banking book.
8. Cf. Basle (1995).
9. Other risks, although more difficult to quantify, like operational risk, legal risk, and liquidity risk, may also represent substantial exposures to the bank.
10. The trading book means the bank's proprietary positions in financial instruments, whether on or off balance sheet which are intentionally held for short-term trading, and/or which are taken on by the bank with the intention of making profit from short-term changes in prices, rates, and volatilities. All trading book positions must be marked-to-market or marked-to-model every day. For market risk capital purposes, an institution may include in its measure of general market risk certain non-trading book instruments that it deliberately uses to hedge trading positions.
11. Cf. Basle (1996a,b). In 1993 the European Commission adopted the Capital Adequacy Directive (CAD), imposing uniform capital requirements for securities trading books of banks and securities houses chartered within the European Community. In many ways, the CAD follows the new BIS guidelines (cf. Elderfield (1995a)). It has been effective since January 1996, two years before the BIS market risk proposal applies, placing banks in the rest of the G-10 countries with a comparative advantage against their European counterparts. It should be noted that in North America, large securities houses like Godman

Sachs, Salomon Brothers, Merrill Lynch, which are not regulated by the Office of the Controller of the Currency (OCC), the Federal Reserve System (FED), or the Federal Deposit Insurance Company (FDIC), in the United States, or the Office of the Superintendent of the Financial Institutions (OSFI) in Canada, will not have to satisfy any such minimum capital adequacy requirements. Instead, they are subject to the rules imposed by the Securities and Exchange Commission (SEC) in the United States, and which are less stringent. However, trading opportunities and the profitability of those securities houses depend heavily on their rating. It is then expected that rating agencies like Moody's and Standard and Poor's will play an active role in promoting similar standards among securities houses, and will condition their attribution of top ratings to the implementation of best practice risk management.

12. These qualitative requirements are consistent with the G-30 (1993) recommendations.

13. The convenience yield for commodities, like energy products, reflects the benefits from direct ownership of the physical commodity, e.g. when there is a risk of shortage. It is affected by market conditions as well as specific conditions like the level of inventory and storage costs. Accordingly, the convenience yield may be positive or negative. When inventory are high, demand is low and marginal storage costs are high, the convenience yield is likely to be negative.

14. The square root of 10 rule is only valid when the changes in the portfolio values are not correlated and identically distributed.

15. The 60-day average includes also the previous day.

16. If historical data are weighted to estimate volatilities and correlations, then the average weighted time lag of the individual observations should be at least half a year, which is what would be obtained if the observations were equally weighted.

17. See Section 1.4 for details.

18. Cf. ISDA (1996) and IIF (1996). ISDA (1996) sets out the conclusions of a Joint Task Force of members of the International Swaps and Derivatives Association (ISDA) and the London Investment Banking Association (LIBA) on aspects of the Basle Committee's standards for the use of the internal models to calculate market risk capital charge. IIF (1996) reports the conclusions on the specific risk issue of a task force composed of the representatives of 15 banks which are members of the Institute of International Finance (IFF).

19. See, for example, Sharpe and Alexander (1990, Chapter 8).

20. The limits on capital used vary slightly from one country to the other. For example, OSFI in Canada limits the use of tier 2 and tier 3 capital to meet market risk requirements to 200 per cent of tier 1 capital used to meet these requirements. In addition, tier 1 and tier 2 capital cannot, in total, exceed 100 per cent of tier 1 capital.

21. VaR is an assessment of the potential loss for a given, static portfolio, i.e. the closing position at the end of the day. Obviously the portfolio is traded all the time, and its actual composition keeps changing during the next trading day. Risk management is also active, and decisions to alter the risk exposure of the bank's position may be taken during the course of the day. This is why VaR should be compared *ex post* to these two measures of P&L.

22. Indeed, 99 per cent one-tail confidence level means that we expect losses, but also profits, to be greated than VaR in absolute value 2.5 days per year.

23. The obligation to backtest will be effective only after a year, i.e. in 1999, when institutions will have accumulated one year of historical market data to be used in backtesting. Initially, at least for 1998, the regulators will require only a comparison of VaR against actual P&L.
From our point of view, a better approach to backtesting would be "historical simulation" where on each day the position would be re-evaluated based on the last 250 days closing market data. Then, the "historical distribution" of the changes in the position value would be compared with the "theoretical distribution" derived from the internal VaR model. This approach would allow us, over time, to revisit some key assumptions made in the VaR model which, according to the historical simulation, are revealed to be inconsistent with market data, and may produce a very biased picture of the bank's exposure.

24. Regulators argue that a scaling factor is an absolute necessity to account for model risk, the underestimation of the tail probabilities of the actual distribution of the market factors,

and time-dependence effects when daily VaR is scaled up by the square root of the holding period.

25. For example, a Fed tightening scenario like in May 1994 could be characterized by a 100 basis point (bp) upward shift in the overnight rate, and 30 bp increase for the 10-year yield for the US curve. The yield curves for the other G-10 countries and Switzerland would also shift upward, but by less than the US curve. G-10 currencies would depreciate against the US dollar. Equity markets would also react negatively, with at least a 2 per cent downward move.

26. In Canada, only the maturity method is allowed by the regulator, OSFI. In this chapter we just present the maturity approach. The duration approach differs only by its more accurate method of calculating the sensitivities, or risk weights (cf. Table 1.9).

27. It is valued at current spot exchange rates, since we are interested in the present value of the forward exposures.

28. See also Fed (1995).

29. To save space we do not show the correlation matrix.

1.8 REFERENCES

Basle (1988) *International Convergence of Capital Measurement and Capital Standards*. Basle: Basle Committee on Banking Supervision, Bank of International Settlements.

Basle (1995) *An Internal Model-Based Approach to Market Risk Capital Requirements*. Basle: Basle Committee on Banking Supervision, Bank of International Settlements.

Basle (1996a) *Amendment to the Capital Accord to Incorporate Market Risks*. Basle: Basle Committee on Banking Supervision, Bank of International Settlements.

Basle (1996b) *Overview of the Amendment to the Capital Accord to Incorporate Market Risks*. Basle: Basle Committee on Banking Supervision, Bank of International Settlements.

Basle (1996c) *Supervisory Framework for the Use of Backtesting in Conjunction with the Internal Models Approach to Market Risk Capital Requirements*. Basle: Basle Committee on Banking Supervision, Bank of International Settlements.

Crouhy, M. and Galai, D. (1986) "An economic assessment of capital requirements in the banking industry". *Journal of Banking and Finance*, **10**, 231–241.

Crouhy, M. and Galai, D. (1991) "A contingent claim analysis of a regulated depository institution". *Journal of Banking and Finance*, **15**, 73–90.

Elderfield, M. (1995a) "Capital countdown". *Risk*, **8**, February, 18–21.

Elderfield, M. (1995b) "Capital incentives". *Risk*, **8**, September, 20–21.

FED (1995) *Request for Comment on the Precommittment Approach for Market Risks*, Docket R-0886. Washington: Board of Governors of the Federal Reserve System.

G-30 (1993) *Derivatives: Practices and Principles*. Washington: Global Derivatives Study Group, Group of Thirty.

Gumerlock, R. (1996) "Lacking commitment". *Risk*, **9**, June, 36–39.

IFF (1996) *Report of the Working Group on Quantitative Issues: Capital Adequacy of Specific Risk*, Washington International Institute of Finance, September.

ISDA (1996) "Amendment to the Capital Accord to incorporate market risks: The use of internal models for supervisory purposes". Comments of the ISDA/LIBA Joint Models Task Force, October.

J.P. Morgan (1997) *CreditMetrics*.

Kupiec, P. and O'Brien, J. (1995a) "The use of bank trading risk measurement models for regulatory capital purposes", FEDS Working Paper 95–11. Washington: Federal Reserve Board.

Kupiec, P. and O'Brien, J. (1995b) "A pre-commitment approach to capital requirements for market risk", FEDS Working Paper 95–34. Washington: Federal Reserve Board.

Kupiec, P. and O'Brien, J. (1995c) "Internal affairs". *Risk*, **8**, May, 43–47.

Kupiec, P. and O'Brien, J. (1995d) "Model alternative". *Risk*, **8**, June, 37–40.

Kupiec, P. and O'Brien, J. (1996) "Commitment is the key". *Risk*, **9**, September, 60–63.

Kupiec, P. and O'Brien, J. (1997) *The Pre-Commitment Approach: Using Incentives to Set Market Risk Capital Requirements*, Washington: Board of Governors of the Federal System. 1997–14.

Merton, R. (1977) "An analytic derivation of the cost of deposit insurance and loan guarantees". *Journal of Banking and Finance*, **1**, 9–13.

Rawnsley, J. (1975) *Going for Broke, Nick Leeson and the Collapse of Barings Bank.* London: Harper Collins.

Sharpe, W. and Alexander, G.J. (1990) *Investments.* Englewood Cliffs: Prentice-Hall.

Standard & Poors (1996) *Bank Ratings Comment: Market Capital Rules.* New York.

2

A Survey of Risk Measurement Theory and Practice

STAN BECKERS

2.1 INTRODUCTION

Financial risk quantification, analysis and control have evolved dramatically over the last decades. The old approach may be illustrated by the advice from the American comic Will Rogers (1879–1935): "Buy a stock. If it goes up, sell it. If doesn't go up, don't buy it." In the old days, individual positions were evaluated separately on their own merits and risk was defined as negative return. Significant advances in academic theory have had a major impact on practical risk measurement. Applications such as risk diversification, portfolio construction and hedging are no longer the esoteric domain of the academic ivory tower but are now widely applied by every bank, market maker, investment management organization and pension fund.

In this chapter, we briefly sketch the major academic developments that are generally considered as milestones in our thinking about risk: the principle of risk diversification, beta as an exponent of the single index model and multiple factor models. This gradual progression reflects an increasingly richer description and quantification of the risk dimension.

As the academic treatment of risk became multidimensional and more "realistic", the resulting interplay between academic and the real world led to ever broader applications. In particular, the idea that risk is a relative rather than absolute concept highlighted the need to identify and clearly specify the neutral or benchmark position. We show that benchmarking is therefore an essential prerequisite for a systematic and structured approach to risk control.

Finally, we briefly dwell upon the added complexity of risk in internationally diversified portfolios or books. In particular, it is not a priori clear what repercussions the growing international economic integration has on the risk profile of "global" positions. The international economic fabric is generally assumed to change rather slowly. Structural

Risk Management and Analysis. Vol. 1: Measuring and Modelling Financial Risk.
Edited by Carol Alexander © 1998 John Wiley & Sons Ltd

change would therefore be hard to detect. The same cannot be said, however, for the associated currency regimes. We therefore also look into the complexities of currency risk management as a special case of international portfolio diversification.

Before we dive into the intricacies of exchange rate risk, we need to return to the roots of all modern risk analysis.

2.2 THE BASICS

2.2.1 Markowitz and the Principle of Diversification

There is no doubt that all modern forms of risk quantification find their origins in the seminal work of Markowitz (1959) *Portfolio Selection: Efficient Diversification of Investments*. Although the idea of not putting all your eggs in one basket was certainly not new, Markowitz was the first to formalize and apply it to financial instruments. He started from the assumption that each portfolio construction decision can be structured in function of the expected mean and standard deviation of the portfolio return.[1] His main insights can be summarized as follows:

1. Whereas the portfolio return is a simple weighted average of the individual asset returns, the portfolio risk will typically be less than the weighted average of the individual asset risks.
2. The portfolio risk will be lower, the lower the correlations between the constituent asset returns (the famous diversification principle).
3. Therefore the risk of each asset can be thought of as consisting of two components: some of it can be made to disappear through a judicious combination of this asset with other assets (the diversifiable risk). The other part will always have to be borne by an investor.

Portfolio selection was reduced to the choice of maximizing the return while at the same time minimizing the risk. An investor who is driven by this mean–standard deviation criterion would make a rational choice that could be formalized in a quadratic programming problem.

As a result of this problem formulation, the correlation between different financial instruments came to the fore as the crucial characteristic that defines the optimal portfolio profile. It also helped to establish the notion that an instrument cannot be evaluated in isolation: its attractiveness will largely depend on its contribution towards the overall portfolio return and standard deviation.

Risk characterization and quantification using Markowitz's approach presupposes a knowledge of the "full covariance matrix", e.g. an exact measure of means, standard deviations and correlations of all assets under consideration. The practical estimation of this covariance matrix is not straightforward since the standard deviations and correlations need to be estimated on the basis of historic time series using daily, weekly or monthly observations. The length of the observation history to be used is partially determined by the number of assets in the matrix: to ensure that the covariance matrix is well behaved (semi-positive definite), the number of observations has to (significantly) exceed the number of assets.

For example, a covariance matrix of 30 different assets will have 435 different entries. Estimating these covariances using 12 observations would result in a matrix with rank 66.

Intuitively, this is equivalent to saying that 66 out of the 435 entries contain information, whereas the remaining 369 estimates would be pure noise.

In addition, at least 200 observations are typically needed to reduce the standard error of the correlation coefficients to reasonable proportions.[2] Although the standard error of the estimates can be reduced by increasing the number of observations, this will also amplify the risk of incompletely capturing a structural change in the relationships. Using long time series, there is a significant danger that fundamental changes in the interrelationships will be lost in the large number of observations. Luckily, the structural behaviour of some asset categories (such as equity markets) will only change slowly relative to each other. In other cases, such as exchange rates, violent and significant structural shifts are commonplace.[3] These structural changes will be picked up slowly using the historical covariance matrix, thereby reducing the practical relevance of the "full covariance" approach.

In sum, the practical implementation of the full covariance approach to risk estimation as developed by Markowitz runs into severe implementation problems when large numbers of assets are involved, and especially when returns are not jointly stationary. This observation naturally leads us to the question of modelling the risk (variances and correlations) in function of the underlying asset characteristics. An important step in this direction was the Capital Asset Pricing Model.

2.2.2 Sharpe and the Distinction Between Systematic and Residual Risk

Markowitz's book revolutionized economic thinking, particularly a little known aspect of it (financial economics). Indeed, until then most academic work had concentrated on corporate finance and financial statement analysis. Structured portfolio selection opened new opportunities for quantitatively oriented financial economists.

(i) The Capital Asset Pricing Model

The next leap forward was achieved by the work of Sharpe (1964), Lintner (1965) and Mossin (1966). They extended the portfolio diversification principle of Markowitz by introducing the (simplifying) assumption of homogeneous expectations: if all interested parties agree on the expected returns, standard deviations and correlations of the available investment alternatives, then they will effectively be facing the same opportunity set. Assuming that they behave rationally, as defined by the Markowitz portfolio selection rule, they will all end up choosing the same portfolio.

The formalization of this analysis led to the Capital Asset Pricing Model (CAPM) that would dominate academic thinking for the next decades. It is important to note that the model is a normative equilibrium model: it prescribes how the world should behave if all investors are rational and markets are efficient.[4] Under these circumstances only the non-diversifiable risk of an asset would be rewarded. (Why would one expect to be compensated for needlessly carrying diversifiable risk?) Formally:

$$E(R_j) = R_f + \beta_j[E(R_M) - R_f)] \tag{1}$$

where

$E(R_j)$ = expected return on asset (portfolio) j,

$\beta_j = \mathrm{Cov}(R_j, R_M)/\mathrm{Var}(R_M)$,

$E(R_M)$ = expected return on the capitalization weighted portfolio of all assets,

$\quad R_f$ = risk-free return.

It is not surprising that the CAPM was not enthusiastically received by the financial community. It effectively says that 99 per cent of all financial analysts, investment managers, brokers and market makers are wasting their time and have no socially redeeming value. Indeed, if the world were to behave exactly as prescribed by the CAPM, then

- all investors would all hold the same portfolio (i.e. the market portfolio), which — by definition — is perfectly diversified, and
- the only thing one would ever need to know about an asset would be its beta with respect to the market portfolio (since the beta fully determines its expected return).

Luckily financial practitioners do not have to feel guilty about their scepticism because the CAPM is very hard to validate empirically: it is set in terms of expected returns which are not directly observable, and the "market portfolio", which contains all assets (not restricted to those traded in financial markets), is impossible to quantify (Roll (1977)).

(ii) Single Factor Models of Risk

The major value of the CAPM must therefore not be sought in its formalization of the (normative) return generating equation, but mainly in the fact that it helped to structure the risk quantification and decomposition. Early attempts to validate empirically the CAPM relied upon time series regressions of the following form:

$$R_{jt} - R_{ft} = \alpha_j + \beta_j(I_{mt} - R_{ft}) + \varepsilon_{jt} \tag{2}$$

where

R_{jt} = return to asset j in period t,

R_{ft} = risk-free rate in period t,

I_{mt} = return to market index m in period t,

α_j = non-index-related return to asset j,

β_j = beta of asset j with respect to index I,

ε_{jt} = residual return of asset j in period t.

If *ex post* realized returns over long periods accurately reflect *ex ante* expectations and if index I_m completely captures the market portfolio, then the regression test would be a direct test of the CAPM. (According to the theory one would then expect $\alpha_j = 0$.) It is now generally accepted that both of these conditions never hold and that therefore the CAPM cannot be empirically (in)validated.

The above equation, however, is much more interesting because it helps to segment the return on an asset in an index-related component and a return that is residual to the index. This segmentation does not require any financial theory and can be performed with respect to any index. It has significant repercussions for the risk decomposition of an asset:

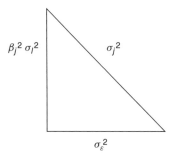

Figure 2.1

- the risk equivalent of equation (2) is

$$\sigma_j^2 = \beta_j^2 \sigma_I^2 + \sigma_\varepsilon^2 \tag{3}$$

where σ_ε^2 = variance of ε_{jt}. In words, the total risk of an asset (portfolio) can be divided into two orthogonal components that can be visualized as shown in Figure 2.1. Note that by construction the residual return will always be independent of the index-related return.

- The crucial risk measure of an asset (portfolio) is the beta of that asset (portfolio), where beta is defined as $\text{Cov}(r_j, r_I)/\text{Var}(r_I)$ and r_j and r_I are the excess return on asset (portfolio) j and the index, respectively.[5] This beta is related to the hedge ratio that determines the number of index futures contracts that need to be sold to eliminate the index-related risk from the portfolio.[6]

Using old capital markets terminology the beta as measured by (2) is nothing more than a quantification of the extent to which a stock is cyclical (high beta) or defensive (low beta) with respect to the prevalent index. In sum, although the single index model (2) finds its origins in the early attempts to test the CAPM, it has now taken on a life of its own as a convenient way to segment the risk of an asset into index-related and residual risk. Since the single index model is not based on any financial theory, it does not presuppose whether a_j should be zero or not.

The practical implementation of the risk segmentation (3) is flawed by the simplifying assumptions underlying (2):

1. The correlation between the different assets arises from a common source, i.e. the index. No other sources of communality (correlation) are recognized.

2. The measure of communality (beta) is assumed to be stationary through time. Relatively long time series are needed to obtain accurate estimates of beta. At best, regression (2) will have an R^2 of 35 per cent for individual equities.[7]

3. The residual risk σ_ε^2 is assumed to be entirely company specific and would diversify very quickly. There is no correlation between the company-specific returns.

As a result, the main use of the single index model (2) is typically concentrated in hedging away the benchmark-related risk in portfolios or books using index-based futures or derivatives. Very few organizations or academics would "model" asset risk based on one explanatory variable. To the contrary, it is now generally recognized that risk is multidimensional and needs to be explained using a multitude of characteristics or attributes. This has naturally led to multiple factor models.

2.3 MULTIPLE FACTOR MODELS

Although the empirical evidence substantiating the multidimensional nature of risk goes back to the late 1960s,[8] its standing was significantly enhanced through the development of the Arbitrage Pricing Theory (Ross (1976)). The Arbitrage Pricing Theory can be thought of as a generalization of the CAPM. Using a somewhat less restrictive set of assumptions (mainly doing away with the need for investors to make decisions on the basis of mean and standard deviation), the theory infers that there may be a multitude of risk premia associated with an individual asset.[9] Unfortunately, the theory does not tell us how many risk factors could be at play. A *fortiori* it cannot identify the exact nature of these risk factors.

The multifactor Arbitrage Pricing Theory can be formulated as follows:

$$E(R_j) = R_f + \beta_{1j}[E(F_1) - R_f] + \beta_{2j}[E(F_2) - R_f] + \beta_{3j}[E(F_3) - R_f]$$
$$+ \beta_{4j}[E(F_4) - R_f] + \cdots \tag{4}$$

where

$$E(R_j) = \text{expected return on asset (portfolio) } j,$$
$$\beta_{ij} = \text{sensitivity of asset } j \text{ to risk factor } i,$$
$$R_f = \text{risk-free return,}$$
$$E(F_i) - R_f = \text{expected risk premium associated with factor } i.$$

The Arbitrage Pricing Theory (like the CAPM) is a normative equilibrium theory. If, indeed, on average assets were to behave as prescribed by the theory, then we would observe

$$R_{jt} - R_{ft} = \alpha_j + \beta_{1j}(F_{1t} - R_{ft}) + \beta_{2j}(F_{2t} - R_{ft}) + \beta_{3j}(F_{3t} - R_{ft})$$
$$+ \beta_{4j}(F_{4t} - R_{ft}) + \cdots + \varepsilon_{jt} \tag{5}$$

where

$$R_{jt} = \text{return to asset } j \text{ in period } t,$$

$$R_{ft} = \text{risk-free rate in period } t,$$

$$F_{it} = \text{risk premium associated with factor } i \text{ in period } t,$$

$$\alpha_j = \text{non-factor-related return to asset } j,$$

$$\beta_{ij} = \text{sensitivity of asset } j \text{ with respect to risk factor } i,$$

$$\varepsilon_{jt} = \text{residual return of asset } j \text{ in period } t.$$

Since α_j should be zero (no free lunch), the stylized matrix notation of equation (5) can be written as

$$\mathbf{R}_t = \mathbf{B}\,\mathbf{f}_t + \mathbf{E}_t \tag{6}$$

where

$\mathbf{R}_t$ = vector of individual asset excess returns (over the risk-free rate) for period t,

$\mathbf{B}$ = matrix of asset exposures to the different risk factors,

$\mathbf{f}_t$ = vector of factor risk premia (in excess over the risk-free rate) for period t,

$\mathbf{E}_t$ = vector of individual asset residual returns for period t,

with corresponding risks

$$\mathbf{V} = \mathbf{B}'\mathbf{FB} + \mathbf{\Omega} \tag{7}$$

where

$\mathbf{V}$ = covariance matrix of asset returns $\mathbf{R}_t$,

$\mathbf{F}$ = covariance matrix of factor risk premia $\mathbf{f}_t$,

$\mathbf{\Omega}$ = (diagonal) matrix of asset residual risks $\mathbf{E}_t$.

Close inspection of equation (7) reveals that in fact the original Markowitz "full covariance" matrix is broken up into factor-related risks and residual risks. The notion of a multitude of risk factors driving asset returns is now widely accepted. Unfortunately, the identification of these risk factors remains an empirical exercise about which there is no consensus. Broadly speaking, three approaches can be used to identify these factors. They can be classified in function of which components of (6) are presupposed to be known: fundamental factor models assume the $\mathbf{B}$ as given and estimate the $\mathbf{f}_t$. Macroeconomics models, on the other hand, take the $\mathbf{f}_t$ as given and estimate the $\mathbf{B}$. Statistical models try to simultaneously estimate $\mathbf{B}$ and $\mathbf{f}_t$. In what follows we briefly discuss each of these alternatives.

2.3.1 Fundamental Factor Models

Fundamental factor models try to fill in equation (6) based on the observation of the day-to-day activity of investment managers, brokers and financial analysts. In their pursuit of return, they use a multitude of decision variables. It is therefore reasonable to assume that these decision variables have some relation to the factor sensitivities $\mathbf{B}$. Although it is virtually impossible to draw up a completely exhaustive list of factor exposures $\mathbf{B}$, there is a fairly large consensus on the company or asset characteristics that are assumed to play a role in explaining differential asset returns. Amongst these are: market capitalization, asset liquidity, price earnings ratio, interest rate sensitivity, stability of earnings growth, dividend yield, exchange rate sensitivity as well as the economic or industrial sectors in which the company operates. The fundamental factor model uses these company or asset attributes as proxies for $\mathbf{B}$. A cross-sectional regression of the type (6) will identify whether, for any time period t, there was a significant risk premium $\mathbf{f}_t$ associated with some or all of these attributes.

Estimating the cross-sectional regressions (6) over consecutive time periods will yield a history of factor risk premia $\mathbf{f}_t$ which can be used to estimate the factor covariance matrix $\mathbf{F}$. The main advantage of this approach is the fact that it allows for quick adaptations to structural changes in asset characteristics: the effect of an exogenous change in the company's dividend yield or leverage (interest rate sensitivity) will feed through immediately in that company's risk characterization in equation (7). Indeed, given $\mathbf{F}$, the volatility and correlation of any asset (not necessarily market traded) can be derived immediately from its attributes **B**.

The disadvantage of the fundamental factor approach derives from the fact that it presupposes that an exhaustive set of mutually exclusive company attributes **B** can be identified and quantified. If an important attribute is overlooked, then the resulting residual variance matrix Ω in (7) will not be diagonal, potentially resulting in an underestimation of the real portfolio risk. Since the matrix Ω is assumed to be diagonal, all specific return correlations are, by definition, set to zero. If unidentified common factors are left undetected in the specific return series, then the true correlations between the specific returns will be non-zero. These specific risks will therefore not diversify as quickly as assumed by the zero correlation assumption.

Fundamental factor models are probably the most widely used for risk estimation and quantification purposes. Separate models have been estimated for about 20 of the leading stock markets across the world. Table 2.1 summarizes the fundamental company attributes that have been found to be relevant in a representative sample of these markets. Note that some attributes are found to contribute consistently to explaining differential stock returns in all markets (such as market capitalization, price earnings ratio, recent performance), whereas others (such as book value to market value) are unique to a given market.

Table 2.1   Fundamental factors

	US	Japan	UK	Germany	France	Switzerland
Historic Volatility	X	X	X	X	X	X
Recent Performance (Momentum)	X	X	X	X	X	X
Market Capitalization	X	X	X	X	X	X
Liquidity	X	X	X		X	
Earnings Growth	X	X	X			X
Price/ Earnings	X	X	X	X	X	X
Book/Price	X					
Earnings Variability	X		X	X		X
Leverage	X	X	X	X	X	X
Foreign Income	X	X	X	X		
Labour Intensity	X		X	X	X	
Yield	X		X	X	X	X
Interest Rate Sensitivity		X				
+ Industries						

Source: BARRA International.

2.3.2 Macroeconomic Factor Models

Instead of taking the asset sensitivities to the different factors as given, macroeconomic models try to approximate the factor risk premia $\mathbf{f}_t$ through a time series of macroeconomic variables. This approach presupposes that the macroeconomic events that have a pervasive impact on the future cash flows (and therefore present values and returns) of different assets can be identified. Since expected changes are already reflected in current prices, this approach tries to link surprises in major macroeconomic events to individual asset behaviour.

The empirical implementation of this approach has many variants. However, the following set of unexpected changes are typically used as proxies for the time series $\mathbf{f}_t$: changes in inflation, industrial production, investor confidence[10] and interest rates. Note that each of these variables can be expected to impact the (real) present value of the future cash flow of most assets.

The predefined time series $\mathbf{f}_t$ (e.g. the realized unexpected changes in the above variables) can then be used in a time series estimation of (6) to identify $\mathbf{B}$, the average sensitivity of each asset to these risk premia. Note that this estimation procedure is conceptually very similar to the time series estimation of beta in the single index model (2). It therefore suffers from the same drawback, namely that the estimated factor exposure of an asset will change only slowly through time. Conversely, it will take some time before a structural change in the characteristics of an asset will feed through in the estimated $\mathbf{B}$.

The macroeconomic model also shares the drawback of the fundamental model in that an accurate estimation of (6) assumes that all pervasive risk premia can be exactly identified and quantified (and that they are more or less mutually exclusive).

A risk analysis using the macroeconomic model would proceed along the same lines as the fundamental factor approach: given $\mathbf{B}$ and $\mathbf{f}_t$, equation (7) can be used to characterize the risk of any combination of assets.

2.3.3 Statistical Models

Statistical models are most closely associated with the original tests of the Arbitrage Pricing Theory. As the name implies, they rely upon pure statistical analysis of the return series to infer $\mathbf{B}$ and $\mathbf{f}_t$. The statistical model pleads total ignorance about the nature of the risk premia or factor sensitivities that are at play within a given market.

The statistical model uses the full covariance matrix $\mathbf{V}$ as a starting point and applies a factor analysis or principal components procedure to decompose $\mathbf{V}$. The statistical procedure will typically yield a set of factor exposures $\mathbf{B}$, which can then be used in cross-sectional regression (6) to yield the factor return $\mathbf{f}_t$. The procedure is conceptually similar to the fundamental factor approach, except that the factor exposures are identified using a statistical procedure rather than (subjective) fundamental analysis. The statistical model has the significant advantage that the factor exposures are completely orthogonal in the estimation sample (but not necessarily out of sample). However, the statistical factors exposures (and associated factor returns) have no direct economic interpretation. Further analysis (and subjective judgement) is needed to attach some economic rationale to the statistical constructs.

The methodology also suffers from the fact that the factor exposures will only change slowly through time and will react to structural changes with a long lag. Obviously the matrix $\mathbf{V}$ can be observed over different time intervals, presumably using the history that is deemed to be most relevant for the forecast horizon. Using slightly shorter or longer histories will yield slightly different factor exposures. However, given the number of observations needed to minimize the estimation error of the (co)variances, in $\mathbf{V}$ it is unlikely that the factor exposures will change significantly from one estimation to the next.

2.3.4 A Comparison

Although each of the three methods has its adherents, arguably the fundamental factor model is used most widely for risk forecasting purposes. This is partially due to the fact that it is couched in a language and uses concepts that most financial analysts, brokers, market makers and investment managers are familiar with. The out of sample risk forecasts will — by nature — also react more quickly to structural changes.

A recent article by Connor (1995) compares the explanatory power of the three models as applied to the US equity market and concludes that the statistical and fundamental models significantly outperform the macroeconomic model. The fundamental model also has a slight edge over the statistical model.

It is interesting to note that the risk breakdown as described in (7) (irrespective of the estimation procedure) also allows for the refined estimation of drift in certain components of $\mathbf{F}$ or Ω. Indeed, the GARCH class of estimation procedures can be applied to the time series of asset-related factor variances or residual variances.

In general the multiple factor models allow for a refined breakdown of the asset risks and correlations and thereby improve upon forecasting accuracy by separating structural sources of variability from the incidental ones.

2.4 ABSOLUTE VERSUS RELATIVE RISK

The risk models we discussed in Section 2.3 form the core of all risk measurement and management activities. In fact, the matrices $\mathbf{V}$ and $\mathbf{F}$ can be thought of as the engines that drive all risk quantification. The usage of these models will differ significantly depending on the objectives and time frame. In what follows we discuss the essential role of the benchmark in all risk control activities. Indeed, risk is always a relative concept and it cannot be discussed meaningfully unless the neutral point has been identified. Whereas market makers and corporate treasurers probably worry most about the absolute value of money at risk, money managers are continually evaluated against their peer group. This leads to two distinct applications of the risk models.

2.4.1 The Role of the Benchmark

Risk quantification is (should be) at the core of all activities for traders, corporate treasurers and market makers. They worry about how much money they stand to make or lose, given their current positions. They typically have a short time frame that is measured in terms of days or (at most) weeks. Their natural risk measure is therefore the value at risk in their current positions.

This value at risk concept can be quantified using the covariance matrix $\mathbf{V}$ as follows. Let $\mathbf{P}$ be the vector of (dollar) value positions in the different instruments (i.e. $\mathbf{P}_i$ is the dollar amount in instrument or asset class i). Note that this vector can contain both positive and negative values. The Value at Risk (VaR) is then derived from $(\mathbf{P'} \ \mathbf{V} \ \mathbf{P})^{1/2}$, after translation into an appropriate confidence interval.

This VaR tells us how much money the aggregate position can make or lose with 66 per cent probability. (Doubling the number will increase the confidence band to 95 per cent.) The time horizon over which this forecast applies depends on the nature of the matrix $\mathbf{V}$. If $\mathbf{V}$ is calibrated within a daily time frame (i.e. it is put together using daily data), then the risk forecast will apply over a one day horizon.[11] VaR implicitly assumes that putting the aggregate value of all positions on short term (one day, a week ...) deposit is the neutral or benchmark position. VaR therefore effectively measures how much more money can be made or lost in comparison with a short-term deposit strategy.

Whether the VaR is acceptable or not crucially depends on the capital backing up the positions. The VaR can be used directly to evaluate whether the minimum solvency requirements are met.

Note that the VaR concept is different from the risk characterization as proposed by the Basle Committee of the Bank for International Settlements and from the European Union Directive (EEC 93/6). These regulatory authorities ignore the impact of the covariance matrix $\mathbf{V}$ and consider the risks in individual positions to be completely additive. This results in more stringent capital requirements than those implied by the VaR number. Banks and traders are consequently required to be better capitalized than strictly necessary given the real risks being incurred. It is somewhat disappointing that these capital adequacy standards make no allowance for the potential diversification effect of offsetting positions.

Whereas market operators have a short time frame and are mainly concerned about not losing (too much) money, investment managers are working with slightly different objectives. Portfolio managers are typically expected to outperform the market average or their peer group (or both). They will be evaluated over longer time frames (typically on an annual cycle).

In fact, the (implicit or explicit) objective of most portfolio managers is to add value relative to a predefined alternative. This alternative is often defined as a market index. Presumably the owner of the funds argues that she does not have to hire a highly paid investment manager to produce the average return as reflected in the market index. Indeed, over the past decade a number of investment managers have specialized in providing nothing more that this "average" index return. These index fund managers typically succeed in very closely mimicking the index return at extremely low costs.[12]

The objective of the portfolio manager is therefore to create a portfolio that is sufficiently different from the index to allow her to outperform it. This leads to a segmentation of the portfolio risk into two components: (i) the risk inherent in the benchmark and (ii) the active risk added onto it by the portfolio manager.

It is fair to argue that the benchmark risk is the responsibility of the owner of the funds: she sets the target and requests the manager to outperform the target. Let us assume that a client decides to invest in a Japanese mutual fund and learns from the manager that this fund targets an outperformance of the Nikkei 225 index. If, subsequently, the Japanese equity market crashes resulting in a negative return on the Nikkei 225, then the client cannot blame the manager for the resulting losses. In fact, a manager can have performed well by losing less money than the benchmark (for example, by turning in a return of -10 per cent when the index does -15 per cent). Conversely, a manager who achieves a return of 30 per cent when the benchmark has a total return of 35 per cent has nothing to be proud of.

The above example illustrates the segmentation of the risk in institutionally managed portfolios: benchmark-related risk is the responsibility of the owner of the funds. The investment manager tries to add value relative to the benchmark by incurring active risk relative to the benchmark. Mathematically this active risk can be expressed as follows. Let $\mathbf{W}_P$ be the vector of portfolio weights (i.e. $\mathbf{W}_{iP}$ is the percentage weight of asset i in portfolio P) and $\mathbf{W}_M$ be the vector of index weights (i.e. $\mathbf{W}_{iM}$ is the percentage weight of asset i in index M). Then the active variance risk of portfolio P is given by

$$(\mathbf{W}_P - \mathbf{W}_M)' \, \mathbf{V}(\mathbf{W}_P - \mathbf{W}_M) \tag{8}$$

Note that the active risk uses percentage weights to measure the exposure to the risk matrix $\mathbf{V}$. The active risk is a direct function of the extent to which individual assets are weighted differently to their weight in the index (if all $\mathbf{W}_P$ are equal to $\mathbf{W}_M$, then the active risk will be zero). The direct implication of this observation is that the neutral (no information) position in an asset is the market weight.

Given that the exposures are expressed in percentage weights, the active risk will be expressed in percentage terms. An active risk of 5 per cent, for instance, would imply that the portfolio has a 66 per cent (95 per cent) chance to obtain a return bounded by the benchmark return plus or minus 5 per cent (10 per cent)

Since the time horizon used to evaluate investment managers usually extends over longer time periods (anywhere from one to three years), the matrix $\mathbf{V}$ will typically be estimated using monthly observations. The resulting risk measures can be annualized by multiplying them by the square root of 12. Active risks are mostly quoted on an annual basis.

2.4.2 The Notion of Tracking Error

The active risk of the portfolio is mostly referred to as the tracking error since it quantifies the extent to which the portfolio can be expected to obtain a differential return from the benchmark. It is a direct quantification of the aggressiveness of the portfolio manager's style: managers who aggressively pursue outperformance of the benchmark will do so by holding assets in wildly different weights $\mathbf{W}_P$ from their benchmark weights $\mathbf{W}_M$. This may result in tracking errors of up to 10 per cent or more. Conservative managers, on the other hand, may have tracking errors of 2–4 per cent. Index fund managers will have tracking errors of less than 0.50 per cent.[13]

An alternative way of looking at the tracking error can be derived from equation (1):

$$E(R_p) - R_f = \beta_p[E(R_M) - R_f] + E(e_p)$$

i.e. the excess return on portfolio p is proportional to the beta of the portfolio with respect to index M. (Note that $E(e_p)$ is zero according to the CAPM.)

Therefore the active return of the portfolio over the market index M is

$$[E(R_p) - R_f] - [E(R_M) - R_f] = \beta_p[E(R_M) - R_f] - [E(R_M) - R_f] + E(e_p)$$

and the variance of the active return is given by $(\beta_p - 1)^2 \sigma_M^2 + \sigma_\varepsilon^2$. This alternative expression for the tracking error variance (which can be shown to be mathematically equivalent to expression (8)), clearly illustrates the two main sources of potential value added: the tracking error will increase as the portfolio beta will deviate significantly from 1 and as the residual risk of the portfolio increases.

Let us illustrate this with a practical example. Assume that the portfolio has a beta of 0.8 and a residual risk of 5 per cent. If the standard deviation of the market index is 20 per cent, then the tracking error will be $\sqrt{[(0.8 - 1)^2 \times 400 + 25]} = 6.40$ per cent, implying that the return on this portfolio will, two years out of three, deviate up to 6.4 per cent from the market index return.

The sources of value added (and associated risks) in a portfolio can be broken down into two components: (i) market timing and (ii) less than perfect diversification (giving rise to residual risk). In practice, very few portfolio managers will aggressively engage in market timing since it is an "all or nothing" strategy. By constructing a portfolio with a beta that is significantly higher (or lower) than 1, the portfolio manager effectively bets on an exceptionally high (low) index risk premium. The market will very quickly prove the manager right or wrong.

Conversely, there are thousands of ways of introducing residual risk in the portfolio. The manager can

- overweight or underweight individual stocks relative to their index weights (stock picking);
- over- or underemphasize individual sectors or industries; or
- take a view with respect to certain types of companies (such as high yield, small capitalization, low price earnings, etc.).

In other words, there are thousands of sources of residual risk in the portfolio. Each investment manager will have her own preferences, giving rise to her own investment style. There are as many styles as there are investment management organizations, although a number of classifications of style have been introduced (such as small capitalization, value, growth, income, etc.). Table 2.2 summarizes the most frequently used investment styles, together with the associated tracking errors.

It is also worth mentioning that the tracking error is directly related to the business risk of the investment manager: portfolios with a high tracking error have a higher probability of significantly outperforming (underperforming) the benchmark. Since there is a high correlation between under (out)performance and client (dis)satisfaction, only investment managers with strong convictions can afford to run portfolios with high tracking errors. The self-preservation instinct of most portfolio managers drives them towards lower (safer)

Table 2.2

Investment Style	Typical Tracking Error relative to Cap Weighted Market Index (%)
Market Timer	>10
Small Capitalization	>7
Growth	>5
Value (Income)	>4
Quantitative	>4
Traditional Stock Picker	2–4
Tilted Fund	2
Index Fund	<.50

tracking errors: they prefer to make many small bets in a portfolio rather than a few big ones.

Very crudely, it can be said that investment management organizations sell tracking error to their clients. It is up to the client to decide how much tracking error she would like to bear and what kinds of tracking error are more likely to give rise to market outperformance. Although there is a bewildering choice of tracking errors and styles on offer, it is a sobering thought that, by definition, the average reward to all these tracking errors is zero.[14]

Although tracking error can be measured with respect to any benchmark, the point of reference that is most frequently used is the market index. However, as is evident from equation (8), the formula can be applied with respect to any externally defined neutral position. In the extreme, a short-term time deposit could be used as the benchmark, in which case (8) reduces to measuring the total volatility of the portfolio (over the appropriate risk-free rate). (The tracking error with respect to the risk-free rate is the total portfolio risk.)

The quantification of the portfolio tracking error only presupposes that a benchmark has been predefined. A portfolio manager will (should) be at a loss as to what to do if the performance benchmark has not been identified a priori (choosing $\mathbf{W}_P$ if $\mathbf{W}_M$ is unknown is virtually impossible). Although this seems a self-evident truth, there are still many portfolio managers who take on mandates without exactly agreeing with the client on the benchmark. Not surprisingly, they feel unfairly treated when *ex post* the client pulls a different performance evaluation benchmark out of a hat.[15]

2.4.3 Concluding Remarks

Although VaR and tracking error both use the matrix $\mathbf{V}$ as the "driving" force, the accuracy of the risk model plays a more important role in the VaR calculation. Indeed, the tracking error typically concentrates on a small proportion of the total portfolio risk (the tracking error rarely makes up more than 20 per cent of the portfolio risk). The VaR calculation, on the other hand, is a direct function of the total volatility of the aggregate position value.

This does not diminish the importance of accurate risk forecasting for both types of applications. It should be kept in mind that there is no such thing as a risk model that will satisfy all needs: traders and treasurers will be interested in short-term fluctuations and short-term risk, whereas portfolio managers' $\mathbf{V}$ should satisfy long-term needs. These different objectives will also be reflected in the factor decomposition of the different $\mathbf{V}$.

Short-term risk models are much more driven by technical factors related to market imbalances (such as liquidity, turnover, bid/ask spread, high–low, open interest, etc.) which help to explain differential short-term volatility of different assets. Long-term risk models in turn are more sensitive to the fundamental characteristics of the underlying instruments (such as the vital signals that are reflected in balance sheet and income statements). A factor decomposition of the matrix $\mathbf{V}$ will therefore crucially depend on the forecast time horizon.

Table 2.3 compares the "fundamental" factors driving a short-term and a long-term risk model for the US and UK equity markets. Note that the explanatory power of the short-term risk model is significantly lower than that of a longer-term model. This is due to the prevalence of more idiosyncratic events in day-to-day observations (whereas the impact of these events would be diversified away through time and therefore have less

Table 2.3 A comparison of short-term versus long-term risk models

Short-Term Risk Factors	US	UK
Capitalization	X	X
Short-Term Beta		X
Short-Term Volatility	X	X
Short-Term Momentum		
+ Industries	X	X
Typical R^2 (Adj)	0.23	0.22
Typical R^2 (Adj) Long-Term Fundamental Factor Model	0.38	0.35

Source: BARRA International

impact on monthly observations). Short-term risk is also much less stable through time given the transient nature of short-term market themes or forces.

However, this does not mean that longer-term risks are immune to structural changes in the underlying relationships. A good risk model will try to adapt as quickly as possible to these changes. This is the theme we turn to in the following section.

2.5 INTERNATIONAL PORTFOLIO DIVERSIFICATION

The benefits of risk diversification derive from the fact that individual positions have less than perfect correlation. Casual empiricism suggests that international capital markets are becoming more integrated, implying that the correlation between markets, sectors and individual instruments is increasing. The question about the extent to which international markets are segmented or integrated has therefore received a fair amount of attention in the financial literature. In Section 2.5.1 we review some of the insights that have been derived from this research.

2.5.1 Integration versus Segmentation

There is currently no clear evidence suggesting that the growing international economic integration (European Economic Community, European Free Trade Association, North American Free Trade Association, GATT, etc.) results in significant increases in correlations. However, it should be pointed out from the outset that economic integration can be perfectly reconciled with low correlations to the extent that different markets or regions are dominated by different types of industrial activity. For example, despite the growing harmonization of monetary, economic and fiscal policies within the European Economic Union, it is perfectly reasonable to observe a continued low correlation between the French equity market (with a relative dominance of oil and consumer goods) and the German market (banks and chemicals).

As long as low correlations are driven by the different industrial fabric, international diversification will continue to yield significant benefits. The situation changes to the extent that countries with a similar economic profile will be less and less impacted by purely domestic (country-specific) events and be influenced more by transnational (global) effects. Under those circumstances, a growing macroeconomic integration will automatically lead to a stronger correlation at the microeconomic level (at least for companies within the same sector). The questions we are effectively asking are: To what extent is the behaviour of individual stocks explained by purely domestic factors or transnational variables? Have the transnational variables been gaining in explanatory power in the recent past?

Several academic studies have investigated these questions (Grinold et al. (1989), Beckers et al. (1992), Heston and Rouwenhorst (1994)). They invariably come to the conclusion that stock price behaviour is dominated by purely local (domestic) forces. For example, Grinold et al. (1989) find, on the basis of a world-wide sample of 2500 companies, that the nationality (domicile) of a company is much more powerful than a company's industrial classification in explaining differential stock returns. A similar conclusion was arrived at by Beckers et al. (1992) for a sample of 1400 European stocks: the R^2 for a typical company is 32 per cent using country of domicile as the explanatory variable, whereas industrial classification only accounts for 21 per cent of the stock variance. Adding the industrial classification as a second explanatory variable to the country of domicile leads to an insignificant increase in R^2. Both studies also conclude that over the decade of the 1980s, the explanatory power of the transnational industry affiliation variable has not increased (i.e. domestic factors appear to be as important and dominant at the end of the 1980s as at the start of the decade). Heston and Rouwenhorst (1994) similarly conclude that over the last 20 years, industrial structure is a weak explanatory variable when analysing cross-sectional return differences. They find that the low correlation between stock markets is almost completely due to country-specific events.

The general evidence therefore points in the direction of markets that continue to be driven by purely domestic factors. This is also reflected in the way in which most portfolio managers and market makers operate: as long as assets are classified, analysed and researched first and foremost on the basis of their "nationality" and as long as portfolios are structured in a top-down fashion (choosing country allocation first before filling in the individual country portfolios), we will continue to observe a dominance of domestic over international factors. There may be a slow shift in the direction of a more global view, mostly at the level of financial analysis where increasingly companies within a given sector are compared with each other, irrespective of their domicile. However, so far this globalization of security analysis has had no discernible impact on individual correlations.

The above analyses suffer somewhat from the relatively weak power of statistical significance tests of differences in correlation coefficients. Given that most correlation coefficients are based on a fairly limited set of observations, their estimation error will typically be large (see endnote 2). It is therefore difficult to prove statistically that correlation coefficients have indeed increased (or decreased) significantly through time.

A related but equally relevant question regarding market correlations concerns their stability across different market regimes. A recent study (Erb et al. (1994)) hints at the possibility that correlations may be the highest in periods when they matter most. There is indeed some evidence that recent crash periods, such as October 1987, have simultaneously and uniformly affected almost all markets. The benefits of international diversification were not as strong during these periods as originally thought on the basis of the average historic correlations. It remains, however, very difficult to establish statistically that correlations are different in down from up markets.

So far we have mainly addressed the question of correlation within and across equity markets. Whereas there is little evidence of significant correlation changes through time,

Table 2.4   Local currency correlations (1991.01–1995.02)

Belgium	Denmark	France	Germany	Italy	Netherlands	Spain	Sweden	UK	
–	0.7123	0.6835	0.7050	0.4901	0.7017	0.6179	0.5644	0.6139	Belgium
	–	0.8343	0.7138	0.5791	0.6984	0.7597	0.5466	0.6698	Denmark
		–	0.8804	0.5856	0.8471	0.6855	0.4991	0.7015	France
			–	0.5032	0.9555	0.5648	0.4598	0.6542	Germany
				–	0.4568	0.7328	0.6049	0.4571	Italy
					–	0.5405	0.4761	0.6780	Netherlands
						–	0.5777	0.5663	Spain
							–	0.4801	Sweden
								–	UK

the same cannot be said for the fixed income markets. For instance, we can observe a high degree of correlation in term structure movements within the European Monetary System (EMS) currencies. Table 2.4 summarizes the (local currency) correlations of bonds returns for the major EMS fixed income markets.

Obviously, the benefits of diversification are much less strong within the European government bond markets (with an average correlation of 0.63) than in the corresponding equity markets. The (slow) emergence of a single currency will eventually eliminate these benefits completely.

When evaluating cross-country correlations for equity and fixed income markets, it is easiest to discuss these in local (excess) return terms (as we have done so far). Otherwise exchange rate and local market effects are mixed together, thereby confusing the picture. In the next section we discuss exchange rate (or currency) correlations in more detail.

2.5.2 The Problem of Currency Risk

The currency exposure should be looked at as a separate decision variable when evaluating the risk of internationally diversified portfolios or market maker positions. Taking on a position outside the non-domestic market does not necessitate carrying the associated currency risk. Let us make this point formally.

Looking at the return received from an internationally diversified position, we will use the following notation. Let r_n be the total rate of return on a foreign asset expressed in the investor's numeraire currency, r_x be the rate of return due to changes in exchange rates, and r_l be the total rate of return on an asset as experienced by a local investor.

Therefore $1 + r_n = (1 + r_x)(1 + r_l)$. Let r_{fl} be the risk-free rate a local investor would receive in her home market, and r_c be the random rate of return due to changes in exchange rate plus any interest received as a result of an investment in the foreign risk-free rate. In other words, $1 + r_c = (1 + r_x)(1 + r_{fl})$. Therefore

$$r_n = (r_x + r_{fl}) + (r_l - r_{fl}) + r_x r_l$$
$$= r_c + (r_l - r_{fl}) + r_x(r_l - r_{fl})$$

The last term of this expression reflects the cross product of exchange rate movements and excess local market returns. It can be shown that this term is typically negligible (see, for instance, Beckers et al. (1992)), such that the above expression reduces to

$$r_n = r_c + (r_l - r_{fl}) \tag{10}$$

In other words, the rate of return received from a "foreign" position is approximately equal to the currency rate of return plus the "foreign" excess rate of return. The risk equivalent of (10) is

$$\sigma_n^2 = \sigma_c^2 + \sigma_l^2 + 2\sigma_{cl} \tag{11}$$

The risk can therefore be straightforwardly broken down into currency risk, local market risk and the covariance between them. Although currency risk and local market risk are not necessarily independent (they clearly are not in the case of fixed income instruments), they can be treated separately for risk management and control purposes.

Currency risk is probably the most unstationary of all asset categories. Currencies are subject to periods of excessive volatility and the behaviour of different currencies relative to each other may change dramatically through time (think of the on-again off-again love affair of Sterling with respect to the EMS). Estimating currency risks and correlations is therefore the most problematic of all risk measurement activity. For example, Tables 2.5 and 2.6 summarize the correlations in exchange rate movements (using the US dollar as base currency) for 1993 and 1994 using daily data. Compared with 1993, the yen/£ correlations almost doubled in 1994. Using the 1993 estimates in 1994 would therefore have resulted in some unpleasant surprises.

One way of mitigating the effect of these instabilities is to measure volatilities and correlations using high-frequency data over short observation periods. Most currency risk measurement (even for longer-term investment purposes) would use daily data. These data may be exponentially weighted to give more weight to recent observations so as to rapidly capture regime changes. Alternatively, there is no doubt that the ARCH class of volatility estimation procedures has proven much more valuable in currency markets than for any other asset category.

There are plenty of tools available to recombine historical currency returns and deduce better risk forecasts. However, there is not a single procedure that has taken the upper hand

Table 2.5 Dollar based exchange rate return correlation: daily data for 1993

GBP	Yen	DM	SFr	DFl	FFr	
–	0.305	0.782	0.733	0.746	0.741	GBP
	–	0.341	0.356	0.305	0.269	Yen
		–	0.858	0.934	0.873	DM
			–	0.838	0.795	SFr
				–	0.891	DFl
					–	FFr

Table 2.6 Dollar based exchange rate return correlation: daily data for 1994

GBP	Yen	DM	SFr	DFl	FFr	
–	0.430	0.783	0.790	0.788	0.790	GBP
	–	0.573	0.548	0.573	0.574	Yen
		–	0.939	0.994	0.983	DM
			–	0.937	0.929	SFr
				–	0.981	DFl
					–	FFr

in this context. Short-term currency risk (and correlation) forecasting therefore remains somewhat more of an art. The artists have a bewildering toolkit of instruments available. Unfortunately, the currency market environment is so unstable that no methodology can be shown always to be superior.

2.5.3 Concluding Remarks

We live in a changing world that is subject to continuous structural change. However, this structural change is harder to prove statistically than originally thought. Except for currency markets, no clear evidence exists that points in the direction of significant drift or regime changes in asset (category) risks and correlations.

Although sophisticated statistical procedures can be used to improve risk forecasting accuracy, it is also widely established that the collective market wisdom is probably a better risk forecaster than any individual (or combined) statistical procedure. These consensus risk forecasts can be derived from the prices of traded options. It is well known that the future volatility of the underlying instrument over the remaining life of the option is the major (and in most cases only unknown) determinant of the value of that option. By observing the market traded price, one can therefore effectively back out the market consensus risk forecast.[16] In a very limited number of cases (such as the option to exchange one instrument for another) it may even be possible to extract the market consensus correlation forecast.

Although the forecasting accuracy of these option implied volatilities is widely recognized, they can only be effectively used for the limited set of instruments on which options are traded. Even then these implied volatilities are extremely valuable to calibrate other (statistical) risk estimation and forecasting procedures.

2.6 CONCLUSION

In this chapter we have tried to give a historical overview of the evolution in risk management and risk measurement. Although the foundations of modern risk measurement were laid by Markowitz almost 40 years ago, his principles and ideas remain as topical as ever. Risk reduction through a judicious spread of money across a wide range of alternatives remains central to all financial practice.

A correct estimation of volatilities and correlations is an essential prerequisite to quantifying accurately the actual risks being run. As a result, much risk forecasting activity has concentrated on identifying and quantifying the structural causes of risk and correlation. Indeed, it is only through the separation of structural from incidental (spurious) risks that more reliable forecasts can be achieved.

This quest for structural risk models started with identifying "the market" as the main source of communality in stock risks. However, this single-minded approach quickly evolved into a richer description of the structural causes of risk as reflected in multiple factor risk models. These models try to identify an exhaustive set of risk factors that help to explain common stock risks and correlations. The application of a multi-factor approach will typically lead to a richer understanding of the nature of the risks being incurred and will also lead to vastly improved risk forecasts.

Once a reliable risk model has been estimated, it can be used to quantify the business risk of brokers, market makers, corporate treasurers and investment managers. Although each of them will probably use the risk model in a slightly different fashion, they are ultimately all concerned about the extent to which they will be able to live up to (externally defined) expectations. In other words, each of the financial market operators lets her actions be determined by a benchmark. Risk and return will be evaluated relative to this benchmark.

In the case of market makers, brokers and corporate treasurers, the benchmark would typically be not to lose money or to make more money than what can be achieved through putting money on deposit. This establishes the Value at Risk concept as an appropriate risk measure since it quantifies the amount of money that can be made or lost over the predetermined time horizon.

Investment managers, on the other hand, are more concerned about their tracking error with respect to the predefined benchmark (typically a market index). They worry about the extent to which they can out- or underperform this benchmark and sell their clients the tracking error that they think will most likely lead to fame and glory (or at least one of these two).

The calculation of Value at Risk and tracking error both use the risk model (covariance matrix) as the central engine. This engine needs to be fine-tuned to the needs of the user. In particular, the time frame over which risks need to be forecast will have an important impact on the way in which the risk model will be estimated. Although more detailed risk model classification models are possible, an important distinction relates to the forecast time horizon: short-term risk models are typically fundamentally different from long-term models.

When forecasting risks, it is always worrisome to note that the historical information used to estimate the risk model may not necessarily reflect the current market conditions and relationships. Historical models will always lag structural changes in the market place. Luckily, there is little statistical evidence of sudden fundamental structural changes in the interrelationships in equity and bond markets. In currency markets, on the other hand, non-stationarity of relationships is common and needs to be accommodated in the risk forecasting procedures. Exponential smoothing, ARCH processes and implied volatilities and correlations can somewhat mitigate these problems, although currency risk forecasting remains more of an art than a science. Luckily the artists have a vast array of highly sophisticated instruments available to practise their artistry.

This chapter has mainly concentrated on the traditional approach to risk quantification using the concepts of variance and standard deviation. As the usage of derivatives (options, futures and warrants) spreads ever more widely, it becomes increasingly obvious that these standard risk measures are no longer appropriate. No single alternative risk measure has, however, become generally accepted. Although concepts such as semi-variance, downside risk and downside probability are slowly coming to the fore, their usage also depends heavily on a more complete and robust characterization of the higher moments of the return distributions of the underlying instruments. The academic who can match the success of the Markowitz concept of diversification to include asymmetric distributions probably has a prize waiting in Stockholm.

2.7 ENDNOTES

1. Markowitz, even in his early work, clearly recognized the limitations of standard deviations as a potential risk measure. In effect, the use of standard deviation presupposes a symmetric return distribution around the expected return. Although this assumption may be acceptable for common stocks and bonds over relatively short observation intervals, it is clearly violated in the case of options and warrants. In his book, Markowitz hints at the potential superiority of other risk measures such as semivariance, shortfall risk or shortfall probability. He rejects them

because of the computational complexity they entail. Whereas improved analytical solutions and vast increases in computing power have mostly remedied these objections, it is fair to say that the majority of the standard risk measurement approaches continue to rely heavily on the basic mean–standard deviation framework.

2. The standard error of a correlation coefficient is proportional to 1 over the square root of the number of observations.

3. The regular realignments of the currencies within the European Monetary System immediately come to mind.

4. Market efficiency is a well-defined concept that refers to the assumption that all relevant information is immediately and accurately reflected in the market prices.

5. Note that we are using beta here to refer to the regression coefficient of the time series regression (2). This beta is distinct from the CAPM beta of equation (1). In other words, there are as many betas as there are indices that can be used in regression (2). It is therefore never possible to talk about "the" beta of an asset.

6. Let Y denote the returns to the portfolio and X denote the returns to the hedging instrument over the hedging period. Then the expected return to the hedged position with hedge ratio δ is

$$E = \mathrm{E}(Y) + \delta\,\mathrm{E}(X)$$

and the variance of the hedged position is

$$V = \mathrm{Var}(Y) + \delta^2\mathrm{Var}(X) + 2\delta\,\mathrm{Cov}(X, Y)$$

Choosing δ to maximize $E - rV$, where $r > 0$ denotes the degree of risk aversion, yields the optimal δ to be

$$\tilde{\delta} = (\mathrm{E}(X) - 2r\,\mathrm{Cov}(X, Y))/2r\mathrm{Var}(X))$$

Now it is usual to assume that the hedge follows a random walk, so $\mathrm{E}(X) = 0$ and in this case

$$\hat{\delta} = -\mathrm{Cov}(X, Y)/\mathrm{Van}(X)$$

is the optimal hedge ratio, which can be obtained as the ordinary least squares (OLS) estimate in the linear regression model

$$Y_t = \alpha + \delta X_t + \varepsilon_t$$

7. These R^2 will differ significantly from country to country. The average R^2 will be about 30 per cent in developed markets such as the United States, Japan and the United Kingdom. In high volatility environments such as Thailand, Taiwan or Mexico, the average R^2 can be as high as 50 per cent or 60 per cent. This is a natural by-product of the fact that on average it is easier to explain what happens to individual stocks in markets that are subject to market-wide violent price corrections. In other words, the index will explain a higher proportion of the total volatility when that total volatility is high.

8. See, for example, King (1966) and Rosenberg (1974).

9. The term Arbitrage Pricing Theory refers to the main insight that assets that have an identical exposure to the different risk factors should also have an identical expected return. Otherwise there would be obvious riskless arbitrage opportunities.

10. Investor confidence is mostly measured as the yield spread between corporate and government bonds.

11. The calibration involves more than the choice of daily, weekly or monthly observation intervals. Indeed, when using a daily time frame, the riskless instrument is a one day time deposit. The excess returns used to calculate the covarianace matrix $\mathbf{V}$ should therefore use the overnight money rate as the risk-free rate. A weekly or monthly risk model would use one week or one month rates as the risk-free rate to calculate excess returns.

12. Since index fund managers do not have to engage in investment research, financial analysis or return forecasting, their operating costs are greatly reduced. As a consequence, the management fee will be several orders of magnitude lower than the one charged by traditional active managers. The transaction costs incurred by index funds will also be low since they pursue a buy and hold strategy as opposed to the active managers who may turn over significant fractions of the portfolio during the course of the year.

13. Although an index fund in theory should have zero tracking error, it is not always possible to continually hold all assets that are part of the index at exactly their index weight. This may be due to irregular cash flows into or out of the portfolio. Alternatively, portfolios trying to duplicate indices consisting of a large number of assets may not always be able to buy all assets in the index. Sampling or optimization procedures are then used to minimize the tracking error.

14. By definition, for every manager who overweights an asset, sector or industry relative to the market, there must be another one who underweights that asset, sector or industry. Relative to the market average, investment management is a zero-sum game: for every investment manager who outperforms the average, there must be another one who underperforms. In this sense the aggregate value added (relative to the market average) of all investment management activity is zero.

15. In these cases the *ex post* benchmark chosen by the client usually happens to be the asset category or market that performed best over the evaluation period.

16. See, for instance, Latane and Rendleman (1976) and Beckers (1981) for early applications of these ideas.

2.8 REFERENCES

Beckers, C. (1981) "Standard deviations implied in option prices as predictors of future stock price variability". *Journal of Banking and Finance*, **5**, 363–381.

Beckers, C., Grinold, R., Rudd, A. and Stefek, D. (1992) "The relative importance of common factors across the European equity markets". *Journal of Banking and Finance*, **16**, 14–38.

Bollersev, T. (1986) "Generalized autoregressive conditional heteroskedasticity". *Journal of Econometrics*, **31**, 307–327.

Bollersev, T., Chou, R. and Kroner, K. (1992) "ARCH modelling in finance: a selective review of the theory and empirical evidence with suggestions for future research". *Journal of Econometrics*, **52**, 5–59.

Connor, G. (1995) "The three types of factor models: A comparison of their explanatory power". *Financial Analysts Journal*, May–June 1995, 42–46.

Engle, R. and Bollersev, T. (1986) "Modelling the persistence of conditional variances". *Econometric Review*, **5**, 1–50.

Erb, B., Harvey Campbell, R. and Viskanta Tadas, E. (1994) "Forecasting international equity correlations". *Financial Analysts Journal*, **November–December**, 32–44.

Grinold, R., Rudd, A. and Stefek, D. (1989) "Global factors: fact or fiction". *The Journal of Portfolio Management*, **Fall**, 79–88.

Heston, S.L. and Rouwenhorst, K.G. (1994) "Does industrial structure explain the benefits of international diversification?". *Journal of Financial Economics*, **36**, 3–27.

King, B. (1966) "Market and industry factors in stock price behavior". *Journal of Business*, **January**, 139–170.

Latane, H. and Rendleman, R. (1976) "Standard deviations of stock price ratios implied in option prices". *Journal of Finance*, **31**, 369–381.

Lintner, J. (1965) "The valuation of risk assets and the selection of risky investments in stock portfolios and capital budgets". *Review of Economics and Statistics*, **February**, 13–37.

Markowitz, H. (1959) *Portfolio Selection: Efficient Diversification of Investments*. New York: John Wiley and Sons,

Mossin, J. (1959) "Equilibrium in a capital asset market". *Econometrica*, **October**, 768–783.

Roll, R. (1977) "A critique of the asset pricing theory's tests. Part I: On past and potential testability of the theory". *Journal of Financial Economics*, **4**, 129–176.

Rosenberg, B. (1974) "Extra-market components of covariance in security returns". *Journal of Financial and Quantitative Analysis*, **9**, 263–274.

Ross, S. (1976) "The arbitrage theory of capital asset pricing". *Journal of Economic Theory*, **13**, 341–360.

Sharpe, W. (1964) "Capital asset prices: a theory of market equilibrium". *Journal of Finance*, **September**, 425–442.

3

Value at Risk

THOMAS C. WILSON

3.1 INTRODUCTION

One of the most important developments in risk management over the past few years has been the implementation of a new class of risk measures that are specifically designed to measure and aggregate diverse risky positions across an entire institution using a common conceptual framework. Although these measures come under any one of many different institution-specific guises (e.g. Bankers Trust's Capital at Risk (CaR), J.P. Morgan's Value at Risk (VaR) and Daily Earnings at Risk (DEaR), other institutions' Dollars at Risk (DaR) and Money at Risk (MaR)), they all have as their foundation a common definition comprising three elements: VaR is generically defined as the maximum possible loss for a given position or portfolio within a known confidence interval over a specific time horizon.

Slightly confusing for the organization considering implementing these measures is the fact that, although all institutions begin with the same generic definition, the actual calculation methods used by each can differ markedly. In fact, it seems that just as each institution has a unique name for its VaR, each also has a unique technical implementation;[1] and, while there is some convergence in terms of high-level approaches for measuring market risk, convergence in technical approaches is much farther off when discussing the measurement of credit, insurance and operational risks. In all fairness, the different technical implementations are based in part on theoretical grounds, in part on systems considerations, and in part on the institutional and strategic context in which the calculations are employed to measure and control risks. But the myriad of different context-specific methods only serves to highlight the need to evaluate carefully the trade-offs between the different methods when deciding which method is best suited to your particular business.

The purpose of this chapter is to give a concise technical overview of some of the most prevalent techniques used for calculating VaR, clearly stating their (implicit) assumptions and their relative strengths and weaknesses from a theoretical as well as a practical perspective. Although VaR measurement techniques are becoming more prevalent for a wide variety of different risk classes (e.g. market, credit, insurance, operational, business volume and behavioral risks), in order to frame the issues in manageable terms we focus

Risk Management and Analysis. Vol. 1: Measuring and Modelling Financial Risk.
Edited by Carol Alexander © Thomas Wilson, McKinsey & Company, Inc.

here primarily on market or price risks and credit risks. Before we go into the technical details, however, we begin by providing some motivation for looking at VaR as a measure of risk for financial institutions and then look at some of the preconditions that typically need to be met in order for VaR and Return On Risk-Adjusted Capital (RORAC) measures to have true business impact.

3.2 USES OF VaR

In this section we attempt to outline the potential uses for VaR, highlighting where it can potentially add value and where not. In addition, we also review the preconditions that need to be met in practice before VaR actually has business impact.

3.2.1 Why Can VaR Have an Impact?

Broadly speaking, there are three areas where VaR can potentially have a significant business impact:

(i) Risk Comparability

First, VaR can be applied consistently across a wide variety of diverse risky positions and portfolios, allowing the relative importance of each to be directly compared and aggregated. How, for example, can the interest rate risk of a futures contract be put on comparable terms with the volatility risk of an option? With the foreign exchange risk of a currency swap? How can these diverse market risk positions be aggregated within a trading book? Across an institution? How can these market risks be made comparable to the credit risks associated with a loan portfolio? With the operational risk of a systems failure or the catastrophe risk of an earthquake?

While there is a wide variety of standard risk measures available for characterizing the individual risks in a trading or derivatives portfolio (e.g. delta, gamma, vega, shifts, rotations)[2] or credit portfolio (e.g. ratings, exposure numbers, watch lists), they provide little guidance when trying to interpret the relative importance of each individual risk factor to the portfolio's bottom line or for aggregating the different risk categories to a business unit or institution level. The ability to do so correctly allows an institution to gain a deeper understanding of the relative importance of its different risk positions and to gauge better its aggregate risk exposure relative to its aggregate risk appetite.

VaR accomplishes these objectives by defining a common metric that can be applied universally across all risk positions or portfolios: the maximum possible loss within a known confidence interval over a given holding period. Besides being able to be applied universally across all risk categories, including market, credit, operational and insurance risks, this metric is also expressed in units that are (or should be) meaningful at all levels of management: dollars (or pounds, francs, etc.). It therefore serves as a relevant focal point for discussing risks at all levels within the institution, creating a risk dialogue and culture that is otherwise difficult to achieve given the otherwise technical nature of the issues.

(ii) Determinant of Capital Adequacy

This leads to the second important reason for calculating VaR: because VaR is calculated in currency units and is designed to cover most, but not all, of the losses that might face a risk business, it also has the intuitive interpretation as the amount of economic or equity capital that must be held to support that particular level of risky business activity. In fact, the definition of VaR given above is completely compatible with the role of equity as perceived by many financial institutions: while reserves or provisions are held to cover expected losses incurred in the normal course of business, equity capital is held to provide a capital cushion against any potential unexpected losses. Since an institution cannot be expected to hold capital to cover all unexpected losses with 100 per cent certainty (as this would require, for example, 100 per cent equity financing of all credits, never selling an equity call option, etc.), the level of this capital cushion must be determined within prudent solvency guidelines over a reasonable time horizon needed to identify and resolve problem situations. The same type of logic is often applied to the determination of the optimum level of exchange margining or collateralization in the over-the-counter (OTC) market (see Longin (1994)).

The philosophy that economically-determined VaR is the relevant measure for determining capital requirements for risk businesses is also being increasingly adopted by regulators and supervisors. In the regulatory context, the Bank for International Settlement's Subcommittee on Banking Supervision recently released a proposal for market VaR adequacy (Basle Committee on Banking Supervision (1995a, b) reviewed in Kupiec and O'Brien (1995a, b)) that would allow banks to use their own internal VaR calculation models to determine the capital needed to support their trading activities. Of interest is the fact that the class of allowable models is only slightly constrained by the proposal, prescribing only a few parameters and guidelines[3] but no specific calculation methodology: each qualifying institution is allowed to use its own proprietary model. To qualify, however, institutions must also have in place a sufficiently developed management control organization and policies.

In the supervisory context, the Derivatives Policy Group (DPG), formed at the suggestion of Chairman A. Levitt of the Securities Exchange Commission (SEC) in August 1994, also makes similar recommendations regarding the determination of capital adequacy for the unregulated affiliates of SEC-registered broker-dealers and the Commodity Futures Exchange Commission (CFTC)-registered futures commission merchants (Derivatives Policy Group (1995)). These recommendations, which would allow institutions to determine the amount of capital needed to support their given trading activities based on proprietary models subject to the same 99 per cent confidence interval/10-day holding period horizon parameters, are also complemented by other recommendations regarding the existence of a well-defined management policy and controlling organization. They are also broadly in line with the industry-sponsored Group of Thirty (G30) Report's recommendations (G30 (1993)).

Unfortunately, while we are seeing convergence in terms of the acceptance of VaR as the relevant determinant of capital adequacy for most risk businesses in concept and even a few of the relevant parameters (e.g. a 99 per cent confidence interval/10-day holding period horizon), the actual calculation rules are left up to the individual institution. This is unfortunate because there exists a wide variety of different methods, each presenting the institution with non-trivial trade-offs. Many of these different methods, as well as their trade-offs, will be described in detail below.

(iii) Performance Measurement

The final important reason for calculating VaR is to help management to evaluate the performance of business units and strategies on a risk-adjusted basis. Given the interpretation of VaR as the minimum equity required to support a risky business, it is natural to use this measure when evaluating the relative performance of different businesses by calculating the return on that equity, where equity is defined as risk, rather than regulatory, capital. In fact, many Risk-Adjusted Performance Measures (RAPMs) such as Bankers Trust's Risk-Adjusted Return on Capital (RAROC) use the concept of VaR in just this manner to adjust returns for the amount of risk undertaken by each position or business.[4]

These RAPM measures are used by management to evaluate the relative and absolute performances of different businesses. For example, how does 25 basis points (bp) on a straight loan compare with 10 bp on an interest rate swap with the same counterparty and maturity? With a different counterparty or maturity? Or, how does a net return of $150 million on proprietary trading compare with $50 million from custodial services? Or $75 million from derivatives trading? It is well known that evaluating performance relative to regulatory capital requirements may lead to the wrong signals being sent to management.[5] What, then, is the relevant measure of capital for a portfolio or business? VaR, with its interpretation as the economic capital needed to support a risky business, is becoming the de facto standard in helping management to adjust returns for the risks involved.

3.2.2 Where is VaR *Unlikely* to Have Impact?

Often, individuals point to two additional areas where VaR measures can potentially have business impact: first, in their use as operational risk limits and, secondly, as a means of preventing large and embarrassing losses. It has been my experience that VaR numbers alone do not typically bring substantive impact in these areas, although they may do so when combined in a broader risk management context. Each of these possible uses is worth discussing in greater detail.

(i) As Operational Risk Limits

It is a common belief that a VaR measure makes a good limit for controlling risk; from an operational, desk-level perspective, this potential role for VaR has probably been overstated. While it is true that a VaR number can be used to control a desk's positions against limits, business unit heads have successfully been controlling, at an operational level, their trader's positions using position and sensitivity limits for years. Furthermore, given the computational cost of calculating VaR accurately for non-linear portfolios, often resulting in a day's delay in getting the information and then only for end-of-day positions, senior management will probably continue to rely on these "unsophisticated" risk measures as the basis for their operational limits for some years to come.

In addition, standard position and sensitivity information, often the basis for operational risk limits, is necessary for managing a risk business, because they convey important position information in a standardized format that can be communicated quickly and understood by the trader, leading to a better understanding of his or her actual positions. For these three reasons (i.e. delay in getting the data; availability of other, operational limits; and the need for the position and sensitivity limits anyway to steer the business), VaR rarely, if ever, forms the cornerstone of an operational, intra-day limit structure.

This implies that if a VaR measure is to have business impact, its potential to do so will be found primarily in its role as a measure of risk or economic capital rather than as an operational limit to be controlled; this important insight is discussed in greater detail in Sections 3.2.3 and 3.2.4.

(ii) Preventing Embarrassing Losses

VaR measures and systems are often touted as being one of the best defenses against large, embarrassing losses such as those arising from fraud, portfolio revaluations caused by model errors, or major market corrections. It has been my experience that VaR measures, by themselves, add little value in terms of preventing such losses in practice.

In terms of helping institutions to avoid embarrassing losses, no risk management or VaR system will prevent the type of embarrassing losses suffered by Barings or Diawa, two of many institutions where traders were arguably able to hide positions, and losses, for long periods of time: these positions were not, and could not, be measured by a VaR system simply because they were never entered into systems correctly in the first place (the old adage "Garbage In, Garbage Out" leaps to mind).

Nor will VaR systems prevent embarrassing revaluation losses suffered by some derivatives and mortgage-backed securities, caused by using the wrong pricing models: no VaR system can determine whether or not a particular pricing model is appropriate for the type of business undertaken.

Finally, VaR systems are not likely to prevent losses from consciously taking large open positions during periods of extreme market turbulence; for example, in Japanese Government Bonds (JGBs) or Treasuries during the 1994 fixed income crisis or emerging markets positions during the Peso crisis of 1995. Arguably, the same houses with fixed income or emerging markets reputations that took the large positions knew their open positions very well before the crisis and were quite happy with them (at least, before the crash). In addition, since these events are typically rolled out of the historical sample used to generate VaR covariance and volatility parameters after only a year or two, many VaR systems have too short an institutional memory to be effective against such historical scenarios.

This implies that if VaR measures are to have impact in terms of helping institutions to prevent large, embarrassing losses, it will only be indirectly: some other element of risk management organization, beyond a pure risk number, must be in place as well. For this reason, virtually all institutions will agree that a clear separation of front-office and back-office responsibilities, coupled with an appropriately skilled and independent risk-controlling function, are a necessary complement to risk management systems — a subject that is worthy of a chapter in itself. In fact, this is one of the necessary conditions that must be met in order to use internal models for the determination of capital adequacy for regulatory purposes (Basle Committee (1995a)).

3.2.3 Preconditions for a VaR Impact: More Than Numbers

In summary, VaR can play three important roles within a modern financial institution: first, it allows diverse risky positions to be directly compared and aggregated; secondly, it is a measure of the economic or equity capital required to support a given level of risk activities and, as such, is increasingly recognized by regulators for this purpose; and, finally, it helps management to make the returns from diverse risky businesses directly comparable on a risk-adjusted basis (e.g. in terms of RAPM). Thus, while there may remain a few open technical issues regarding its calculation, VaR is potentially a very useful tool for helping management to steer and control diverse risk-absorption and intermediation businesses for those institutions that are able to exploit its potential.

Nonetheless, we have also seen through some examples (e.g. preventing losses and operational limit structures) that generating VaR numbers, by itself, is no guarantee of business impact. Going further, my experience has been that very few institutions are capable of capturing the full potential from their complicated VaR and RAPM methods and systems simply because they do not have the risk management organization capable of using the information. To emphasize the importance of the organizational issues in terms of generating an impact, I would point to a few institutions that are able to generate a far greater business impact with far less than what would be considered "state of art" or "industry best practice", precisely because they put equal emphasis on making sure that their risk management organization is capable of using the important information provided by VaR and RAPM numbers and also has the incentives to do so. Because this is (intentionally) a controversial statement, it is worth illustrating with two additional examples.

(i) A Trading Example

Consider, first, the hypothetical institution that has worked for a long time, investing heavily in systems, data warehouses and theoretical discussions, to implement a global VaR system covering its global trading activities, primarily driven by regulatory reporting concerns. After successful implementation, on Monday morning, Friday afternoon's close-of-business positions are reported to the Head of Trading as usual, but now the report is complemented by the "one number that senior management really needs to see", VaR, which will be controlled every day against limits allocated once a year. In the meantime, business is being lost to competitors in some business areas because the business units with opportunities may have fully utilized their own market or credit limits, even though, from an aggregate perspective, there is still some risk-bearing capacity available. On Monday morning, what position decisions will be taken differently by the foreign exchange desk? By the fixed-income derivatives desk? Will VaR have any impact at all on the operational management decisions of the trading desks, or will it simply satisfy regulatory reporting requirements?

(ii) A Credit Example

Consider, as a second example, the hypothetical commercial bank that has developed a "RAROC" approach to be applied "bottom-up" for pricing at the transaction level as well as a credit portfolio VaR measurement approach designed to measure the risk of a portfolio of commercial banking assets. The objective of the credit portfolio VaR approach is to provide a basis for better steering the origination process as well as more actively managing the portfolio of retained risks.

After being implemented, credit portfolio VaR is reported to the central Credit Committee on a monthly basis. However, given that individual deals continue to be reviewed, case by case, because they are originated with only the highest level portfolio guidelines in terms of country risk actually binding in practice (industry or segment risk limits, if defined at all, are rarely binding if the "right deal" is brought in by the account executive), what impact will credit VaR measures actually have in terms of steering the bank's origination? In addition, given that the business units, who ultimately own the assets originated, have revenue objectives to be met, what potential is there for a central portfolio management group to use loan sales, credit derivatives or securitization techniques to manage actively the portfolio of retained risks?

3.2.4 Three Preconditions for a VaR Impact

For these hypothetical examples, what went wrong? Why were these institutions unable to capture more than cursory returns in terms of management impact from their investments in VaR methods and systems? The bottom line is that while advanced methods and systems are a necessary condition for having a business impact, they are not by themselves a sufficient condition. Experience has shown that at least two other preconditions, in addition to having the proper VaR methods and systems, need to be met in practice before VaR will have a significant business impact: the risk management organization must be capable of using VaR information to its advantage and, secondly, it must have the incentives to do so.

(i) Risk Management Organization and Processes

The first precondition that must be met in order for an institution to leverage VaR and, by extension, RAPM measures into a true business impact is that the institution be organizationally capable of using the information to support its decision-making process. And, while the existence of the skilled and independent risk-controlling function that we discussed earlier is important, the organizational readiness issues of which I speak now are far more subtle.

Consider the trading example again, where the VaR numbers appeared at the bottom of the Head Trader's exposure report a day late, only to be compared against limits that were allocated once a year. Clearly, this type of process is not designed for optimal business impact in a dynamic business environment. As we have already mentioned, two of the most important advantages of VaR are that it makes diverse risks directly comparable and its interpretation as equity, a fungible commodity. The trading organization in this example is taking advantage of neither of these two potential advantages, choosing instead to use VaR only as a risk-controlling, as opposed to a risk management, tool.

Risk comparability and the fungibility of risk capital imply that risk capital limits can, and should, be dynamically allocated across diverse business activities, allowing it to flow to wherever attractive business opportunities emerge. Many organizations find that market or credit risk lines are "sticky" and that, as a consequence, opportunities are being lost; those institutions that have managed to gain the most impact from VaR behave as if it is fungible, with senior management working together as a team, ensuring that while the overall risk capital limits are respected across the trading businesses, risk capital nonetheless flows to where it is needed within the trading organization. This implies a fundamental redesign of the capital management processes and limit structures in addition to a robust and technically correct VaR methodology.

As a second example illustrating the importance of organization in terms of capturing the potential impact of VaR and RAPM measures, consider again our credit example where very little active portfolio management has been achieved, even after the implementation of credit VaR. Many institutions would agree with the principle that "those who manage the returns also must manage the risks". In this instance, this rule has been subtly broken, with the originators responsible for managing the returns while the credit function is responsible for managing the risk. This type of disconnect leads to a stalemate and an inability to actually use VaR information to support proactive portfolio management. And, while each of the two possible organizational realignment options (e.g. put both return and risk management responsibilities with the front or within portfolio management) can be optimal in practice, depending upon the type of business being considered, and therefore may coexist within the same organization, it is clear that one must be chosen before active portfolio management based on credit VaR can proceed.

As these simple examples illustrate, for many institutions the main challenges to getting business impact is not necessarily developing VaR and RAPM methods and systems, but rather ensuring that the risk management organization, processes and culture are in place to utilize, and take advantage of, the information.

(ii) Incentives and Opportunities to Use the Numbers

The second precondition that must be met in order for an institution to leverage VaR and, by extension, RAPM measures into a true business impact is that the institution have the incentive and opportunities to use the information. To illustrate this, consider again the credit example: what motivation does the front have to manage actively its portfolio of retained assets if it is measured solely on a revenue basis? How can the management of credit risk capital, or for that matter the pricing of risk capital via RAROC measures, ever be expected from an organization that is revenue driven and puts no real opportunity cost on capital? Where are the incentives? It has been my experience working in Europe and Asia that managing capital and using RAPM measures bottom-up at the transaction level typically do not succeed until senior management recognizes top-down that capital is not a free good. As an aside, this typically does not occur until management wakes up to the fact that an 8–12 per cent Return on Equity (ROE) is simply not adequate. Until then, there is often very little incentive for the organization to use VaR and RAPM information, even if it were available and the management organization were in place.

As a second illustration of the importance of aligning the organization's incentives, consider again the trading example: just suppose that business opportunities were not, in fact, dynamic, with very little need to shift capital around from one activity to another. What motivation would the institution have to set up a very dynamic management process? While this hypothetical situation is a bit of a stretch in terms of trading businesses, consider banks with a pure retail strategy, which are arguably more stable businesses: many of the best run retail institutions such as Lloyds TSB in the United Kingdom get along very well by focusing management attention on ROE instead of RAROC, simply because they do not necessarily face important, dynamic trade-offs within their strategy and because regulatory capital, and not risk capital, is the binding constraint.

In general, experience has shown that the incentive to use VaR information is driven by two important considerations: first, the organization must view capital as a scarce resource that needs to be adequately compensated and, secondly, the organization must face non-trivial choices in terms of the types of businesses that could be undertaken given that scarce capital base. Broadly speaking, if management recognizes that capital is scarce and must be allocated between real business alternatives, then VaR and RAPM measures will begin to have real business impact.

(iii) Methods and Systems

It is often thought that the third and final precondition for achieving business impact from VaR numbers is that they be technically correct. A more accurate (and more controversial) statement would be that they be directionally correct, adequate for the business and, most importantly, are actually used to support risk management decisions.

In summary, VaR measures and systems are not by themselves sufficient to guarantee business impact: they must also be complemented by changes in the risk management organization and incentives. In point of fact, I have seen some institutions that have obtained far more impact out of far less in terms of technical sophistication simply because they have put equal focus on these other two dimensions.

3.3 CALCULATING MARKET VaR

3.3.1 Measurement Issues

The main problem with calculating market VaR is that there is a wide variety of different ways to implement the definition of VaR, each having distinct advantages and disadvantages. Although perhaps surprising to hear in the context of this chapter, it is important to recognize at the outset that all VaR methods are, with probability one, wrong; each alternative relies on assumptions that are invariably false. This fact does not diminish the potential role that VaR may play within the organization, however, once the trade-offs are understood by management.

To get a better feeling for the trade-offs implicit in each of the methods, it is important first to understand the issues surrounding the calculation of VaR, many of which are currently being discussed at great length in the financial literature.[6] In this context, VaR can be thought of as comprising two distinct elements (Figure 3.1):

1. The *sensitivity of a portfolio's market value to changes in market rates*, illustrated in (a). The slanted line is a stylized representation of the aggregate change in the mark-to-market value of a portfolio as market rates change, with the change in value on the Y axis and the change in market rates on the X axis.

2. The *(joint) probability distribution of changes in market rates over the desired reporting period horizon*, illustrated in (b). The stylized curve in the diagram can be thought of as the (marginal) probability density function for changes in the market rate of a given size, with probability on the Y axis and the change in market rates on the X axis.

When "combined", as is intuitively done in (c), the desired definition of VaR is implemented: the maximum possible loss within a known confidence interval over a predetermined holding period horizon. In practice, however, the calculation of VaR

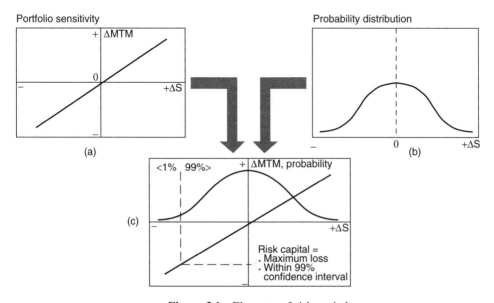

Figure 3.1 Elements of risk capital

requires that simplifying assumptions need to be made with regard to one or both of these components, e.g. the portfolio's sensitivity or the joint distribution of market rate innovations. To illustrate this, consider the closed-form VaR formula, described and motivated in greater detail in Subsection 3.3.3.

$$\text{VaR} = z_\alpha \sqrt{\boldsymbol{\omega}' \boldsymbol{\Sigma} \boldsymbol{\omega}} \sqrt{\Delta t},$$

where z_α is defined as the constant that gives the appropriate one-tailed confidence interval for the standardized normal distribution, e.g. $z_\alpha = 2.33$ for a 99 per cent confidence interval, $\boldsymbol{\omega}$ is the $N \times 1$ vector of portfolio position weights, $\boldsymbol{\Sigma}$ is the $N \times N$ annualized covariance matrix of position returns and Δt is the holding period horizon as a fraction of a year. Very often, $\boldsymbol{\omega}$ is taken to be the net asset positions themselves or, in the case of derivatives, the delta position equivalents of the portfolio.

This formula, most often associated with variations on RiskMetrics[TM] (J.P. Morgan (1994–95)), comprises two clearly identifiable sets of assumptions: first, a set of assumptions regarding position sensitivities embodied in the risk position weights ($\boldsymbol{\omega}$), and secondly, a set of assumptions and calculation rules regarding the probability distribution of market rate innovations embodied in the covariance matrix of position returns ($\boldsymbol{\Sigma}$).

The most common critiques of the popular VaR calculation methods, including RiskMetrics[TM], can therefore be thought of as critiques of these two component assumptions rather than of the concept itself.[7] In the rest of this section we will therefore highlight some of the most important critiques commonly made regarding the price sensitivity and distribution assumptions.

(i) Portfolio Sensitivity Assumptions

The first set of critiques is aimed at the portfolio sensitivity assumptions often made in practice. Broadly speaking, these critiques can be divided into three categories: risk factor coverage, adequacy of local measures and model risks.

Risk Factor Coverage.   The first concern is whether or not the local measures used in calculating VaR recognize all of the potential sources of risk that might affect the value of the portfolio. For example, some VaR calculations ignore the volatility or vega risk of option portfolios for convenience, even though this can be one of the most significant sources of risk for the trading book (especially when the trading strategy and limit structures constrain the book to have no directional price, or delta, risk). Some methods solve this issue by treating the term structure of implied volatilities as another "market price", treating the "vega" as another "delta" or directional price sensitivity, and incorporating it directly into such standard methods as the RiskMetrics[TM] or Delta–Normal methods (more on this issue later in the chapter).

Non-linearity.   More problematic by far is the fact that many calculation rules ignore second-order or gamma effects (e.g. the calculation of VaR is often only on the basis of the portfolio's delta or directional price risk), although risk managers and options traders know that higher-order terms such as the portfolio's gamma or even cross-gamma terms can be equally important, especially for option portfolios. To illustrate this point, consider the (linear) portfolio sensitivity illustrated in Figure 3.2(a); while this line represents exactly the pay-off profile for a straight equity position, the same linear, or delta, representation may be a poor representation for a portfolio containing options. Figure 3.2(b) represents

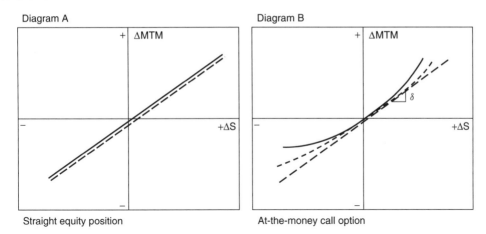

Figure 3.2 Stylized portfolio sensitivity profiles. Key: _____ analytic solution; _ _ _ _ delta approximation; - - - - delta–gamma approximation

both an exact call option pay-off profile and its delta, or first-order, representation and its delta–gamma, or second-order, representation. It is interesting to note that the approximation error arising from a delta representation typically increases with the size of the unexpected market rate innovation (an effect also discussed in J.P. Morgan (1994–95)); unfortunately, large market events are exactly the events that we are concerned about when calculating VaR. This approximation error decreases, however, when the Delta–Gamma, or second-order, representation is used (an observation that motivates the Delta–Gamma method developed in later).

While all traders will agree that delta as a risk measure is not sufficient to manage an options book and, in fact, many options books are run with an explicit strategy of being delta–neutral at all times, paradoxically, many of the most popular VaR techniques (e.g. the Delta–Normal, covariance or RiskMetrics[TM] methods) recognize *only* directional price or delta risks. This is one reason that J.P. Morgan does not recommend that their RiskMetrics[TM] technique be applied to portfolios including options.[8]

Along a similar line, many methods ignore potentially important cross-gamma effects.[9] Consider, for the simplest example, an at-the-money foreign currency interest rate forward rate agreement (FRA) where the profit and loss (P&L), and therefore VaR, is reported in the domestic currency. Because this position is at-the-money, it has no foreign currency value and therefore no first-order currency risk.[10] However, if foreign interest rates were to move in an adverse manner, therefore creating a foreign currency loss, their impact could be mitigated or exacerbated by foreign exchange rate movements when translating the loss into your reporting currency. The net impact on VaR depends on whether foreign interest rates are positively or negatively correlated with exchange rate movements. This cross-rate effect caused by P&L translation may be of substantial importance for all standard, first-generation products such as forward rate agreements, straight equity positions, FX forwards, interest rate and currency swaps. Second-order, cross-rate effects become even more important for some second-generation correlation products (e.g. choosers, diff swaps or quantos), which are expressly designed to play a view on correlation risks.

A Delta–Gamma Approximation overcomes many of these problems by capturing the direct- and cross-gamma or convexity risks of the portfolio and incorporating them into the

VaR calculation. In the past, the problem was one of how to incorporate gamma into the VaR calculation in a simple manner that could be easily implemented. This problem has been resolved with the development of the Delta–Gamma method, described in detail below.

Local Measures Are Not Sufficient.   Standard local sensitivity measures or "Greeks" such as deltas, gammas and vegas are often used as the basis for representing the portfolio pay-off profile when calculating VaR. The measures themselves are "local" in the sense that they measure the sensitivity of the portfolio's value to infinitesimal changes in market rates around current rates. These local measures are then often used to construct a Taylor Series Expansion to represent the portfolio pay-off profile in order to simplify greatly the calculations (for details, refer to the description of the Delta–Normal and Delta–Gamma methods described in Subsections 3.3.2–3.3.4).

Unfortunately, these representations of the portfolio pay-off profile based on local measures may not be sufficient fully to characterize the portfolio pay-off for large market events. Consider Figure 3.3, which illustrates a stylized pay-off profile for a short-dated, deep in-the-money or out-of-the-money option portfolio. Such portfolios can exhibit large swings in their deltas and gammas, and therefore values, under extreme market movements. Although the Delta–Gamma method captures the portfolio's convexity or gamma risk for small market movements, it still suffers from the fact that it is based on *local* as opposed to *global* risk measures (as illustrated by the dotted line in Figure 3.3), with the approximation error most likely to increase with extreme market rate movements. Thus, using local risk measures alone may be inadequate when calculating VaR. These observations are reflected in Estrella (1994) and in the following quotation by Bob Gumerlock of the Swiss Bank Corporation:

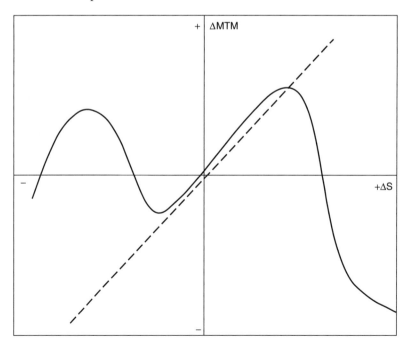

Figure 3.3   "Non-local" risks. Key: ——— analytic pay-off profile; _ _ _ delta–gamma approximation

When O'Connor set up in London at Big Bang, I built an option risk control system incorporating all the Greek letters — deltas, gammas, vegas, thetas and even some higher order ones as well (the delta of the gamma and the gamma of the vega). And I'll tell you that during the crash it was about as useful as a US theme park on the outskirts of Paris (Chew (1994b)).

As we discuss later, simulation techniques are the only methods available that can capture these non-local risks for complex options portfolios.

Model Risks.   Many of the derivatives pricing models used to value transactions and calculate their risk profiles are based on some simplifying assumptions about market liquidity or the way that market rates evolve and these assumptions often contradict the spirit of VaR calculations.

For example, many models assume that markets remain liquid when faced with large price movements, thereby allowing the book to be re-balanced or dynamically hedged on a continuous basis. In fact, many of the models used to price derivatives implicitly assume that a delta hedge, re-balanced continuously, is sufficient to create an exact replicating portfolio, thereby allowing the transaction to be priced based on a "no-arbitrage" argument. In addition to ignoring transaction costs, these models ignore the fact that when large market movements do occur, they typically take what little market liquidity there is with them and what little liquidity there is left tends to be in one direction only — that of the stampeding herd. This phenomena arguably was the death knell for the concept of portfolio insurance, which relied on the concept of option replication, when the crash came in 1987. Thus, while it might have been theoretically correct to allocate no VaR at the time to equity portfolios covered by portfolio insurance, the practical realities based on lessons learnt from the 1987 crash are somewhat different.

Some institutions face a more fundamental and serious problem with regards to model risk, however; over the past few years, many banks and securities firms have had to write off significant amounts because they historically marked their book to model and not to market and, when the market finally caught up to them, they had to restate their profits accordingly. To illustrate the issues, consider a hypothetical institution using a modified-Black option pricing model (relatively standard in the caps and floors market) to value longer-dated interest rate swap or bond options; while there are enough degrees of freedom in terms of defining the current forward rate volatility surface to match market prices for generic caps, floors and swaptions today, it is not likely that using the same surface to value on-the-run, in- and out-of-the-money options positions will give values anywhere near to current market prices for similar, off-market structures. This divergence occurs because the bank is using a pricing model that is inappropriate for the type of business in which it is engaged. The divergence between the market values and the model values is often not recognized until it is too late. Since risk is defined as the potential change in value, the odds are that if the institution is not pricing the positions correctly, then it is also not measuring their risks correctly either.

(ii) Market Rate Distribution Assumptions
To calculate the maximum possible loss within a known confidence interval, as in Figure 3.1, portfolio sensitivity measures must somehow be combined with a probability measure defining how likely adverse movements actually are. Simplifying assumptions are therefore also often made with regard to the distribution of market rate innovations, generating several standard criticisms in their own right:

Fat Tails.   Many calculation methods assume that (proportional) market rate innovations are jointly normally distributed with independent realizations. This assumption has direct and controversial implications for the implied probability of extreme events as well as the shape of the distribution itself and its evolution over time.

Several empirical studies[11] have demonstrated that the historical return distributions in a wide variety of markets demonstrate a far higher incidence of very large market rate movements than is predicted by the normal distribution (a statistical property called kurtosis or fat tails) and have a higher peak at the mean than is predicted by the normal distribution (a property called leptokurtosis). These properties are demonstrated in Figure 3.4, which graphically illustrates the phenomena, and Table 3.1, which shows how dramatic this effect can be in various government bond markets. The table indicates that three standard deviation movements occurred with a frequency of 2.3 per cent of the time (respectively, 2.8 per cent and 1.5 per cent) over the sample period for the 10-year sterling (respectively, dollar and Deutschmark) government bond markets although the normal distribution suggests that such events should only occur 0.3 per cent of the time.

The consequence in terms of VaR calculations is dramatic: although we think that we should be looking at 2- or 3-sigma events based on the assumed normal distribution, we should really be looking at 4- to 6-sigma events based on the empirical distribution. This could lead both to a gross under-allocation of VaR and an exacerbation of the problem of local sensitivity measures discussed earlier.

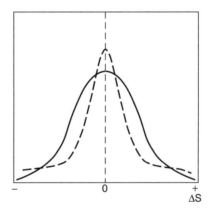

Figure 3.4   Fat tails. Key: ⎯⎯ normal distribution; ⎯ ⎯ ⎯ empirical distribution. *Source:* Chew (1994b)

Table 3.1   Actual vs. expected frequency of extreme market movements: weekly returns on 10 years government bonds over the last five years

SDs	£	$	DM	Expected probability
3	2.3%	2.8%	1.5%	0.300%
4	0.6%	0.4%	0.2%	0.006%
5	0.2%	0.4%	0.0%	<0.000%
6	0.2%	0.1%	0.0%	<0.000%
Max SD move	6.4	7.6	4.1	

This has led many authors to investigate the properties of other distributions with "fatter tails" than the normal distribution, e.g. the Stable Paretian and Student-t distributions, as well other price processes such as jump-diffusion and subordinated stochastic processes,[12] in an effort to model better the evolution of market prices.

Stable and Exploitable Relationships.   Most methods of calculating VaR rely on estimates of the volatilities and correlations of market rate innovations in order to aggregate diverse risky positions. These parameters are estimated on the basis of specific statistical models, many of which require that the parameters be constant over the sample period or, even more trivially, that they exist at all.

The motivation for recognizing correlations is clear: the aggregate VaR needed for a spread position consisting of a long DM/$ and a short £/$ position based on the high historical or implied correlation estimates between the DM/$ and £/$ rates may be significantly less than the sum of the VaR for the two positions when considered in isolation. The problem is that this correlation may be highly unstable, as the ERM crisis of 1992 demonstrated. So, while the risk manager might believe that he or she has entered into a relatively riskless spread trade, the amount of VaR should actually be much higher since the relationship itself, although historically quite stable, might prove to be quite unstable in times of stress. These same qualitative statements can also be made regarding the stability of market rate volatilities.

Many authors are moving towards alternative statistical models to describe and forecast market rate dynamics,[13] such as factor-GARCH and cointegration representations. There have even been attempts to integrate the fact that volatilities and correlations may not be constant into the calculation of VaR (see, for example, Alexander (1994), Chapter 4 by Carol Alexander in this volume and Wilson (1993)), although they will only be mentioned in passing here. It should be noted, however, that many of these attempts are aimed at generating a better forecast for the covariance matrix that will govern next period's returns, rather than for incorporating the correlation and volatility forecast uncertainty itself into the VaR calculation; one exception is Wilson (1993) who finds that forecast uncertainty may lead to the fat tails phenomena described earlier.

Nonetheless, similar critiques may be valid for these "next generation" methods — their representation of correlations and volatilities may only be valid in "normal", 2-sigma periods — but what happens in times of stress, e.g. 5-sigma events, when these unobservable parameters also exhibit extreme movements that exceed what the model predicts? Although some of the implications from following such a modeling strategy are desirable, specifically a more accurate estimate of VaR and a better understanding of market rate dynamics, senior management should not delude itself into thinking that these models are a panacea and become complacent in their implementation: the models merely push the assumptions regarding constant distribution parameters to a lower, more obscure level. While quite useful for calculating VaR as well as supporting front-office activities, the performance of these models (as with *all* models) must be tested continuously against market developments.

Arbitrage Relationships Violated.   When implementing VaR calculations, it is often expedient to ignore certain no-arbitrage conditions in order to make the problem tractable. For example, some institutions simply assume that proportional innovations in the DM/$, £/$ and DM/£ rates follow a highly correlated, jointly normal process when calculating the

VaR for an exchange rate book, thereby ignoring the triangular no-arbitrage relationship between the three currency pairs. This no-arbitrage relationship dictates that if the innovations in any two of the three rates is given, then the third is uniquely determined; otherwise, a triangular arbitrage between the resulting spot rates would exist. The result from ignoring the no-arbitrage condition is that VaR may be allocated to cover events that can never occur, such as an appreciating DM/$ and a depreciating £/$ at the same time as a depreciating DM/£ rate. Similarly, it is often assumed that interest rates follow an arbitrary geometric Brownian motion process estimated using market data without checking whether or not the implied process is arbitrage free.

Miscellaneous Distribution Assumptions.   Another problem with the assumption of normally distributed market rate innovations is that the normal distribution is symmetric, whereas the empirical distributions tend to be skewed (see J.P. Morgan (1994–95)), implying that we may have under- or over-allocated VaR depending on whether we have long or short positions. A more critical issue related to the symmetry of the distribution is that depending on how the market rate process is discretized, assuming the normality of market rate innovations could imply that interest rates, equity prices or exchange rates may become negative with positive probability[14] for extreme innovations in the assumed geometric Brownian motion process. This is clearly not a desirable property for many market price processes.

Finally, it is often assumed that market rate innovations are independently distributed (see, again, J.P. Morgan (1994–95)). This contradicts many of the empirical studies and no-arbitrage models that have found, for example, mean reversion in interest rates, the reliability of the forward rate hypothesis or interest rate parity theorem.

Model Risks.   Furthermore, most option pricing models are based on assumptions regarding market rate processes that are at odds with price dynamics during stress periods. For example, many models assume that market prices evolve in a continuous fashion; e.g. that they are governed by a diffusion rather than a jump process, and that market rate innovations are symmetrically distributed. As an example of the inadequacy of these assumptions, consider the ERM crisis of 1992 when various European currencies came under speculative attack: it was clear at the time that if the sterling rate was going to move out of its band, it was going to make a big move and then only in one direction — depreciation. While some market practitioners were rumored to have models that were capable of coping with such a market rate process, many did not and had to rely on "rule of thumb" adjustments to volatility parameters (see Chew (1992)). These model risks not only had implications for the way that institutions priced transactions during this volatile period, but also for the way that they measured risks and hedged the positions, and therefore for the amount of VaR needed to support the business.

(iii) Parameter Assumptions

The final major source of criticism for standard models is the relative arbitrariness of the key parameters (e.g. confidence interval and reporting period horizon), which determine to a great extent the amount of capital that should be held against any given risky position. While many institutions have chosen an overnight time horizon combined with a 95 per cent confidence interval (see, for example, Chew (1994b), the Group of Thirty Report (1993) and J.P. Morgan (1994–95)), many others have chosen to set different parameters.

For example, Bankers Trust uses a one-year time horizon for all positions (see, again, Chew (1994b)). Still other institutions, such as Barclays de Zoete Wedd, set their time horizons equal to an "orderly liquidation period" on a risk-by-risk basis in order to bring it into line with the individual market's liquidity (see Lawrence and Robinson (1995b)). The actual liquidation period therefore depends on both the markets considered as well as the size of the position. This assumption has the admirable consequence that positions in illiquid markets will bear more VaR for the same volatility owing to their illiquidity. These assumptions differ from those advocated by the Basle Committee and DPG proposals discussed earlier.

Complicating the time horizon issue is the problem of how to scale VaR trading limits up into yearly VaR numbers that might be used for planning and budgeting as well as limit setting purposes; while many techniques are used in practice (e.g. the square root of time rule, augmented stop-loss rules), few are compelling and often management must simply settle for the rationale that it finds most practical and convincing. Some interesting new work done by Bahar et al. (1997) addresses these issues in more detail.

In conclusion, there are several criticisms of the most common VaR calculation methods (summarized in Table 3.2). These critiques are directed less at the concept of VaR itself and more at the underlying assumptions used technically to implement the concept. For example, many methods rely too heavily on local risk measures and specific models when approximating the portfolio pay-off profile, while others make assumptions about the process generating market rate innovations that are violated in reality (e.g. fat tails, negative rates, stable or predictable correlations, diffusion processes).

Although many of the critiques may seem quite problematic, the practitioner should not despair: methods for calculating VaR are continuously evolving and improving as new analytical techniques are being developed and computational algorithms improved, a wide variety of which are discussed in Subsections 3.3.2–3.3.4. A word of caution is perhaps in order, however: as the techniques become more and more complex, their implicit assumptions and pitfalls also tend to become less and less transparent and, worse yet,

Table 3.2 Common critiques of capital calculations

Portfolio Sensitivity Assumptions	Distributional Assumptions	Arbitrary Parameter Assumptions
"Local" measures are not sufficient • Delta ignores gamma or convexity risk • Delta and gamma do not provide good approximations for extreme movements	Fat tails Stable and exploitable relationships • Correlations • Volatilities	Confidence intervals Reporting horizon • Overnight • Liquidity-based • Yearly
Other risks often ignored • Volatility or vega risk • Rho or rate risk	Arbitrage relationships violated • Triangular arbitrage of spot exchange rates • Interest rate processes	Time aggregation rules
Model risk • Continuous re-balancing in liquid markets • Symmetric, diffusion processes	Skewed and unrealistic distributions • Non-symmetric distributions • Negative rates • Independent increments	

management tends to become overly complacent with their implementation. Fortunately, the efficacy of the individual techniques is also dependent on the specific risk portfolio or trading strategy as well as the risk management and controlling procedures employed by the institution. In this context, the sentiments of Daniel Mudge, Bankers Trust, are relevant: "I would prefer a C-rated model with weaknesses and have people with experience and intuition to run our risk management than an A-rated model with a C-rated team of people who don't understand the model and are therefore unable to question the numbers that the system churns out" (Chew (1994b)).

Therefore, when choosing between the various popular methods described below, risk managers will always need to make informed trade-offs in terms of computational efficiency, information requirements and theoretical "correctness". The bottom line is that if the short-comings of each particular method are well understood and controlled, risk managers are finding that the information that even the simplest calculation methods provide can be invaluable in spite of their limitations.

3.3.2 Internal Models

As mentioned earlier, there is no single "best" method of calculating market VaR. Each of the popular methods reviewed below involves explicit (or implicit) trade-offs between computational efficiency and theoretical accuracy; all are subject to at least one of the critiques outlined earlier. Complicating matters further is the fact that many of the adverse trade-offs can be mitigated through the tailored design of risk management control procedures and limit structures, as discussed earlier. This implies that the best method for a particular institution, or even a particular trading book within an institution, depends on the risk characteristics of the portfolio in question, its business strategy and the management and control procedures and organization designed to support its risk management objectives.

Below, we describe several different methods for calculating market VaR that represent different trade-offs between theoretical accuracy and the cost of implementation. These methods range from the simple "building block" approach preferred by some regulators in lieu of more complex proprietary models, to the complex and computationally expensive simulation methods preferred by industry professionals. For each of these methods, we discuss the calculation rules, the implicit assumptions and their applicability. For convenience, we have summarized our analysis in Table 3.3, including how well each of these methods stands up to the most common criticisms leveled at VaR calculation methods.

In addition, we also arbitrarily differentiate these methods into two groups for convenience, one group that is suitable for "linear" products, i.e. primarily those products without an option component, and another group that is suitable for "non-linear" products, i.e. primarily those products comprising an option component. In the following, we discuss each of these categories in turn, reserving for the end a discussion of several methods that do not readily fall into any specific category.

3.3.3 "Linear" Methods

The following calculation methods typically make the joint assumption that the portfolio's profit and loss profile is linear and that the position returns are normally distributed. One must balance the issues discussed earlier with regard to these assumptions against the relative ease of implementation of these methods; the major benefits in terms of implementation are, first, that these methods can be implemented in a simple spreadsheet with

Table 3.3 Comparison of selected methods

Method	Regulator's "Building Block" Approach	Portfolio Normal	Asset-/Delta-Normal or RiskMetrics Methods	Delta-Gamma Methods	Simulation Methods, Historical or Monte Carlo
Description	General and specific charges with predefined, tabular offsets between selected, bucketed positions	Assume directly that portfolio returns are normally distributed. Using standard formula: $\mathbf{VaR} = z_\alpha \sigma_p$	Assume that asset returns are jointly normal, implying linear asset pay-off profiles and normally distributed portfolio returns. Using formula: $$\mathbf{VaR} = z_\alpha \sigma_p = z_\alpha \sqrt{\delta' \Sigma \delta}$$	Assume that market rate innovations are normal but that pay-off profiles approximated by local, second-order terms	Approximates portfolio profit/loss distribution based on simulated rate movements, either historical or model based
Advantages/ disadvantages	+ Simplicity − Overly conservative − No recognition of cross-market correlations, even within risk class − Draconian measures applied to option risks (e.g. gamma, vega)	+ Simplicity + Useful for top-down, business unit capital attribution − Assumes normality of business unit returns, ignoring fat tails, skewness, kurtosis, etc. − Assumes constancy of risk strategy and portfolio characteristics	+ Simplicity — can be calculated using a spreadsheet + Based on Markowitz/CAPM concepts − Assumes normality of returns; ignoring fat tails, skewness, etc. − Assumes predictable covariances − Assumes linear pay-off profile, not viable for convex products or non-local movements	+ Simplicity + Captures gamma − Assumes normality of returns − Assumes predictable covariances − Does not capture risks of non-local movements	+ Captures local and non-local price movements + Not subject to model risks (historical simulation) − Model risk for empirical simulation − Computer intensive

existing staff, hardware, software and market data; secondly, they are quick to calculate and therefore can be implemented close to the decision-makers; and, finally, since they capture only the portfolio's linear risk, which can be summarized by net positions or "deltas", they do not require that the institution gain access to every position at the transaction level, thereby saving considerable systems expenditure in terms of accessing and warehousing data and methods from existing systems. Because of these benefits, many institutions feel that the trade-off between accuracy and complexity is in favor of these models when the underlying portfolios are relatively "linear" and when the time horizon is "reasonably" short.

(i) Portfolio–Normal Methods

Calculation Rules.   This method calculates VaR as a multiple of the standard deviation of the portfolio's or business unit's returns, e.g.

$$\text{VaR} = z_\alpha \sigma_p \sqrt{\Delta t}$$

where z_α is defined as the constant that gives the appropriate one-tailed confidence interval for the standardized normal distribution (e.g. $z_\alpha = 2.33$ for a 99 per cent confidence interval), σ_p is the (annualized) standard deviation of the portfolio/business unit's returns and Δt is the holding period horizon as a fraction of a year.

Assumptions and Implications.   This calculation rule is justified if portfolio or business unit returns are normally distributed, e.g. $\Delta P \sim N(\mu_p, \sigma_p)$, with μ_p assumed to equal 0, since it is a well-known property of the normal distribution that confidence intervals can be expressed as a multiple of the standard deviation. The normal assumption is valid for a portfolio in one of three situations:

- If the portfolio is comprised of a large number of positions whose limiting distribution is the normal distribution (see below for an example) or,

- If the portfolio returns are, in fact, normal and the portfolio strategy and composition is "constant", implying that the returns are drawn from a distribution with constant mean and variance, or

- If the portfolio is comprised of a set of asset positions, each of which is normally distributed. These assumptions define the assumptions underlying RiskMetrics^{TM} and will therefore be discussed in the next subsection.

Given these (implicit) assumptions, almost all of the common critiques (e.g. local measures, model risks, fat tails, non-constant parameters, symmetry) can therefore be applied to this method.

Applications.   As discussed, the Portfolio–Normal method is typically used in one of two contexts. The first involves portfolios comprising a large quantity of identical but independent positions whose limiting distribution can be reasonably approximated by a normal distribution. For example, consider calculating the VaR of a large, well-diversified portfolio of small consumer credits where we are interested in the amount of the portfolio that might go into default. Since, in the limit, the distribution of the sum of binomial variates converges in probability to the normal distribution, the portfolio's absolute return distribution will approach that of a normal distribution in the limit as the number of credits increases. Since we are justified in assuming a normal distribution in the limit, we might feel comfortable assuming that for very large portfolios of identical and independent positions, the return distribution is approximately normal. This method is therefore often used to calculate the VaR for large, well-diversified portfolios of consumer credits, credit card receivables, or the credit risk of mortgage pools (see Section 3.4 on measuring credit risk for a more exact approach).

The second potential use of the Portfolio–Normal method is to develop a quick and dirty capital VaR methodology based on historical profit and loss information *at the business unit level*. For example, consider calculating VaR for an equity trading unit by dividing monthly net income over the past 3–5 years by the market value of its equity holdings. On the basis of this time series, one could estimate the standard deviation of returns per dollar invested in the equity portfolio; using the formula, this would be used to estimate the VaR needed to support each dollar's worth of open "equity" position. This method assumes that beyond changes in the volume, the composition or trading strategy of the equity trading book is constant — an obviously unreasonable assumption.

While this application may prove useful in terms of getting a first cut at business unit VaR for performance measurement purposes, it is not a long- (or even medium-) term solution in terms of risk control. Nonetheless, it is quite useful as a starting point for the top-down evaluation of a business unit's risk-adjusted performance, especially in the context of a portfolio of businesses (see Matten (1996), D. Wilson (1995) and T. Wilson (1992)).

(ii) Asset–Normal or RiskMetrics[TM] Methods

Calculation Rules.   As with the Portfolio–Normal method, this method also calculates VaR as a multiple of the standard deviation of the portfolio's or business unit's returns, e.g.

$$\text{VaR} = z_\alpha \, \sigma_p \sqrt{\Delta t}$$

where z_α and Δt are defined as above. The only difference is that the standard deviation of the portfolio returns, σ_p, is calculated using a set of portfolio weights, $\boldsymbol{\omega}$, and the covariance matrix of position returns, $\boldsymbol{\Sigma}$, using the formula $\sigma_p = \sqrt{\boldsymbol{\omega}' \boldsymbol{\Sigma} \boldsymbol{\omega}}$.

Assumptions and Implications.   The Asset–Normal method assumes that the $N \times 1$ vector of position returns is jointly normal, e.g. $\Delta P \sim \text{N}(\boldsymbol{\mu}, \boldsymbol{\Sigma})$ where $\boldsymbol{\mu}$ is the $N \times 1$ vector of expected returns for one unit of each position usually assumed to be equal to zero and $\boldsymbol{\Sigma}$ is the $N \times N$ covariance matrix of position returns, respectively.[15] Note that we are assuming that the returns on market positions (e.g. zero bonds, equity index positions, equity options) are normally distributed[16] and not that market rate innovations (e.g. changes in interest rates, exchange rates) are normally distributed; this latter assumption is made in the Delta–Normal method described below. Since a portfolio is a weighted sum of its underlying positions and since the sum of normal variates is itself normally distributed, it follows that the expected returns of the portfolio are also normally distributed with mean $\mu_p = \boldsymbol{\omega}' \boldsymbol{\mu}$ and variance $\sigma_p^2 = \boldsymbol{\omega}' \boldsymbol{\Sigma} \boldsymbol{\omega}$.

If the market prices for individual positions are assumed to be governed by a diffusion process similar to the geometric Brownian motion process described earlier, then this assumption can be justified on theoretical grounds but only over infinitesimally short time intervals and for "small" market rate innovations (see Wilson (1992, 1993)); thus, this assumption can be thought of as valid only "locally". Almost all of the common critiques (e.g. linear approximations, local measures, model risks, fat tails) are therefore valid for this method of calculating VaR.

Applications.   The Asset–Normal method has a longer history of being applied to investment portfolios than many people actually realize; in fact, its assumptions (e.g. that position returns are normally distributed and that the variance or standard deviation of portfolio returns is a good measure of risk) are at the heart of the CAPM developed by Sharpe (1964) and Lintner (1965), as well as the portfolio optimization techniques of Markovitz (1952). As such, investors have been calculating VaR for a long time without even knowing it every time they considered the standard deviation of returns as a risk measure in the CAPM framework.

In addition, the asset–normal assumptions form the basis for RiskMetrics[TM] VaR methodologies. At its core, RiskMetrics[TM,17] comprises two basic components: first, a set of techniques to map a wide variety of products into standardized risk positions (e.g. zero coupon bonds, equity positions and net open exchange rate positions) and, secondly, advanced techniques applied to the estimation of the covariance matrix (e.g. the handling of missing data, exponential weighted average covariance estimation). Notwithstanding the extensive mathematics and theory utilized as well as the tremendously beneficial impact for the industry, it should be noted that this approach makes basically the same assumptions about position returns (e.g. normally distributed) and position sensitivities (e.g. linear) that Markovitz made in 1952. As such, the advantages and disadvantages of the model have been well understood and documented over the years.

One important problem is that since position returns are assumed to be normally distributed, the covariance methodology is not suitable for products with non-symmetric return distributions (e.g. options). The issue of non-linear pay-offs, and therefore non-symmetric return distributions, can only be addressed through other models such as the Delta–Gamma method, simulation techniques or the factor push method.

(iii) Delta–Normal Methods
A natural problem with the covariance approach arises when the number of positions (N) is quite large relative to the number (M) of market rates (S) that determine the value of the portfolio. Consider the following examples:

- Suppose we are interested in capturing the volatility risks of options. To capture option risks, we would either have to estimate the covariance between each individual option's returns or try to come up with some mapping technique to map an arbitrary option position into standardized risk positions as is done in RiskMetrics[TM] for non-contingent cash flows by mapping bonds, FRAs, etc. into a cash flow grid. This would be a very complicated and inaccurate mapping since the price of an option depends on many different factors, including volatility, degree of "moneyness", time to expiration, etc. The easier approach would be to focus on volatility itself as a risk factor and try to characterize how the portfolio's value changes with changes in volatilities rather than try to model the covariance between position returns as is done in the covariance approach.

- As a further example, suppose that we have 16 zero coupon maturity bucket grid points per currency that are all highly dependent on the level of interest rates. Rather than estimating the correlations and variances of all 16 positions for a large number of currencies, it might make sense instead to reduce the dimensionality of the problem by focusing on only two or three"risk factors" that capture most of the variation in the level and shape of the term structure. So, instead of modeling the highly correlated returns of 16 individual positions, one would instead measure the risk of a portfolio under 2–3 independent interest rate scenarios. This reduction in dimensionality can be accomplished through principle components or factor analysis techniques as described in Kaarkki and Reyes (1995) and Wilson (1994a) and implemented in a VaR framework by understanding the correlation between interest rate shifts and rotations rather than between position values directly.

The ability to reduce the dimensionality of the problem is accomplished by the Delta–Normal approach because it focuses on risk factors instead of risk positions. As such, it is a slightly more useful method of calculating VaR for complicated portfolios that cannot easily be "mapped" into standard positions.

Calculation Rule.   This method calculates VaR as a multiple of the portfolio's standard deviation, e.g.

$$\text{VaR} = z_\alpha \sigma_p \sqrt{\Delta t} \tag{1}$$

where z_α and Δt are as defined above. Here, however, σ_p is calculated using the portfolio's delta sensitivities to market rates as the portfolio weights, using the following formula: $\sigma_p = \sqrt{\delta' \Sigma \delta}$, where δ is the $M \times 1$ vector of portfolio sensitivities to market rates and Σ is the $M \times M$ market rate covariance matrix.

Assumptions and Implications.   Implicitly, the assumption is made that the portfolio returns are normally distributed. This result follows from making market rate assumptions similar to those made for the Delta–Gamma methods: market rate innovations are assumed to be jointly normally distributed, e.g.

$$\Delta \mathbf{S} \sim \text{N}(\boldsymbol{\mu}, \Sigma \Delta t), \tag{1*}$$

where rates are defined as interest rates, exchange rates, etc. rather than position prices (e.g. zero coupon bonds) as is the case for the Asset–Normal approach. Often, the mean vector is assumed to be equal to zero, a reasonable assumption if the time horizon is relatively short.

Given that the market rate innovations are assumed to have a joint normal distribution, the only way that the portfolio returns can also be normally distributed is if all of the price functions are linear in terms of changes in the underlying market prices. This follows directly since a linear combination of normal variables is itself normally distributed. The implicit assumption is that the price functions can be reasonably approximated by a first-order Taylor Series Expansion around the current market prices. We will call this expansion a Delta Approximation to differentiate it from the second-order, Delta–Gamma Approximation discussed later. More concretely:

$$\Delta P(\mathbf{S}) = \theta \Delta t + \delta' \Delta \mathbf{S} + o(2)$$

$$\Delta P(\mathbf{S}) \approx \theta \Delta t + \delta' \Delta \mathbf{S}$$

where θ is the portfolio's theta, or $\partial P(\mathbf{S})/\partial t$, $\boldsymbol{\delta}$ is the portfolio's $M \times 1$ vector of delta sensitivities expressed in dollar amounts, or $\partial P(\mathbf{S})/\partial \mathbf{S}$, and $o(2)$ represents the approximation error, which is of order 2. Again, this approximation error can be theoretically ignored if market rates are governed by a diffusion process and if time horizons are very "short"; see, for example, Wilson (1992, 1993) for a discussion. Using the properties of the normal distribution, it follows directly that portfolio returns are normally distributed, e.g.

$$\Delta P \sim \mathrm{N}(\theta_p, \boldsymbol{\delta}'_p \boldsymbol{\Sigma} \boldsymbol{\delta}_p \Delta t)$$

The VaR calculation rule given in equation (1) above follows directly where we define $\sigma_p = \sqrt{\boldsymbol{\delta}'_p \boldsymbol{\Sigma} \boldsymbol{\delta}_p}$.

To incorporate vega or volatility risk into the analysis in an internally consistent manner, institutions often treat the K-period ahead implicit market volatilities, where $K > 1$, as market rates just like any other market rates, e.g. they assume that innovations in market rate volatilities are also jointly normally distributed, and they then treat the portfolio's vega as the portfolio's linear sensitivity to changes in implicit volatilities just like any other delta or first-order, linear approximation term. By redefining market rates to include volatilities as well and by redefining delta sensitivities to include all first-order expansion terms, including vega terms, one can integrate volatility risk into the closed-form Delta–Normal approach.

Applications.   As mentioned, this method may be a reasonable method for calculating VaR if the time horizon is very short, e.g. intraday, and if the products themselves have a relatively linear pay-off profile, or, because it is easy to calculate, if a quick and dirty method is required. Thus, it may be very well suited for measuring and controlling intraday risks of a money market or foreign exchange book with few option positions. Its advantages over the RiskMetrics^{TM} approach is that it can be used to capture volatility risks as well as to reduce significantly the dimensionality of the problem. In addition, its calculation also relies on the portfolio's deltas, which should be readily available without the need to develop complex mapping techniques.

(iv) Variations on the Normal Assumption

Various approaches have been suggested to resolve some of the distribution issues associated with linear–normal methods. For example, several authors attempt to capture implicitly the "fat tails" characteristics displayed by many financial time series by making alternative distribution assumptions. For example, Wilson (1993) assumes that market rate volatilities are not known with certainty but that the risk manager has some Bayesian prior distribution for volatilities in mind. The result is that both the financial time series as well as portfolio returns have a Student-t distribution as opposed to a normal distribution, implying that large market rate movements will occur with greater frequency than would be predicted by the normal distribution. Alexander (1997), Hull and White (1997), Zangari (1997) and Venkataraman (1997) achieve similar results by assuming that market rate innovations are generated by a mixture of normal distributions, also generating kurtosis or fat tails in the implied market rate innovation time series.

Another approach for replacing the assumption that all market rates are normally distributed is to simulate the linear component of the portfolio's profit/loss profile using either a Monte Carlo or Historical simulation technique. More specifically, one would simulate the delta approximation to the portfolio profit/loss profile (ΔP) given below using market rate innovations ($\Delta\mathbf{S}$) generated either from historical data or using Monte Carlo techniques:

$$\Delta P(\mathbf{S}) = \theta\Delta t + \boldsymbol{\delta}'\Delta\mathbf{S} + o(2)$$

$$\Delta P(\mathbf{S}) \approx \theta\Delta t + \boldsymbol{\delta}'\Delta\mathbf{S}$$

After simulating the change in portfolio value a sufficient number of times, a loss histogram is generated and the required critical value is tabulated. By using historical market rate innovations, one avoids any possible "model risk" associated with a specific distribution assumption; depending upon the distribution assumed for generating the simulation samples using Monte Carlo techniques, one can match higher moments of the actual market rate innovation time series as well as their mean and covariance structure, thereby also capturing the "fat tails" effects. This approach is one variant of the historical or Monte Carlo simulation approaches that are typically used to capture the risks of a non-linear portfolio, with a non-linear portfolio sensitivity profile used instead of the delta approximation described here. As such, it will be discussed in greater detail in Section 3.3.4.

Another line of research focuses on improving the estimate of the covariance matrix needed to calculate VaR using single- or multi-factor GARCH techniques; much of the current work assumes that, conditional on current information, the innovations in market rates tomorrow are normally distributed but otherwise exhibit kurtosis or fat tails unconditionally. See Chapter 4 by Carol Alexander in this volume for an excellent overview and references.

3.3.4 Non-Linear Methods

As discussed earlier, the problem with the "linear" methods described in the last section is that they are not appropriate when applied to profit/loss profiles that are inherently "non-linear", such as those that would be generated by a portfolio containing options, callable or convertible bonds, mortgage-backed securities with large convexity, etc. In general, there are two different approaches that are used: second-order approximations (e.g. Delta–Gamma methods) or simulation techniques.

(i) Delta–Gamma Methods

As discussed earlier, one of the main benefits of a delta-based VaR calculation method is that deltas are essentially "free" — they are almost always calculated as a by-product in the front office systems; they offer a parsimonious parameterization of the portfolio's risk profile without having to capture detailed transaction-level information; the methods themselves are simple and do not require large, technically proficient staff to implement them and, finally, they are computationally quite efficient, giving a VaR result using only matrix multiplication. The problem is that they do not capture the non-linear risks.

There have, therefore, been many attempts at developing a simple approach based on a portfolio's delta and gamma representation that is also computationally efficient. The main benefit of such an approach, if it could be developed, would again be the fact that the institution would not have to collect transaction-level information but could continue to rely on a small number of portfolio-level risk measures that are calculated as a by-product of standard exposure reporting processes. This benefit alone has the potential to offer significant savings in terms of systems integration expenses.

There are at least four different numerical approaches for calculating VaR that could be considered a Delta–Gamma approach. Each of these different calculation methods is described in detail below.

Assumptions and Implications.   Just as with the Delta–Normal approach, most Delta–Gamma approaches assume that market rate innovations are normally distributed, e.g. $\Delta S \sim N(\mu, \Sigma \Delta t)$ with μ typically assumed to equal zero. The key difference is that the Delta–Gamma approach explicitly uses the standard risk measures that risk managers use every day to manage and control the risk of their portfolios, e.g. the portfolio's delta and gamma sensitivities (as well as the portfolio's vega sensitivities, as discussed earlier). To motivate this approach, we begin by taking a second-order Taylor Series Expansion of the portfolio's value function around current market rates. We will call this a Delta–Gamma Approximation to contrast it with the first-order expansion used by the Delta–Normal approximation technique described earlier.

Delta–Gamma Approximation:

$$\Delta P(\mathbf{S}) = \theta \Delta t + \boldsymbol{\delta}' \Delta \mathbf{S} + \Delta \mathbf{S}' \boldsymbol{\gamma} \Delta \mathbf{S}/2 + o(3)$$

$$\Delta P(\mathbf{S}) \approx \theta \Delta t + \boldsymbol{\delta}' \Delta \mathbf{S} + \Delta \mathbf{S}' \boldsymbol{\gamma} \Delta \mathbf{S}/2,$$

(2)

where θ is the portfolio's theta, or $\partial P(\mathbf{S})/\partial \mathbf{t}$; $\boldsymbol{\delta}$, an $M \times 1$ vector, is the portfolio's vector of delta sensitivities to changes in market rates that we have already discussed in the section on Delta–Normal methods; $\boldsymbol{\gamma}$, an $M \times M$ symmetric matrix, is the portfolio's gamma matrix with respect to the various market risk factors; and $o(3)$ is the approximation error term, which is of order 3.

More specifically, the gamma matrix is defined as the second derivative, or Hessian, of the portfolio's value function (e.g. $\gamma_{ij} = \partial^2 P(\mathbf{S})/\partial \mathbf{S}_i \partial \mathbf{S}_j$ for the i, jth element of the matrix), which is also the sum of the individual positions' gammas. These gamma terms are more readily recognizable for $i = j$, in which case gamma i is defined as $\partial^2 P(\mathbf{S})/\partial \mathbf{S}_i^2$, or the change in delta i for a change in market rate i. We may ignore the cross-product terms of the expansion (e.g. when $i \neq j$) if the individual prices are functions of only one market price or if the cross-product effects are trivial, a potentially dangerous assumption that is often made implicitly by risk managers. For other, correlation-dependent products such as diff swaps and choosers, the cross-product terms can be significant and should not be ignored. For an additional discussion, see Rouvinez (1997), Schaefer (1995), Jorion (1997) and Estrella (1994).

Calculation Rules.   Based on these assumptions, there are at least four different numerical algorithms for calculating market VaR that are referenced in the literature: the exact distribution approach used by Rouvinez (1997); the approximating distribution approach; the numerical optimization approach discussed in Wilson (1994b) and, finally, Monte Carlo or historical simulation approaches. Each of these approaches is discussed below.

• *Exact distribution approach.*   Following Wilson (1994b), Rouvinez (1997) and Schaefer (1995) begin by performing a linear transformation of the market rates:

$$\Delta \mathbf{S}^* = \mathbf{TP} \Delta \mathbf{S} = L \Delta \mathbf{S}$$

where $\mathbf{P}$ is the inverse of the Cholesky decomposition of Σ, e.g. the non-singular matrix that satisfies the equation $\mathbf{P} \Sigma \mathbf{P}' = \mathbf{I}$, and $\mathbf{T}$ is the orthogonal matrix that satisfies the equation $L'^{-1}\gamma L^{-1} = \mathbf{T}'(\mathbf{P}'^{-1}\gamma\mathbf{P}^{-1})\mathbf{T} = \gamma$, where γ is the diagonal matrix of the eigenvalues of the matrix $\mathbf{P}'^{-1}\gamma\mathbf{P}^{-1}$ and $\mathbf{T}$ is the matrix of eigenvectors of $\mathbf{P}'^{-1}\gamma\mathbf{P}^{-1}$, where γ is the Hessian or gamma matrix of the second-order Taylor Series Expansion discussed earlier. This transformation leaves $\Delta\mathbf{S}^*$ as a vector of independently distributed normal random variates with unit variance, e.g. $\Delta\mathbf{S}^* \sim N(0, \mathbf{I})$. This follows immediately since

$$\Sigma = \mathbf{TP}\Sigma\mathbf{P}'\mathbf{T}' \text{ by definition}$$

$$= \mathbf{TT}' \text{ by the definition of } \mathbf{P} \text{ (e.g. } \mathbf{P}\Sigma P' = \mathbf{I})$$

$$= \mathbf{I} \text{ by the definition of } \mathbf{T} \text{ as normalized eigenvectors}$$

Sheffe (1959) demonstrates that for any quadratic form of $\Delta\mathbf{S}$ defined by $Q = \Delta\mathbf{S}'\gamma\Delta\mathbf{S}$, with γ symmetric, by using the above transformation using matrices $\mathbf{T}$ and $\mathbf{P}$, we can define Q in the following manner:

$$Q^* = \Delta\mathbf{S}^{*'}\gamma^*\Delta\mathbf{S}^*$$

where $\gamma^* = L'^{-1}\gamma L^{-1}$, with Q^* equivalent to $Q = \Delta\mathbf{S}'\gamma\Delta\mathbf{S}$ in distribution. This is easy to demonstrate since

$$\Delta\mathbf{S}^{*'}\gamma^*\Delta\mathbf{S}^* = \Delta\mathbf{S}'L'(L'^{-1}\gamma L^{-1})L\Delta\mathbf{S} = \Delta\mathbf{S}'\gamma\Delta\mathbf{S}$$

This transformation therefore allows us to rewrite (2) in a much simpler manner, e.g.

$$\Delta\mathbf{P(S)} \approx \theta\Delta t + \delta^{*'}\Delta\mathbf{S}^* + \Delta\mathbf{S}^{*'}\gamma^*\Delta\mathbf{S}^*/2 \tag{2*}$$

with $\delta^* = L'^{-1}\delta$, γ^* diagonal and as described above, and $\Delta\mathbf{S}^* \sim N(0, \mathbf{I})$ by construction. To see this, first note that $\Delta\mathbf{S}^{*'}\gamma^*\Delta\mathbf{S}^*$ is equivalent in distribution to $\Delta\mathbf{S}'\gamma\Delta\mathbf{S}$ under the linear transformation as a consequence of Sheffe's observation stated above. Secondly, note that $\delta^{*'}\Delta\mathbf{S}^* = \delta'\Delta\mathbf{S}$ by definition. It follows that (2) and (2*) are equivalent in distribution under the linear transformation. Following Wilson (1994b), Schaefer (1995) and Rouvinez (1997), given that γ^* is diagonal and $\Delta\mathbf{S}^*$ are independent, we can rewrite (2*) as the sum of linearly separable, independent, non-central chi-squared random variables, e.g.

$$\Delta\mathbf{P(S)} \approx \theta\Delta t + \sum_{i=1...N}(\delta_i^*\Delta\mathbf{S}_i^* + 1/2\gamma_{ii}^*\Delta\mathbf{S}_i^{*2}) \tag{2*}$$

for γ_{ii}^* non-zero; otherwise, (2*) reduces to the sum of independent, non-central chi-squared *and* normal variates.

The exact distribution method was developed by Rouvinez (1997); using this transformation, Rouvinez specifies the moment generating function for this sum of independent chi-squared and normal variates and then demonstrates how to compute numerically the exact cumulative distribution function (cdf) of (2*) by first inverting the characteristic function for (2*); once this is done, one only needs to invert numerically the cdf at the required confidence level in order to calculate the portfolio's VaR. These calculations can be done relatively quickly using standard numerical recipes.

- *Approximate Distribution Methods.* Other, proprietary Delta–Gamma methods take a similar approach but change direction slightly after defining the moment generating function for the sum of independent chi-squared variables. Intuitively, these approximate distribution methods use a parametric distribution with easy-to-calculate confidence intervals as an approximating distribution by choosing the appropriate parameters of the approximating distribution in such a manner so as to match the first few moments of the actual distribution that were tabulated using the moment generating function. The benefit of this approach is potentially speed with potentially some sacrifice in terms of approximation errors.

- *Optimization techniques.* Wilson (1994b) develops a method for capturing a portfolio's second-order or gamma risk using numerical optimization techniques. Following industry standards, we define VaR as the maximum possible loss over a specific time horizon within a given confidence interval. The solution technique that was developed by Wilson (1994b) takes a new approach by taking this definition literally. If interpreted literally, the definition can be seen to outline a very concrete and well-defined optimization program: solve for the market event that maximizes potential losses subject to the constraint that the event and all events generating less losses are within a given confidence interval. We can formulate this problem very generally in the following manner:

$$\text{VaR} = \max_{\{S\}} -\Delta P(S) = \sum_{l}[P_i(S) - P_i(S_0)]$$

$$\text{subject to } F(S) \leq \kappa \tag{3}$$

where $\Delta P(S)$ is defined as the change in portfolio value, $P_i(S)$ is the price function for each of the individual transactions, $i = 1 \ldots N$, as a function of market rates, S is the $M \times 1$ vector of market rates with S_0 being the current market rates, $F(S)$ is defined as the probability that this event or one of greater negative impact will actually occur (note that this constraint is very complex unless simplified in some manner) and κ is the confidence level that the risk manager wants to achieve, expressed in per cent (e.g. the maximum loss within a 1 per cent confidence interval). Using the assumptions that market rate innovations are normally distributed and that the portfolio's price profile is well approximated by a Delta–Gamma representation, we can rewrite this optimization problem in the following manner:

$$\text{VaR} = \max_{\{\Delta S\}} -[\delta'\Delta S + \Delta S'\gamma\Delta S/2] \tag{4}$$

$$\text{subject to } \Delta S'\Sigma^{-1}\Delta S \leq z_\alpha^2,$$

where we have taken advantage of the normality assumption to rewrite the constraint in a quadratic form. The $\Delta S'\Sigma^{-1}\Delta S$ term represents the M-dimensional confidence ellipsoid for the jointly normal innovations to market rates and α in equation (4) is the number of standard deviations required to give the appropriate one-tailed confidence interval for κ in equation (1), e.g. $z_\alpha = 2.33$ for $\kappa = 1$ per cent. Since market rate events lying outside of this ellipsoid occur with probability less than the desired confidence interval, we can restrict our search for worst-case market rate events by looking in the interior and at the boundary of this ellipsoid. If the worst-case scenario occurs at an extreme value of this ellipsoid, then this constraint will be binding (e.g. $\Delta S'\Sigma^{-1}\Delta S = z_\alpha^2$); otherwise, if the worst-case scenario occurs when rates do not move "too much", e.g. an interior solution, then the constraint will not be binding (e.g. $\Delta S'\Sigma^{-1}\Delta S < z_\alpha^2$).[18]

Equation (4) is now a quadratic programming problem (the objective function is quadratic, as is the constraint) and, as such, many numerical methods exist for solving it. One method is to set up the appropriate Lagrangian or Kuhn–Tucker equation and differentiate, where we find that the first-order, Kuhn–Tucker conditions[19] that describe the solution to (4) are as follows:

$$[-\gamma - \lambda \Sigma^{-1}]\Delta S = \delta \text{ or } A(\lambda)\Delta S = \delta \tag{5a}$$

$$\Delta S' \Sigma^{-1} \Delta S \leq z_\alpha^2 \tag{5b}$$

with

$$\lambda(\Delta S' \Sigma^{-1} \Delta S - z_\alpha^2) = 0 \text{ and } \lambda \geq 0 \tag{5c}$$

where λ is the Kuhn–Tucker multiplier associated with the constraint. Equation (5c) states that if the worst-case scenario occurs at an extreme value and the constraint is binding, then the Kuhn–Tucker multiplier must have a value greater than zero; conversely, if the worst-case scenario is an interior solution, implying that the constraint is not binding, then the multiplier will have zero value. The Kuhn–Tucker multiplier has a useful interpretation: it measures the marginal amount of additional VaR that will need to be allocated to the portfolio if the confidence interval (squared), or α^2, is increased. This system of equations can be solved numerically. One method of solving this system of equations is to do a numerical search over $\lambda \geq 0$, inverting the matrix $A(\lambda)$ for each λ to solve for ΔS using equation (5a) and then checking to see whether the constraints (5b) and (5c) are satisfied to some tolerance level.

The speed can be increased if we diagonalize A and transform the risk factors into independent variables. Using the transformation discussed earlier, we can rewrite (4) as (6) below:

$$\text{VaR} = \max_{\{\Delta S\}} -[\delta^{*'} \Delta S^* + \Delta S^{*'} \gamma^* \Delta S^* /2]$$

$$\text{subject to } \Delta S^{*'} \Delta S^* \leq z_\alpha^2 \tag{6}$$

The first-order conditions for equation (6) can now be rewritten in the following form:

$$[-\gamma^* - \lambda I]\Delta S^* = \delta^* \text{ or } A^*(\lambda)\Delta S^* = \delta^* \tag{7a}$$

$$\Delta S^{*'} \Delta S^* \leq z_\alpha^2 \tag{7b}$$

$$\lambda(\Delta S^{*'} \Delta S^* - z_\alpha^2) = 0 \text{ and } \lambda \geq 0. \tag{7c}$$

where $A^*(\lambda)$ is a diagonal matrix, implying that the values of ΔS^* that solve (7a) for each λ can be determined analytically. This further implies that the matrix A^* does not have to be inverted with each iteration of the search, thereby reducing the time it takes to solve for the solution of the system of equations given by (7). More concretely, the solution to (7a) for each ΔS_i is given by the following equation:

$$\Delta S_i^* = \delta_i^* /(\gamma_{ii}^* + \lambda) \tag{8}$$

Nonetheless, the system of equations defined by (7) must still be solved numerically by searching over $\lambda \in [0, \infty)$, calculating the values of ΔS^* that solve (8) and then checking the constraints in (7b) and (7c). Unfortunately, there may be many solutions to this system of equations in λ; Rouvinez (1997) discusses an approach for defining the region (λ_{min}, λ_{max}), which contains the λ that gives the global maximum of (6).

- *Factor-push approach.*   If we are willing to make one more approximation, however, then we can develop a closed-form solution to the problem and avoid this time-intensive numerical search. Let us expand equation (6) and concentrate on only those terms that involve ΔS_i, the ith transformed market rate, in the objective function:

$$\delta_i^* \Delta S_i + \gamma_{ii}^* \Delta S^2/2 \tag{9}$$

Equation (9) measures the contribution of the ith transformed market rate, ΔS_i^*, which is by construction a standardized, independent unit normal variable, to the change in value of the portfolio. By construction, equation (9) passes through zero and has no cross-product terms owing to the transformation. Furthermore, for non-zero γ^*, it may have any one of the shapes shown in Figure 3.5.[20]

Since we are ultimately concerned about the behavior of equation (9) when the ith variable is at its extreme, consider constructing a piecewise linear function to approximate equation (9). This piecewise linear function is illustrated in Figure 3.6 and is chosen to have its breakpoint at zero, passing through zero as well as the extreme values of the function when evaluated at the confidence interval that we

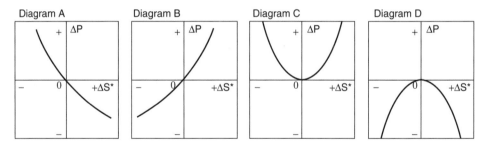

Figure 3.5   Impact of diagonal risk factors

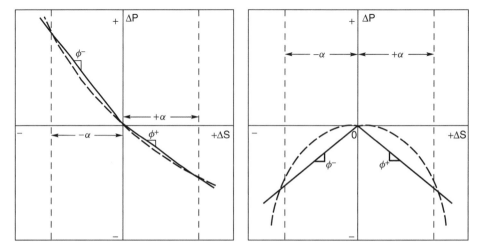

Figure 3.6   Piecewise linear approximation

desire. The formula for this equation is given below:

$$\delta_i^* \Delta S_i^* + \gamma_{ii}^* \Delta S^{*2}/2 \approx \phi_i^{+*} \Delta S_i^* \text{ for } \Delta S_i^* > 0$$

$$\approx \phi_i^{-*} \Delta S_i^* \text{ for } \Delta S_i^* \leq 0 \qquad (10)$$

where $\phi_i^- = (\delta_i^* - \gamma_{ii}^* \alpha/2)$, $\phi_i^+ = (\delta_i^* + \gamma_{ii}^* \alpha/2)$ and α is the number of standard deviations required to achieve the desired confidence interval. Define $\phi_i = \min[\phi i^-, \phi_i^+, 0]$. We interpret ϕ_i as the delta or linear pay-off profile that approximates the actual pay-off profile in the region of the (joint) worst-case scenario. Our rationale for doing so is as follows: it is clear that, along a given risk factor dimension, the solution to the optimization program defined by equation (6) occurs in the region for which equation (9) is best approximated by $\phi_i^* \Delta S_i^*$ for $\phi_i < 0$. Furthermore, inspection of the quadratic constraint in equation (6) indicates that if $\phi_i > 0$ (e.g. the contribution of the ith transformed market rate is always positive as in Figure 3.5(c)), then the solution is to set $\Delta S_i^* = 0$.[21] These observations are incorporated in the definition of ϕ_i.

Substituting $\phi_i^* \Delta S_i^*$ for each $\delta_i^* \Delta S_i^* + \gamma_{ii}^* \Delta S^{*2}/2$ in equation (6) linearizes the objective function by eliminating the quadratic term. Solving the first-order conditions for this transformed problem, we find that the worst-case scenario is defined by the following transformed market rate factors:

$$\Delta S_i^* = \begin{cases} -\alpha\phi_i / \sqrt{\displaystyle\sum_i \phi_i^2}, & \text{for } \phi_i \leq 0 \\ \\ 0, & \text{for } \phi_i > 0 \end{cases} \qquad (11)$$

Substituting equation (11) into the linearized objective function, we find that we can express the arbitrary portfolio's VaR in the following form:

$$\text{VaR}_{\delta\gamma} = z_\alpha \sigma_{\delta\gamma} \sqrt{\Delta t} \qquad (12)$$

where $\sigma_{\delta\gamma} = \sqrt{\Sigma_i \phi_i^2}$ or $\sqrt{\phi'\phi}$. This is the same formula as for the Delta–Normal or covariance method described earlier, only we have substituted a different volatility parameter that is adjusted to capture the convexity of the portfolio into the calculation rule. Furthermore, given that the actual market rate innovations, e.g. ΔS_i are a linear transformation of the optimal, transformed innovations, e.g. ΔS_i^*, we find that the "worst-case" scenario in terms of market rates is the following:

$$S_{\text{worst}} = S_0 + P^{-1} T^{-1} \Delta S^* \qquad (13)$$

where ΔS^*, T and P are as defined by the linear transformation described earlier and in equation (11).

There is some intuition behind this calculation method: by using the transformation, we have effectively made the individual risk factors independent from one another and therefore have isolated their first- and second-order influence on the portfolio's value. By isolating the impact of each individual risk factor, we can then approximate each factor's influence via a piecewise linear function that is valid only at the extremes where the worst-case scenario is likely to occur; since the transformed market rate innovations are independent of one another, we can simply choose the "worst" section of the piecewise linear approximation and create a linear approximation. Having effectively linearized the portfolio's sensitivities to the transformed risk factors at the extremes, we could then use the properties of the standard normal and the familiar RiskMetrics™ formula to calculate VaR.

- *Simulation approach.*   The final approach is to simply simulate the Delta–Gamma or second-order Taylor Series approximation directly using either Monte Carlo or historical simulation techniques, just as we discussed earlier in terms of simulating the Delta or first-order Taylor Series Expansion. After simulating the change in portfolio value a sufficient number of times, a loss histogram is generated and the required critical value is tabulated. By using historical market rate innovations, one avoids any possible "model risk" associated with a specific distribution assumption; depending upon the distribution assumed for generating the simulation samples using Monte Carlo techniques, one can match higher moments of the actual market rate innovation time series as well as their mean and covariance structure, thereby also capturing the "fat tails" effects. This approach is one variant of the historical or Monte Carlo simulation approaches that are typically used to capture the risks of a non-linear portfolio, with a non-linear portfolio sensitivity profile used instead of the delta approximation described earlier. Structured Monte Carlo approaches that simulate the portfolio's profits or losses using each transaction's actual price function will be discussed in greater detail in the next subsection.

Applications.   The Delta–Gamma methods discussed in this section use a second-order approximation of the portfolio's value function to represent the portfolio's sensitivity to market rate innovations. These methods therefore eliminate several of the criticisms described earlier (e.g. they capture the portfolio's direct and cross-market gamma or convexity risks as well as their vega risks), but they do so using local rather than global risk measures. Because they use local measures, however, these new methods have the advantage that they can be calculated using the standard risk measures (e.g. delta, gamma, vega and theta) that are readily available for most portfolios; their main advantages are therefore that their implementation requires significantly less systems integration effort than other methods and that they can be calculated quickly for portfolios based on aggregate risk measures. Against this must be balanced the fact that they are based on local, rather than global, measures.

(ii) Empirical Simulation Methods

Calculation Rule.   This method, although often difficult to implement in a cost-effective manner at the transaction level for arbitrary portfolios involving any but the simplest derivatives, is the one most often chosen by regulators to set the optimal parameters for the "building block" approach because it is considered more robust and intuitive than other, model-based methods.

The method is based on a three-step simulation technique using historical rate movements and is therefore quite intuitive (see Figure 3.7).

- Take a suitably long historical time series of market rates, $\{S_t\}_{t=-T...0}$, typically 3–5 years of daily data, where S_t is the vector of market rates at time t.
- Calculate a time series of the change in value of the portfolio of interest over the assumed liquidation period using the actual price functions, $P_i(S_t)$ (e.g. the Black–Scholes or Garman–Kohlhagen formulas for simple options, zero coupon discount functions for cash flows), where $P_i(S_t)$ represents the price of position i

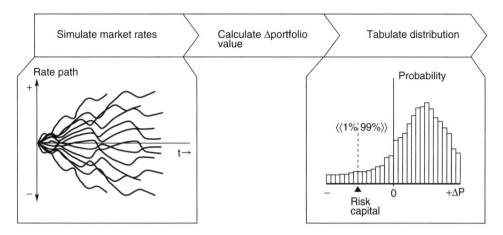

Figure 3.7   Simulation procedure

given market rates at time *t*. Alternatively, define and simulate an approximating portfolio pay-off function over this region, perhaps using a local, quadratic function, an *N*-dimensional cubic spline, a polynomial spline, linear interpolation, etc. based on portfolio sensitivities evaluated at 1-sigma intervals (including crosses) around the initial market rates. This pay-off function approximation step is optional if all of the portfolio's transactions can be accessed and evaluated directly in an efficient manner.

- Finally, tabulate the empirical return distribution generated from these historical rates and determine the appropriate VaR for the portfolio by examining the extreme values of that distribution.

Assumptions and Implications.   This method makes very few assumptions about the market price processes generating the portfolio's returns: it simply assumes that market price innovations in the future are drawn from the same empirical distribution as those market price innovations generated historically; it is, however, dependent on the specific historical context chosen. This implies that the exact time frame used is somewhat critical as it could arbitrarily include or exclude extreme price movements actually observed. For example, a five-year period would capture the bond crash of 1994 and the Peso crisis of 1995 but not the stock market crash of 1987 and the Euro crisis of 1992, whereas a 10-year period would do so.

To its benefit, by using the empirical distribution, one avoids many of the problems inherent in explicitly modeling the evolution of market prices, e.g. the fact that market prices tend to have "fatter tails" and be slightly more skewed than predicted by the normal distribution; the fact that correlations and volatilities can vary over time. The main advantage of this method, therefore, is that one does not inadvertently introduce model risk (beyond the assumption that the future can be summarized using today's empirical distribution) into the calculation of VaR, except to the extent to which models of the stochastic behavior of market rates are required to calculate non-observable parameters such as volatilities and correlations.

Also to its benefit is the fact that if one follows this method exactly, then there are no assumptions made regarding the price functions (except that they are appropriate for the positions being valued): one would use the exact price functions, $P_i(\mathbf{S}_t)$, to generate the historical distribution of portfolio returns. This implies that the actual pay-off profile of the portfolio is captured globally, rather than having to rely on local approximations. If an approximating pay-off profile is used, model risk or approximation error is introduced, which might be mitigated by the choice of a tighter grid for calculating the approximation.

The full simulation method is quite costly, however, to implement from a systems perspective. First, it requires that all of the institution's positions be accessible by the same system in some form or another or, equivalently, that the organization have an institution-wide, transaction-oriented database. This presents certain challenges in itself for institutions that have to integrate a wide variety of legacy systems, or whose operations are geographically disperse or that innovate new products frequently. Secondly, it requires that all of these transactions be able to be priced centrally on the back of this transaction database. Again, this may be a difficult task if new product structures are being introduced frequently, because there may be a lead time before the new structures are implemented centrally. Thirdly, it requires substantial computing power in order to calculate the empirical return distribution, essentially entailing the marking-to-market of the portfolio every day over the 3–5 year historical period in order to calculate a single VaR number. It may be the case that such computing capacity is not warranted from a risk control perspective alone, in which case the implementation of the full simulation method must find at least partial justification from the trading or front division as well. Finally, it requires that an adequate historical time series of market rates be constructed. This method may therefore be difficult to apply in emerging markets that have no "history" or when attempting to capture market risk factors that are not directly observable, such as rate volatilities and correlations for correlation dependent options.

Applicability.   As mentioned earlier, the full simulation method is robust to most of the common criticisms leveled at VaR calculations (e.g. local measures, model risk, fatter tails). It is therefore most useful in the context of portfolios that meet two conditions: first, the computing infrastructure is justified by both the front divisions as well as risk controlling and, secondly, the products covered are highly complex with pay-off profiles that cannot be easily approximated at the extremes by other, simpler methods.

(iii) Monte Carlo Simulation Methods
Calculation Rules.   Just like the empirical simulation method, the Monte Carlo simulation method calculates VaR by using the same three-step procedure outlined in Figure 3.7, except that the simulations are based on specific models for market rate innovations rather than on the historical innovations.

Assumptions and Implications.   The joint evolution of each market risk factor must be explicitly modeled in order to implement this method. Although some complex representations of single and multi-country, arbitrage-free rate dynamics are implemented (e.g. Heath–Jarrow–Morton, Langstaff–Schwartz or other representations for single currency rate environments as well as other multi-currency, multi-asset class representations), they are very complex to implement because they require the estimation of non-observable parameters and significant intellectual and systems infrastructure to make them operational. Owing to the complexity of their implementation, these models are most commonly used for calculating VaR only if they are used by the front for the pricing and risk management of complex derivative portfolios. The most common (and the simplest) Monte Carlo implementation involves the assumption that market rates follow a joint geometric Brownian motion (GBM) process with constant drift and volatility parameters as given below:

$$\mathrm{d}\mathbf{p}(t) = \boldsymbol{\mu}(t)\mathbf{p}(t)\,\mathrm{d}t + \boldsymbol{\sigma}(t)\mathbf{p}(t)\,\mathrm{d}\mathbf{Z}(t)$$

implying the stochastic integral

$$\mathbf{p}(t + \Delta t) = \mathbf{p}(t)^* \exp\left[\int_{\Delta t} \boldsymbol{\mu}(s)\,\mathrm{d}s + \left(\int_{\Delta t} \boldsymbol{\sigma}(s)\,\mathrm{d}s\right)\sqrt{\Delta t}\boldsymbol{\omega}\right],$$

where $\mathbf{p}(t)$ is the $N \times 1$ vector of market rates at time t, $\boldsymbol{\mu}(t)$ is the $N \times 1$ vector of instantaneous drift terms at time t (often set so that the process fits the implied forward rates), $\boldsymbol{\sigma}(t)$ is the $N \times 1$ vector of instantaneous, annualized volatilities of the process, $\mathrm{d}\mathbf{Z}$ is an $N \times 1$ serially independent standard Wiener process with correlation matrix $\boldsymbol{\Sigma}$, and $\boldsymbol{\omega} \sim \mathrm{N}(\mathbf{0}, \boldsymbol{\Sigma})$.

To implement the Monte Carlo method assuming a GBM process, one would follow the following process:

- First, estimate the relevant parameters of this representation (e.g. $\boldsymbol{\sigma}$ and $\boldsymbol{\Sigma}$) along the following lines (this is described in great detail in many standard textbooks on options such as Hull (1988)):
  - Calculate a new series by taking the first difference of the natural log of the market rate observations.
  - Estimate the correlation matrix ($\boldsymbol{\Sigma}$) and standard deviations (or the square root of the variances) of these series.
  - Scale the standard deviations so that they represent annualized values. For example, if data used to estimate the parameters were daily and there are 250 working days in the year, then this standard deviation vector would be scaled by multiplying it by $\sqrt{250/1}$.

- Secondly, set the drift term as desired (e.g. consistent with the risk neutral price path/to fit the implied forward curve or to generate a random walk/zero expected drift).

- Thirdly, simulate the innovations to the $N \times 1$ market rate vector:
  - Typically, this will be done by first generating a random sample of an $N \times 1$ vector of independent, $\mathrm{N}(\mathbf{0}, \mathbf{I})$ random variables, $\bar{\boldsymbol{\omega}}$. The next step would be to use the Cholesky decomposition of the covariance matrix, $\boldsymbol{\Sigma} = \mathbf{X}\mathbf{X}'$, to create a new, correlated set of innovations that have the same covariance structure as the market rate innovations, e.g. $\boldsymbol{\omega} = \bar{\boldsymbol{\omega}}\mathbf{X}$, so that $E(\boldsymbol{\omega}\boldsymbol{\omega}') = E(\bar{\boldsymbol{\omega}}\mathbf{X}\mathbf{X}'\bar{\boldsymbol{\omega}}') = \boldsymbol{\Sigma}$ (see J.P. Morgan (1994–95) for a discussion).
  - These innovations will then be used to calculate additive changes in observable market rates using a discretized version of the market rate model, e.g. $\Delta\mathbf{p}(t) \equiv \mathbf{p}(t + \Delta t) - \mathbf{p}(t) \approx \mathbf{p}(t)\boldsymbol{\mu}\Delta t + \mathbf{p}(t)\boldsymbol{\sigma}(t)\sqrt{\Delta t}\boldsymbol{\omega}$, where $\boldsymbol{\mu}(t)$ may be set equal to zero to achieve a random walk process; alternatively, $\boldsymbol{\mu}(t)$ can be set so that the implied process is consistent with the implied forward curves (see above).
  - In theory, simulating the P&L distribution will provide us with an estimate of the actual distribution, with the estimate converging to the actual as the number of simulations increases to infinity. Since it is impractical to simulate the P&L

an infinite number of times, there will always remain some estimation error. For this reason, some type of variance reduction techniques, e.g. antithetic or control variates, quasi-random sequences,[22] are typically employed to improve the efficiency of the Monte Carlo sampling procedure.

- Finally, re-value the portfolio for each simulation run using either the actual transactions or an approximating pay-off profile as described in the section on empirical simulation.

Depending upon which models are chosen, this approach is subject to many of the standard distribution criticisms, e.g. fat tails, symmetric distributions. More disturbing for regulators is the fact that this method introduces model risks for the market rate processes that need to be modeled before being simulated. In addition, some models (e.g. the GBM assumption) do not necessarily restrict the market rate processes to be arbitrage free, whereas other models may have the desired arbitrage-free properties. Although some assumptions regarding the price functions may be made, normally the simulated distribution is generated using the actual price functions. If an approximating pay-off profile is used, then approximation errors may be introduced.

This method is therefore as challenging to implement in terms of systems as the empirical simulation method. An additional cost arises, however, in that the institution must also be in a position to estimate the relevant model parameters, thus increasing the skilled resources required.

Applications.   Nonetheless, if the modeling is correctly done, it is one of the most robust methods available in terms of its ability to be applied to many diverse product structures. Furthermore, the skills and systems built up through its implementation may lead the institution to be a stronger player in the derivatives markets, allowing it better to structure solutions for their clients. Because of these points, it is probably not cost effective to implement a Monte Carlo method based solely on a risk measurement mandate: if the institution has already developed Monte Carlo models to price and manage complex structures for their clients, then these can be leveraged in terms of risk assessment. Otherwise, their implementation probably does not make sense on a stand-alone basis except in a simplified way.

(iv) Factor-Push Methods

Calculation Rule.   The Factor-Push method, often used for calculating the potential credit exposure from derivatives transactions, determines the most disadvantageous direction that market prices can go and then "pushes" the prices in that direction in order to calculate VaR. The amount by which the individual factors are pushed typically depends on their volatilities but not on their correlations; for example, the DM/$ and HFL/$ rates may each be "pushed" by 2.33 standard deviations if a 99 per cent confidence interval is desired, but perhaps in opposite directions even though the rates are themselves very highly correlated. More concretely, the Factor-Push method calculates VaR through the following process (see Figure 3.8(A)):

1. For $m = 1 \ldots M$, define P_{m+} equal to the value of the portfolio when evaluated when the mth market price is "pushed" up by α standard deviations (e.g. $S_m = S_{m0} + \alpha^* \sigma_m$, where α equals the number of standard deviations required to give the desired confidence interval and σ_m is the volatility of the mth market rate innovation), all other market prices being held constant. Define P_{m-} analogously.

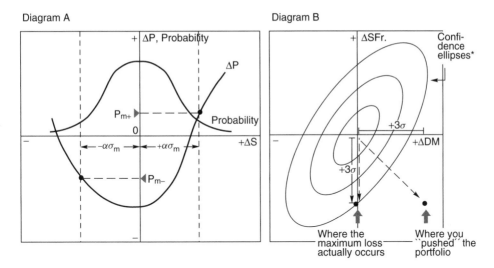

Figure 3.8   Factor-Push methods

2.   Define a "worst-case" scenario that "pushes" all of the variables in the worst possible direction. This is accomplished by valuing the portfolio using $+\alpha\sigma_m$ if $P_{m+} < P_{m-}$ and $-\alpha\sigma_m$ otherwise for each of the M market rates.

3.   The VaR for this portfolio is calculated as the difference between this "worst-case scenario" and the portfolio's value at current market prices. Alternatively, sometimes the sum of the individual deviations is taken (e.g. take the sum of $(\min[P_{m+}, P_{m-}] - P_0)$ over all M.

There are several problems with this methodology that are illustrated by Figure 3.8(B).

• First, it does not optimally recognize factor sensitivity trade-offs, e.g. it pushes all of the factors by two or three standard deviations, regardless of the portfolio's sensitivity to the individual factors. Consider, for example, Figure 3.8(B), which illustrates this effect for a portfolio that has a small short DM position with relatively low sensitivity to an appreciating DM/$ rate but a very large long £/$ position and therefore high sensitivity to a depreciating £/$ rate. For this example, the maximum possible loss within a 97.5 per cent confidence interval does not occur when both rates are pushed equally by two standard deviations; this would only be the case if the portfolio was equally as sensitive to both rates. Rather, it occurs when the £/$ rate is pushed by more than two standard deviations and the DM/$ rate by less. Intuitively, by pushing the DM/$ rate by the same amount, even though it has less of a negative impact on the value of the portfolio, you are wasting valuable probability–probability that could better be used by pushing the £/$ rate in a direction that pushes the portfolio even further into the red.

• Secondly, by pushing each rate based on its marginal distribution, it ignores specific properties of their joint distribution. For example,

  –   It ignores correlations between the rates. In the example above, based on the high correlation between the DM/$ and £/$ exchange rates, both rates are more likely to either appreciate or depreciate rather than go in separate directions (as is illustrated by Figure 3.8).

- In addition, even if the rates are uncorrelated, pushing each of the rates by two standard deviations based on their marginal distribution actually describes an event that is much less likely to occur given the joint distribution of the exchange rates.

• Thirdly, it assumes that the maximum possible loss will occur at the extreme values of the price distribution. Consider again, for example, Figure 3.8(A), which illustrates a position for which the losses occur when rates remain stable, not when they reach their extremes. Because we are pushing each of the market prices by α standard deviations, we are actually pushing the position further into the money; for this example, the maximum possible loss is found closer to, rather than farther from, the current market prices.

The critique that the Factor-Push method does not capture correlation effects can be mitigated to some extent by first using principle components or factor analysis to create independent risk factors with unit variance (see Kaarkki and Reyes (1995) and Wilson (1994a) for a description) that can then be "pushed" independently of one another. Unfortunately, this process ignores (or creates) second-order effects that can be significant. To see this, consider the second-order Taylor Series Expansion given by (2) earlier:

Delta–Gamma Approximation:

$$\Delta P(\mathbf{S}) \approx \theta \Delta t + \boldsymbol{\delta}' \Delta \mathbf{S} + \Delta \mathbf{S}' \boldsymbol{\gamma} \Delta \mathbf{S} / 2 \tag{2}$$

where $\Delta \mathbf{S} \sim N(0, \boldsymbol{\Sigma})$ with $\boldsymbol{\Sigma}$ non-diagonal. To aid the exposition, assume that $\boldsymbol{\gamma}$ is diagonal, implying that to the extent that there are cross-product effects, they come only through the covariance matrix, $\boldsymbol{\Sigma}$. Next, consider creating a new set of independent risk factors by applying the linear transformation implied by the principle components technique. More specifically, define

$$\Delta \mathbf{S}^* = \mathbf{P}^* \Delta \mathbf{S}$$

where $\mathbf{P}^* = \mathbf{P} \boldsymbol{\Lambda}^{-1/2}$ is defined as in the discussion of the Delta–Gamma methods earlier. Inserting this relationship into (2) gives the following:

$$\Delta P(\mathbf{S}) \approx \theta \Delta t + \boldsymbol{\delta}^{*'} \Delta \mathbf{S}^* + \Delta \mathbf{S}^{*'} \boldsymbol{\gamma}^* \Delta \mathbf{S}^* / 2$$

where $\boldsymbol{\delta}^* = \boldsymbol{\delta} \mathbf{P}^{*-1}$ and $\boldsymbol{\gamma}^* = \mathbf{P}^{*'-1} \boldsymbol{\gamma} \mathbf{P}^{*-1}$. Inspection of $\boldsymbol{\gamma}^*$ reveals that even if there were no cross-product terms initially (e.g. $\boldsymbol{\gamma}$ was diagonal), cross-product terms will have been introduced after the factorization of the market rate innovations. The only way to eliminate these (second-order) cross-product effects is to use the results of the linear transformation discussed for the Delta–Gamma methods earlier.

Applications.   As mentioned, this method is most often used for evaluating the potential credit exposure arising from derivative transactions, particularly for evaluating in isolation a single swap transaction whose value depends on a single market rate (thereby avoiding the problematic correlation issue); the end products of such an effort typically include potential credit exposure envelopes for standard swap transactions used to replace the BIS haircuts and the ability to "push" a portfolio of single-factor, counterparty transactions "on the fly" to aid marketers. This method is preferred because it is easier to implement under an arbitrary netting set definition.

Unfortunately, the rationale for using this method is based more on systems limitations than on measurement accuracy: by implementing this method, the institution potentially sacrifices correlations and interior solutions but gains the ability to calculate counterparty potential exposure in the "front" applications where the transaction data and pricing algorithms reside, implying that less systems integration work and a less comprehensive modeling effort need to be undertaken. As such, this method should be considered an interim solution at best.

(v) Numerical Search Methods

Calculation Rule.   This method, described by M. Allen of the Swiss Bank Corporation (Allen (1994)), is an attempt to reflect the fact that statistical relationships such as correlations and volatilities, while valid during "normal" market periods, are most likely to fall apart with extreme market movements. In an effort to calculate the VaR needed to support extreme market movements when "normal" correlations may no longer be valid, it ignores statistical relationships entirely (see Figure 3.9) through the following process:

- First, specify a region in $\mathfrak{R}^N$ within which to search for the worst possible outcome. In this example, we have chosen a two-dimensional rectangle where the length of each side is set arbitrarily equal to a 10 standard deviation innovation in the underlying market rates.
- Secondly, use the actual pay-off profile or an approximating pay-off function over this region, perhaps using an N-dimensional cubic spline, a polynomial spline, linear interpolation, etc. based on portfolio sensitivities evaluated at 1-sigma intervals around the initial market rates. As for the simulation techniques, the creation of an approximating pay-off profile is optional if all of the portfolio's transactions can be accessed and evaluated directly.

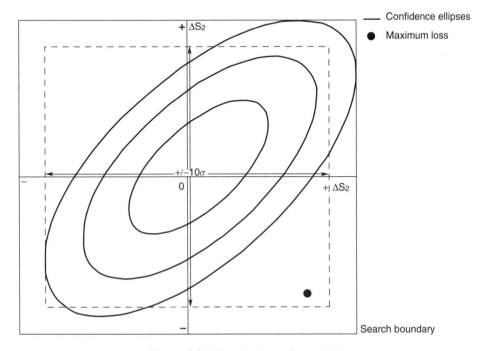

Figure 3.9   Numerical search methods

- Thirdly, "search" the pay-off profile over this region for the worst possible event. If a gradient search method is used, then use various initial conditions to ensure that a global rather than a local minimum is achieved.

Assumptions and Implications.   This numerical search method makes no assumptions regarding the stochastic process generating return innovations (except, perhaps, with regard to the maximum possible innovations, which is a parameter to be set by management, e.g. 10-sigma in the example) in an attempt to capture the absolute maximum VaR required to cover truly extreme market rate movements when "normal" statistical relationships tend to break down. It therefore also ignores potentially useful information and relationships that might govern markets during more "normal" periods. As such, it is impossible to give the result a confidence interval interpretation. Both of these criticisms are reflected in Figure 3.9, where the solution to the numerical search (represented by the dot) lies clearly outside the confidence intervals of the joint process (represented by the ellipsoids).

In terms of price sensitivities, this method may or may not assume that the portfolio's pay-off function is closely approximated by an approximating function over the relevant search region, depending upon whether or not transaction data is available.

Applications.   This method was developed to answer a specific question: what is absolutely the worst-case scenario for the portfolio if absolutely everything goes against the book, ignoring all historical correlations and volatilities? As such, it may be interpreted as an extreme type worst-case scenario and therefore provides some useful information. Nonetheless, it needs to be supplemented by other measures of VaR that are valid as well during more "normal" times in order for it to be made operational and provide the information required by management to run their risk businesses.

(vi) Extreme Value Methods
Calculation Rule.   A relatively new development, and one that is clearly still in its infancy, is the use of asymptotic extreme value theory to calculate VaR. Longin (1994) proposes a method for calculating the optimal margining requirement for futures markets based on the asymptotic extreme value distribution; the potential is further discussed in Bassi et al. (1996). The question of the optimal margin requirement is directly related to the concept of VaR given above, e.g. as the amount of capital needed to support a given risky position over some time horizon. Towards this end, Longin uses extreme value theory that gives the exact form for the asymptotic distribution of the minimum of a random variable (in this case, position returns), and as such is independent of the distribution of daily price changes: different processes of daily price changes imply different parameters (a location parameter, β, a scale parameter, α, and a tail index, τ) but the same (generalized) functional form of the asymptotic extreme value distribution (see equation 5 in Longin (1994)).

Assumptions and Implications.   The functional form of the extreme distribution is relatively robust, covering, for example, serially correlated price changes, innovations that exhibit "fat tails", ARCH processes, and mixtures of jump-diffusion processes. Nonetheless, one is modeling directly the extreme value of the price of a given product or portfolio and estimating the relevant parameters directly rather than using a "building block" approach to build the portfolio distribution from the joint distribution of the underlying positions.

Applications.   As mentioned, the use of asymptotic extreme value distributions for the calculation of VaR is still in its infancy. Longin suggests that there needs to be several important extensions in this area before it can be implemented in practice. The first and most important is the extension of the results to a multivariate context in order to capture spread or open positions in correlated markets; the second is the extension of the results to positions such as options that do not have a symmetric pay-off distribution. These extensions may prove to be extremely challenging.

(vii) Regulator's Building Block Approach[23]

Calculation Rules.   As a matter of practicality, most regulators prior to 1995 had been advocating simple rules or algorithms for the calculation of VaR. This approach "builds" the capital required to support a trading book out of several "building blocks", the two most important being a charge for specific and general risks. The specific risk charge is "designed to protect against an adverse movement in the price of an individual security owing to factors related to the individual issuer" (Basle Committee (1995a)). The general risk component is designed to capture the risk of loss arising from changes in market rates and is often based on a banding or bucketing of risk positions into homogeneous groups or maturity buckets similar to those for RiskMetrics[TM] with inter-band offsets used to recognize correlations between groups rather than using the actual correlations as is done in the covariance approach. The practicality of this approach is underscored by the fact that it is the fall-back solution proposed under the Basle Committee 1995 proposals for institutions that choose not to develop their own internal VaR models since it is (arguably) less costly to implement in terms of systems and skilled resources than are proprietary models (see Basle Committee (1995a)). Following the Basle Committee proposals of 1996 (Basle Committee (1996a,b)) the "internal model" approach has subsequently been accepted by most regulators.

As an example to illustrate the original, building block approach, consider the band and bucket structure that the Basle Committee has proposed to cover interest rate risks, illustrated in Figure 3.10 (Basle Committee (1995a)). In addition to a specific risk charge depending on the remaining life of the instrument and the issuer,[24] a general risk charge is also calculated. This general risk charge is calculated by summing four values:

1. The net short or long position for the entire trading book.

2. The "vertical disallowance" calculated using the following rule: first, weight the gross long and short positions with the factors in Table A to reflect their interest rate sensitivity, with the weighting determined by the remaining life for fixed rate positions and the time to the next interest rate reset for floating rate positions. A charge of 10 per cent is then allocated against the smaller of the gross long and short positions to reflect basis and gap risk (called the "vertical allowance").

3. The "horizontal disallowance" calculated by allowing the gross long and short positions to offset one another using Table B in Figure 3.10. For example, the "horizontal disallowance" is equal to 40 per cent of the net exposure in Zone 1 plus 30 per cent of the net in Zones 2 and 3 plus 40 per cent of the net residual between Zones 1 and 2 and Zones 2 and 3 plus 100 per cent of the residual between Zones 1 and 3.

4. Finally, a charge for option positions to capture convexity and volatility risks. Using the "simplified approach", these charges are calculated in the following manner:
    - For gamma risk, multiply the net negative gammas per maturity band by a weight and by the square of the market value of the underlying.

Table A:"Vertical Disallowance" Weights			Table B:"Horizontal Disallowance" Weights		
Coupon of 3 per cent or more	Coupon less than 3 per cent	Risk weight	Off-set within zone	Between adjacent zones	Between zones 1-3

Zone 1
≤ month	≤ month	0.00%
1-3 months	1-3 months	0.20%
3-6 months	3-6 months	0.40%
6-12 months	6-12 months	0.70%

40%

Zone 2
1-2 years	1-1.9 years	1.25%
2-3 years	1.9-2.8 years	1.75%
3-4 years	2.8-3.6 years	2.25%

30%   40%   150%

Zone 3
4-5 years	3.6-4.3 years	2.75%
5-7 years	4.3-5.7 years	3.25%
7-10 years	5.7-7.3 years	3.75%
10-15 years	7.3-9.3 years	4.50%
15-20 years	9.3-10.6 years	5.25%
>20 years	10.6-12 years	6.00%
	12-20 years	8.00%
	>20 years	12.50%

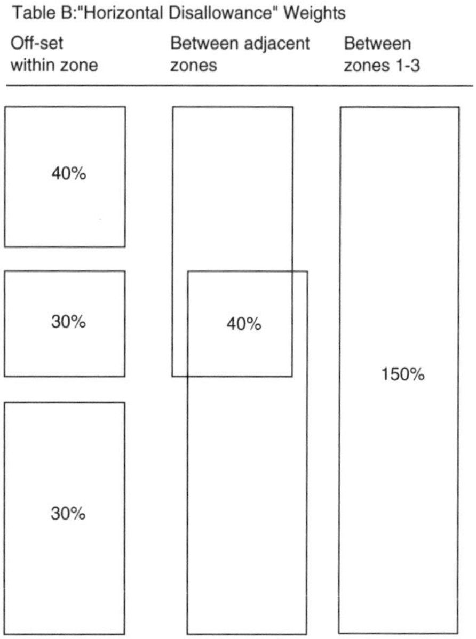

30%

Figure 3.10 Regulators "building block" approach

- For vega risk, the net vega amount per time band calculated using a ±25 per cent proportional shift in volatility.

The offset rules designed to capture correlations between changes in position values were defined after empirically simulating the rules against a wide variety of portfolios designed specifically to stress those rules. The rules are only then set once they have been shown not only to cover the worst-case market rate development but also to cover the "worst-case portfolio" within the band structures. In addition, the offset rules never extend between the most obvious correlated pairs, e.g. net long DM interest rate positions are not allowed to offset net short HFL positions; net short vega is not allowed to offset net long vega in a different maturity band; short gamma is not allowed to offset long gamma, even though the pairs of risks may be highly correlated.

Assumptions and Implications.   The simple bucketing and banding rules may work well for positions with simple structures that can be decomposed, mapped and represented by non-contingent cash flows, e.g. swaps, forwards, futures. All option positions, however, do not naturally lend themselves to being "bucketed" without making heroic assumptions (e.g. bucketing their delta equivalents) and levying draconian surcharges to cover gamma and vega risks.

If the institution relies on the arbitrary bucketing or banding techniques as described, then it may be consistently over-allocating VaR for three reasons; first, because, as mentioned earlier, the banding or bucketing techniques are essentially designed to cover the worst possible portfolio within the band structure in the worst-case market scenario. This differs subtly from allocating VaR to cover the worst possible market rate event for the actual portfolio of interest. Second, because the arbitrary netting between buckets or bands do not extend between different risk factors, any cross-market hedges using highly correlated instruments will not be recognized. Finally, because the proposed methods used to capture gamma and vega risk are relatively Draconian by design in an effort to "keep it simple".

Applicability.   Based on our observations, the most likely application of these bucketing techniques is in the regulatory context where it is arguably necessary to develop simple rules so that all financial institutions can implement them in a cost-effective manner and so satisfy their regulatory reporting requirements (although this is questionable given the current industry concern over the costs of implementing the CAD guidelines). For the internal management and control of an institution's risk positions, its efficacy is less clear, especially given the availability of other methods that are just as easy to implement (e.g. the Delta–Normal or Delta–Gamma methods), which have synergies with other risk management and trading applications (e.g. the calculation or correlations and volatilities) and which recognize the convexity and correlations between positions.

3.4 CALCULATING CREDIT VaR

When compared with the measurement of market risk, the application of VaR techniques to credit risk is still in its infancy. While the need to do so is arguably just as compelling, both in terms of helping management better to allocate and price the economic capital required to support a given portfolio of credit-risky transactions and potentially to affect regulatory reform, the uptake of VaR techniques for credit risk has probably been hampered by several factors: first, a lack of data and standard, accepted techniques; secondly, relatively illiquid markets traditionally offering few opportunities dynamically to manage the portfolio of retained risks; and, finally, in some instances, an institutional barrier within some organizations, causing them to manage credit risk differently from market risk.

Fortunately, most of these barriers to implementing VaR techniques to cover credit risk are beginning to fall. In particular, significant advances have been made with regards to applying these same concepts to credit risk, spurred most notably by the introduction of CreditMetrics® by J.P. Morgan (J.P. Morgan (1997)), CreditRisk+ by Credit Suisse First Boston (CSFB(1997)) and CreditPortfolioView by McKinsey & Company (Wilson (1997a,b,c,d), McKinsey (1998)), as well as the pioneering work of many companies and individuals, such as KMV (Kealhofer (1995b)). In addition, risk management tools such as credit derivatives, securitization, syndication and secondary loan trading are increasing in their liquidity, giving financial institutions more options in terms of actively managing their portfolio of retained risks. Nonetheless, given the relative lack of convergence on any one method, the relative infancy of the approaches and their inherent complexity, this section attempts only to give a broad overview of the issues and techniques.

3.4.1 Measurement Issues

Similar to market risk, credit risk is often defined as the potential for losses due to credit events, e.g. counterparty defaults and rating migrations. To make the definition of credit risk more precise in the context of loss uncertainty, the financial industry is converging on two statistics derived from a credit loss distribution: expected losses and a critical value of the loss distribution often defined as the portfolio's credit VaR; these risk measures are used as complements to the more standard exposure and rating measures for reporting and measuring credit risk. Each of these measures serves a distinct and useful role in supporting management decision making and control (see Figure 3.11).

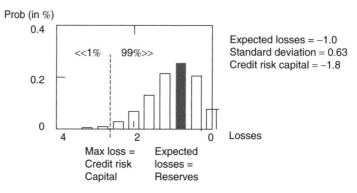

Loss distribution for $100 portfolio, 250 equal and independent credits with prob(default) = 1%

Figure 3.11   Operational risk measures

- *Expected losses,* illustrated as the mean of the distribution in Figure 3.11, often serve as the basis for management's reserve policies: the higher the expected losses, the higher the reserves that need to be set aside to cover them. Increasingly, auditors and local regulators (but not tax authorities) are accepting actuarial methods as a means for determining a bank's reserves, recognizing expected losses rather than recognizing losses on a risk-occurrence basis, thereby smoothing earnings; examples include the reserving policies of the Swiss Bank Corporation (now the United Bank of Switzerland) and the Credit Suisse Group. In addition, expected losses are also an important component for determining whether the pricing of the credit risky position is adequate: normally, each transaction should be priced with sufficient margin to cover its contribution to the portfolio's expected credit losses.

- *Credit VaR,* defined as the maximum loss within a known confidence interval (e.g. 99 per cent) over some time horizon, illustrated in Figure 3.11, is often interpreted as the additional economic capital that needs to be held against a given portfolio, above and beyond the level of credit reserves, in order to cover its unexpected credit losses. Since it would be uneconomic to hold capital against all potential losses (as this would imply that equity is held against 100 per cent of all credit exposures), some level of capital must be chosen to support the portfolio of transactions in most, but not all, cases. Just as with expected losses, VaR also plays an important role in determining whether the credit risk of a particular transaction is appropriately priced: typically, each transaction or treaty must be priced with sufficient margin to cover not only its expected losses, but also the cost of its marginal VaR contribution.

Figure 3.11 illustrates expected losses and credit VaR with a simple example portfolio with a total notional of $100 million, consisting of 250 equal-sized, independent credits, each a probability of default of 1 per cent. For this portfolio, the expected losses are equal to $1 million, while the additional maximum losses will be less than, or equal to, $1.8 million with 99 per cent confidence. Note that as the loss distribution is not "normal", this additional unexpected loss is not well approximated by some multiple of the portfolio's standard deviation of losses (e.g. 2.31 times the standard deviation, or $1.45 million, in the case of a 99 per cent one-tailed confidence interval for the normal distribution).

Unlike capital adequacy rules covering the market risk for trading portfolios, internal models used to calculate credit VaR are not currently accepted by regulators as a means for determining adequacy to support credit portfolios. It is generally accepted that current capital adequacy rules; for example, the Cooke capital ratios requiring an 8 per cent capitalization ratio for any unsecured loan to a corporate regardless of the corporate's credit quality, are a blunt instrument and may actually lead institutions to make imprudent decisions as they search for higher ROEs in increasingly competitive markets. Given the current forces at work in the area (e.g. acceptance of internal models for determining capital adequacy for market risk, convergence in techniques for credit risk VaR, increased competitive pressure, especially in the large corporate segments), one could anticipate that some form of regulatory reform would take place in the context of credit risk capital adequacy rules within the next two to three years.

One notable difference between this definition of credit VaR and the definition of market VaR described earlier is the role of expected losses: while it is standard in the industry to calculate credit VaR as the maximum potential loss within a given confidence interval less the portfolio's expected losses, no such term typically appears in the formula for market VaR. Implicitly, most standard market risk calculation rules assume that expected losses (or gains) are equal to zero. This assumption is justified when measuring market-risk VaR if the holding period horizon is sufficiently short, if stable earnings streams not related to absorbing market risks such as those generated by a strong customer franchise or unearned credit spreads are eliminated from the profit stream of a trading desk and/or if management wishes to avoid relatively fruitless discussions regarding the expected returns from holding pure market-risk positions. Given the nature of credit risk, where there is often very little upside and losses are a fact of life for all but the most secure, sovereign positions, expected losses are a necessary component of the calculation of VaR.[25]

Just as the calculation of market VaR depended upon assumptions regarding the joint distribution of future market rates and the potential impact on the value of the portfolio that such market rate changes imply, the calculation of credit VaR relies on similar assumptions. In the case of credit VaR, however, we are not necessarily interested in how market rate changes impact the value of the portfolio but rather how changes in credit quality affect the value of the portfolio. More specifically, to calculate credit VaR, management must implicitly or explicitly make enough assumptions so that it can answer two important questions (see Figure 3.12):

- First, what is the (joint) likelihood of credit events, e.g. defaults or credit migrations, across different counterparties? Or, what are the expected default frequencies as well

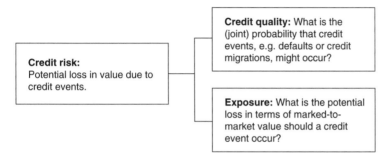

Figure 3.12   Credit measurement framework

as default correlations for counterparties within a given portfolio? An answer to this question concerns itself primarily with the quality of the individual exposures. Implicitly or explicitly, credit risk managers have to make assumptions regarding the distribution of future credit events, much as market risk managers must make assumptions about the distribution of future market rates, with different assumptions leading to different results.

- Secondly, what is the economic loss in value should such events occur? Or, in other terms, what is the loss given default? An answer to this question concerns itself implicitly with determining the quantity of the exposure. Implicitly or explicitly, credit risk managers have to make assumptions regarding the impact of credit events on the value of the portfolio, much as market risk managers have to make assumptions regarding the impact of rate changes on the value of the portfolio, with different assumptions leading to different results.

Paralleling our discussion of market risk VaR methods, we discuss critically in the remainder of this section the implicit assumptions commonly made for each of these components as well as some of the typical calculation approaches used in practice.

(i) Credit Event Distribution Assumptions

There are typically four areas where issues may arise when modeling the joint distribution of future counterparty defaults and/or credit migrations: the first is in delineating market and credit risk and ensuring that both are captured by some risk management system; the second is in the area of modeling an individual counterparty's credit quality or probability of default or credit migration; the third is in the area of modeling default correlations across different counterparties and the last is in the area of modeling the cyclical behavior of defaults over time.

Delineating Market and Credit Risks.   In today's increasingly liquid financial markets where secondary traded loans and credit derivative volumes are growing exponentially, the difference between market and credit risk is becoming increasingly blurred. What is the distinction between the market risk of a bond and the credit risk of a loan to the same counterparty, especially if that loan can be traded in a relatively liquid secondary market? Before we define how credit events can influence the value of a position, we first have to define clearly what credit events are and how they differ from market rate movements.

Consider, for example, the discount rate for a credit-risky bond. This rate can be seen as comprising at least two distinct components: a risk-free rate consistent with the maturity of the asset and a credit spread consistent with the creditworthiness of the asset. The risk factors used for measuring the market risk of these credit-risky positions is typically defined in one of two different ways: either by treating the combined discount rate as the market rate whose volatility and correlations need to be modeled or by defining the risk-free rate as one market risk factor and separate credit spreads for each rating category in addition, thereby separating basis interest rate risk from credit spread risk. The former method is typically preferred by institutions or trading desks with relatively homogeneous credit exposures such as would be found in some OTC derivatives books or the investment grade inventory of a bond trading book, while the latter is often chosen by institutions with heterogeneous credit quality exposures. In either case, however, the potential variation in the average credit spread level is captured, either implicitly or explicitly, in the market VaR calculation.

What, then, remains for credit VaR to capture for traded assets? The only remaining risk of these hypothetical bond (or loan) positions is that the counterparty might migrate or jump from one rating category to another. Therefore, most credit VaR calculations focus on capturing only the risk that a counterparty's credit quality changes, leaving the level of general interest rates and average credit spread levels to be captured by the institution's market risk measurement system. One important issue that needs to be explicitly addressed within many institutions is whether or not all of these components (e.g. the level of interest rates, the level of average credit spreads by rating category and, finally, the impact of migrating to a new rating category) are, in fact, being covered by their risk measurement framework for both their loan book and their trading book. Although this generalization is not always true, most market VaR systems capture the basis and spread risks for fixed income products, leaving the spread risk on loans uncovered, with most credit VaR systems focusing on measuring the economic impact of a change in credit rating for both loans and traded securities.

Modeling Counterparty Events. Most institutions answer the first question (e.g. what is the probability of a credit event occurring?) by consistently classifying each individual counterparty into a specific rating category or rating class; each of these classes typically has implicitly or explicitly associated with it a unique probability of default and/or rating migration over some time horizon. This counterparty rating is typically accomplished by combining a subjective evaluation of the counterparty's quality, perhaps supported by cash flow and industry analysis,[26] with some form of quantitative scoring technique. Although some would criticize the use of subjective criteria and judgment in the assessment of counterparty quality, it is, in practice, unavoidable given the lack of historical data and methods to cover the majority of the credit segments to which a typical financial institution is exposed.

Examples of quantitative methods applied in practice include the Z-score and Zeta models as well as standard and behavioral scoring models (see, for example, Altman (1983) or Thomas et al. (1992) for applications in the corporate and retail segments, respectively). More recently, neural networks and genetic learning algorithms have also been applied to the problem of discriminating between different qualities of counterparty classes. Most of these techniques are criticized for either being relatively static in their assessment, relying on firm specific financial data that is updated only periodically, or for focusing only on counterparty specific factors using cross-sectional data, thereby ignoring the current macro-economic environment in which the counterparty must operate.

In addition to these models based on micro-data, e.g. financial statement and account information, another class of models has been developed based on the observation made by Merton (1973) that the equity and debt of a company can be viewed as a call-and-put option on the firm's assets, respectively. This relationship has been exploited to create a default prediction model based on the volatility of a firm's asset value implied by its equity price as well as its current market value of debt and equity. See, for example, Kealhofer (1995a,b) and McQuown (1995). The probability of default for a particular counterparty is calculated by determining the probability that the firm's asset value is insufficient to cover all of its debt obligations. These methods are sometimes criticized either for being applicable to only a small part of an institution's overall portfolio (e.g. quoted companies as opposed to middle-market and retail segments) or for overreacting and reflecting market sentiment as opposed to market fundamentals. In addition, since this method relies on an estimate of the firm's asset volatilities, this technique is also subject to all of the criticisms related to estimating market rate volatilities.

Given the relative lack of historical data and verifiable models, most institutions will continue to use qualitative judgment complemented by a combination of these quantitative techniques for assessing the probability of default or credit migration for individual counterparties.

Modeling Default Correlations.   Successful completion of the rating process yields the marginal default or migration probabilities for individual counterparties over some time horizon, with the joint distribution being determined by the correlations between different rating classes and segments. At the portfolio level, the next step is therefore to model the joint distribution of credit events across all of the counterparties contained in the portfolio. Roughly speaking, this is done by estimating the correlation or covariance between credit events for the different counterparties contained within the portfolio.

The most simplistic models assume that credit events between counterparties are independent, implying that all credit risk can be fully diversified away by holding a large enough portfolio of equal size exposures; in fact, if credit events were independent or uncorrelated, then portfolios with as few as 250 to 500 counterparties of equal size and rating would have very little capacity to surprise management with significant losses as almost all of the risk could, in theory, be diversified away (see McKinsey (1998)). This is not a particularly satisfying assumption, especially in light of the recent behavior of relatively large mortgage and credit card portfolios in Central Europe and the United States.

Other approaches assume that default correlations are equal to a constant across all counterparty segments, thus assuming that some non-diversifiable or systematic risk remains in any portfolio. This approach is also not very satisfying for two reasons: first, as is well documented, because default correlations are directly related to the rating of the counterparty, increasing as ratings decrease, all other things being equal; thus, the default correlation between two triple-A counterparties will be an order of magnitude smaller than the correlation between two single-B counterparties (see Kealhofer (1995b) for more details). Secondly, because it is both empirically and theoretically unpalatable to assume that the default correlations between any two arbitrary counterparty segments are equal to the same constant: consider, for example, the correlations between US Construction and US Retail counterparties and between US Construction and Japanese public utilities.

Figure 3.13 illustrates the need for a multi-factor model, as opposed to a single-factor or equal correlation model, for determining default rate correlations. Performing a factor analysis of different countries' average insolvency rates, it emerges that the first "factor" only captures 77.5 per cent of the total variation in systematic default rates for "Moody's", the US, UK, Japanese and German markets; the fact that this is significantly larger than 20 per cent indicates that the assumption of independence or zero correlation is incorrect. In addition, since the 77.5 per cent number corresponds to the amount of systematic risk "captured" by most single-factor or average correlation models, the rest of the variation is implicitly assumed to be independent and uncorrelated in average correlation models. Unfortunately, the first factor only explains 23.9 per cent of the US systematic risk index, 56.2 per cent for the United Kingdom and 66.8 per cent for Germany. Figure 3.12 demonstrates that the substantial remaining correlation is explained by the second and third factors, covering an additional 10.2 per cent and 6.8 per cent, respectively, of the total variation and the bulk of the risk for the United States, the United Kingdom and Germany. A similar decomposition of default correlations between industries yields similar results.

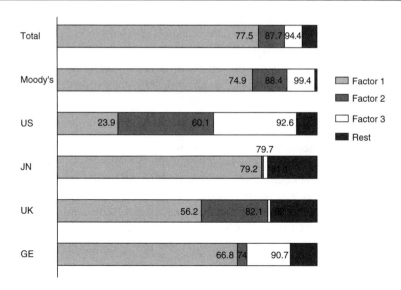

Figure 3.13   Multi-factor default risk model

Another approach estimates default correlations using asset value correlations calculated using equity and debt price information as discussed earlier (again, see Kealhofer (1995b)). In principle, a joint default probability can be calculated from both firms' debt levels, their asset value volatilities and correlations; these joint default probabilities can then be used to construct default correlations across the entire sample of firms. In practice, one would need to calculate $N(N-1)/2$ individual pair-wise correlations for N individual counterparties, a very large number for even investment grade portfolios; as such, it is often expedient to model segment-specific correlations based on some multi- or single-factor model of asset value innovations as alluded to in Kealhofer (1995b). Along similar lines, J.P. Morgan uses equity index correlations as a proxy for segment-specific default correlations (see J.P. Morgan (1997)). Many of the same criticisms with regards to this equity-based approach that were discussed earlier, e.g. applicability to non-listed firms or retail segments such as cards or mortgages, volatility of the estimates, apply to these approaches as well.

Using another multi-factor approach, Gollinger and Morgan (1993) model the joint risk of a credit portfolio by measuring the correlation of different industry segments' Zeta score over time based on an historical sample. As with the asset value approach, this approach can be criticized for being specific to only a sub-set of a financial institution's overall portfolio, focusing primarily on the largest corporate counterparties.

Wilson (1997a,b,c,d) and McKinsey (1998) also use time series data of segment-specific historical default or average loss rates, average migration probabilities and both of their relationships over the economic cycle to develop a Monte Carlo model of average default and migration rates. The approach outlined in Wilson (1997a,b,c,d) and implemented in McKinsey & Company's CreditPortfolioView (McKinsey (1998)) relies on intuition accepted by most credit professionals: if asked, many people would agree that higher defaults are associated with, or even caused by, weaker economies or recessions: as unemployment rates increase and GDP growth declines, defaults and insolvencies tend to increase. This intuition is strongly supported by the empirical facts. Figure 3.14 plots the actual insolvency rate history for Germany over the period 1960–1994 against the predicted default rate, where the predicted value was estimated on the basis of statistical techniques using only macro-economic variables such as GDP innovations and unemployment rates as explanatory variables.

As can be seen in Figure 3.14, the predicted default rates (which depend only on aggregate or macro-economic data) fit the actual default rates very well. Table 3.4 gives some impression of the model fit on a country-by-country basis. As is illustrated by the relatively high R-squareds (a measure of the percentage of total variation explained by the statistical model) found in the table, a country's average insolvency rate can be well explained by our prediction equation, which uses only macro-economic variables as explanatory variables. Similar results have been obtained when examining the behavior of retail mortgage or credit card portfolios, although the optimum choice of explanatory variables differs (e.g. housing price indices, local economic indicators, debt to income ratios, etc.). Again, this confirms what every credit professional has intuitively understood for years: credit cycles are inexplicably linked to the underlying macro-economic cycle; what is often surprising to many credit professionals is how strong this relationship actually is and why it has not been exploited before.

In models that link credit cycles to macro-economic cycles, correlations between segments are captured both because the average default rates by segment are driven by common, macro-economic factors, and these also covary across different countries.

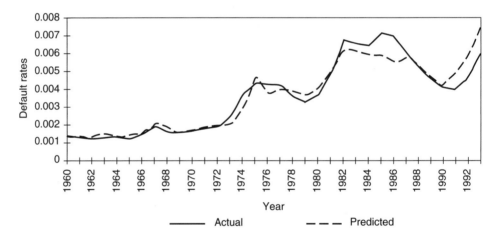

Figure 3.14   Macro-economic influence on credit cycles: actual vs. predicted default rates

Table 3.4   Predicting cyclical default behavior: default prediction model R-squared

Country	R-Square* (%)	Explanatory Variables
Belgium	96.9	Unemployment rates
France	89.1	GDP growth
Germany	95.7	Long-term interest rates
Spain	95.3	Foreign exchange rates
Switzerland	89.3	Public disbursement
United Kingdom	85.6	Aggregate savings rate
United States	82.6	

*Adjusted regression R-squared.

This approach has the benefit that it can be applied equally well to portfolios of retail products, such as retail mortgages, credit cards, personal overdrafts, as well as to corporate segments; this is important as it is sometimes difficult to find equity indices or publicly available rating surrogates that reflect the characteristics of some of these segments. In addition, it anchors the average default levels and correlations by segment using the current point in the economic cycle, allowing institutions to undertake "what-if?" analysis with regard to the potential credit risk impact of different macro-economic scenarios. Nonetheless, these approaches are "backwards"- as opposed to "forwards"-looking, relying on historical data to model credit events that will only occur in the future.

Modeling the Time Series Properties of Credit Events.   As mentioned earlier, conventional wisdom has it that "credit cycles" exist, e.g. that recessionary economic periods leading to higher-than-average default rates are more likely than not to be followed by further recessionary times with high default rates rather than expansionary times with lower default rates. We crudely tested this intuition by estimating second-order auto-regressive (AR(2)) processes for US, German and Japanese average corporate insolvency rates over the period 1970–1994, of the following form:

$$p_t = \alpha_0 + \alpha_1(p_{t-1} - \mu) + \alpha_2(p_{t-2} - \mu) + \varepsilon_t$$

where p_{t-i} are the realized corporate insolvency rates at time $t - i$; μ is the average corporate insolvency rate over the period; α_0, α_1 and α_2 are coefficients to be estimated; and, ε_t is a random error term, assumed to be independently and normally distributed. If credit "cycles" did in fact exist, one would expect that α_1 would be greater than zero and significant, implying that higher than average defaults last period would indicate higher than average default rates this period. For the process to be mean-reverting or stationary, the sum of coefficients on the lagged insolvency rates would have to be less than one; thus, one could consider the sum of the α_is to be the amount of "momentum" in average insolvency rates. Looking at Table 3.5, we see that our intuition regarding the existence of credit cycles is confirmed by the data.

This table plots the coefficients, t-statistics and adjusted R-squareds for the AR(2) processes that we estimated for Germany, Japan and the United States. In all of the cases, credit cycles appeared to be present given the large and positive value of the α_1s and the significance of all of the αs within a 99 per cent confidence interval. Similar results also hold when one investigates other countries or the time series behavior of different public rating classes. Thus, our intuition regarding credit cycles appears to be supported by this casual empirical evidence. This result is intuitively plausible: during the first year of a

Table 3.5   Evidence of credit "cycles": AR(2) process, 1970–1994

| Country | Coefficients (and t-statistics) | | | R-squared |
	Constant	$p(t-1)$	$p(t-2)$	(adjusted) (%)
Germany	0.0044	1.48*	−0.55*	92
	1.63	8.58	−3.22	
Japan	0.0107*	1.09*	−0.30*	76
	2.53	6.28	−1.82	
US	0.0061*	1.41*	−0.55*	87
	1.83	8.75	−3.24	

*Significant at the 99 per cent level.

recession, a company may face a squeeze on its free cash flow and therefore its ability to service its debt; this situation is typically exacerbated if the first year of a recession is followed by subsequent years, leading to a liquidity crisis and ultimately to default.

In practice, the different methods for modeling the joint credit event probabilities make different assumptions regarding "credit cycle" momentum. For example, the methods based on equity prices such as Kealhofer (1995a,b), McQuowen (1995) and J.P. Morgan (1997) implicitly assume that there are no "credit cycles", or, rather, that the path a particular economy or counterparty took to get to today's rating or expected default frequency is of no use in predicting future credit events or the volatility of future credit events.

For example, the equity-driven models of Kealhofer (1995a,b) and McQuowen (1995) use a specific assumption regarding the evolution of future asset values in order to calculate the implicit asset value volatility needed to calculate expected default frequencies. Using the appropriate option pricing model, they derive asset value volatilities from equity and debt prices (e.g. the value of a call and a put on the firm's asset value); typically, it is assumed that asset values follow a geometric Brownian motion (GBM) process with drift so that standard Black–Scholes option pricing techniques can be used to imply the underlying asset volatilities. The GBM process itself is driven by innovations with independent increments over time, e.g. there is no cyclical behavior in equity prices and therefore credit default rates.

CreditMetrics® makes a similar assumption that there are no credit cycles by using a constant rating transition matrix as both the unconditional and conditional migration matrix (J.P. Morgan (1997)); thus, credit events for individual counterparties are drawn from the same basic distribution year after year based only on their rating. CreditMetrics® then uses equity market data as a surrogate for credit migration and default correlations only.

On the other hand, the methods outlined in Wilson (1997a,b,c,d) and implemented in CreditPortfolioView (McKinsey (1998)), which we discussed earlier, explicitly model these credit cycle momentum terms by linking the average default and migration rates, as well as their volatilities, to the macro-economic cycle.

While potentially of less importance in terms of measuring the short-term behavior of defaults, understanding the cyclical behavior of credit events over the longer term can be critical for longer dated, less liquid portfolios. While current counterparty ratings may be explicitly linked with an expected default frequency over some time horizon, typically one year, it is really the counterparty's behavior over different expansionary and recessionary cycles that will determine the final risk profile of an illiquid, longer-term commitment.

(ii) Portfolio Sensitivity Assumptions

Continuing the analogy to measuring market VaR, measuring credit VaR also requires the institution to understand how changes in credit quality might affect the value of their positions; in terms of understanding a portfolio's sensitivity to credit events, critical assumptions must be made in two specific areas: first, how to measure overall exposures to a particular counterparty or country, an issue that is especially interesting for derivatives and some contingent commercial banking products such as committed lines of credit, and, secondly, how to recognize gains and losses from credit events for liquid, illiquid and "retail" assets. Each of these is discussed in detail below.

Measuring Exposures.   The first challenge that needs to be resolved in order to map credit events into a change in the portfolio value concerns the measurement of the amount of (potential) exposure to a particular counterparty. The measurement of your institution's exposure to a credit event for a particular counterparty is a trivial exercise for many standard commercial banking products: if a \$100 million, unsecured loan is in default, then the lending institution stands to lose \$100 million in value, subject to any recoveries, plus or minus some small amount due to changing interest rates. For many other of today's banking products, however, answering this question is a non-trivial exercise.

Consider, for example, the credit exposure to a particular counterparty arising from the purchase of a stock option written by that counterparty: if the counterparty should default on its obligations, your loss is not the premium that you had paid for the option, but rather the replacement value of the option at the time that the counterparty goes into receivership. Unfortunately for credit risk managers, this value can change substantially over time as the underlying stock price changes, approaching zero if the option is very far out-of-the-money and the value of the stock less the strike price if the option is very far in-the-money. Similarly, your exposure to a particular counterparty can vary substantially for other products as well, including committed but undrawn lines of credit, swaps, forwards, collateralized loans, all of whose net replacement value can change substantially as the draw-down rate, interest rates, commodity, equity and real estate prices change.

It is clear from these examples that the potential severity of loss, or the loss given default, is determined by many different factors, including the actual structure of the individual transaction (or portfolio of transactions), the current state of financial markets that influence its value and the potential evolution of these variables in the future, the potential recovery amount, the current and future value of the collateral used to support the positions, etc. Thus, exposure to a particular counterparty or group of counterparties is itself a random variable, with the exposure level increasing or decreasing depending upon the evolution of financial markets.

It is, in general, extremely difficult intuitively to compare the potential credit exposure of an equity option with that of a loan or a commodity swap without some method to make them comparable. For this reason, the industry is converging on a standard measure of credit exposure, or a "Loan Equivalent Exposure", which allows such diverse exposures to be put on a comparable basis. Following industry best practices,[27] we define the Loan Equivalent Exposure as the sum of two distinct elements (see Figure 3.15):

- *Current Exposure (CE)*, defined as the loss or replacement cost if the counterparty were to default today, recognizing valid netting and collateral agreements.

- *Potential Exposure (PE)*, defined as some measure of the additional potential loss, above and beyond the current exposure, if the counterparty were to default some time

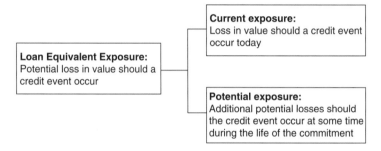

Figure 3.15   Loan equivalent exposure framework

in the future, recognizing valid netting and collateral agreements. Typically, potential exposure is calculated in one of three ways:

- *Basle Committee potential exposure add-ons*, a set of multiplicative factors that are applied against the notional of the particular transaction, determined by the remaining maturity of the transaction and the key risk factor that determines its value.
- *Expected Potential Exposure*, which measures the expected exposure to the counterparty at any point in time over the life of the commitment, and
- *Maximum Potential Exposure*, which measures the maximum exposure that could occur within some given confidence interval (e.g. 99 per cent) at any point in time over the life of the commitment.

While most market participants use some variation on the Basle Committee Current Exposure method for derivatives, more and more are actively experimenting with or actually implementing alternative methods using Monte Carlo or Factor-Push methods (see Lawrence (1995) and Rowe (1995), as well as the discussion of each of these techniques earlier in this chapter for a description). To calculate the Loan Equivalent Exposure for an arbitrary derivatives contract or netting set using one of these methods, the institution first needs to be able to value all of its commitments and associated collateral at any point in time in the future and, secondly, to simulate those values under different market rate scenarios in order to calculate the transaction's potential value that might be put at risk in the event of a counterparty default.

Some standard commercial products also raise comparable challenges: for standard commercial lines of credit, an institution must know a counterparty's current utilization and limit and make an assumption how future limit utilization might evolve, especially should the counterparty suffer a rating degradation and suddenly draw down the line substantially; in addition, it must also understand how rapidly a potential problem situation can be identified and the limit reduced, if necessary. For bank loans, an institution must make certain assumptions regarding the future value of the loan's collateral as well as various prepayment scenarios. These are only some examples of the types of assumptions that management must make and that therefore can go wrong. For a more detailed discussion, see J.P. Morgan (1997).

Quantifying Credit Portfolio Sensitivities.   Once the institution's overall exposure to a counterparty has been determined, it is then possible to calculate its change in value should a counterparty event occur. This can be accomplished in several different ways, depending upon the characteristics of the underlying risky asset: for example, if the asset is "liquid", then the potential impact of rating migrations and defaults over some liquidation period can be calculated by recognizing the theoretical change in marked-to-market value of the position due to the change in credit rating; if the asset is illiquid, then one can choose to use the discounted value of potential future losses given default. Alternatively, other approaches can be used for retail portfolios. Each of these methods is described in detail in the following sections.

- *Liquid Positions: Migration Approach.*   Many credit-risky assets, such as traded corporate bonds and commercial paper, can be bought or sold in relatively liquid markets and the markets for other assets, such as bank and syndicated loans, are increasing in their liquidity. For these asset classes, the appropriate way to calculate the potential impact of credit events is on a marked-to-market basis using a holding period horizon that reflects the potential liquidation period of the individual asset.

It is clear that if the position can be liquidated prior to its maturity, then all credit events (e.g. both credit migrations as well as defaults) within the liquidation period will affect its marked-to-market value. For example, if you have locked in a single-A spread and the credit rating of the counterparty decreases to a triple-B rating, then you would suffer an economic loss: while the market would demand a higher, triple-B spread, your commitment only provides a lower, single-A spread.

Therefore, in order to calculate the marked-to-market loss distribution for positions that can be liquidated prior to their maturity, we must be in a position to tabulate the change in marked-to-market value of the exposure for every possible change in credit rating. In the case of traded loans or debt, a pragmatic approach is simply to define a table of average credit spreads, in basis points per annum, as a function of rating and the maturity of the underlying exposure. The potential loss (or gain) from a credit migration can then be tabulated by calculating the change in marked-to-market value of the exposure due to the changing of the discount rate implied by the credit migration; this is the approach taken by CreditMetrics® (J.P. Morgan (1997)) where all assets are treated implicitly as liquid with the same liquidation period. The CreditPortfolio View approach described in Wilson (1997a,b,c,d) and McKinsey (1998) allows one to define which assets are "liquid", and therefore should be treated on a theoretical marked-to-market basis, and, in addition, to define a specific liquidation period for each individual asset.

The results of applying this approach are illustrated in Figure 3.16, where we have tabulated the potential profit and loss profile from a single traded credit exposure, originally rated triple-B, which can be liquidated prior to one year. Should the counterparty default, the loss would amount to -100 per cent of the exposure, assuming no recovery; should the counterparty be downgraded to a double-B rating, the loss would be in the order of -0.4 per cent of the exposure given market conditions during 1996; conversely, should the counterpart be upgraded to a single-A rating, the potential gain would have been roughly 0.4 per cent. As is clear from Figure 3.16, it is inappropriate to talk about "loss distributions" in the context of marked-to-market loan or

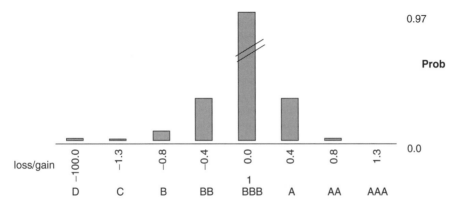

Figure 3.16 MTM approach for liquid assets: market-to-market credit event profit/loss distribution

debt securities since a profit or gain in marked-to-market value can also be created by an improvement in the counterparty's credit standing.

Potential issues for implementing these loss tabulation methods arise in two areas: first, the calculation of the average credit spreads to be used for discounting often involves complex securities selection, e.g. eliminating all callable bonds, and statistical bootstrapping techniques to create a yield curve per rating class based on on-the-run securities. Fortunately, J.P. Morgan is making this data available. An alternative approach is to use indicative new syndicated loan prices for the shorter-term, higher-grade segments and bootstrap longer maturities and lower ratings with the help of the leveraged funding desk. Secondly, the institution must be able to price appropriately each type of exposure for different counterparty credit classes; this issue is often resolved by creating discount rates that are rating and maturity dependent and applying them against the outstanding loan equivalent exposures as if they were known cashflows.

- *Illiquid Exposures: Migration Approach.*   The examples in the last section illustrated how one might calculate the potential losses of liquid assets to changes in the credit quality of individual counterparties. While the assumption of liquidity may be appropriate for many institutional investors' or syndicated loan portfolios, the bulk of the credit risk for many financial institutions is in portfolios that are substantially less liquid and can only be sold, if at all, for a substantial discount. These portfolios typically comprise middle-market or retail names, e.g. markets that are inherently less transparent than those for large, international and capital market-oriented corporate names. Because of the non-transparency of these markets, financial institutions may only be able to sell these assets at a discount relative to what they believe to be their fair market value due to the perception of adverse selection and/or moral hazard. As such, the risk of most of these assets, once originated, will remain with the originator until they mature.[28] The logical conclusion is that capital and reserves should be built up when the asset is originated to cover the potential default risk over the life of the asset as opposed to potential changes in the assets theoretical marked-to-market value over some short-term horizon.

To calculate the sensitivities of illiquid assets to credit events, the most common approach is to recognize only the loss from defaults over some time horizon; this is the approach taken by CSFP in their CreditRisk+ approach (CSFB (1997)) as well as the approach described by Kealhofer (1995a,b), which both build binomial default/no-default distributions over some time horizon based on the counterparty's cumulative probability of default over that time horizon. This loss typically reflects an assumption regarding the amount the institution stands to recover in the event of default and is often discounted at an appropriate discount rate in order to calculate the net present value of the potential loss. Credit migrations are captured by using the cumulative default rate, which explicitly recognizes the possibility of credit migrations prior to default.

Complicating this sensitivity calculation is the fact that the counterparty's exposure profile can change substantially over time; for example, it is well known that the potential exposure profiles generated by swaps, futures or options is not constant. This effect is even common for simpler, commercial banking products; for example, more is at stake if a counterparty goes default in the first year than in the second year if your total exposure to the counterparty consists of a current account and a medium-term financing position.

The resulting loss distribution or, equivalently, the sensitivity of the position to credit defaults, is therefore not the typical binomial, default/no default distribution commonly used, but rather a multi-nomial loss distribution that reflects the exact timing of default. Figure 3.17 illustrates the impact of non-constant loss exposures in terms of tabulating loss distributions.

With a constant exposure profile, the loss distribution for a single exposure is bi-modal — either it goes into default at some time during its maturity, with a cumulative default probability covering the entire three-year period equal to $p_1 + p_2 + p_3$ in Figure 3.17, implying a loss of 100, or it does not; if the exposure is non-constant, however, you stand to lose a different amount depending upon the exact timing of the default event. In the example, you would stand to lose 100 with probability p_1, the marginal probability that the counterparty goes into default during the first year, 50 with probability p_2, the marginal probability that the counterparty goes into default during the second year, etc.

Addressing both of these issues requires that one works with marginal, as opposed to cumulative, default probabilities: whereas the cumulative default probability tells you the probability of observing a default in any of the prior years, the marginal default probability tells you the probability of observing a loss in each specific year, assuming that the loss has not already occurred in a previous period. McKinsey's CreditPortfo-lioView (McKinsey (1998)) approach uses the multi-nomial, marginal probability of default approach for illiquid positions, which can be overridden by management fiat should a binomial approach be desired.

The critical issues facing many institutions are, first, to define concretely which assets are liquid, and, if they are liquid, what the appropriate liquidation period is; secondly, for the remaining, illiquid positions, whether to recognize multi-period losses as opposed to single period losses; and, finally, what are the appropriate recovery rates or recovery distributions for each asset class.

- *Retail or Average Loss Rate Portfolios.* Many institutions have portfolios comprising a large number of small, homogeneous assets; often, for such products as cards, mortgages or overdrafts, or even proportional credit and surety contracts, the institution does not choose to rate each individual asset and then track its migration from one risk category to another (although some form of behavioral scoring may be used), but rather chooses initially to use scoring techniques to evaluate the counterparty but

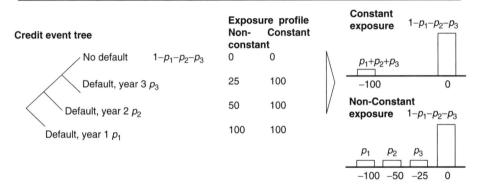

Figure 3.17   Loss distributions for illiquid assets

then monitor the portfolio's average loss rate for VaR measurement purposes. For these types of portfolios to be integrated into a credit VaR measurement framework, many institutions simply model how this average loss rate may evolve over time, especially its mean and variance (and sometimes higher moments as well), and then apply different loss scenarios directly against the portfolio's run-off profile in order to tabulate the portfolio's loss, either using Monte Carlo techniques or by applying the worst-case average loss rate scenario directly. If the average loss rate is gross of recoveries, then a suitable recovery distribution is assumed; otherwise, if it is already on a net basis, it is applied directly.

While this approach is relatively easy to use when considering the "retail" portfolio in isolation, one key challenge facing many institutions is to model these losses in the context of the overall portfolio: how are losses from these portfolios correlated with losses from other portfolios, for example? What are the drivers of these losses? Are they related to regional cycles? Housing price indices? While many institutions simply add the VaR from these "retail" segments to that calculated for their other lines, other approaches such as that used by CreditPortfolioView (Wilson (1997a,b,c,d) and McKinsey (1998)) incorporate these types of portfolios into a consistent framework.

- *Asset– and Portfolio–Normal Approaches.*   An alternative approach for modeling credit events and transaction separately is simply to model the return process for individual assets or the entire portfolio directly, making the assumption that the return process is either lognormally or normally distributed in a manner very similar to the Asset– and Portfolio–Normal approaches outlined in Subsections 3.3.2–3.3.3 on market VaR calculations.

For example, one portfolio approach makes the assumption that the total return for an individual bond is normally distributed. This approach often provides a good first cut at risk numbers and is particularly useful in developing simple risk/return portfolio optimization models; unfortunately, it is primarily applicable to speculative grade portfolios whose individual asset returns more resemble equity prices rather than investment grade portfolios where credit risk is "small" and asymmetric.

As another example, some institutions model the average loss ratio for a portfolio directly using historical loss rates. Often, a particular distribution assumption is made for aggregate portfolio losses, e.g. lognormal, normal or a beta distribution, which is then "fit" to historical data. Prior to the estimation of the distribution's parameters, the historical data is sometimes "adjusted", with some institutions choosing to take out extreme historical events so that the distribution more closely resembles "normal" default scenarios, while others choose to add adverse threat scenarios, e.g. depression era experiences, which were not in the historical time series. As discussed in the market risk section, this approach may be useful to get a quick, top-down first-cut at the portfolio's riskiness; unfortunately, it makes several assumptions that are not always valid in practice, e.g. that the portfolio composition did not change in the past and will not change in the future; that the portfolio and its losses comprise a large number of relatively small exposures.

3.4.2 Comparison of Different Methods

Relative to market VaR calculations, the techniques used to model credit portfolio VaR are still in their infancy; nonetheless, there are a few emerging approaches that bundle some of the assumptions discussed earlier together to form an integrated approach. The implicit or explicit assumptions that these emerging approaches make are summarized in Table 3.6; for a more detailed description of each of the assumptions, please refer to the earlier discussion in this section.

(i) CreditMetrics® (J.P. Morgan (1997))

In terms of distribution assumptions, CreditMetrics® assumes that the counterparty's ratingfully determines its rating migration and default probabilities; note that this rating can be determined using any one of several methods, including implied expected default frequencies using equity market data. Correlations are captured by using equity price index correlations as surrogates and the rating migration matrix is assumed to be constant over time, e.g. no credit cycles occur with each year's losses being drawn from the same distribution in terms of expected default and migration rates. In terms of portfolio sensitivity assumptions, CreditMetrics® assumes that all transactions can be liquidated over some constant, user-defined time horizon. It is difficult to incorporate retail portfolios into the CreditMetrics® approach, both in terms of modeling their correlations and their average losses.

(ii) KMV (Kealhofer (1995a,b) and McQuown (1995))

In terms of distribution assumptions, KMV uses equity price information to characterize the counterparty's default probability as well as the default correlations between different counterparty segments; as with CreditMetrics®, KMV's modeling approach precludes the existence of credit cycles, deriving default levels, volatilities and correlations using equity data using a Geometric Brownian Motion assumption for the evolution of asset values. In terms of portfolio sensitivity assumptions, KMV assumes that all transactions are either

Table 3.6 Comparison of standard models

Assumptions	Model			
	CreditMetrics® (JPM(97))	KMV (Kealhofer (1995a,b))	CreditPortfolio View (McKinsey (1998))	CreditRisk+ (CSFP(1997))
Distribution assumptions Expected default frequencies				
• Discretionary (including asset volatility based)	√	√	√	√
Correlations:				
• Independent	—	—	—	√
• Equity based	√	√	√	—
• Based on own portfolio performance	—	—	√	—
Credit cycle momentum	—	—	√	—
Portfolio sensitivities Quantifying losses				
• Mark-to-market™	√	√	√	—
• Default only, binomial	—	√	√	√
• Default only, multinomial	—	—	√	—
• Retail portfolios	—	—	√	—

illiquid or liquid. For illiquid asset treatment, these loss profiles are calculated using a binomial marginal distribution, precluding the recognition of non-constant exposure profiles. It is difficult to incorporate retail portfolios into KMV's approach, both in terms of modeling their correlations and their average losses.

(iii) CreditPortfolioView (Wilson (1997a,b,c,d) and McKinsey (1998))

In terms of distribution assumptions, CreditPortfolioView assumes that the counterparty's rating determines its expected rating migration and default probabilities over the next year; these ratings may be determined using expected default frequencies implied by equity markets. Default volatilities and correlations are captured on the basis of historical loss experiences, including those for retail portfolios; thus, while double-A construction and public utility companies may have the same expected default and migration rates over a one-year horizon, they will have different default rate volatilities due to the cyclical behavior of the two segments. In addition, CreditPortfolioView uses the historical behavior of average default rates to incorporate credit cycle momentum behavior. In terms of portfolio sensitivity assumptions, CreditPortfolioView can incorporate liquid, illiquid and retail portfolios into a consistent risk measurement framework and can also recognize the impact of non-constant exposure profiles.

(iv) CreditRisk+ (CSFB (1997))

Credit Suisse First Boston has developed an analytic approach for tabulating the loss distribution for a portfolio of exposures leveraging actuarial techniques developed primarily in the property and casualty insurance industry. This approach is able to gain analytic solutions by making several simplifying approximations regarding the segmentation of the portfolio by exposure size. To use the approach, one has to enter the expected cumulative default frequency by rating category and time horizon, as well as the volatility of expected cumulative default probabilities; these parameters are usually taken from historical public rating agency or own portfolio experiences. Modeling correlation structures is more complicated, however, as one must first decompose the correlation structure into orthogonal components before applying it. Losses are tabulated on a binomial, default/no-default basis over a constant time horizon consistent with the time horizon for the cumulative expected default frequencies.

(v) Simulation and Binomial Techniques

In addition to those publically available models, many institutions have developed proprietary models. Many in-house models simulate the average cumulative default rates by rating category on the basis of historical data from the public rating agencies. These relationships, e.g. expected default probabilities and volatilities, are assumed to be constant throughout the credit cycle; since historical default data is typically not available to cover each customer segment/rating pair, correlations between different segments are often set to zero or to a constant determined by the volatility of the average default rate. In terms of portfolio loss sensitivities, these methods resemble the default/no-default approach taken by KMV and CSFP's CreditRisk+: all transactions are illiquid, e.g. in that default events alone determine the portfolio's losses over some, user-defined time horizon. In addition, the loss profiles are typically calculated using a binomial distribution, precluding the recognition of non-constant exposure profiles. To the extent to which segment-specific default rates are not modeled explicitly, it is difficult to incorporate retail portfolios into these approaches, both in terms of modeling their correlations and their average losses. As such, these approaches capture the impact of counterparty concentration as well as uncertainty regarding the average default rate level; they typically do not capture segment diversification, marked-to-market losses for liquid positions or non-constant exposure profiles.

3.5 ACKNOWLEDGEMENTS

The author would like to thank many individuals in McKinsey & Company, especially Wolfgang Hammes, as well as industry professionals in Frankfurt, London, New York, Tokyo and Zurich for providing valuable comments. This work draws substantially on previous work published over the past years in *Risk Magazine*; thanks are therefore also due to *Risk Magazine* and its publisher, Peter Fields, for providing an excellent forum for the exchange of ideas. This chapter corrects an error in a previous article (Wilson (1994b)); any remaining errors remain those of the author. Please direct any comments or questions to: Thomas C. Wilson, McKinsey & Company, 55 E. 52nd Street, New York, NY 10006, USA or via e-mail on tom_wilson@mckinsey.com

3.6 ENDNOTES

1. Although there seems to be a general convergence in the area of market risk in terms of high-level methods (e.g. delta–normal or covariance methods for linear portfolios and some form of simulation methods for non-linear portfolios, either historical or Monte Carlo), their detailed implementations often differ markedly across institutions in terms of which correlations to recognize, which interest rate or volatility model to estimate, etc.
2. See Hull (1988) for a concise description of many of the most important risk measures used in practice.
3. For example, a 99 per cent confidence interval, a 10-day holding period, a minimum of one year of market data, a minimum of six bands for interest rates and an ability to capture non-linear options-related risks.
4. For a discussion of RAPM methodologies from a practical and theoretical standpoint, see Chew (1994a), S. Punjabi (1998), D. Wilson (1995) and T. Wilson (1992).
5. For example, when evaluating credit risks, there is a bias towards lower-rated counterparties if returns are measured relative to regulatory capital since regulatory capital adequacy rules are not sufficiently differentiated by credit risk or rating.
6. See, for example, Alexander (1994), Allen (1994), Chew (1994b), Jorion (1997), Lawrence and Robinson (1995a), Longerstaey and Zangari (1995) and Wilson (1993, 1994b).
7. Although it is certainly correct to ask under what conditions VaR is a meaningful measure of risk for an individual or in market equilibrium. In addition, some financial institutions question whether or not Expected Maximum Loss (EML) or the probability of ruin would not be better measures of aggregate institution risk.
8. See, again, J.P. Morgan (1994–95), Lawrence and Robinson (1995a) and Longerstaey and Zangari (1995).
9. See Ashraff et al. (1995) for cross-rate hedging techniques.
10. To see this, consider the explicit formula for the mark-to-market (MTM) value of this position in terms of the domestic currency:

$$\text{MTM}_t = e_t[df(t_1) - (1 + {}_t f_{t_1 \to t_2}(t_2 - t_1)/360)\, df(t_2)],$$

where MTM_t is the mark-to-market value at time t, e_t is the spot exchange rate, domestic currency/foreign currency, $df(t)$ are the foreign currency discount factors for a single currency unit to be paid/received at time t, ${}_t f_{t_1 \to t_2}$ is the forward rate, at t, from t_1 to t_2. Since the FRA is assumed to be concluded at time t and at current market rates, the expression in brackets (e.g.

$[df(t_1) - (1 + {}_t f_{t_1 \to t_2}(t_2 - t_1)/360)\, df(t_2)])$ is equal to zero. Taking the partial derivative of the MTM expression with respect to the spot exchange rate gives

$$\partial MTM/\partial e_t = [df(t_1) - (1 + {}_t f_{t_1 \to t_2}(t_2 - t_1)/365)\, df(t_2)] = 0.$$

Thus, this position has no first-order foreign exchange risk. Nonetheless, it does have a second-order foreign exchange risk, represented by the second (cross-rate) derivative

$$\partial^2 MTM/\partial e_t \partial r_t = \partial[df(t_1) - (1 + {}_t f_{t_1 \to t_2}(t_2 - t_1)/365)\, df(t_2)]/\partial r_t.$$

11. See, for example, Blattberg and Gonedes (1974) and Praetz (1972) for equity prices, Rogalski and Vinso (1978) and Wilson (1993) for foreign exchange rates; see also J.P. Morgan (1994–95) for a multi-market evaluation.
12. See the references cited earlier. In addition, it is interesting to note that stochastic volatility models predict a similar "fat tails" phenomena as is demonstrated by historical price series. See, for example, Chapter 4 by Carol Alexander in this volume. Other authors have examined models that use mixtures of normal variables in order to get similar fat tail results (see, for example, Hull & White (1997), Venkataraman (1997), Wilson (1993) and Zangari (1997)).
13. For a very good overview, see Alexander (1994)
14. Consider the standard geometric Brownian motion (GBM) process given by:

(a) $dp(t) = \mu(t)p(t)\, dt + \sigma(t)p(t)\, dZ$

with the stochastic integral given by:

(b) $p(t + \Delta t) = p(t)^* \exp\left[\int_{\Delta t} \mu(s)\, ds + \left(\int_{\Delta t} \sigma(s)\, ds\right)\left(\int_{\Delta t} dZ\right)\right]$

This process is typically discretized using the following approximation:

(c) $\Delta p(t) = \mu(t)p(t)\Delta t + \sigma(t)p(t)z$

where z is assumed to be a unit normal variable. While the stochastic integral of (a) given by (b) guarantees strictly positive rates, its equivalent discrete version given by (c) does not.

15. Note that the assumption of a zero mean return vector can be relaxed easily.
16. Note that we could have assumed that the percentage returns rather than the absolute returns on market positions were normally distributed as is done in standard CAPM situations. For short time intervals, these are roughly the same. What is important here is that it is the *position* (e.g. zero bonds, options) returns that are roughly normal rather than market rates (e.g. interest rates, exchange rates).
17. The discussion and evaluation of the RiskMetrics™ techniques in this chapter is not complete. Interested individuals should read J.P. Morgan (1994–95), Longerstaey and Zangari (1995) and Lawrence and Robinson (1995a).
18. Roughly speaking, under the normality assumption and the delta–gamma or second-order approximation, interior solutions can only occur if the γ matrix is positive definite and if δ is "sufficiently" small in absolute value, implying that the portfolio pay-off function is represented (roughly) by a quadratic, M-dimensional hyperbole; this would be the equivalent to a long-straddle position in all risk dimensions. In practice, these conditions are rarely met for multi-market portfolios, implying that interior solutions will be rare using this method.
19. See Varian (1984) for a discussion of constrained optimization, Lagrangian and Kuhn–Tucker conditions.
20. For ease of exposition, we have sketched only those hyperbolic cases with $\delta = 0$ (e.g. Figure 3.5 (c) and (d)). The methods specified later in this subsection provide reasonable approximations when this is not the case.
21. See note 20.
22. See Brotherton-Ratcliff (1994) for a discussion.
23. The discussion and evaluation of the regulator's "building block" approach is not meant to be comprehensive, but only to illustrate the concept and issues. Interested individuals should read the references cited in the section for a more detailed description.

24. For example, 0.00 per cent for government issuers; 0.25 per cent (for remaining life less than six months), 1.00 per cent (between 6 and 24 months) and 1.60 per cent (greater than 24 months) for qualifying issues (essentially, qualifying issues are investment grade issues); and 8 per cent for all other issuers.
25. Analogously, some implementations of VaR for investment portfolios with a longer investment horizon (e.g. one year) also recognize the expected returns from holding the portfolio, implying a non-zero mean for the loss distribution.
26. Determination of the probability of default, and therefore rating, for many structured or project finance transactions also rely heavily on cash flow analysis.
27. See, for example, G30 (1993), DPG (1995), Rowe (1995) and Lawrence (1995).
28. Note that this is also the case for most asset-backed or securitized structures where, in the majority of cases, the originator ultimately provides the credit enhancement to the structure, and therefore bears the credit risk, either through a retention of a subordinated tranche, through an equity participation or through over-collateralization.

3.7 REFERENCES

Alexander, C. (1994) "History debunked". *Risk Magazine*, December.

Allen, M. (1994) "Building a role model". *Risk Magazine*, September.

Altman, E. (1983) "Aggregate influences on business failture rates", in *Corporate Financial Distress: A Complete Guide*.

Ashraff, J., Tarczon, J. and Wu, W. (1995) "Safe crossing". *Risk Magazine*, July.

Bahar, R. (1997) "Making the best of the worst". *Risk Magazine*, August.

Basle Committee on Banking Supervision (1995a) *An Internal Model-Based Approach to Market VaR Requirements*, April.

Basle Committee on Banking Supervision (1995b) *Planned Supplement to the Capital Accord to Incorporate Market Risks*, April.

Basle Committee on Banking Supervision (1996a) *Amendment to the Capital Accord to Incorporate Market Risks*.

Basle Committee on Banking Supervision (1996b) *Supervisory Framework for the Use of "Backtesting" in Conjunction with the Internal Models Approach to market VaR Requirements*.

Bassi, F., Embrechts, P. and Kafetzaki, M. (1996) "A Survival Kit on Quantile Estimation". Working Paper, Department of Mathematics, ETHZ, CH-8092, Zurich, Switzerland.

Blattberg, R. and Gonedes, N. (1974) "A comparison of the stable and Student-*t* distributions as statistical models for stock prices". *Journal of Business*, April.

Brotherton-Ratcliff, R. (1994) "Monte Carlo motoring". *Risk Magazine*, December.

Chew, L. (1992) "Editorial". *Risk Magazine*, October.

Chew, L. (1994a) "Conscious efforts". *Risk Magazine*, April.

Chew, L. (1994b) "Shock therapy". *Risk Magazine*, September.

CSFB (1997) *CreditRisk+ Approach Documentation*.

Derivatives Policy Group (1995) *Voluntary Oversight of OTC Derivatives*.

Estrella, A. (1994) "Taylor, Black and Scholes: Series Approximations and Risk Management Pitfalls". Working Paper, Federal Reserve Bank of New York.

Gollinger, T.L. and Morgan, J.B. (1993) "Calculation of an efficient frontier for a commercial loan portfolio". *Journal of Portfolio Management*, **19**, no. 2, Winter.

Group of Thirty (G30) (1993) *Derivatives: Practices and Principles*. Washington: Global Derivatives Study Group.

Hull, J. (1988) *Options, Futures and Other Derivative Securities*. New York: Prentice-Hall.

Hull, J. and White, A. (1997) "Taking Account of the Kurtosis in Market Variables when Calculating Value at Risk". Working Paper.

Jorion, P. (1997) *Value at Risk: The New Benchmark for Controlling Market Risk*, Irwin Professional Publishing.

J.P. Morgan (1994–95) *RiskMetrics–Technical Documentation*, Releases 1–3. New York: J.P. Morgan.

J.P. Morgan (1997) *CreditMetrics–Technical Documentation*, Release 1. New York: J.P. Morgan.

Kaarkki, J. and Reyes, C. (1995) "Model relationship". *Risk Magazine*, December.

Kealhofer, S. (1995a) "Managing default risk in portfolios of derivatives", in *Derivative Credit Risk: Advances in Measurement and Management*. London: Risk Publications.

Kealhofer, S. (1995b) "Portfolio management of default risk". Proprietary documentation. San Francisco: KMV Corporation.

Kupiec, P. and O'Brien, J. (1995a) "Internal affairs". *Risk Magazine*, May.

Kupiec, P. and O'Brien, J. (1995b) "Model alternative". *Risk Magazine*, June.

Lawrence, D. (1995) "Aggregating credit exposures: the simulation approach", in *Derivative Credit Risk: Advances in Measurement and Management*. London: Risk Publications.

Lawrence, C. and Robinson, G. (1995a) "How safe is RiskMetrics?". *Risk Magazine*, January.

Lawrence, C. and Robinson, G. (1995b) "Liquid measures". *Risk Magazine*, July.

Lintner, J. (1965) "The valuation of risk assets and the selection of risk investments in stock portfolios and capital budgets". *Review of Economic Studies*, **47**.

Longerstaey, J. and Zangari, P. (1995) "A transparent tool". *Risk Magazine*, January.

Longin, F. (1994) "Optimal Margin Level in Futures Markets: A Parametric Extreme-Based Method". IFA Working Paper 192–94, London Business School.

Markowitz, H. (1952) "Portfolio selection". *Journal of Finance*, **7**.

Matten, C. (1996) *Managing Bank Capital*. Chichester: Wiley.

McKinsey (1998) *CreditPortfolioView Approach and User's Documentation*, New York: McKinsey & Company.

McQuown, M. (1995) "Evaluating credit risk: a market-based approach". Proprietary documentation. San Francisco: KMV Corporation.

Merton, R. (1973) "The theory of rationale option pricing". *Bell Journal of Economics and Management Science*, **4**.

Praetz, P. (1972) "The distribution of share price changes". *The Journal of Business*, **45**, January, 49–55.

Punjabi, S. (1998) "Many Happy Returns". *Risk Magazine*, June.

Rogalski, R. and Vinso, J. (1978) "Empirical properties of foreign exchange rates". *Journal of International Business Studies*, **9**, Fall, 69–79.

Rouvinez, C. (1997) "Going Greek with VaR". *Risk Magazine*, February.

Rowe, D. (1995) "Aggregating credit exposures: the primary risk source approach", in *Derivatives Credit Risk: Advances in Measurement and Management*. London: Risk Publications.

Schaefer, S. (1995) "Value at risk". Conference presentation. London.

Sharpe, W. (1964) "Capital asset prices: A theory of market equilibrium under conditions of risk". *Journal of Finance*, **19**.

Sheffe, (1959) *Analysis of Variance*

Thomas, L.C., Crook, J.N. and Edelman, D.B. (1992) *Credit Scoring and Credit Control*. Oxford: Clarendon Press.

Varian, H. (1984) *Microeconomic Analysis*. New York: W.W. Norton.

Venkataraman, S. (1997) "Value at risk for a mixture of normal distributions: The use of quasi-Bayesian estimation techniques". *Federal Reserve Bank of Chicago*, March/April, 2–13.

Wilson, D. (1995) "Marriage of ideals". *Risk Magazine*, July.

Wilson, T. (1992) "Raroc remodeled". *Risk Magazine*, September.

Wilson, T. (1993) "Infinite wisdom". *Risk Magazine*, June.

Wilson, T. (1994a) "Debunking the myths". *Risk Magazine*, April.

Wilson, T. (1994b) "Plugging the gap". *Risk Magazine*, November.

Wilson, T. (1997a) "Measuring and managing credit portfolio risk: Part 1: Modeling systematic risk". *Journal of Lending and Credit Risk Management*, July.

Wilson, T. (1997b) "Measuring and managing credit portfolio risk: Part 2: Tabulating loss distributions". *Journal of Lending and Credit Risk Management*, August.

Wilson, T. (1997c) "Portfolio credit risk (1)". *Risk Magazine*, September.

Wilson, T. (1997d) "Portfolio credit risk (2)". *Risk Magazine*, October.

Zangari, P. (1997) "An improved methodology for measuring VaR". *RiskMetrics Monitor*, Reuters/J.P. Morgan.

$$\text{---------} \quad 4 \quad \text{---------}$$

Volatility and Correlation: Measurement, Models and Applications

CAROL ALEXANDER

4.1 INTRODUCTION

The most widely accepted approach to "risk" in financial markets focuses on the measurement of volatility in certain returns distributions.[1] The volatility of portfolio returns depends on the variances and covariances between the risk factors of the portfolio, and the sensitivities of individual assets to these risk factors. In linear portfolios, sensitivities are also measured by variances and covariances. So the primary objective of this chapter is to account for the standard methods of estimating and forecasting covariance matrices. The practical and theoretical advantages and limitations of each method are discussed in detail. Later in the chapter it is shown how to employ them effectively in value at risk systems, capital allocation models, investment management and the pricing and hedging of derivative products. The chapter concludes with a short review of other methods for measuring market risk: downside risk and regret, expected maximum loss, and cointegration.

What is volatility? A standard non-parametric definition is that x is "more volatile" than y if

$$P(|x| > c) > P(|y| > c)$$

for all c. So if y is a time series it becomes more volatile when $P(|y_{t+1}| > c) > P(|y_t| > c)$ for all c. But when y has a symmetric distribution, such as a normal distribution, this occurs if and only if $\sigma_{t+1}^2 > \sigma_t^2$, where σ_t^2 denotes the conditional variance of y.[2] However, variance is not standardized. If we were to plot a term structure of variances, across different maturities, variance would simply increase with the holding period of returns. So volatility is usually quoted as an annualized percentage standard deviation:

$$\text{volatility at time } t = (100\sigma_t\sqrt{A}) \text{ per cent} \tag{1}$$

Risk Management and Analysis. Vol. 1: Measuring and Modelling Financial Risk.
Edited by Carol Alexander © 1998 John Wiley & Sons Ltd

where A denotes the number of observations per year. We do this so that volatilities of different maturities may be compared on the same scale — as the variance increases with the holding period, so the annualizing factor decreases. In this way, volatilities are standardized.

If one takes two associated returns series x and y — returns on two Gilts for example — we can calculate their correlation as

$$\text{Corr}(x, y) = \text{Cov}(x, y)/\sqrt{\text{Var}(x)}\sqrt{\text{Var}(y)} \tag{2}$$

that is,

$$\rho_{xy} = \sigma_{xy}/\sigma_x\sigma_y \tag{3}$$

Note that joint stationarity[3] is necessary for the existence of correlation, and that it is the exception rather than the rule. Two arbitrary returns series, such as a Latin American Brady bond and a stock in the FTSE 100, should be unrelated and are not likely to be jointly stationary, so correlations between these two time series do not exist. Of course, one can calculate a number based on the correlation formulae given in this chapter, but it does not measure unconditional correlation unless the two series are jointly stationary. In such cases "correlation" is found to be very unstable. Correlation estimates will jump about a lot over time — a sign of non-joint stationarity.

Correlation does not need to be annualized, as does volatility, because it is already in a standardized form: correlation always lies between -1 and $+1$. A negative value means that returns tend to move in opposite directions and a positive value indicates synchronous moves in the same direction. The greater the absolute value of correlation, the greater the association between the series.[4]

Volatilities and correlations are just standardized forms of the variances and covariances between returns, so the information necessary to measure portfolio risk is usually summarized in a covariance matrix. Based on a set of n returns series $y_1, \ldots, y_n$, this is a square, symmetric matrix of the form

$$
\begin{pmatrix}
\text{Var}(y_1) & \text{Cov}(y_1, y_2) & \ldots & \ldots & \text{Cov}(y_1, y_n) \\
\text{Cov}(y_1, y_2) & \text{Var}(y_2) & \ldots & \ldots & \text{Cov}(y_2, y_n) \\
\text{Cov}(y_1, y_3) & \text{Cov}(y_2, y_3) & \text{Var}(y_3) & \ldots & \text{Cov}(y_3, y_n) \\
\ldots & \ldots & \ldots & \ldots & \ldots \\
\text{Cov}(y_1, y_n) & \ldots & \ldots & \ldots & \text{Var}(y_n)
\end{pmatrix}
$$

The next two sections of this chapter describe the two most commonly used methods of estimating and forecasting covariance matrices in financial markets. Section 4.2 assesses the moving average volatility and correlation estimation methods that most financial institutions use today: the equally weighted "historic" method and the exponentially weighted moving average method. Section 4.3 gives an overview of the huge technical literature on GARCH modelling in finance and Section 4.4 covers implied volatility and correlation forecasts, their use in trading being covered elsewhere (see Chapter 9 in *Risk Management and Analysis. Volume 2: New Markets and Products*). Section 4.5 surveys the use of volatility and correlation forecasts in risk management, with particular emphasis on value at risk (VaR) models. The final section of this chapter covers certain special issues, such as estimating volatilities from "fat-tailed" distributions using normal mixtures, evaluation of the accuracy of different models, and new directions, such as "downside risk" measures and cointegration.

4.2 MOVING AVERAGES

A moving average is an arithmetic average over a rolling window of consecutive data points taken from a time series. Moving averages have been a useful tool in financial forecasting for many years. For example, in technical analysis, where they exist under the name of "stochastics", the relationship between moving averages of different lengths can be used as a signal to trade. Traditionally they have also been used in volatility estimation. Usually volatility and correlation estimates are based on daily or intra-day returns, since even weekly data can miss some of the turbulence encountered in financial markets. Moving averages of squared (or cross products) of returns are estimates of variance (or covariance). These are converted to volatility and correlation as described above, or employed in a covariance matrix for measuring portfolio variance.

4.2.1 "Historic" Methods

This section describes the uses and misuses of the traditional "historic" volatility and correlation forecasting methods. Recent advances in time series analysis allow a more critical view of the efficiency of these methods, and they are being replaced by exponentially weighted moving average or GARCH methods in most major institutions today.

The *n-period historic volatility* at time T is the quantity $(100\hat{\sigma}_T \sqrt{A})$ per cent, where A is the number of returns r_t per year and

$$\hat{\sigma}_T^2 = \sum_{t=T-n}^{t=T-1} r_t^2 \bigg/ n \tag{4}$$

Thus $\hat{\sigma}_T$ is the unbiased estimate of standard deviation over a sample size n, assuming the mean is zero.[5]

"Historic" correlations of maturity n are calculated in an analogous fashion: if x and y are two returns series, then n-period historic correlations may be calculated as[6]

$$r_T = \frac{\displaystyle\sum_{t=T-n}^{t=T-1} x_t y_t}{\sqrt{\displaystyle\sum_{t=T-n}^{t=T-1} x_t^2 \sum_{t=T-n}^{t=T-1} y_t^2}} \tag{5}$$

Traditionally, the estimate of volatility or correlation over the last n periods has been used as a forecast over the next n periods. The rationale for this is that long-term volatility predictions should be unaffected by "volatility clustering" behaviour, and so we need to take an average squared return over a long historic period. However, short-term volatility predictions should reflect current market conditions, whether volatile or tranquil, which means that only the immediate past returns should be used.

However, when we examine the time series properties of "historic" volatilities and correlations we see that they have some undesirable qualities: a major problem with equally weighted averages is that extreme events are just as important to current estimates whether they occurred yesterday or a long time ago. Even just *one* unusual return will continue to keep volatility estimates high for exactly n days following that day, although the underlying volatility will have long ago returned to normal levels. Thus volatility

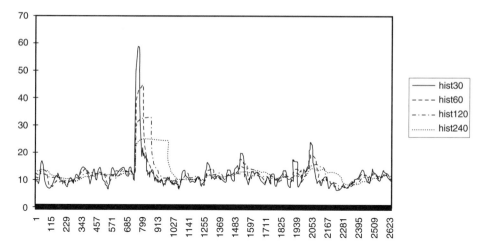

Figure 4.1   Historic volatilities of the FTSE from 1984 to 1995, showing "ghost features" of Black Monday and other extreme events

estimates will be kept artificially high in periods of tranquillity, and they will be lower than they should be during the short bursts of volatility that characterize financial markets.[7]

Figure 4.1 illustrates equally weighted averages of different lengths on squared returns to the FTSE. Daily squared returns are averaged over the last n observations for $n = 30$, 60, 120, 240, and this variance is transformed to an annualized volatility in Figure 4.1. Note that the one-year volatility of the FTSE jumped up to 26 per cent the day after Black Monday and it stayed at that level for a whole year because that one, huge squared return had exactly the same weight in the average. Exactly one year after the event the large return falls out of the moving average, and so the volatility forecast returned to its normal level of around 13 per cent. In shorter term equally weighted averages this "ghost feature" will be much bigger because it will be averaged over fewer observations, but it will last for a shorter period of time.

Ghost features are even more of an issue with equally weighted moving average correlation estimates, where they can induce an apparent stability in correlations. It may be that "instantaneous" correlations are very unstable, because the two returns are not jointly stationary. But whatever the true properties of correlations between the two returns series, the longer the averaging period, the more stable will moving average correlations appear to be. It may also be that, by some fluke, the series both have large returns on the same day. This will cause a ghost feature in correlation, making it artificially high for the n periods following that day.

Even with two closely related series such as the FTSE 100 and the S&P 500, we will obtain correlation estimates that appear more stable as the averaging period increases. This point is illustrated in Figure 4.2, where correlations between the two equity indices are shown for a 60-day averaging period, compared with the 30-day period. Stability of correlation estimates increases with the averaging period, rather than being linked to the degree of joint stationarity between the variables, because the equally weighted moving average method is masking the underlying nature of the relationship between variables. Thus we could erroneously conclude that correlations are "stable" if this method of estimation is employed.

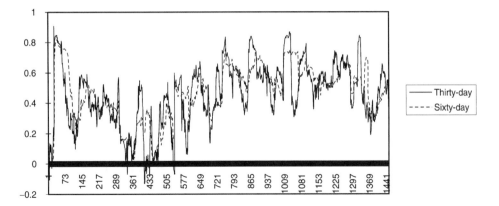

Figure 4.2 Historical correlations between UK and US equities from just before Black Monday to Spring 1993

Equally weighted moving averages should be used with caution, particularly for correlation, on the grounds of these ghost features alone. But there is another, finer point of consideration. Perceived changes in volatility and correlation can have important consequences, so it is essential to understand what is the source of variability in any particular model. In the "historic" model, all variation is due only to differences in samples: a smaller sample size yields a less precise estimate, the larger the sample size the more accurate the estimate. So a short period moving average will be more variable than a longer moving average. But whatever the length of the averaging period we are still estimating the same thing: the unconditional volatility of the time series. This is one number, a constant, underlying the whole series. So variation in the n-period historic volatility model, which we perceive as variation over time, is actually due to sampling error alone. There is nothing else in the model that allows for variation. There is no estimated stochastic volatility model in any moving average method — they are simply estimates of unconditional moments, which are constants.[8] The estimated series does change over time, but as the underlying parameter of interest is a *constant* variance, all the observed variation in the estimate is simply due to sampling variation. The "historic" model also takes no account of the dynamic properties of returns, such as autocorrelation. It is essentially a "static" model that has been forced into a time-varying framework. So, if you "shuffle" the data within any given n-period window, you will get the same answer, provided of course for correlation the two returns series are shuffled "in pairs".

4.2.2 Exponentially Weighted Moving Averages

The "historic" models explained above weight each observation equally, whether it is yesterday's return or the returns from several weeks or months ago. It is this equal weighting that induces the "ghost features", which are clearly a problem. An exponentially weighted moving average (EWMA) places more weight on more recent observations, and this has the effect of eliminating the problematic "ghost features".

The exponential weighting is done by using a "smoothing constant" λ: the larger the value of λ the more weight is placed on past observations and so the smoother the series becomes. An n-period EWMA of a time series x is defined as

$$\frac{x_{t-1} + \lambda x_{t-2} + \lambda^2 x_{t-3} + \cdots + \lambda^{n-1} x_{t-n}}{1 + \lambda + \lambda^2 + \cdots + \lambda^{n-1}} \tag{6}$$

Since the denominator converges to $1/(1 - \lambda)$ as $n \to \infty$, an infinite EWMA may be written

$$(1 - \lambda) \sum_{i=1}^{\infty} \lambda^{i-1} x_{t-i} \tag{7}$$

It is an EWMA that is used for volatility and correlation forecasts in J.P. Morgan and Reuter's RiskMetrics^{TM}. The forecasts of volatility and correlation over the next day are calculated by taking $\lambda = 0.94$ and using squared returns r^2 as the series x in (7) for variance forecasts and cross products of two returns $r_1 r_2$ as the series x in (7) for covariance forecasts. Note that the same value of λ should be used for all variances and covariances in the matrix, otherwise it may not be positive semi-definite (see J.P. Morgan (1996)).

In general this type of EWMA behaves in a reasonable way — see Alexander and Leigh (1997) for an evaluation of their accuracy. In fact, an EWMA on squared returns is equivalent to an IGARCH model (see Section 4.3.2). To see this, consider equation (7) with $x = r^2$:

$$\hat{\sigma}_t^2 = (1 - \lambda) \sum_{i=1}^{\infty} \lambda^{i-1} r_{t-i}^2$$

This may be re-written in the form

$$\hat{\sigma}_t^2 = (1 - \lambda) r_{t-1}^2 + \lambda \hat{\sigma}_{t-1}^2 \tag{8}$$

which shows the recursion normally used to calculate EWMAs. Comparison with equation (13) shows that an EWMA is equivalent to an IGARCH model without a constant term.

In Section 4.3.3 we describe how the GARCH coefficients can be interpreted: the coefficient on the lagged squared return determines the degree of reaction of volatility to market events, and the coefficient on the lagged variance determines the persistence in volatility. In an EWMA these two coefficients are not independent — they sum to one. For the RiskMetrics^{TM} data set, the persistence coefficient is 0.94 for all markets, and the reaction coefficient is 0.06 for all markets. But if one estimates these coefficients rather than imposes them, it appears that $\lambda = 0.94$ is too high for most markets.

For example, in the FTSE series shown in Figure 4.3, the GARCH persistence coefficient is 0.88, and so the GARCH volatility series dies out more quickly than the RiskMetrics^{TM}. However, their reaction coefficient is about the same (0.06) and so both volatilities exhibit a similar size of market reaction in Figure 4.3.

The RiskMetrics^{TM} daily data do have some other problems, which are explained in Alexander (1996), but these are not insurmountable.[9] However, the RiskMetrics^{TM} forecasts of volatility over the next month behave in a rather strange fashion. Since the EWMA methodology is only really applicable to one-step-ahead forecasting, the correct thing would be to smooth 25-day returns, but there is not enough data. Instead, J.P. Morgan have applied exponential smoothing with a value of $\lambda = 0.97$ to the 25-day equally weighted variance. But this series will be full of 25-day "ghost features" (see Figure 4.1)

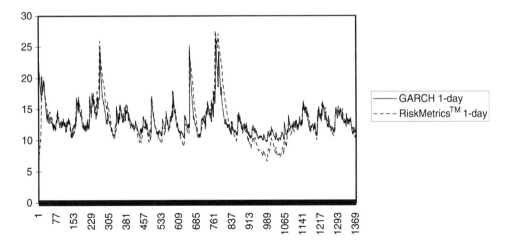

Figure 4.3   GARCH and exponentially weighted moving average one-day volatility forecasts of the FTSE: 1988–1995

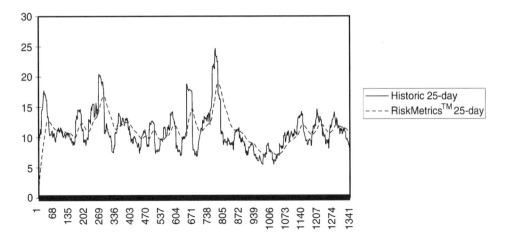

Figure 4.4   25-day "historic" and RiskMetrics^{TM} monthly volatility forecasts of the FTSE: 1988–1995

so the exponential smoothing has the effect of augmenting the very "ghost features" which they seek to diminish. After a major market movement the equally weighted 25-day series jumps up immediately — as would any sensible volatility forecast. But the RiskMetrics^{TM} monthly data hardly reacts at all, at first, then it gradually increases over the next 25 days to reach a maximum exactly 25 days *after* the event. The proof of this is simple: denote by s_t^2 the 25-day "historic" variance series, so the monthly variance forecast is $\hat{\sigma}_t^2 = (1 - \lambda)s_{t-1}^2 + \lambda\hat{\sigma}_{t-1}^2$. Clearly, $\hat{\sigma}_t^2 > \hat{\sigma}_{t-1}^2 \Leftrightarrow s_{t-1}^2 > \hat{\sigma}_{t-1}^2$. At the "ghost feature" s_t^2 drops dramatically, and so the maximum value of $\hat{\sigma}_t^2$ will occur at this point.

Figure 4.4 compares the RiskMetrics^{TM} monthly forecasts for the FTSE with the equally weighted 25-day "historic" forecasts, during the same period as in Figure 4.3. Neither forecast is useful: the "historic" forecast peaks at the right time, the day after a significant market movement, but it stays high for 25 days, when it should probably be declining. The RiskMetrics™ 25-day forecast hardly reacts at all to a market movement, but it slowly increases during the next 25 days so that the largest forecast of the volatility over the next month occurs 25 days too late.

4.2.3 Volatility Term Structures in Moving Average Models: The Square Root of Time Rule

Term structure volatility forecasts which are consistent with moving average models are constant, because that is the underlying assumption on volatility. Moving average models are, after all, estimation methods, not forecasting methods. We can of course say that our current estimate of volatility is to be taken as all future forecasts, and this is what is generally done. The current one-day volatility estimate is taken to be the one-day forward volatility forecast at every point in the future.

Term structure forecasts — forecasts of the volatility of h-day returns for every maturity h — are then based on the "square root of time" rule. This rule simply calculates h-day standard deviations as $\sqrt{h}$ times the daily standard deviation. It is based on the assumption that daily log returns are independently and identically distributed, so the variance of h-day returns is just h times the variance of daily returns. But since volatility is just an annualized form of the standard deviation, and since the annualizing factor is — assuming 250 days per year — $\sqrt{250}$ for daily returns but $\sqrt{(250/h)}$ for h-day returns, the square root of time rule is equivalent to the Black–Scholes assumption that current levels of volatility remain the same.

The square root of time rule implies the assumption of constant volatility. This follows from the assumption that log returns are independent and identically distributed. To see this, we introduce the notation $r_{t,h}$ for an h-day return forecast at time t, so approximately

$$r_{t,h} = \ln(P_{t+h}) - \ln(P_t)$$

where P_t denotes the price at time t. Clearly

$$r_{t,h} = r_{t,1} + r_{t+1,1} + \cdots + r_{t+h-1,1}$$

and if we assume that one-day returns are independent and identically distributed with constant variance σ^2 we have $\mathrm{Var}(r_{t,h}) = h\sigma^2$. Annualizing this into a volatility requires the use of an annualizing factor $250/h$, being the number of h-periods per year:

$$h\text{-period vol} = 100\sqrt{(250/h)}\sqrt{\mathrm{Var}(r_{h,t})} = 100\sqrt{(250/h)}\sqrt{(h\sigma^2)} = 100\sqrt{(250\sigma^2)}$$
$$= \text{one-period vol}$$

That is, volatility term structures are constant. Constant term structures are a limitation of exponentially weighted moving average methods. The reason for this is that financial volatility tends to come in "clusters", where tranquil periods of small returns are interspersed with volatile periods of large returns.[10] Thus volatility term structures should mean-revert, with short-term volatility lying either above or below the long-term mean depending on whether current conditions are high or low volatility. Clearly moving averages are quite limited in this respect. Substantial mispricing of volatility can result from these methods, as a number of large banks have recently discovered.

4.3 GARCH MODELS IN FINANCE

4.3.1 Introduction

The unfortunate acronym "GARCH" is nevertheless essential, since it stands for *generalized autoregressive conditional heteroscedasticity*! Heteroscedasticity means "changing variance", so conditional heteroscedasticity means changing conditional variance. A time series displays conditional heteroscedasticity if it has highly volatile periods interspersed with tranquil periods: i.e. there are "bursts" or "clusters" of volatility. Autoregressive means "regression on itself", and this refers to the method used to model conditional heteroscedasticity in GARCH models.

Most financial time series display autoregressive conditional heteroscedasticity. A typical example of conditionally heteroscedastic returns in high frequency data — minute-by-minute data on cotton futures – is shown in Figure 4.5. Note that two types of news events are apparent. The first volatility cluster shows an anticipated announcement, which turned out to be good news: the market was increasingly turbulent before the announcement, but the large positive return at that time shows that punters were pleased, and the volatility soon decreased. The later cluster of volatility shows increased turbulence following an unanticipated piece of bad news — the large negative return — what is often referred to as the "leverage" effect (see Section 4.3.2(iv)).

At the root of understanding GARCH is the distinction between conditional (stochastic) and unconditional (constant) volatility. These ideas are based on different stochastic processes which are assumed to govern the returns data. Figure 4.6 illustrates the difference between conditional and unconditional distributions of returns. In Figure 4.6(a) the stochastic process that generates the time series data on returns is assumed to be independent and identically distributed. This same distribution governs each of the data points, and since they are independent we may as well redraw the data without taking account of the dynamic ordering, along a line. The data are then considered to be random draws from a single distribution, called the unconditional distribution (Figure 4.6(b)). However,

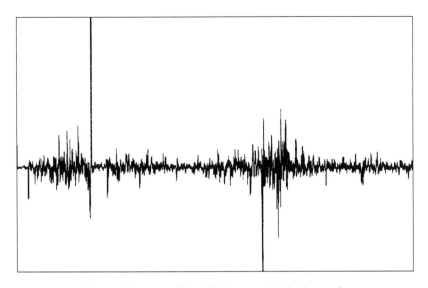

Figure 4.5   A conditionally heteroscedastic time series

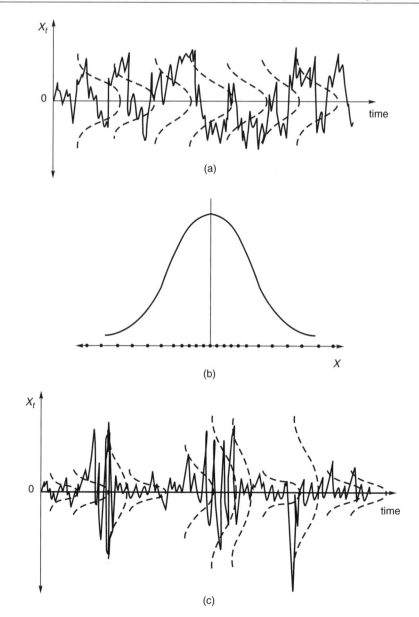

Figure 4.6   Conditional and unconditional distributions

in Figure 4.6(c) the same data are assumed to be generated by a stochastic process with time-varying volatility. In this case it is not realistic to collapse the data into a single distribution, ignoring the dynamic ordering. The conditional distribution changes at each point in time, and in particular the volatility process is stochastic.

The first ARCH model, introduced by Engle (1982), was later generalized by Bollerslev (1986), and many variations on the basic "vanilla" GARCH model have been introduced in the last 10 years.[11] The idea of GARCH is to add a second equation to the standard regression model — an equation that models the conditional variance. The first equation in the GARCH model is the conditional mean equation.[12] This can be anything, but because the focus of GARCH is on the conditional variance equation[13] it is usual to have a very simple conditional mean equation, such as $r_t = \text{constant} + \varepsilon_t$.

Note that the dependent variable (the input to the GARCH model) is always the returns series, and in the simple case that $r_t = \text{constant} + \varepsilon_t$ the unexpected return ε_t is just the mean deviation return, because the constant will be the average of returns over the data period. Of course we can put whatever explanatory variables we want in the conditional mean equation of a GARCH model, but should err on the side of parsimony if we want the model estimation procedure to converge properly (see Section 4.3.4). The conditional mean equation $r_t = \text{constant} + \varepsilon_t$ is fairly standard. A GARCH model conditional variance equation provides an easy analytic form for the stochastic volatility process in financial returns. GARCH models differ only because the conditional variance equations are specified in different forms, or because of different assumptions about the conditional distribution of unexpected returns.

In normal GARCH models we assume that ε_t is conditionally normally distributed with conditional variance σ_t^2. The unconditional returns distributions will then be *leptokurtic* — that is, have fatter tails than the normal — because the changing conditional variance allows for more outliers or unusually large observations. However, in high frequency data there may still be insufficient leptokurtosis in normal GARCH to capture the full extent of kurtosis in the data, and in this case a t-distribution could be assumed (Baillie and Bollerslev (1989, 1990)), or a GARCH model defined on a mixture of normals (see Section 4.6).

Square rooting the GARCH conditional variance series, and expressing it as an annualized percentage in the usual way yields a time-varying volatility estimate. But unlike the moving average methods just described, the current estimate is not taken to be the forecast of volatility over all future time horizons. Instead, by first estimating the GARCH model parameters, we can then construct mean-reverting forecasts of volatility as explained in Section 4.3.3. GARCH is sufficiently flexible that these forecasts can be adapted to any time period. For example, when valuing Asian options, volatility options, or measuring risk capital requirements it is often necessary to forecast forward volatility, such as a one-month volatility but in six months time. This flexibility is one of the many advantages of GARCH modelling over the moving average methods just described.

Very many different types of GARCH models have been proposed in the academic literature, but only a few of these have found good practical applications. The Bibliography contains only a fraction of the most useful empirical research papers on GARCH. In the next section we review some of the univariate models that have received the most attention: ARCH, GARCH, IGARCH, AGARCH, EGARCH, Components GARCH and Factor ARCH. There is little doubt that these GARCH volatility models are easy and attractive to use. A summary of their useful applications in financial risk management is given in Section 4.5. However, in a climate where firm-wide risk management is the key, there is a pressing need to model volatilities and correlations in the context of large covariance matrices that cover all the risk factors relevant to the operations of a firm. Unfortunately, it is not easy to use GARCH for large systems. In Section 4.3.7 we look at the problems with direct estimation of high dimensional multivariate GARCH models and propose a new method for generating large GARCH covariance matrices.

4.3.2 A Survey of GARCH Volatility Models

(i) ARCH

The original model of autoregressive conditional heteroscedasticity introduced in Engle (1982) has the conditional variance equation

$$\sigma_t^2 = \alpha_0 + \alpha_1 \varepsilon_{t-1}^2 + \cdots + \alpha_p \varepsilon_{t-p}^2$$

$$\alpha_0 > 0, \quad \alpha_1, \ldots, \alpha_p \geq 0 \tag{9}$$

where the constraints on the coefficients are necessary to ensure that the conditional variance is always positive. This is the ARCH(p) conditional variance specification, with a memory of p time periods. This model captures the conditional heteroscedasticity of financial returns by using a moving average of past squared unexpected returns: if a major market movement in either direction occurred m periods ago ($m \leq p$), then the effect will be to increase today's conditional variance. This means that we are more likely to have a large market move today, so "large movements tend to follow large movements ... of either sign".

(ii) Vanilla GARCH

The generalization of Engle's ARCH(p) model by Bollerslev (1986, 1987) adds q autoregressive terms to the moving averages of squared unexpected returns: it takes the form

$$\sigma_t^2 = \omega + \alpha_1 \varepsilon_{t-1}^2 + \cdots + \alpha_p \varepsilon_{t-p}^2 + \beta_1 \sigma_{t-1}^2 + \cdots + \beta_q \sigma_{t-q}^2$$

$$\omega > 0, \quad \alpha_1, \ldots, \alpha_p, \quad \beta_1, \ldots, \beta_q \geq 0 \tag{10}$$

The parsimonious GARCH(1,1) model, which has just one lagged error square and one autoregressive term, is most commonly used:

$$\sigma_t^2 = \omega + \alpha \varepsilon_{t-1}^2 + \beta \sigma_{t-1}^2$$

$$\omega > 0, \quad \alpha, \beta \geq 0 \tag{11}$$

It is equivalent to an infinite ARCH model, with exponentially declining weights on the past squared errors:

$$\sigma_t^2 = \omega + \alpha \varepsilon_{t-1}^2 + \beta \sigma_{t-1}^2$$
$$= \omega + \alpha \varepsilon_{t-1}^2 + \beta(\omega + \alpha \varepsilon_{t-2}^2 + \beta(\omega + \alpha \varepsilon_{t-3}^2 + \beta(\cdots$$
$$= \omega/(1 - \beta) + \alpha(\varepsilon_{t-1}^2 + \beta \varepsilon_{t-2}^2 + \beta^2 \varepsilon_{t-3}^2 + \cdots)$$

The above assumes that the GARCH(1,1) lag coefficient β is less than 1. In fact, a few calculations show that the unconditional variance corresponding to a GARCH(1,1) conditional variance is

$$\sigma^2 = \omega/(1 - \alpha - \beta) \tag{12}$$

and so not only must the GARCH return coefficient α also be less than 1, but the sum $\alpha + \beta \leq 1$.

In financial markets it is common to find GARCH lag coefficients in excess of 0.7 but GARCH returns coefficients tend to be smaller, usually less than 0.25. The size of these

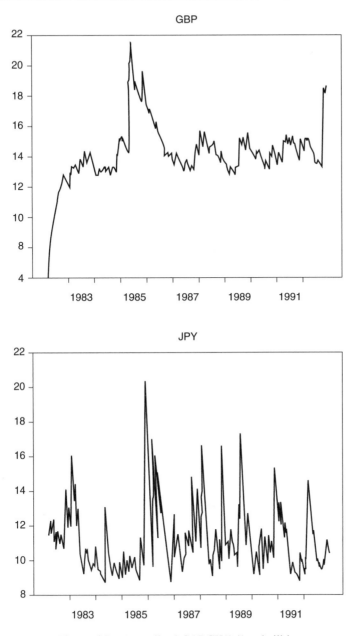

Figure 4.7 Annualized GARCH(1,1) volatilities

parameters determines the shape of the resulting volatility time series: large GARCH lag coefficients indicate that shocks to conditional variance take a long time to die out, so volatility is "persistent"; large GARCH returns coefficients mean that volatility is quick to react to market movements, and volatilities tend to be more "spiky". Figure 4.7 shows US dollar rate GARCH(1, 1) volatilities for Sterling and the Japanese Yen. Cable volatility is more persistent (its lag coefficient is 0.931 compared with 0.839 for the Yen/$) and the Yen/$ is more spiky (its return coefficient is 0.094 compared with 0.052 for Cable).[14] See Alexander (1995) for more details.

The constant ω determines the long-term average level of volatility to which GARCH forecasts converge (see Section 4.3.3). Unlike the lag and return coefficients, its value is quite sensitive to the length of data period used to estimate the model.[15] If a period of many years is used, during which there were extreme market movements, then the estimate of ω will be high. So current volatility term structures will converge to a higher level. Consider, for example, the generation of a GARCH volatility term structure on the FTSE. Long-term average volatility levels in the FTSE were around 13 per cent, but if we include the Black Monday period in the data used to estimate the GARCH model, we would obtain long-term volatility forecasts at around 15 per cent.

(iii) Integrated GARCH

When $\alpha + \beta = 1$ we can put $\beta = \lambda$ and re-write the GARCH(1,1) model as

$$\sigma_t^2 = \omega + (1 - \lambda)\varepsilon_{t-1}^2 + \lambda\sigma_{t-1}^2, \quad 0 \le \lambda \le 1 \tag{13}$$

Note that the unconditional variance (12) is now undefined; indeed, we have a non-stationary GARCH model called the Integrated GARCH (I-GARCH) model, for which term structure forecasts do not converge. Our main interest in the I-GARCH model is that when $\omega = 0$ it is equivalent to an infinite EWMA, such as those used by RiskMetrics[TM]. This may be seen by repeated substitution in (13):

$$\begin{aligned} \sigma_t^2 &= \omega + (1 - \lambda)\varepsilon_{t-1}^2 + \lambda(\omega + (1 - \lambda)\varepsilon_{t-2}^2 + \lambda(\omega + (1 - \lambda)\varepsilon_{t-3}^2 + \lambda(\ldots \\ &= \omega/(1 - \lambda) + (1 - \lambda)(\varepsilon_{t-1}^2 + \lambda\varepsilon_{t-2}^2 + \lambda^2\varepsilon_{t-3}^2 + \cdots) \end{aligned} \tag{14}$$

Currency markets commonly have close to integrated GARCH models, and this has prompted major players such as Salomon Bros to formulate new models for currency GARCH, such as the components GARCH model described below.

(iv) Asymmetric GARCH

The asymmetric GARCH (A-GARCH) model of Engle and Ng (1993) has the conditional variance equation

$$\sigma_t^2 = \omega + \alpha(\varepsilon_{t-1} - \xi)^2 + \beta\sigma_{t-1}^2, \quad \omega > 0, \quad \alpha, \beta, \xi \ge 0 \tag{15}$$

In this model, negative shocks to returns ($\varepsilon_{t-1} < 0$) induce larger conditional variances than positive shocks. Thus the A-GARCH model is appropriate when we expect more volatility following a market fall than following a market rise. This "leverage effect" is a common feature of financial markets, particularly equities.

(v) Exponential GARCH

The non-negativity constraints of the GARCH models considered so far can unduly restrain the dynamics of conditional variances so obtained. Nelson (1991) eliminated the need for such constraints in his exponential GARCH model by formulating the conditional variance equation in logarithmic terms:

$$\log \sigma_t^2 = \alpha + g(z_{t-1}) + \beta \log \sigma_{t-1}^2 \tag{16}$$

where $z_t = \varepsilon_t / \sigma_t$, so z_t is standard normal, and

$$g(z_t) = \omega z_t + \lambda \left(|z_t| - \sqrt{\frac{2}{\pi}} \right) \tag{17}$$

The asymmetric response function $g(\cdot)$, which is illustrated in Figure 4.8, provides the leverage effect just as in the A-GARCH model. Many studies have found that the E-GARCH model fits financial data very well (for example, see Taylor (1994), Heynen et al. (1994), and Lumsdaine (1995)) but it is much more difficult to obtain volatility forecasts using this model.

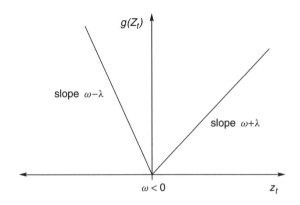

Figure 4.8

(vi) Components GARCH

In practice, estimation of a GARCH model over a rolling data window will generate a term structure of volatility forecasts for each day. In each of these term structures, as volatility maturity increases, GARCH forecasts should converge to a long-term level of volatility (see Section 4.3.3). As the data window is rolled different long-term levels will be estimated, corresponding to different estimates of the GARCH parameters. The components model extends this idea of time-varying "baseline" volatility to allow variation within the estimation period (Engle and Lee (1993) and Engle and Mezrich (1995)).

To understand the components model, note that when $\alpha + \beta < 1$ the GARCH (1,1) conditional variance is often estimated by imposing ω. The model may be written in the form

$$\begin{aligned} \sigma_t^2 &= (1 - \alpha - \beta)\sigma^2 + \alpha \varepsilon_{t-1}^2 + \beta_1 \sigma_{t-1}^2 \\ &= \sigma^2 + \alpha(\varepsilon_{t-1}^2 - \sigma^2) + \beta(\sigma_{t-1}^2 - \sigma^2) \end{aligned} \tag{18}$$

where σ^2 is the long-term variance. We now replace σ^2 by a time-varying permanent component in conditional variance:

$$q_t = \overline{\omega} + \rho(q_{t-1} - \overline{\omega}) + \phi(\varepsilon_{t-1}^2 - \sigma_{t-1}^2) \tag{19}$$

and then the formulation (18) for the conditional variance becomes

$$\sigma_t^2 = q_t + \alpha(\varepsilon_{t-1}^2 - q_{t-1}) + \beta(\sigma_{t-1}^2 - q_{t-1}) \tag{20}$$

Equations (19) and (20) together define the components model. If $\rho = 1$, then the permanent component — to which long-term forecasts mean revert — is just a random walk.

(vii) Factor GARCH

Factor GARCH allows individual volatilities and correlations to be estimated and forecast from a single GARCH volatility — the volatility of the market. In the simple capital asset pricing model, individual asset or portfolio returns are related to market returns M_t by the regression equation

$$r_{it} = \alpha_i + \beta_i M_t + \varepsilon_{it}, \quad i = 1, 2, \ldots, n \tag{21}$$

Denoting by σ_{it} the standard deviation of asset i at time t and by σ_{ijt} the covariance between assets i and j at time t, equation (21) yields

$$\sigma_{it}^2 = \beta_i^2 \sigma_{Mt}^2 + \sigma_{\varepsilon_{it}}^2$$
$$\sigma_{ijt} = \beta_i \beta_j \sigma_{Mt}^2 + \sigma_{\varepsilon_{it}\varepsilon_{jt}} \tag{22}$$

From a simultaneous estimation of the n linear regression equations in (22) we can obtain estimates of the factor sensitivities β_i and the error variances and covariances. These, and the univariate GARCH estimates of the market volatility σ_M, are then used to generate individual asset volatilities and correlations using (22). The idea is easily extended to a model with more than one risk factor, see Engle et al. (1990).

4.3.3 GARCH Volatility Term Structure Forecasts

One of the beauties of GARCH is that volatility and correlation forecasts for any horizon can be constructed from the one estimated model. First, we use the estimated GARCH model to give us forecasts of instantaneous forward volatilities, that is the volatility of r_{t+j}, made at time t and for every step ahead j. The instantaneous GARCH forecasts are calculated analytically: for example, in the GARCH(1,1) model

$$\hat{\sigma}_{t-1}^2 = \hat{\omega} + \hat{\alpha}\varepsilon_t^2 + \hat{\beta}\hat{\sigma}_t^2 \tag{23}$$

and the j-step-ahead forecasts are computed iteratively[16] as

$$\hat{\sigma}_{t+j}^2 = \hat{\omega} + (\hat{\alpha} + \hat{\beta})\hat{\sigma}_{t+j-1}^2 \tag{24}$$

To obtain a term structure of volatility forecasts from these forward volatilities note that the (logarithmic) return at time t over the next n periods is

$$r_{t,n} = \sum_{j=1}^{n} r_{t+j}$$

The volatility term structure is a plot of the volatility of these returns for $n = 1, 2, 3, \ldots$. Since

$$\text{Var}_t(r_{t,n}) = \sum_{i=1}^{n} \text{Var}_t(r_{t+i}) + \sum_i \sum_j \text{Cov}_t(r_{t+i}, r_{t+j}) \tag{25}$$

the GARCH forecast of n-period variance is the sum of the instantaneous GARCH forecast variances, plus the double sum of the forecast autocovariances between returns. This double sum will be very small compared with the first sum on the right-hand side of (25); indeed, in the majority of cases the conditional mean equation in a GARCH model is simply a constant, so returns are independent and the double sum is zero.[17] Hence we ignore the autocovariance term in (25) and construct n-period volatility forecasts simply by adding the j-step-ahead GARCH variance forecasts (and then square-rooting and annualizing in the usual way).[18]

Figure 4.9 shows one-day, 10-day, 30-day, 60-day, and 120-day volatility forecasts for the FTSE from 1988 to 1995. Note how the forecasts of different maturities converge to the long-term volatility level of around 13 per cent. During a volatile period GARCH term structures converge to this level from above (Figure 4.10(a)) and during a tranquil period they converge from below (Figure 4.10(b)).

The speed of convergence in GARCH(1,1) depends on $\alpha + \beta$. Currency markets generally have the highest values of $\alpha + \beta$, and hence the slowest convergence. The speed of convergence in equity and commodity GARCH models tends to be faster, and bond markets often have the lowest $\alpha + \beta$ and the fastest convergence of volatility term structures to the long-term level (see Section 4.3.4).

4.3.4 Estimating GARCH Models: Methods and Results

Most of the models described above are available as pre-programmed procedures in econometric packages such as S-PLUS, TSP, EVIEWS and MICROFIT, and in GAUSS and RATS, GARCH procedures can be written as explained in the manuals. The method used to estimate GARCH model parameters is maximum likelihood estimation, which is a powerful and general statistical procedure, widely used because it always produces consistent estimates.

The idea is to choose parameter estimates to maximize the likelihood of the data under an assumption about the shape of the distribution of the data generation process. For example, if we assume a normal data generation process with mean μ and variance σ^2,

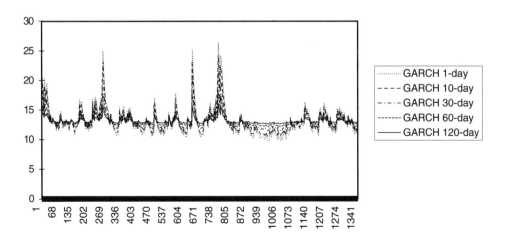

Figure 4.9 GARCH volatility term structure forecasts of the FTSE: 1988–1995

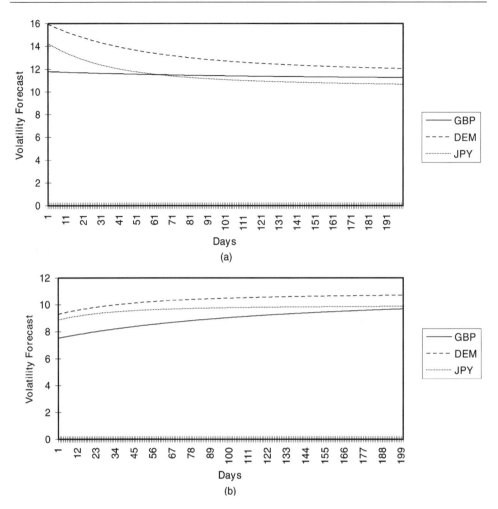

Figure 4.10   GARCH Volatility term structures of US dollar rates (a) on 13 April 1995 and (b) on 2 March 1995

then the likelihood of getting returns $r_1, r_2, \ldots, r_T$ is

$$L(\mu, \sigma^2 | r_1, r_2, \ldots, r_T) = \prod_{t=1}^{T} f(r_t) \tag{26}$$

where

$$f(r) = \frac{1}{\sqrt{2\pi\sigma^2}} \exp\left\{-\frac{1}{2}\left(\frac{r-\mu}{\sigma}\right)^2\right\} \tag{27}$$

Choosing μ and σ^2 to maximize L (or equivalently to minimize $-2\log L$) yields the maximum likelihood estimates of these parameters.

In GARCH models there are more than just two parameters to estimate, and the likelihood functions are more complex but the principle is the same (see, for example, Engle

(1982) and Bollerslev (1986)). Problems arise, though, because the more parameters in the likelihood function the "flatter" it becomes, and therefore more difficult to optimize. For this reason the GARCH(1,1) model is preferred to an ARCH model with a long lag, and parameterizations of conditional mean equations are as parsimonious as possible — often we use just a single constant in the conditional mean.

Convergence problems with GARCH models can arise because gradient search algorithms used to maximize the likelihood functions fall off a boundary. Sometimes this problem can be mitigated by changing the starting values of the parameters,[19] or knocking a few data points off the beginning of the data set so the likelihood function has a different gradient at the beginning of the search. The time taken for GARCH models to converge will be greatly increased unless analytic derivatives are used to calculate the gradient in the search. For leptokurtic data, t-distributed GARCH models have lost ground in favour of normal mixture GARCH models since they require numerical derivatives to be calculated at each iteration.

However, most univariate GARCH models should encounter few convergence or robustness problems if they are well specified. Care should be taken over the re-specification of initial conditions if the coefficient estimates hit a boundary value, and sometimes minor changes in the returns data can induce the occasional odd value of coefficients. These will be evident in rolling GARCH models, where convergence conditions may need re-setting. In some cases the coefficient values take some time to settle down, but once the model is properly tuned to the data it can be updated daily or weekly with few problems.

Table 4.1 gives an idea of what to expect when estimating GARCH(1,1) parameters in some of the major currency and equity markets. Note that very few of these markets have persistence parameters which are as large as the value 0.94 used for the RiskMetrics[TM] data. Of course, the GARCH parameters depend on the data frequency and estimation period, but they should be fairly robust to these differences. When rolling the estimation of a GARCH model day by day, significant changes in the parameters should occur consequent to major market movements only. Bond market GARCH models are more difficult to estimate, particularly since some maturities can be quite illiquid. To estimate

Table 4.1 Approximate GARCH(1,1) parameters for equity markets and US dollar exchange rates

	Alpha	Beta
Equities		
UK	0.105	0.810
GE	0.188	0.712
US	0.271	0.641
JP	0.049	0.935
NL	0.146	0.829
US Dollar Rates		
DEM	0.113	0.747
JPY	0.102	0.763
GBP	0.028	0.935
NLG	0.125	0.735
ESP	0.160	0.597
AUD	0.241	0.674

and forecast volatilities and correlations for an entire yield curve, the orthogonal GARCH model is highly recommended (see Section 4.3.7).

4.3.5 Choosing the Data Period and the Appropriate GARCH Model

The plain "vanilla" GARCH(1,1) model, even without asymmetric or leptokurtic effects, already offers many advantages over the moving average methods described in Section 4.2, and many financial institutions are currently basing their systems on this model. One of the questions that senior management will want to address is whether such a simple GARCH model does the trick. Is it capturing the right type of volatility clustering in the market, or should we be using some sort of complex fractionally integrated GARCH model like the house next door? In this section we show how to diagnose whether you have a good GARCH model or not, and how to employ data to the best advantage.

A test for the presence of ARCH effects in returns is obtained by looking at the autocorrelation in the time series of squared returns. Standard autocorrelation test statistics may be used, such as the Box–Pierce $Q \sim \chi^2(p)$:

$$Q = T \sum_{n=1}^{p} \varphi(n)^2 \tag{28}$$

where $\varphi(n)$ is the nth order autocorrelation coefficient in squared returns:

$$\varphi(n) = \frac{\displaystyle\sum_{t=n+1}^{T} r_t^2 r_{t-n}^2}{\displaystyle\sum_{t=1}^{T} r_t^4} \tag{29}$$

One of the main specification diagnostics in GARCH models is first to standardize the returns by dividing by the estimated GARCH standard deviation, and then to test for autocorrelation in squared standardized returns. If it has been removed, then the GARCH model is doing its job. But what if several GARCH models account equally well for GARCH effects? In that case choose the GARCH model that gives the highest likelihood, either in-sample or in post-sample predictive tests.

The two important considerations in choosing data for GARCH modelling are the data frequency and the data period. It is usual to employ daily or even intra-day data rather than weekly data since convergence problems could be encountered on low frequency data due to insufficient ARCH effects. If tic data are used, then the time bucket should be sufficiently large to ensure that there are no long periods of no trades, and by the same token bank holidays may cause problems so it is often better to deviate from the standard time series practice of using equally spaced daily data, and not fill in the zero returns caused by bank holidays.

When it comes to choosing the amount of historical data for estimating GARCH models, the real issue is whether you want major market events from several years ago to influence your forecasts today. As we have already seen, including Black Monday in equity GARCH models has the effect of raising long-term volatility forecasts by several percent. In the orthogonal GARCH model of Section 4.3.7 it is also important not to take too long a data period, since the principal components are only unconditionally orthogonal so the model will become ill-conditioned if too long a data period is chosen. On the other hand, a certain amount of data is necessary for the likelihood function to be sufficiently well defined. Usually at least one or two years of daily data are necessary to ensure proper convergence of the model.

4.3.6 Multivariate GARCH

Univariate GARCH models commonly converge in an instant, the only real problems being lack of proper specification by the user, or inappropriate data. But there are very serious computational problems when attempting to build large positive definite GARCH covariance matrices which are necessary if one is to net the risks from all positions in a large trading book.

This section reviews the basic multivariate GARCH models, discussing the inevitable computational problems if one attempts direct estimation of full GARCH models in large dimensional systems. The unconditional variance of a multivariate process is a positive definite matrix, the covariance matrix, already defined in the Introduction. The conditional variance of a multivariate process is a time series of matrices, one matrix for each point in time. It is not surprising therefore that estimation of these models can pose problems! The convergence problems outlined in Section 4.3.4 can become insurmountable even in relatively low dimensional systems, so parameterizations of multivariate GARCH models should be as parsimonious as possible. There are many ways that multivariate GARCH can be constrained in order to facilitate their estimation but these methods often fall down on at least one of two counts: either they are only applicable to systems of limited dimension (something like 5–10 factors being the maximum) or they need to make unrealistic assumptions on parameters that are not confirmed by the data (see Engle and Kroner (1995)). However, Section 4.3.7 presents a new method that falls down on neither count. It uses orthogonal approximations to generating arbitrary large GARCH covariance matrices using only univariate GARCH models.

Consider first the bivariate GARCH model, appropriate only if we are just interested in the correlation between two returns series, r_1 and r_2. There will now be two conditional mean equations, which can be anything we like but for the sake of parsimony we shall assume that each equation gives the return as a constant plus error:

$$r_{1,t} = \varphi_{11} + \varepsilon_{1,t}$$

$$r_{2,t} = \varphi_{21} + \varepsilon_{2,t}$$

In a bivariate GARCH model there are three conditional variance equations, one for each conditional variance and one for the conditional covariance. Since all parameters will be estimated simultaneously the likelihood can get *very* flat indeed, so we need to use as few parameters as possible. In this section we introduce the two standard parameterizations of multivariate GARCH models: the vech and the BEKK.

In the vech parameterization each equation is a GARCH(1,1):

$$\sigma_{1,t}^2 = \omega_1 + \alpha_1 \varepsilon_{1,t-1}^2 + \beta_1 \sigma_{1,t-1}^2$$

$$\sigma_{2,t}^2 = \omega_2 + \alpha_2 \varepsilon_{2,t-1}^2 + \beta_2 \sigma_{2,t-1}^2 \tag{30}$$

$$\sigma_{12,t} = \omega + \alpha_3 \varepsilon_{1,t-1} \varepsilon_{2,t-1} + \beta_3 \sigma_{12,t-1}$$

As usual, constraints on the coefficients in (30) are necessary to ensure positive definiteness of the covariance matrices. To obtain time series of GARCH correlations we simply divide the estimated covariance by the product of the estimated standard deviations, at every point in time (see Figure 4.11).

When considering systems with more than two returns series, we need matrix notation. The matrix form of equations (30) is

$$\text{vech } (\mathbf{H}_t) = \mathbf{A} + \mathbf{B} \text{ vech } (\xi_{t-1}\xi'_{t-1}) + \mathbf{C} \text{ vech } (\mathbf{H}_{t-1}) \tag{31}$$

where $\mathbf{H}_t$ is the conditional variance matrix at time t. So vech $(\mathbf{H}_t) = (\sigma_{1t}^2, \sigma_{2t}^2, \sigma_{12t})'$, and $\xi_t = (\varepsilon_{1t}, \varepsilon_{2t})'$, $\mathbf{A} = (\omega_1, \omega_2, \omega_3)'$, $\mathbf{B} = \text{diag}(\alpha_1, \alpha_2, \alpha_3)$ and $\mathbf{C} = \text{diag}(\beta_1, \beta_2, \beta_3)$, with the obvious generalization to higher dimensions.

There are severe cross equation restrictions in the vech model, for example the conditional variances are not allowed to affect the covariances and vice versa. In some markets these restrictions can lead to substantial differences between the vech and BEKK estimates, so the vech model should be employed with caution.

A more general formulation, which involves the minimum number of parameters whilst imposing no cross equation restrictions and ensuring positive definiteness for any parameter values, is the BEKK model (after Baba, Engle, Kraft and Kroner who wrote the preliminary version of Engle and Kroner (1995)). This parameterization is given by

$$\mathbf{H}_t = \mathbf{A}'\mathbf{A} + \mathbf{B}'\xi_{t-1}\xi_{t-1}{}'\mathbf{B} + \mathbf{C}'\mathbf{H}_{t-1}\mathbf{C} \tag{32}$$

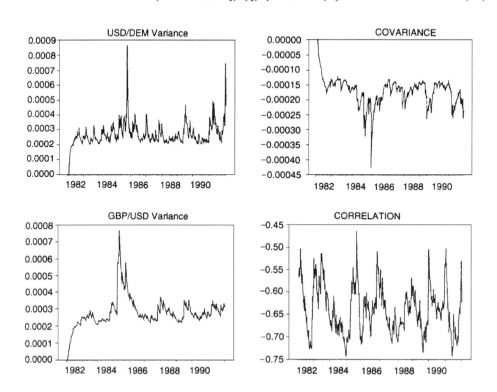

Figure 4.11   Calculation of GARCH correlation

where **A**, **B** and **C** are general $n \times n$ matrices (**A** is triangular). The BEKK parameterization for a bivariate model involves 11 parameters, only two more than the vech. But for higher dimensional systems the extra number of parameters increases, and completely free estimation becomes very difficult indeed. Often it is necessary to let **B** and **C** be scalar matrices, to reduce the number of parameters needing estimation and so improve the likelihood surface and, hopefully, achieve convergence. More details are given in Bollerslev et al. (1992, 1994).

A useful technique for calibrating multivariate GARCH is to compare the multivariate volatility estimates with those obtained from direct univariate GARCH estimation. The multivariate GARCH volatility term structure forecasts are computed as outlined in Section 4.3.4, and correlation forecasts are calculated in a similar fashion: simply by iterating conditional covariance forecasts and summing these to get n-period covariance forecasts.[20] These are then divided by the product of n-period volatility forecasts for correlation term structures:

$$\rho_{t,n} = \sigma_{12,t,n} / \sigma_{1,t,n} \sigma_{2,t,n}$$

4.3.7 Generating Large GARCH Covariance Matrices: Orthogonal GARCH

The computations required to estimate very large GARCH covariance matrices by direct methods are simply not feasible at the present time. However, indirect "orthogonalization" methods can be used to produce the large covariance matrices necessary to measure risk in large portfolios. This method is introduced, explained and verified for all major equity, currency and fixed income markets by Alexander and Chibumba (1997).

In orthogonal GARCH the risk factors from all positions across the entire firm are first divided into reasonably highly correlated categories, according to geographic locations and instrument types. Principal components analysis is then used to orthogonalize each sub-system of risk factors, univariate GARCH is applied to the principal components to obtain the (diagonal) covariance matrix, and then the factor weights from the principal components analysis are used to "splice" together the large covariance matrix for the whole enterprise.

An example explaining the method for just two risk factor categories can easily be extrapolated to any number of risk factor categories. Suppose $\mathbf{P} = (P_1, \ldots, P_n)$ are the principal components of the first system (n risk factors) and let $\mathbf{Q} = (Q_1, \ldots, Q_m)$ be the principal components of the second system (m risk factors).[21] Denote by **A** ($n \times n$) and **B** ($m \times m$) the factor weights matrices of the first and second systems. Within-factors covariances are given by $\mathbf{AV(P)A'}$ and $\mathbf{BV(Q)B'}$, respectively, and cross factor covariances are $\mathbf{ACB'}$, where **C** denotes the $m \times n$ matrix of covariances of principal components.

An illustration of this method applies to a system of equity indices and US dollar (USD) exchange rates (Alexander (1997a)). The system is just small enough to compare the "splicing" method with full multivariate GARCH estimation and Figure 4.12 shows one of the resulting correlations obtained by each method—between the GBP/USD exchange rate and the Nikkei during the period 1 January 1993 to 17 December 1996.

Some care must be taken with the initial calibration of orthogonal GARCH, but once calibrated it is a useful technique for generating large GARCH covariance matrices, with all the advantages offered by these models. It is particularly useful for yield curves, where the more illiquid maturities can preclude the direction estimation of GARCH volatilities.

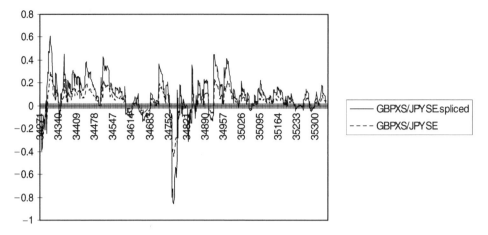

Figure 4.12 Comparison of orthogonal GARCH and BEKK correlations between the Cable rate and the Nikkei index: 1993–1996

The orthogonal method not only provides estimates for maturities with inadequate data, but a substantial reduction in dimensionality is also possible.

The factors that must be taken into account when calibrating an orthogonal GARCH are the time period used for estimation, and the sub-division into risk factor categories. For example, if a market that has very idiosyncratic properties is taken into a sub-system of risk factor categories, then the volatilities and correlations of all other markets in the system will be erroneously affected. Therefore one has to compare the volatilities and correlations obtained by direct GARCH, EWMA, or option implieds with those obtained from the orthogonal GARCH, to ensure successful calibration of the model.

4.4 "IMPLIED" VOLATILITY AND CORRELATION

Implied volatility and correlation are those volatilities and correlations that are implicit in the prices of options. When an explicit analytic pricing formula is available such as the Black–Scholes formula (see *Risk Management and Analysis. Volume 2: New Markets and Products*, Chapter 2) the quoted prices of these products, along with known variables such as interest rates, time to maturity, exercise prices and so on, can be used in an implicit formula for volatility. The result is called the implied volatility. It is a volatility forecast — not an estimate of current volatility — the volatility forecast that is implicit in the quoted price of the option, with an horizon given by the maturity of the option.

Although they forecast the same thing (the volatility of the underlying assets over the life of the option) implied volatilities must be viewed differently from statistical volatilities because they use different data and different models.[22] If the option pricing model were an accurate representation of reality, and if investors' expectations were correct so that there is no over- or under-pricing in the options market, then any observed differences between implied and statistical volatility would reflect inaccuracies in the statistical forecast. Alternatively, if statistical volatilities are correct, then differences between the implied and statistical measures of volatility would reflect a mispricing of the option. In fact, rather than viewing implied volatility and statistical methods as complementary forecasting procedures, when implied volatilities are available they should be taken along-side the statistical forecasts. For example, in the "volatility cones" described below, or in Salomon Brothers "Gift" (GARCH index forecasting tool) the relationship between implied volatility and GARCH volatility is used to predict future movements in prices (see Chew (1993)).

4.4.1 Black–Scholes Implied Volatility

The Black–Scholes formula for the price of a call option with strike price K and time to maturity t on an underlying asset with current price S and t-period volatility σ is

$$C = SN(x) - Ke^{-rt}N(x - \sigma\sqrt{t}) \tag{33}$$

where r denotes the "risk-free" rate of interest, $N(\cdot)$ is the normal distribution function and

$$x = \ln(S/Ke^{-rt})/\sigma\sqrt{t} + \sigma\sqrt{t}/2$$

Option writers would estimate a statistical volatility and use the Black–Scholes or some other option model to price the option. But if C is observed from the market, and so also are S, K, r and t, then (33) may be used instead to "back-out" a volatility implied by the model. This is called the (Black–Scholes) implied volatility, σ. Options of different strikes and maturities on the same underlying attract different prices, and therefore different implied volatilities. A plot of these volatilities against strike price and maturity is called the "volatility smile" (see Figure 4.13).

Long-term options have little variation in prices, but as maturity approaches it is typical that out-of-the-money options would imply higher volatility in the underlying than at-the-money options, otherwise they would not be in the market. Thus, implied volatility is often higher for out-of-the-money puts and calls than for at-the-money options, an effect which is termed the "smile". Equity markets exhibit a "leverage effect", where volatility is often

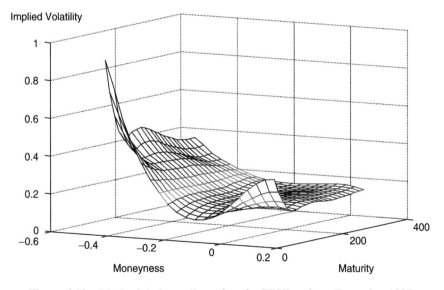

Figure 4.13   Black–Scholes smile surface for FTSE options, December 1997

higher following bad news than good news (see Section 4.3.2(iv)). Thus out-of-the money puts require higher volatility to end up in-the-money than do out-of-the-money calls, and this gives rise to the typical "skew" smiles of equity markets, such as in Figure 4.13.

The volatility smile is a result of pricing model bias, and would not be found if options were priced using appropriate stochastic volatility models (see Dupire (1997)). For example, when options are priced using the Black–Scholes formula, which assumes lognormal prices, we observe volatility smiles because empirical returns distributions are not normal. Most noticeable in currency markets, returns distributions have much fatter tails than normal distributions, so out-of-the-money options have more chance of being in-the-money than is assumed under Black–Scholes. This underpricing of the Black–Scholes model compared with observed market behaviour yields higher Black–Scholes implied volatilities for out-of-the-money options.

"Volatility cones" are graphic representations of the term structure of volatility, used for visual comparison of current implied volatility with an empirical historical distribution of implied volatilities. To construct a cone, fix a time to maturity t and estimate a frequency distribution of implied volatility from all t-maturity implied volatilities during the last two years (say), recording the upper and lower 95 per cent confidence limits. Repeat for all t. Plotting these confidence limits yields a cone-like structure because the implied volatility distribution becomes more peaked as the option approaches maturity (see *Risk Management and Analysis. Volume 2: New Markets and Products*, Chapter 9). Cones are used to track implied volatility over the life of a particular option, and under- or over-shooting the cone can signal an opportunity to trade. Sometimes cones are constructed on "historic" volatility because historic data on implied volatility may be difficult to obtain. In this case cones should be used with caution, particularly if over-shooting is apparent at the long end. Firstly, differences between long-term "historic" and implied volatility are to be expected, since transactions costs are included in the implied volatilities but not the statistical. But also the Black–Scholes bias, which tends to under-price ATM options and over-price OTM options, can increase with maturity.

4.4.2 Implied Correlation

The increase in derivatives trading in OTC markets enables implied correlations to be calculated from three implied volatilities by rearrangement of the formula for the variance of a difference: if we denote by ρ the correlation between x and y, then

$$\sigma^2_{x-y} = \sigma^2_x + \sigma^2_y - 2\sigma_x\sigma_y\rho$$

or

$$\rho = \frac{\sigma^2_x + \sigma^2_y - \sigma^2_{x-y}}{2\sigma_x\sigma_y} \qquad (34)$$

Putting implied volatilities in formula (34) gives the associated implied correlation–we just need traded options on three associated assets or rates X, Y and $X - Y$. For example, X and Y could be two USD FX rates (in logarithms) so $X - Y$ is the cross rate. In the above formulae, the implied correlation between the two FX rates is calculated from the implied volatilies of the two USD rates σ_x and σ_y and the implied volatility of the cross rate σ_{x-y}.

Similar calculations can be used for equity implied correlations: assuming the corre-lation between all pairs of equities in an index is constant allows this correlation to be approximated from implied volatilities of stocks in the index (see Kelly (1994)). Of course, the assumption is very restrictive and not all equities will be optionable, so the approximation is very crude and can lead to implied correlations that are greater than 1. Another way in which implied correlations can be obtained is by inverting the quanto pricing formula. When we know the quanto price, the interest rate, the equity and FX implied volatilities and so on, we can invert the Black–Scholes quanto pricing formula to obtain an implied correlation between the equity and the FX rate.

There are a limited number of ways in which implied correlations can be backed out from option prices, and even when it is possible to obtain such implied correlations, they will be very unstable. Not only are the underlying correlations often unstable, but with implied correlations there are a number of model assumptions that may be questionable. In short, these correlations should be used with even more caution than implied volatilities.

4.5 A SHORT SURVEY OF APPLICATIONS TO MEASURING MARKET RISK

4.5.1 Factor Models

Simple factor models describe returns to an asset or portfolio in terms of returns to risk factors and an idiosyncratic or "specific" return. For example, in the simple Capital Asset Pricing Model (CAPM) the return to a portfolio, denoted r_t, is approximated by the linear regression model

$$r_t = \alpha + \beta R_t + \varepsilon_t$$

where R_t is the return to the market risk factor, the error process ε_t denotes the idiosyncratic return and β denotes the sensitivity (or "beta") of the portfolio to the risk factor. Standard regression models would then estimate this beta by the ratio of the covariance (between the portfolio and the risk factor) to the variance of the risk factor:

$$\beta = \text{Cov}(r, R)/\text{Var}(R)$$

Thus beta is the relative volatility times the correlation between the risk factor and the portfolio. Although relative volatilities may be quite stable, the same cannot be said of the correlation. This means that portfolio betas tend to jump around quite a bit, although this will not be apparent if equally weighted averaging methods are used to estimate them.[23] But this is the case in standard ordinary least squares (OLS) regression. Many analytics firms will be using OLS for their betas, so their estimates just reflect an average beta over whatever data period is used for their estimation. If, on the other hand, we use a time-varying estimate such as EWMA or GARCH for the covariance and variance (as in Kroner and Claessens (1991)) the beta estimate will more accurately reflect current market conditions.

Figure 4.14 shows the time-varying beta for the National Westminster (NatWest) Bank in the FTSE, calculated using an exponentially weighted moving average for correlation and the volatility of the FTSE. It shows significant variation from day to day, ranging from less than 0.2 to over 2, and many other stocks have *negative* betas from time to time. Unfortunately, many analytics firms still employ equally weighted averages in the OLS procedures commonly used to calculate market betas, so they provide only an average of the beta during the estimation period. Clearly this can produce very inaccurate measures of the current beta when compared with time-varying methods.

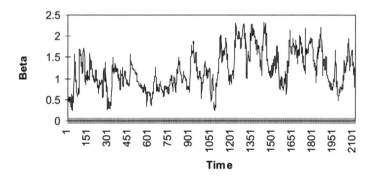

Figure 4.14   EWMA time-varying beta for NatWest bank vs. the FTSE: 1985–1991

More generally, in multivariate factor models, portfolio returns are attributed to several risk factors: the portfolio return is given by

$$r_t = \alpha + \beta_1 R_{1t} + \beta_2 R_{2t} + \cdots + \beta_n R_{nt} + \varepsilon_t$$

where $R_1, \ldots, R_n$ are the returns to different risk factors, $\beta_1, \ldots, \beta_n$ are the net port-folio sensitivities (i.e. the weighted sum of the individual asset sensitivities) and ε is the idiosyncratic or specific return of the portfolio (i.e. that part of the return not attributed to the different risk factors). The net betas with respect to each risk factor can be calculated from the covariances (between risk factors and between the portfolio and risk factors) and the variances of the risk factors. We denote by $\mathbf{X}$ the $T \times n$ matrix of data on the risk factors and by $\mathbf{y}$ the $T \times 1$ vector of data on the portfolio returns. Then we estimate β as the inverse of the covariance matrix between risk factors, times the vector of covariances between the portfolio and the risk factors:

$$\beta = (\mathbf{X'X})^{-1}\mathbf{X'y}$$

Again, time-varying methods for calculating these variances and covariances should be employed in order to obtain a true reflection of current market conditions. The use of OLS in factor models is a major source of error, which has implications for risk management whenever these models are used: in mean–variance analysis, in VaR models, and in other methods for capital allocation.

4.5.2 Capital Allocation

Suppose first that capital allocation decisions are made on the basis of risk characteristics alone. The standard problem is of choosing a vector of weights $\mathbf{w} = (w_1, \ldots, w_n)$ in a portfolio to minimize its variance (although variance is not necessarily the best measure of risk — see Dembo (1997) and Chapter 7 of this volume). In mathematical notation:

$$\min_{\mathbf{w}} \quad \mathbf{w'Vw} \quad \text{such that} \quad \Sigma w_i = 1$$

where $\mathbf{V}$ is the covariance matrix of asset returns. Assuming that weights can be negative or zero this is a straightforward linear programming problem, having the solution

$$w_i = \psi_i / \Sigma \psi_i \text{ where } \psi_i = \Sigma i\text{th column of } \mathbf{V}^{-1}$$

Remarks about the appropriate use of covariance matrices **V** are made below. For example, we may take **V** to be a time-varying covariance matrix such as the GARCH matrix. This will give time-varying weights $w^*_{i,t}$ that can be used to re-balance the portfolio within certain limits as volatilities and correlations between the assets change.

However, capital allocation decisions made on the basis of risk alone may be inappropriate since the return characteristics are ignored. More risk may be acceptable if it is accompanied by higher returns, and managers are in danger of under-utilizing capital if insufficient capital is allocated to high-risk high-return activities. Hence capital allocation is commonly viewed within the framework of risk–return analysis. The problem is to allocate capital between assets $\mathbf{R} = (R_1, \ldots, R_n)'$ with optimal weights $\mathbf{w} = (w_1, \ldots, w_n)'$. Efficient allocations lie on the "efficient frontier", where it is not possible to adjust allocations $w_1, \ldots, w_n$ to gain higher return for the same level of risk, or less risk for the same level of return (see Figure 4.15). Assuming markets are efficient, so that it is not possible to gain return for no risk, the optimal allocation for a risk-neutral investor will be at the point X in Figure 4.15, and the risk-adjusted return on capital is given by the reciprocal of the slope of the tangent at that point.

In simple portfolios, which can be described by a weighted sum of the constituent assets, the current return to the portfolio is $\mathbf{w}'\mathbf{R}$, where $\mathbf{w}$ is the vector of portfolio weights and $\mathbf{R}$ is the vector of asset returns. The portfolio risk is commonly measured as variance, although this has its drawbacks, as described in Chapter 7. The portfolio variance is $\mathbf{w}'\,\mathbf{V}\,\mathbf{w}$, where $\mathbf{V}$ is the covariance matrix of $\mathbf{R}$.[24] In larger linear portfolios, which are best described not at the asset level but by the factor models described above, the portfolio variance is measured using the covariance matrix of risk factor returns and the vector of sensitivities to different risk factors. If we ignore the idiosyncratic risk, the portfolio return is $\beta'\mathbf{R}$ and its variance is simply $\beta'\mathbf{V}\beta$, where β is the vector of net portfolio sensitivities and $\mathbf{V}$ is the covariance matrix of risk factor returns. Both $\mathbf{V}$ and β are obtained from variances and covariances, and again the remarks already made about the dangers of using equally weighted measures for these apply. The problem is that covariance matrices, and in particular correlations, are often unstable. This instability may be masked by inappropriate use of equally weighted averages (see Section 4.2.1), but when more realistic measures such as EWMA or GARCH are used, the efficient frontier, and

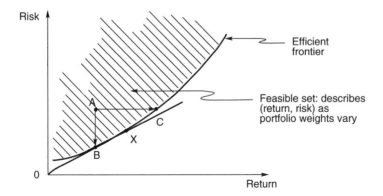

Figure 4.15 Efficient frontier. Portfolio A is not efficient since either less risk is possible for the same return (portfolio B) or greater return is possible for the same risk (portfolio C). The efficient frontier is the set of efficient (return, risk) pairs

hence also the optimal capital allocation, may vary significantly as correlations change. This implies that efficient portfolios chosen according to risk–return analysis may need constant re-balancing to remain optimal. Realistic transactions costs should therefore be factored into this type of capital allocation framework.

4.5.3 Option Pricing and Hedging

There are many basic applications of volatility and correlation to pricing and hedging options. For example:

1. Statistical forecasts of average volatility and/or correlation over the life of an option can be "plugged" into the closed form solution (e.g. into the Black–Scholes formula for vanilla options).
2. Volatilities and correlations are used in numerical option pricing methods (lattices, partial differential equations).
3. The covariance matrix is used to simulate correlated risk factor returns for a terminal price distribution (see Chapter 5).
4. In two-factor models, where the underlying price process has stochastic volatility (see Hull and White (1987)).

This section outlines some uses of GARCH models in option pricing and hedging. First consider an example of the fourth application above: a simulation method for an option based on a single risk factor where a GARCH model is employed in a two-factor model with stochastic volatility. To fix ideas, it will be seen in Chapter 5 how simulation can be used to price and hedge a call option on an underlying price $S(t)$ which follows the Geometric Brownian Motion diffusion:

$$d S(t)/S(t) = \mu \, dt + \sigma \, dZ$$

where Z is a Wiener process. Since volatility σ is constant this is a one-factor model, and it is only necessary to use Monte Carlo on the independent increments dZ of the Wiener process to generate price paths $S(t)$ over the life of the option. This is done on the discrete form of Geometric Brownian Motion,[25] namely

$$S_t = S_{t-1} \exp(\mu - 0.5\sigma^2 + \sigma z_t)$$

where $z_t \sim \text{NID}(0,1)$. So, starting from the current price S_0, Monte Carlo simulation of an independent series on z_t for $t = 1, 2, \ldots, T$ will generate a terminal price S_T. Thousands of these terminal prices should be generated starting from the one current price S_0, and the discounted expectation of the option pay-off function gives the price of the call. For example, for a plain vanilla option

$$C(S_0) = \exp(-rT)\text{E}(\max\{S - K, 0\})$$

where r is the risk-free rate, T the option maturity and K is the strike. So from the simulated distribution $S_{T,i}$ ($i = 1, \ldots, N$) of terminal prices we get the estimated call price:

$$\hat{C}(S_0) = \exp(-rT) \left(\sum_i \max\{S_{T,i} - K, 0\}/N \right)$$

Simulation deltas and gammas are calculated using finite difference approximations, such as the central differences

$$\delta = [C(S_0 + \eta) - C(S_0 - \eta)]/2\eta$$

$$\gamma = [C(S_0 + \eta) - 2C(S_0) + C(S_0 - \eta)]/\eta^2$$

In this example, with constant volatility GBM for the simulations, the delta and gamma should be the same as those obtained using the Black–Scholes formula. But in practice, simulation errors can be very large unless the time is taken to run large numbers of simulations for each option price.[26]

Now consider how to extend the standard GBM model to a two-factor model, where the second factor is GARCH(1,1) stochastic volatility.[27] The two diffusion processes in discrete time are

$$S_t = S_{t-1} \exp(\mu - 0.5\sigma_t^2 + \varepsilon_t)$$

$$\sigma_t^2 = \omega + \alpha\varepsilon_{t-1}^2 + \beta\sigma_{t-1}^2$$

where $\varepsilon_t = \sigma_t z_t$. Starting with current price S_0 and unconditional standard deviation σ_0, an independent set of Monte Carlo simulations on z_t ($t = 0, 1, \ldots, T$) will now generate σ_t at the same time as S_t for $t = 1, \ldots, T$. Note that the simulated price paths are already based on expected volatility levels, so the GARCH delta and gamma hedge ratios do not require additional vega hedging (see Duan (1993) and Engle and Rosenberg (1995)).[28]

GARCH models can also be used to forecast option prices from the volatility smile. The idea is to estimate the GARCH parameters using cross-section data on the market implied smile surface, and then the dynamics of the GARCH model can be used to predict the smile. Initial values for the GARCH model parameters are fixed, and then GARCH option prices obtained, as explained above, for options of different strikes and maturity. These prices are put into the Black–Scholes formula, and the GARCH "implied" volatility is then backed out of the formula (just as one would do with ordinary market implied volatilities, only this time the GARCH price is used instead of the price observed in the market). Comparison of the GARCH smile surface with the observed market smile surface leads to a refinement of the GARCH model parameters (that is, iteration on the root mean square error between the two smiles) and so the GARCH smile is fitted. It turns out that the GARCH parameters estimated this way are very similar to those obtained from time series data, so using the GARCH smile to predict future smiles leads to sensible results (see Duan (1996)).

4.5.4 Value-at-Risk Models

Value at Risk (VaR) has become central to financial decision making — not just for risk managers and regulators, but for anyone concerned with the actual numbers produced: traders, fund managers, corporate treasuries, accountants, etc. Not only is capital set aside for regulatory compliance on the basis of these measures, but such things as trading limits or capital allocation decisions may be set. Providing accurate VaR measures therefore becomes a concern for many.

VaR is the level of loss that is expected to be exceeded, in normal market circumstances, if the portfolio is left unmanaged during a fixed holding period. Since we cannot state this level with certainty, we must provide a measure of confidence associated with this figure. For example, a 1 per cent 10-day VaR of $10,000 means that if the portfolio is not managed for 10 days, in normal market circumstances we would be 99 per cent sure that we would not lose more than $10 000.

A VaR measure depends on two parameters, the holding period h and the significance level α (0.01 in the above example). A good VaR report should provide a convergent and consistent sequence of VaR measures for every holding period from one day (or even less than a day) to several years. Uncertainties generally increase with time, so the VaR measure will increase as the holding period increases. However, the significance level is just a matter of personal choice: is it relevant to reflect potential losses one day in 20 ($\alpha = 0.05$) or one day in 100 ($\alpha = 0.01$)? The VaR measure will of course increase with its associated significance level. Current recommendations of the Basle committee are that 1 per cent VaR measures, calculated over a holding period of 10 working days, are used to calculate capital reserves for the central banks.

Two of the VaR models in common use ("covariance" methods for linear portfolios and Monte Carlo methods for options portfolios) require an accurate, positive definite covariance matrix. The "covariance" method is commonly referred to as the "RiskMetrics" method, since it was popularized by J.P. Morgan in their RiskMetrics[TM] database. This, and other common methods for calculating VaR, are described fully in Chapter 3. In this section we only give a brief overview of the two methods that employ covariance matrices.

We denote by ΔP_t the forecast P&L over the next h days and by μ_t and σ_t^2 its mean and variance. A mathematical formulation of VaR is that number x such that

$$Pr(\Delta P_t < -x) = \alpha$$

That is, the VaR is the lower 100α per cent quantile of the P&L distribution. The covariance method assumes P&Ls are conditionally normally distributed, and in that case we have[29]

$$\text{VaR} = z_\alpha \sigma_t - \mu_t$$

where z_α denotes the critical value from the standard normal distribution corresponding to the choice of significance level. It is often assumed that μ_t is zero,[30] and z_α is just looked up in tables, so the sole focus of this method is on σ_t, the standard deviation of forecast P&L over the holding period. This is given by

$$\sigma_t^2 = \mathbf{p}'\mathbf{V}\mathbf{p}$$

where $\mathbf{V}$ is the covariance matrix of asset returns (or risk factor returns) over the holding period and $\mathbf{p}$ is a vector of the current mark-to-market values of the assets (or the current mark-to-market values of the risk factors times their respective sensitivities or cash flows amounts).[31] Since $\mathbf{V}$ is the main stochastic part of the covariance VaR model[32] it is important to obtain good estimates of the parameters in $\mathbf{V}$, i.e. the variance and covariance forecasts of asset (or factor) returns over the holding period. For example, the model may give zero or negative VaR measures if $\mathbf{V}$ is not positive definite.[33]

The covariance method is subject to a number of errors, or inappropriate usage. For example, factor models may be misspecified, sensitivities or covariances may be inaccurately measured, and the assumption of normality may be violated. Also it is only applicable to linear portfolios, and the obvious non-linearities of options pay-offs have prompted the BIS to require different methods for VaR in options portfolios. An example of the inappropriate use of this linear method is given in Figure 4.16. It shows the P&L

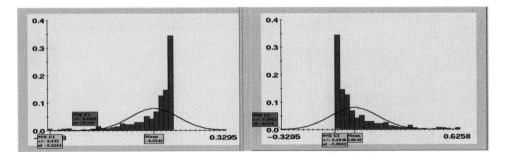

Figure 4.16   VaR of a single barrier option using covariance and simulation methods
© Algorithmics Inc.

distribution of a barrier option, where the covariance method would give the same 1 per
cent one-day VaR whether long or short the position ($0.26 in both cases). A simulation
method, such as "historical" or Monte Carlo simulation, would give a much more accurate
measure of VaR ($0.05 for the short and $0.63 for the long).[34]

VaR measures for options portfolios may be calculated using Monte Carlo methods to
simulate a more realistic distribution of P&Ls over the forthcoming holding period than
that which would be obtained using normal approximations. To calculate this distribution,
correlated vectors of underlying returns are simulated over the holding period. These are
generated by first simulating independent returns to the risk factors and then applying the
Cholesky decomposition of the covariance matrix of returns to the underlyings to obtain
correlated paths for risk factors,[35] as illustrated in Figure 4.17.

Each set of correlated simulations — e.g. each yield curve in Figure 4.17 — gives one
value of the portfolio at the end of the holding period. Lots of such curves are simulated
and then used to calculate a simulated P&L distribution from which the VaR measure can
be read off directly as the lower 100α per cent quantile, as in Figure 4.18.

Many financial institutions are using the "historic simulation" method for computing
VaR, which has many advantages — and limitations. Since this method does not employ
covariance matrices, it is not discussed here, but is fully described in Chapter 3.

The main problem with simulation VaR methods is the time it takes to re-value the
portfolio for each simulation of the underlying factors. There are two ways in which

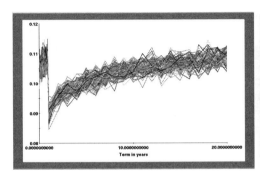
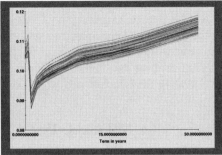

Figure 4.17   Uncorrelated and correlated yield curve scenarios.
© Algorithmics Inc.

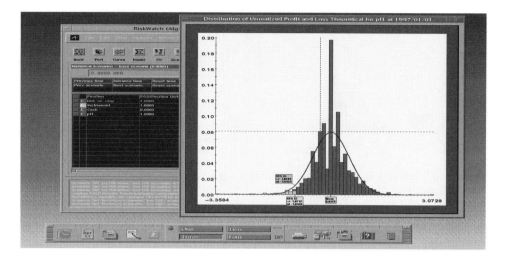

Figure 4.18   Simulated P&L distribution showing VaR compared with normal curve VaR.
© Algorithmics Inc.

computational time can be reduced. First, advanced sampling techniques such as low-discrepancy sequences may be applied to reduce the number of simulations required (see Chapter 5). Secondly, a form of portfolio compression may be used: for example, delta–gamma approximations could be used instead of full portfolio re-valuation at each stage, or the portfolio may be replicated using more simple instruments that are quick to re-value (as in the Algorithmics product RiskWatch™).

The current emphasis on integrated risk systems, to measure VaR across all the risk positions of a large bank, requires very large covariance matrices. How should these be constructed? Regulators currently require the use of at least one year of historic data, so exponentially weighted moving average methods are ruled out.[36] Currently there are only two realistic alternatives: equally weighted moving averages or GARCH. Direct multivariate GARCH models of enterprise-wide dimensions would be computationally impossible. One way that one can construct large dimension covariance matrices using GARCH is to employ the orthogonal GARCH model. However, much care should be taken over the calibration of the orthogonal GARCH model, as outlined in Section 4.3.7. Equally weighted moving average covariance matrices are easy to construct, and should be positive definite (assuming no linear interpolation of data along a yield curve) but these forecasts will be contaminated by any stress events which may have occurred during the last year, as already explained in Section 4.2.1. Therefore the stress events should be filtered out of the data before the moving average is applied, and saved for later use when investigating the effect of real stress scenarios on portfolio P&Ls.

4.6 SPECIAL ISSUES AND NEW DIRECTIONS

4.6.1 Evaluating Volatility and Correlation Forecasts

It is not unusual to read statements such as "... we employ fractionally integrated GARCH volatilities because they are more accurate". But the accuracy of volatility forecasts is extremely difficult to assess. Results will depend on the method of evaluation employed, so no single answer can be given to the question: which method is more accurate? Assessing the accuracy of correlation forecasts is an even more difficult problem, not only because correlations can be so unstable, but also because a proper statistical evaluation requires the full multivariate distribution to be known — which it is not.

If one decides to embark on the treacherous path of forecast evaluation, the first point to note is that different models should be ranked according to how they perform according to a certain benchmark. But problems arise when applying this type of ranking: unlike prices, volatility is unobservable, so what should the volatility benchmark be? I would consider taking the unconditional standard deviation over a very long data period as the benchmark against which to test different volatility forecasting models. If a model cannot improve upon this simplest of models there is no point in using any greater degree of sophistication!

The next problem along the route of evaluating a volatility model is: what do we mean by "better"? Is it preferable to use a statistical evaluation criterion or to assess models purely on a P&L basis, when possible? Much research has been published in this area, mostly on statistical evaluation, because this has a greater degree of subjectivity (Alexander and Leigh (1997), Brailsford and Faff (1996), Dimson and Marsh (1990), Figlewski (1994), Tse and Tung (1992), and West and Cho (1995)). P&L evaluations are based on specific trading metrics so this type of operational evaluation is quite objective — and it is difficult to come to any broad conclusions.

If statistical evaluation is used it should be emphasized that however well a model fits *in-sample* (i.e. within the data period used to estimate the model parameters) the real test of its forecasting power is in *out-of-sample* predictive tests. A certain amount of historic data should be withheld from the period used to estimate the model, and then forecasts made from the model may then be evaluated by comparing them to the out-of-sample returns data. The appropriate statistical criteria to use is the maximization of out-of-sample likelihoods, but the effectiveness of this method relies on correct specification of the returns distributions. Some of the literature uses *root mean square errors* to evaluate volatility and correlation forecasts, since this is a simple distance metric, not based on a statistical distribution of returns which in many cases is erroneously assumed to be normal.[37]

Alexander and Leigh (1997) look at both statistical and operational evaluation of the three types of volatility forecasts which are in standard use: equally weighted moving averages, exponentially weighted moving averages and GARCH. Given the remarks just made, it is impossible to draw any firm conclusions about the relative effectiveness of any volatility forecasting method for an arbitrary portfolio. But, using data from the major equity indices and foreign exchange rates during 1996 it appears that whilst EWMA methods perform well for predicting the "centre" of a normal distribution, the GARCH and equally weighted moving average methods are generally more accurate for the "tails" prediction required by VaR models.

4.6.2 Modelling "Fat-Tailed" Distributions

One way of retaining normality assumptions whilst allowing for "fat-tails" is to model returns distributions using mixtures of normals. Mixtures of normals with different variances generate leptokurtic distributions, and if means are also allowed to vary, then this will capture the skewness or multi-modal nature of some portfolio returns distributions (see Figure 4.19).[38]

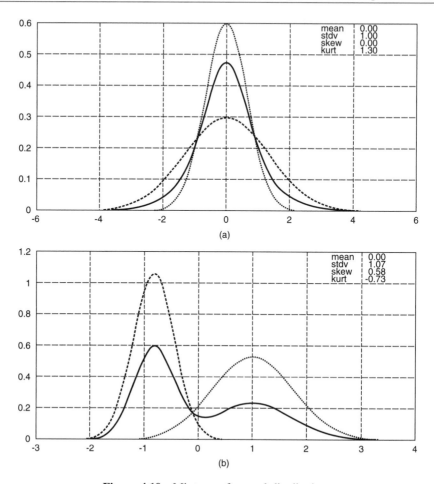

Figure 4.19 Mixtures of normal distributions

Hull and White (1997, 1998) have developed a model for estimating mixtures of two normal distributions with constant parameters. Their means are both assumed to be zero, and their standard deviations are $u\sigma_t$ and $v\sigma_t$, where $u < 1$, $v > 1$ and σ_t is the standard deviation of market returns at time t. In the empirical work of Hull and White, on 12 major US dollar exchange rates between 1988 and 1994, σ_t is either assumed constant or an exponentially weighted moving average estimate of σ_t is obtained (for example, using RiskMetrics^{TM} data). The proportions of the two normals in the mixture are assumed constant through time, denoted p and $1 - p$, respectively, so that

$$pu^2 + (1 - p)v^2 = 1 \qquad (35)$$

Hull and White propose a maximum likelihood method to estimate the model parameters which are consistent with (35). Direct maximization of the likelihood of the normal mixture is not robust to outliers, so the empirical data are divided into four categories: the first category consists of returns that are less than one standard deviation, the second category contains returns that are between one and two standard deviations, the third category of returns is between three and four standard deviations and the fourth is for those returns more than four standard deviations. A maximum likelihood method is employed where p, u and v are chosen to match the observed number of returns in each category with the predicted number of returns from the normal mixture in that category. Results are tested out-of-sample using standard diagnostics. The model fits better when EWMA rather than constant volatilities are assumed, and when parameters are estimated for individual exchange rates rather than using the same parameters for all. It has natural extensions to modelling correlations and the calculation of VaR using simulation techniques. Further details are given in Hull and White (1998).

Another robust statistical technique for estimating mixtures of normals is with a neural network that trains on the whole likelihood function rather than the simple error surface used in standard neural networks packages. Many neural networks output only a single vector, and back-propagation is then used to minimize the root mean square error of the output, compared with the actual data in the training set. But minimizing a root mean square error is equivalent to maximum likelihood estimation of the mean of a single normal distribution with constant variance, and is therefore very restrictive. Packaged neural networks also have the reputation of fitting well in sample, but predicting poorly out-of-sample. This can be due to over-fitting the data: a neural network is a universal approximator, and so needs to be constrained in its complexity if sufficient flexibility is to be retained for generating future scenarios.

A method for constraining complexity which is more advanced than simply cutting off the network after a certain point, is to use a penalized likelihood function where the value of the in-sample likelihood is offset by an amount proportional to the number of weights and connections in the network. In Williams (1995, 1996) a network is trained by maximizing the likelihood function of a normal mixture. The training is automatically regularized to avoid over-fitting, by using a penalized likelihood function to estimate weights and biases. Simulation of the conditional returns distributions from such a neural network then produces term structure forecasts of all the moments of the normal mixture — including the variance, skewness and kurtosis. Alexander and Williams (1997) show that for US dollar exchange rates, kurtosis term structures generated by this neural network are much closer to empirically expected levels than the GARCH kurtosis term structures, although their volatility term structures are similar.

4.6.3 Downside Risk and Expected Maximum Loss

One of the problems with using variance to measure "risk" is that it does not distinguish between upside and downside risk — that is, positive returns and negative returns are regarded as equally unfavourable. Short-term hedging based on mean–variance analysis without frequent re-balancing can lead to very skewed distributions of longer-term returns (see Section 4.6.4) and for these portfolios the standard variance operator is totally inadequate. A risk measure that focuses purely on downside risk, proposed by Markovitz, is the semi-variance

$$SV = E(\min(0, r - E(r))^2)$$

When returns are greater than average, $\min(0, r - E(r)) = 0$, so only below-average returns are counted in this risk measure. Many software and data providers are now incorporating more flexibility into their risk measures, including some measure of downside risk such as semi-variance (see Chapter 2).

Algorithmics Inc. have patented an optimizer based on "regret", a well-known concept from the decision sciences, which is similar to semi-variance. Returns are measured relative to a benchmark B, which can be empirically defined, or simulated, based on user requirements. The regret of a portfolio is given by

$$regret = -E(\min(0, r - B))$$

Portfolios that appear to have similar risk attributes when standard variance or VaR is employed can be distinguished by their regret. If variance is concentrated on the "upside", then the regret is small, but "bad" portfolios with distributions that are skewed on the downside will have large regret. The use of the benchmark also has attractive applications in many areas of allocation and risk measurement, see Chapter 7 for more details.

Finally, we mention briefly a risk measure that focuses on the actual decisions faced by risk managers. VaR only gives the frequency with which a fixed loss (or worse) should occur, but risk managers are more likely to be concerned with the nature of losses — are they consecutive small losses or intermittent large ones? What is the maximum loss I can expect to incur from this portfolio during a given holding period? Both these questions are addressed with a risk measure called "expected maximum loss" (Acar and Prieul (1997)). By utilizing more information about the dynamic nature of returns, this risk measure can be usefully employed in the simultaneous allocation of capital and setting of trading limits.

4.6.4 Cointegration

Cointegration has had an astounding impact on applied economic modelling during the last decade. Since the seminal work of Engle and Granger (1987), the many thousands of papers published on the theory and application of cointegration to economics bears testimony to the huge resources now devoted to this approach. Every modern econometrics textbook will contain details of the statistical theory necessary to master the application of cointegration to time series data.

However, the financial community has been less aware of the potential for cointegration modelling. Traditionally, a portfolio risk analysis takes as its starting point the distribution of financial returns, so the log price, rate or yield data are differenced before the analysis is even begun. This removes any long-term trends in the price, rate or yield data and, although these trends are implicit in the returns data, the analysis of any common trends (cointegration) in the raw data is often precluded.

Cointegration and correlation are related, but different, concepts. Correlation measures co-movements in returns, so it is intrinsically a short-run measure, liable to instabilities over time since returns typically have low autocorrelation. Cointegration measures long-run co-movements in prices (rates or yields) and high correlation of returns does not necessarily imply high cointegration in prices. An example is given in Figure 4.20, with a 10-year daily series on US dollar spot exchange rates of the German mark (DEM) and the Dutch guilder (NLG) from, say, 1975 to 1985. Their returns are very highly correlated: the correlation coefficient is approximately 0.98 (Figure 4.20(a)). Also, the rates move together over long periods of time, and they appear to be cointegrated (Figure 4.20(b)). Now suppose that we add a very small daily incremental return of, say, 0.0002 to NLG. The returns on this NLG "plus" and the DEM still have a correlation of 0.98,

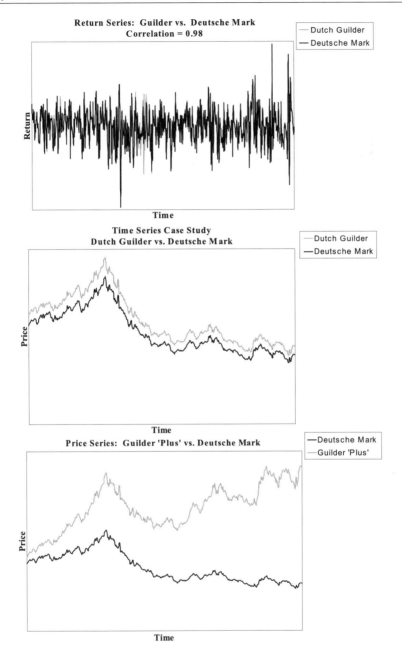

Figure 4.20   (a) NLG and DEM returns; (b) NLG and DEM rates; (c) NLG "plus" vs. DEM

but the price series diverge more and more as time goes on — they are not cointegrated (Figure 4.20(c)).[39]

To introduce cointegration we first define the notion of an *integrated* series. An example of an integrated series is a random walk

$$y_t = \alpha + y_{t-1} + \varepsilon_t$$

where α denotes the drift and the error process ε_t is an independent and identically distributed (i.i.d.) stationary process.[40] If financial markets are efficient, then prices (or log prices), rates or yields are all random walks. In the random walk model we could take $y_t = \log P_t$, where P_t is a financial price series, and in this case ε_t denotes the return at time t.

Now if returns are stationary i.i.d. processes, then log prices are random walks, but what if returns are not i.i.d., because they are not independent and there is some autocorrelation in returns? Provided returns are still stationary, log prices will be an integrated series of order 1. A time series is integrated of order 1, denoted I(1), if the stochastic part is non-stationary, but it is stationary after first differencing.[41]

Two or more integrated series are termed "cointegrated" if there is a weighted sum of these series (called the *cointegrating vector*) which is stationary. Consider a simple case: x and y are random walks, but $x-y$ is stationary. This means that x and y cannot drift too far apart, because $x-y$ is stationary, mean-reverting. So cointegrated series are "tied together" by the cointegrating vector in the long run, even though they can drift apart in the short run.

The mechanism that ties cointegrated series together is a "causality" — not in the sense that if we make a structural change to one series the other will change too, but in the sense that turning points on one series precede turning points in the other. This is called *Granger causality* (see Engle and Granger (1987)). The strength and directions of Granger causality can change over time, there can be bi-directional causality, or the direction of causality can change. For example, in the "price discovery" relationship between spot and futures there may be times when futures lead spot, whereas at other time spot prices can lead futures prices. The necessity for causality between cointegrated series is revealed by the *error correction model*, which is a dynamic model of returns where deviations from the long-run equilibrium are corrected. More details may be found in Alexander and Johnson (1992, 1994) and in any standard econometrics text.

Consider two cointegrated series. Each is individually a random walk, which means that given enough time they could be anywhere (because they have infinite unconditional variance) and the best forecast of any future value is the value today. But since they are cointegrated we know that, wherever one series is in x years time, the other series will be right there along with it.

When only two integrated series are considered for cointegration, there can be at most one cointegrating vector, because if there were two cointegrating vectors the original series would have to be stationary. More generally, taking n series in cointegration analysis, the maximum number of cointegrating vectors is $n - 1$. Each cointegrating vector is a "bond" in the system, and so the more cointegrating vectors found the more the coherence and co-movements in the prices. Yield curves have very high cointegration; if each of the $n - 1$ independent spreads is mean-reverting, then there are $n - 1$ cointegrating vectors.

Examples of cointegrated series abound in financial markets:

- Spot and futures prices: If spot and futures prices are tied together, then the basis can never get too large–it will be mean-reverting. The basis is the cointegrating vector (see Beck (1994) and Schwarz and Szakmary (1994)).
- Yields of different maturities: Yields are random walks–they could be anywhere given enough time. But wherever the one-month yield is in x years time, the three-month yield will be right along there with it, because the spread can never get too large.

The spreads are mean-reverting, so they are the cointegrating vectors (see Bradley and Lumpkin (1992) and Hall et al. (1992)).

- Any pair of series with a mean-reverting spread: For example two different equity indices (or bond indices) or pairs of bond and equity indices in the same country can be cointegrated, but they are not always so. It depends on the time series properties of the spread (see Alexander (1995), Alexander and Thillainathan (1996), and Clare et al. (1995)).

- Related commodities: Carry costs represent the difference in prices between related commodities. If carry costs are mean-reverting, then commodities based on the same underlying market will be cointegrated (see Brenner and Kroner (1995)).

- Equities within an index: Since the index is, by definition, a weighted sum of the constituents, there should be some sufficiently large basket that is cointegrated with the index. The cointegrating vector is the tracking error between that basket and the index. Baskets found by cointegration will have mean-reverting tracking errors, so the basket cannot drift away from the index, they are "tied together" in the long run (see Alexander (1999)).

4.7 CONCLUSION

This chapter has covered a very wide subject area, which is of central importance for effective measurement of market risks. It is a very active area for both practical and academic research, and in places the chapter gives only a brief indication of the key issues, but with supporting references for further reading whenever possible.

The first part of the chapter provides a critical overview of some of the most commonly used methods for estimating volatility and correlation: moving averages and GARCH models. Common pitfalls in the use of these models are explained, and the chapter should provide the reader with enough information to employ these statistical models appropriately for market risk measurement.

After a short discussion of implied volatility and correlation, its calculation and use in trading and risk management, the chapter has focused on the main applications of volatility and correlation for market risk systems. Special issues, such as the use of GARCH models in option pricing and smile fitting, and the proper implementation of covariance matrices in Value at Risk models, have been explored. The chapter closes with an overview of some of the key areas of current research: in particular we have examined the use of alternative risk measures such as regret and cointegration for market risk analysis.

4.8 ACKNOWLEDGEMENTS

I wish to thank Dr Aubrey Chibumba of Citibank, UK; Dr Ian Giblin of Pennoyer Capital Management, US; Christopher Leigh of CAL-FP Bank, UK; Wayne Weddington of Pennoyer Capital Management, US; and Dr Peter Williams of the University of Sussex, UK. Also a huge thank you to Dr Ron Dembo of Algorithmics Inc., from whose vision I have benefited enormously, and to Professor John Hull of University of Toronto, Canada, for his encouragement and support. Figures 4.16, 4.17 and 4.18 reproduced by permission of Algorithmics Inc.

4.9 ENDNOTES

1. Returns are given by the relative change in prices (or rates) over a fixed holding period h. The return at time t is given by $(P_t - P_{t-h})/P_{t-h}$ which, for small h, is well approximated by $\ln P_t - \ln P_{t-h}$. Value at Risk (VaR) is, however, based on the volatility of a portfolio's change in market price (the profit and loss, P&L). Both returns and P&L are generally stationary (mean reverting) variables. But some confusion may be caused by the term "price volatility", since prices (or rates) are random walks in efficient markets, and hence have infinite (unconditional) variance.

2. We use the notations Var (for variance) and σ^2 interchangeably, similarly Cov(x, y) and σ_{xy}. The standard deviation is the square root of the variance. Conditional and unconditional variance are explained in Section 4.3.1.

3. Loosely speaking, this means that not only are the two individual returns series stationary (mean reverting), but their joint distribution has stationarity properties such as constant auto-correlations.

4. It is important to bear in mind that returns series can be perfectly correlated even when the prices are in fact moving in opposite directions. Correlation only measures short-term co-movements in returns, and has little to do with any long-term co-movements in prices. For the common trend analysis in prices, rates or yields the technique of *cointegration* offers many advantages, and this is reviewed in the final section of the chapter.

5. It is usual to apply moving averages to squared returns r_t^2 ($t = 1, 2, 3 \ldots, n$) rather than squared mean deviations of returns $(r_t - \bar{r})^2$, where $\bar{r}$ is the average return over the data window. Although standard statistical estimates of variance are based on mean deviations, empirical research on the accuracy of variance forecasts in financial markets has shown that it is often better not to use mean deviations of returns, but to base variances on squared returns and covariances on cross products of returns (Figlewski (1994), Alexander and Leigh (1997)).

6. Again assuming zero means is simpler, and there is no convincing empirical evidence that this degrades the quality of correlation estimates and forecasts in financial time series.

7. For this reason I suggest removing extreme events from the returns data before the moving average is calculated. This will give a better "everyday" volatility estimate, for example, in VaR models. For stress-testing portfolios, these extreme events can be put back into the series; indeed, they could even be bootstrapped back into the series for more creative stress-testing.

8. This is a limitation of moving average methods. When the estimation method also gives a model for stochastic volatility (as it does, for example, in GARCH models) the stochastic volatility model has very useful applications for pricing and hedging (see Sections 4.5.2 and 4.5.3)

9. In fact all the RiskMetrics™ matrices have low rank — either because EWMA use insufficient data for the size of matrix, or because of the linear interpolation of yield curve data.

10. As long ago as 1963 Benoit Mandlebrot observed that financial returns time series exhibit periods of volatility interspersed with tranquillity, where "Large returns follow large returns, of either sign...".

11. For excellent reviews of the enormous literature on GARCH models in finance see Bollerslev et al. (1992, 1994).

12. The unconditional mean of a stationary time series y is a single number, a constant. It is denoted $E(y)$ or μ, and is usually estimated very simply by the sample mean. On the other hand, the conditional mean varies over time, and is commonly measured by a linear regression model. The conditional mean is denoted $E_t(y_t)$ or μ_t or $E(y_t|\Omega_t)$, where Ω_t is the *information set* available at time t (so Ω_t includes y_{t-1} and any other values that are known at time t).

13. The unconditional variance of a stationary time series y is a constant, denoted Var(y) or σ^2. It is often estimated by a moving average, as explained in the previous section. On the other hand, the conditional variance σ_t^2 is often denoted Var$_t(y_t)$ or Var$_t(y_t|\Omega_t)$. Like the conditional mean, its estimates will form a time-varying series.

14. These are slightly different from the values given in Table 4.1, because first they use daily data (Table 4.1 exchange rates are based on weekly data), and secondly a different data estimation period is used.

15. For this reason it is common to impose a value of $\omega = (1 - \alpha - \beta)\sigma^2$ from equation (12), using an unconditional volatility estimate for σ^2.

16. We only know the unexpected return at time t, not ε_{t+j} for $j > 0$. But $E(\varepsilon_{t+j}^2) = \sigma_{t+j}^2$.

17. Even in an AR(1)–GARCH(1,1) model (with autocorrelation coefficient ρ in the conditional mean equation) (25) becomes

$$\hat{\sigma}_{t,n}^2 = \sum_{i=1}^{n} \hat{\sigma}_{t+1}^2 + \hat{\sigma}_t^2 [\rho(1 - \rho^n)/(1 - \rho)]^2$$

and the first term clearly dominates the second.

18. In this way we can also construct any sort of forward volatility forecasts, such as three-month volatility, but for a period starting six months from now.

19. The starting value $\sigma_0 = 0$ can produce features at the beginning of the estimation period such as those in the Cable and DEM rates in Figures 4.7 and 4.11.

20. To see this, note that

$$\text{Cov}_t(r_{1,t,n}, r_{2,t,n}) = \sum_{i,j=1}^{n} \text{Cov}_t(r_{1,t+i}, r_{2,t+j})$$

Ignoring non-contemporaneous covariances gives

$$\hat{\sigma}_{12,t,n} = \sum_{i=1}^{n} \hat{\sigma}_{12,t+i}$$

21. One of the advantages of principal components analysis is to reduce dimension, and this is certainly an attractive proposition for the yield curve (see Chapter 5 in *Risk Management and Analysis. Volume 2: New Markets and Products*), or for systems when the reduction in "noise" obtained by using only a few principal components makes correlations more stable. However, it is the orthogonality property of principal components that is the primary attraction here, and if one does not retain the full number of principal components, then we cannot ensure positive definiteness of the final covariance matrix.

22. Implied methods use current data on market prices of options and so implied volatility contains all the forward expectations of investors about the likely evolution of the underlying. Statistical methods use only historic data on the underlying asset price. Apart from differences in data, the mathematical models used to generate these quantities are totally different: implied methods assume risk neutrality and use a diffusion process for the underlying asset price; statistical methods assume stationarity and use a random walk model for prices.

23. It is exactly the same problem of "ghost features", which have already been described with respect to "historic" volatilities and correlations, that makes market betas appear more stable than they really are.

24. Provided **V** is a positive definite matrix, the portfolio risk will always be positive, whatever the weights in the portfolio.

25. To derive this from the continuous form use Ito's lemma on $\log S$ and then make time discrete.

26. Simulation errors are reduced by using correlated random numbers — the variance of delta estimates is reduced when $C(S_0 + \eta)$ and $C(S_0 - \eta)$ are positively correlated.

27. Note that moving average methods do not yield stochastic volatility models and so these methods cannot be used to generate option prices and hedge ratios which already account for stochastic volatility.

28. Note that in a world with stochastic volatility a perfect hedge does not always exist, so the risk-neutral pricing assumption that underlies this method does not, in fact, hold.

29. Apply the standard normal transformation to ΔP_t.

30. However, this may be an unrealistic assumption for insurance companies, corporates and pension funds, who commonly look at very long holding periods in VaR. In this case, an exogenously determined mean P&L may be used to offset the final VaR figure.

31. Large portfolios of cash or futures will be represented either as a linear model of risk factor returns, or as a map in cash-flow space. The **p** vector is $(w_1\mathbf{p}_1, w_2\mathbf{p}_2, \ldots, w_n\mathbf{p}_n)$, where $\mathbf{p}_i$

are the MTM values of the n risk factors ($I = 1, \ldots, n$). In the linear factor model w_i is the sensitivity of the portfolio to the ith risk factor. In the cash-flow model the w_i are the amount invested in the ith risk factor.

32. But the accurate measurement of sensitivites is also crucial, as explained earlier in this section.
33. The RiskMetrics™ data are not always positive definite. See Alexander (1996a).
34. Many thanks to Algorithmics Inc. for permitting the use of Figures 4.16, 4.17 and 4.18.
35. If r is a vector of standard independent returns, and $C'C = V$, where C is the (triangular) Cholesky matrix, then $C'r$ is a vector of returns with variance–covariance matrix V. If the covariance matrix is not positive semi-definite, then the Cholesky decomposition does not exist. So what can be done with the non-positive semi-definite matrices, produced by RiskMetrics™? *Ad hoc* methods — such as shooting the negative or zero eigenvalues to something small and positive — must be resorted to. Unfortunately, this changes the original covariance matrix in an arbitrary way, without control over which volatilities and correlations are being affected.
36. Unless one tailors the tolerance level to the smoothing constant. For example, a smoothing constant of 0.9 would mean that 250 days of past data are taken into account for the EWMA if the tolerance level is 10^{-12}.
37. As a statistical criterion the root mean square error criterion comes from a normal likelihood function — minimizing the sum of squared differences between the actual observations and the predicted means will maximize the normal likelihood when volatility is constant (see (27)). Hence root mean square errors are applicable to *mean* predictions rather than variance or covariance predictions. Of course, a variance is a mean, but the mean of the *squared* random variable, which is chi-squared distributed, not normally distributed, so the likelihood function is totally different and does not involve any sum of squared errors.
38. Many thanks to Peter Williams of Sussex University for providing these figures.
39. Many thanks for Wayne Weddington of Pennoyer Capital Management for providing these figures.
40. A (covariance) stationary series has constant, finite mean and variance, and an autocorrelation that depends only on the lag. The constant, finite variance implies that stationary series are "mean-reverting". Typically, financial returns data are stationary. We use the notation $I(n)$ to denote a series which is non-stationary, and only stationary after differencing a minimum of n times. Stationary series are denoted $I(0)$, and random walks are $I(1)$.
41. Series with deterministic trends are not integrated, they are $I(0) +$ trend. If a deterministic trend is removed from a random walk, than the result is another random walk, without a drift term. Thus standard technical analysis methods of "detrending" data by fitting a line are not removing the stochastic trend, and the result will be a random walk and not a mean-reverting series.

4.10 REFERENCES

Acar, E. and Prieul, D. (1997) "Expected maximum loss". *NetExposure*, 1 (www.netexposure.co.uk)

Alexander, C. (1994) "History debunked". *RISK*, 7, no. 12, 59–63.

Alexander, C. (1995) "Common volatility in the foreign exchange market". *Applied Financial Economics*, 5, no. 1, 1–10.

Alexander, C. (1996a) "Evaluating RiskMetrics as a risk measurement tool for your operation: What are its advantages and limitations?". *Derivatives: Use, Trading and Regulation*, 2, no. 3, 277–285.

Alexander, C. (ed.) (1996b) *The Handbook of Risk Management and Analysis*. Chichester: John Wiley and Sons.

Alexander, C. (1997a) "Splicing methods for generating large covariance matrices". *Learning Curve of Derivatives Week*, 3, 140–142.

Alexander, C. (1997b) "Estimating and forecasting volatility and correlation: methods and applications", in S. Das (ed.), *Risk Management and Financial Derivatives: A Guide to the Mathematics*. LBC Publications, pp. 337–354.

Alexander, C. (1999) "Optimal hedging of international equity portfolios using cointegration". Forthcoming in *Philosophical Transactions of the Royal Society* special issue on Imperfect Markets.

Alexander, C. and Chibumba, A. (1997) "Orthogonal GARCH: An empirical validation in equities, foreign exchange and interest rates". Mimeo.

Alexander, C. and Giblin, I. (1997) "Multivariate embedding methods: Forecasting high-frequency data in the first INFFC". *Journal of Computational Intelligence in Finance*, **5**, no. 6, 17–24.

Alexander, C. and Johnson, A. (1992) "Are foreign exchange markets really efficient?". *Economics Letters*, **40**, 449–453.

Alexander, C. and Johnson, A. (1994) "Dynamic Links". *RISK*, **7**, no. 2, 56–61.

Alexander, C. and Leigh, C. (1997) "On the covariance matrices used in VaR models". *Journal of Derivatives*, **4**, 50–62.

Alexander, C. and Riyait, N. (1992) "The world according to GARCH". *RISK*, **5**, no. 8, 120–125.

Alexander, C. and Thillainathan, R. (1996) "The Asian connections". *Emerging Markets Investor*, **2**, no. 6, 42–47.

Alexander, C. and Williams, P. (1997) "Modelling the term structure of kurtosis: A comparison of neural network and GARCH methods". Mimeo.

Andersen, T.G. (1994) "Stochastic autoregressive volatility: A framework for volatility modelling". *Mathematical Finance*, **4**, no. 2, 75–102.

Baillie, R.T. and Bollerslev, T. (1989) "The message in daily exchange rates: A conditional-variance tale". *Journal of Business and Economic Statistics*, **7**, no. 3, 297–305.

Baillie, R.T. and Bollerslev, T. (1990) "Intra-day and inter-market volatility in foreign exchange rates". *Review of Economic Studies*, **58**, 567–585.

Beck, S.E. (1994) "Cointegration and market efficiency in commodities futures markets". *Applied Economics*, **26**, no. 3, 249–257.

Bollerselv, T. (1986) "Generalised autoregressive conditional heteroskedasticy". *Journal of Econometrics*, **31**, 307–327.

Bollerslev, T. (1987) "A conditional heteroskedasticity time series model for security prices and rates of return data". *Review of Economics and Statistics*, **69**, 542–547.

Bollerslev, T. (1988) "On the correlation structure for the generalised autoregressive conditional heteroskedastic process". *Journal of Time Series Analysis*, **9**, 121–131.

Bollerslev, T., Chou, R.Y. and Kroner, K.F. (1992) "ARCH modeling in finance". *Journal of Econometrics*, **52**, 5–59.

Bollerslev, T., Engle, R.F. and Nelson, D. (1994) "ARCH models", in R.F. Engle and D.L. McFadden (eds), *Handbook of Econometrics*, Volume 4. Amsterdam: North-Holland, 2959–3038.

Bradley, M. and Lumpkin, S. (1992) "The Treasury yield curve as a cointegrated system". *Journal of Financial and Quantitative Analysis*, **27**, 449–463.

Brailsford, T.J. and Faff, R.W. (1996) "An evaluation of volatility forecasting techniques". *Journal of Banking and Finance*, **20**, 419–438.

Brenner, R.J. and Kroner, K.F. (1995) "Arbitrage, cointegration, and testing the unbiasedness hypothesis in financial markets". *Journal of Financial and Quantitative Analysis*, **30**, no. 1, 23–42.

Brenner, R.J., Harjes, R.H. and Kroner, K.F. (1996) "Another look at alternative models of the short term interest rate". *Journal of Financial and Quantitative Analysis*, **31**, no. 1, 85–108.

Cerchi, M. and Havenner, A. (1988) "Cointegration and stock prices". *Journal of Economic Dynamics and Control*, **12**, 333–346.

Chew, L. (1993) "Summer of content". *RISK*, **6**, no. 8, 28–35.

Chowdhury, A.R. (1991) "Futures market efficiency: Evidence from cointegration test". *The Journal of Futures Markets*, **11**, no. 5, 577–589.

Clare, A.D., Maras, M. and Thomas, S.H. (1995) "The integration and efficiency of international bond markets". *Journal of Business Finance and Accounting*, **22**, no. 2, 313–322.

Dembo, R. (1997) "Value at Risk and return". *NetExposure*, **1** (www.netexposure.co.uk).

Dickey, D.A. and Fuller, W.A. (1979) "Distribution of the estimates for autoregressive time series with a unit root". *Journal of the American Statistical Association*, **74**, 427–429.

Dimson, E. and Marsh, P. (1990) "Volatility forecasting without data-snooping". *Journal of Banking and Finance*, **14**, 399–421.

Duan, J.C. (1993) "The GARCH option pricing model". *Mathematical Finance*, **4**, no. 2, 13–32.

Duan, J.C. (1996) "Cracking the smile". *RISK*, **9**, 55–59.

Dupire, B. (1997) "A unified theory of volatility". Mimeo.

Dwyer, G.P. and Wallace, M.S. (1992) "Cointegration and market efficiency". *Journal of International Money and Finance*, **11**, 318–327.

Engle, R.F. (1982) "Autoregressive conditional heteroscedasticity with estimates of the variance of United Kingdom inflation". *Econometrica*, **50**, no. 4, 987–1007.

Engle, R.F. (ed.) (1995) *ARCH: Selected Readings*, Advanced Texts in Econometrics. Oxford University Press, Oxford.

Engle, R.F. and Granger, C.W.J. (1987) "Co-integration and error correction: representation, estimation, and testing". *Econometrica*, **55**, no. 2, 251–276.

Engle, R.F. and Lee, G. (1993) "A permanent and transitory component model of stock return volatility". Mimeo.

Engle, R.F. and Kroner, K.F. (1995) "Multivariate simultaneous generalized ARCH". *Econometric Theory*, **11**, 122–150.

Engle, R.F. and Mezrich, J. (1995) "Grappling with GARCH". *RISK*, **8**, no. 9, 112–117.

Engle, R.F. and Ng, V. (1993) "Measuring and testing the impact of news on volatility". *Journal of Finance*, **48**, 1749–1778.

Engle, R.F. and Rosenberg, J. (1995) "GARCH-Gamma". *Journal of Derivatives*, **2**, no. 4, 47–59.

Engle, R.F., Ng, V. and Rothschild, M. (1990) "Asset pricing with a factor ARCH covariance structure: Empirical estimates for treasury bills". *Journal of Econometrics*, **45**, 213–238.

Figlewski, S. (1994) "Forecasting volatility using historical data". New York University Salomon Center (Leonard N. Stern School of Business) Working Paper Series no. S-94-13.

Hall, A.D., Anderson, H.M. and Granger, C.W.J. (1992) "A cointegration analysis of Treasury bill yields". *The Review of Economics and Statistics*, 116–126.

Heynen, R., Kemna, A. and Vorst, T. (1994) "Analysis of the term structure of inplied volatilities". *Journal of Financial and Quantitative Analysis*, **29**, no. 1, 31–56.

Ho, T., Chen, M. and Eng, F. (1996) "VaR analytics: Portfolio structure, key rate convexities and VaR betas". *Journal of Portfolio Management*, **23**, no. 3, 89–98.

Hull, J. and White, W. (1987) "The pricing of options on assets with stochastic volatilities". *Journal of Finance*, **42**, 281–300.

Hull, J. and White, A. (1997) "Evaluating the impact of skewness and kurtosis on derivatives prices". *NetExposure*, **3**, (www.netexposure.co.uk).

Hull, J. and White, A. (1998) "Value at Risk when daily changes are not normally distributed". *Journal of Derivatives*, **5**, no. 3, 9–19.

Johansen, S. and Juselius, K. (1990) "Maximum likelihood estimation and inference on cointegration — with applications to the demand for money". *Oxford Bulletin of Economics and Statistics*, **52**, no. 2, 169–210.

Jorion, P. (1996a) *Value at Risk: The New Benchmark for Controlling Market Risk*. Homewood: Irwin.

Jorion, P. (1996b) "Risk2: Measuring the risk in VaR". *Financial Analysts Journal*.

J.P. Morgan, (1996) RickMetrics™, Technical Document, 3rd edn. (www.jpmorgan.com).

Kelly, M. (1994) "Stock answer". *RISK*, **7**, no. 8, 40–43.

Kroner, K.F. and Claessens, S. (1991) "Optimal dynamic hedging portfolios and the currency composition of external debt". *Journal of International Money and Finance*, **10**, 131–148.

Kroner, K.F., Kneafsey, D.P. and Claessens, S. (1993) "Forecasting volatility in commoditiy markets". World Bank Policy Research Paper 1226.

Kroner, K.F. and Sultan, J. (1991) "Exchange rate volatility and time varying hedge ratios". *Pacific-Basin Capital Markets Research*, **II**, 397–412.

Lumsdaine, R.L. (1995) "Finite sample properties of the maximum likelihood estimation in GARCH(1,1) and IGARCH(1,1) models: A Monte Carlo investigation". *Journal of Business and Economic Statistics*, **13**, no. 1, 1–10.

Magdon-Ismail, M. and Abu-Mostafa, Y.S. (1996) "Validation of volatility models". Caltech Discussion Paper.

Nelson, D.B. (1991) "Conditional heteroskedasticity in asset returns: A new approach". *Econometrica*, **59**, no. 2, 347–470.

Schwarz, T.V. and Szakmary, A.C. (1994) "Price discovery in petroleum markets: Arbitrage, coin-tegration, and the time interval of analysis". *Journal of Futures Markets*, **14**, no. 2, 147–167.

Taylor, S.J. (1994) "Modelling stochastic volatility". *Mathematical Finance*, **4**, no. 2, 183–204.

Tse, Y.K. and Tung, S.H. (1992) "Forecasting volatility in the Singapore stock market". *Asia Pacific Journal of Management*, **9**, 1–13.

Wang, G.H.K. and Yau, J. (1994) "A time series approach to testing for market linkage: Unit root and cointegration tests". *Journal of Futures Markets*, **14**, no. 4, 457–474.

West, K.D. and Cho, D. (1995) "The predictive ability of several models of exchange rate volatility". *Journal of Econometrics*, **69**, 367–391.

Williams, P. (1995) "Bayesian regularization and pruning using a Laplace prior". *Neural Computation*, **7**, 117–143.

Williams, P. (1996) "Using neural networks to model conditional multivariate densities", *Neural Computation*, **8**, 843–854.

5

Simulation for Option Pricing and Risk Management

MARK BROADIE AND PAUL GLASSERMAN

5.1 INTRODUCTION

Three broad classes of methods are used to price derivatives and measure their risks: formulas, deterministic numerical methods (including binomial trees and partial differential equation methods), and Monte Carlo simulation. Moving from each of these categories to the next expands the class of models encompassed but can also represent a significant increase in the computational effort required. As the complexity of derivative portfolios and the models used to price and hedge them increases, simulation becomes the only method general enough to fully capture this complexity. With continuing increases in computing power and innovation in the effective application of simulation, the use of the method in option pricing and risk management is destined to grow.

This chapter discusses some of the key issues and developments in simulation, including both introductory and advanced topics. Section 5.2 gives an overview of the types of processes typically simulated in option pricing; later sections use these as illustrative examples. Section 5.3 discusses basic path generation including random number generators, methods for sampling random variables and vectors, and ultimately the simulation of complex stochastic processes. Section 5.4 discusses methods for making simulation more computationally efficient through improved path generation and estimation. Section 5.5 gives an introduction to *quasi Monte Carlo* or *low discrepancy* methods, which also seek to reduce the computational effort required to produce accurate results. Finally, Section 5.6 discusses simulation issues arising in the estimation of value at risk.

5.2 UNDERLYING PROCESSES

Before discussing the mechanics of simulation, we briefly describe some of the underlying stochastic processes commonly used in financial simulations. Our intent is by no means

Risk Management and Analysis. Vol. 1: Measuring and Modelling Financial Risk.
Edited by Carol Alexander © 1998 John Wiley & Sons Ltd

to be exhaustive, but rather to highlight some distinct classes of processes and the issues they raise in simulation.

The most basic example of an underlying process is geometric Brownian motion, described by the stochastic differential equation (SDE)

$$\frac{dS_t}{S_t} = \mu \, dt + \sigma \, dW_t \tag{1}$$

in which W_t is a standard Wiener process and the drift and volatility parameters μ and σ are constants.[1] This is a rare example of an explicitly solvable SDE; its solution is

$$S_t = S_0 \exp\left(\left[\mu - \tfrac{1}{2}\sigma^2\right] t + \sigma W_t\right) \tag{2}$$

Thus, simulating values of S_t reduces to simulating values of W_t.

The solvability of (1) extends to the case in which μ and σ are functions of time but not, in general, to the case

$$\frac{dS_t}{S_t} = \mu \, dt + \sigma(S_t, t) \, dW_t \tag{3}$$

in which $\sigma(\cdot)$ is a deterministic function of the current price S_t and possibly also of time. This type of model has attracted attention as a means of reproducing implied volatility smiles and skews; see Dupire (1994). The intractability of (3) means that a simulation of this model cannot advance directly from time 0 to time t, as in (2), but must instead progress through a series of smaller approximating steps. We return to this issue later in the chapter.

At the next level of complexity are stochastic volatility models, such as that proposed by Hull and White (1987):

$$dS_t = \mu S_t \, dt + \sigma_t S_t \, dW_t^{(1)} \tag{4}$$

$$dV_t = \nu V_t \, dt + \xi V_t \, dW_t^{(2)} \tag{5}$$

with $V_t = \sigma_t^2$. The correlation $\rho = t^{-1} E[W_t^{(1)} \cdot W_t^{(2)}]$ need not be zero (or ± 1). From the perspective of simulation, the main difference between this model and the previous one is that simulating (4)–(5) entails simulating two sources of randomness.

GARCH models of asset prices allow return volatilities to be stochastic without necessarily introducing additional random factors. To describe an asset price through a GARCH model, one must first specify a sampling frequency at which the price is observed. A simple example is the GARCH-(1,1) model described by

$$S_n = S_{n-1} \exp\left(r + \lambda\sqrt{h_n} - \tfrac{1}{2}h_n + \sqrt{h_n}\,\varepsilon_n\right) \tag{6}$$

$$h_n = \alpha_0 + \alpha_1 h_{n-1}\varepsilon_{n-1}^2 + \beta h_{n-1} \tag{7}$$

Here, S_n is the asset price at the nth sampling instant and h_n is the conditional variance of the nth return, given the price history up to the $(n-1)$th observation. The constants r and λ are, respectively, a risk-free interest rate and risk premium associated with the sampling frequency. The random inputs $\varepsilon_1, \varepsilon_2, \ldots$, are independent with mean 0 and variance 1 — possibly, though not necessarily, normally distributed. The positive constants α_1 and β make the squared returns serially correlated, and α_0 then determines the unconditional return variance. Unlike (1), (3), and (4)–(5), GARCH models are intrinsically discrete-time processes.[2] Often, simulating a continuous-time asset price requires discretizing time, but there is an important distinction between a discrete approximation to a continuous path and a model of a price process at discrete instants only. (For further background on GARCH see Chapter 4 in this volume.)

Next we consider some interest rate models. The simplest models specify a diffusion for the (instantaneous, continuously-compounded) short rate r_t. The Vasicek (1977) model, for example, specifies an Ornstein–Uhlenbeck process

$$dr_t = \alpha(b - r_t)\,dt + \sigma\,dW_t \tag{8}$$

with the reversion speed α, the reversion level b, and the volatility σ all constant. The mean-reverting form of the drift is an attractive feature in modeling interest rates. Like (1), this equation is solvable; it remains solvable if b is made time-varying, as is usually necessary to match an initial term structure. In this case, the solution is

$$r_t = e^{-\alpha t} r_0 + \alpha \int_0^t e^{-\alpha(t-s)} b(s)\,ds + \sigma \int_0^t e^{-\alpha(t-s)}\,dW_s \tag{9}$$

Although the second integral on the right is stochastic, its integrand is deterministic; the integral is therefore normally distributed with mean 0 and variance

$$\int_0^t e^{-2\alpha(t-s)}\,ds = \frac{1}{2\alpha}(1 - e^{-2\alpha t}).$$

Thus, simulating values of r_t reduces to simulating values from a normal distribution.

The Cox, Ingersoll and Ross (1985) model (CIR model) specifies

$$dr_t = \alpha(b - r_t)\,dt + \sigma\sqrt{r_t}\,dW_t \tag{10}$$

The presence of the $\sqrt{r_t}$ in the diffusion coefficient keeps this process from becoming negative (if $r_0 \geq 0$), and 0 is inaccessible if $2\alpha b > \sigma^2$. Though not explicitly solvable, this model retains some of the tractability of (1) and (8) because it has a known (non-central chi-square) transition density. If, however, b is made time-varying to match an initial term structure, then even this degree of tractability is lost.

At the next level of complexity among interest rate models are the finite-dimensional "state variable" models. Examples of two-variable models include those of Fong and Vasicek (1992)

$$dr_t = \alpha(\bar{r} - r_t)\,dt + \sqrt{v_t}\,dW_t^{(1)}$$

$$dv_t = \gamma(\bar{v} - v_t)\,dt + \eta\sqrt{v_t}\,dW^{(2)}$$

which has a mean-reverting stochastic volatility, and Longstaff and Schwartz (1992)

$$r_t = c_1 Y_t^{(1)} + c_2 Y_t^{(2)}$$

$$dY_t^{(1)} = a_1(b_1 - Y_t^{(1)})\,dt + \sqrt{Y_t^{(1)}}\,dW_t^{(1)}$$

$$dY_t^{(2)} = a_2(b_2 - Y_t^{(2)})\,dt + \sqrt{Y_t^{(2)}}\,dW_t^{(2)} \tag{11}$$

in which the $Y_t^{(i)}$, $i = 1, 2$, though lacking a simple interpretation, are selected so that $W^{(1)}$ and $W^{(2)}$ are independent. From the perspective of simulation, these models are of a complexity similar to that of (4)–(5).

The most general processes we consider are those of the Heath–Jarrow–Morton (1992) framework. These describe the evolution of the entire term structure through the forward rate curve f, in which $f(t, s)$ is the instantaneous rate contracted at time t for borrowing at time $s, t \leq s \leq T$, for some ultimate maturity T. The dynamics of the forward curve are given by

$$\mathrm{d}f(t, s) = \alpha(t, s, f)\,\mathrm{d}t + \sum_{i=1}^{m} \sigma_i(t, s, f)\,\mathrm{d}W_t^{(i)} \tag{12}$$

where m is the number of factors or independent Wiener processes $W_t^{(i)}$, and the drift α and volatilities σ_i potentially depend on time t, maturity s and the current forward curve f. (The drift and volatility parameters could even depend on past forward rates.) This is clearly a rather more complex class of processes than those considered above because they describe the evolution of a continuum of rates. These models do not offer any analytical tractability beyond state-variable models of the type in (8)–(11), though they allow for much more flexible modeling of interest rates.

We return to these examples as we discuss various simulation techniques. At this point, the key issue to notice — one to which we will return — is the distinction between processes whose distributions at fixed times given values at previous times are known and can be sampled (such as (1), (6)–(7), (8), and (10)), and processes whose distributions can only be approximated ((4)–(5), and (12)). Simulations of both types of processes exhibit statistical variability, but simulations of the second type are subject to discretization error as well.

5.3 GENERATING PATHS

We now turn to the mechanics of generating paths of the underlying processes of interest in financial simulations, drawing on some of the examples of the previous section for illustration. The generation of paths usually proceeds in layers: at the core is the generation of (pseudo-) random numbers; these are transformed to non-uniform random variables and vectors, which are then used to build paths.

5.3.1 Random Number Generation

The random number generator is the heart of most stochastic simulations. As such, it is vitally important to the accuracy of simulation, and there is an extensive literature on the design of good generators. Because this topic is quite removed from the focus of this chapter, we will simply mention a few examples of generators and provide references where more complete discussions can be found.

The output of a random number generator is a sequence of numbers between 0 and 1. Ideally, these numbers would be indistinguishable from a sequence of values of independent random variables uniformly distributed over [0, 1]. Approximate uniformity is relatively easy to achieve but — because the numbers are generated deterministically — approximate independence is not. Various tests for serial correlation have been proposed and studied; see L'Ecuyer (1994) for a recent survey discussing a range of methods and tests.

The most commonly used generators are the *linear congruential generators*. These are algorithms of the form[3]

$$x_n = (ax_{n-1} + c)(\text{mod } m)$$

$$u_n = x_n/m$$

$n = 1, 2, \ldots$, with output $u_1, u_2, \ldots$. The *seed* x_0 is specified by the user. Such a generator produces at most m different values, so m is ordinarily very large. The properties of the sequence produced depend crucially on the values of a, c, and m. The values $m = 2^{31} - 1$, $a = 950\,706\,376$, and $c = 0$ were recommended by Fishman and Moore (1986). The main shortcoming of this class of generators is that vectors of their consecutive values lie on a lattice within the unit hypercube. L'Ecuyer (1994) recommends the only slightly more complicated generator

$$x_n = (ax_{n-1} + bx_{n-5})(\text{mod } m)$$

$$u_n = x_n/m$$

with $a = 107\,374\,182$, $b = 104\,480$, and $m = 2^{31} - 1$.

Any set of pseudo-random numbers will, by definition, fail on some problem, so it is occasionally useful to have a second generator available for comparison. In this case it may be more useful to compare results with a fundamentally different generator, rather than simply with a different choice of parameters. Effective alternative generators are analyzed in Hellekalek (1995) and Marsaglia and Zaman (1991). For an overview of many different types of generators and tests, see the survey article by L'Ecuyer (1994).

5.3.2 Random Variables and Vectors

The next layer in a typical simulation transforms the output $U_1, U_2, \ldots$ of the random number generator (henceforth treated as a true independent and identically distributed (i.i.d.) uniform sequence) into non-uniform random variables and vectors. As the examples in Section 5.2 indicate, the normal (Gaussian) case is the most fundamental one, so we give it particular emphasis.

There are many ways of transforming uniform random variables into normal random variables; Devroye (1986) lists several, varying in their speed, accuracy, and simplicity. Among the most popular methods is the Box–Muller transform: from a pair U_1, U_2 of independent uniforms it generates

$$X_1 = \sqrt{-2 \log U_1} \cos 2\pi U_2, \qquad X_2 = \sqrt{-2 \log U_1} \sin 2\pi U_2 \qquad (13)$$

which are then independent standard (mean 0, variance 1) normals. Its popularity stems from its simplicity rather than any other particular advantage. It is rather slow, and it maps the lattice structure of a linear congruential generator onto spirals; see the discussion in Bratley et al. (1987). Treating X_1 and X_2 as genuinely independent is therefore risky.

The fastest methods use a combination of table look-ups and different approximations in different regions. We will see, however, that the *inverse transform* method carries other advantages that frequently compensate for the loss in speed. Let

$$\Phi(x) = \frac{1}{\sqrt{2\pi}} \int_{-\infty}^{x} \exp\left(-\frac{t^2}{2}\right) dt$$

be the standard normal cumulative distribution and let Φ^{-1} denote its inverse. Since Φ takes values between 0 and 1, Φ^{-1} is a function on the unit interval $(0, 1)$; and if U is uniform on the unit interval, then $\Phi^{-1}(U)$ has the standard normal distribution. Indeed, for any cumulative distribution function F, the random variable $F^{-1}(U)$ has distribution F. (Figure 5.1 illustrates this transformation.) The function Φ^{-1} is not available in closed form but can be approximated to a high degree of accuracy by rational functions; see Moro (1995) for details of an implementation and Marsaglia et al. (1994) for an alternative. Once we know how to generate a sample $Z = \Phi^{-1}(U)$ from the standard normal distribution, we can generate a sample X from the normal distribution with mean μ and standard deviation σ by setting $X = \mu + \sigma Z$.

The most useful property of the transformation $U \mapsto Z = \Phi^{-1}(U)$ is that it *preserves percentiles*: if U falls between the ath and bth percentiles of its distribution, then $\Phi^{-1}(U)$ falls between the same percentiles of its distribution. Suppose we want to generate a value from the standard normal distribution conditioned to lie between, say, the 98th and 99th percentiles. We can do this by choosing U uniformly between 0.98 and 0.99 and then applying Φ^{-1} to U. To sample U uniformly between a and b (with, for example, $a = 0.98$ and $b = 0.99$) set $U = a + (b - a)U_0$, with U_0 uniform on $(0, 1)$.

The percentile-preserving property of the inverse transform is useful in generating *stratified* samples from a distribution. Suppose, for example, that we want to generate 100 values $Z_1, Z_2, \ldots, Z_{100}$ approximating the standard normal distribution. A random sample of independent draws from the distribution will tend to leave gaps and underrepresent the tails. A more regular sample can be generated as follows. First set

$$V_i = (i - 1) + \frac{U_i}{100}, \quad i = 1, \ldots, 100$$

with $U_1, U_2, \ldots$ i.i.d. uniforms; each V_i is uniformly distributed between the $(i-1)$th and ith percentiles. Now set $Z_i = \Phi^{-1}(V_i)$; then Z_i falls between the $(i-1)$ and ith percentiles of the standard normal distribution. This method gives equal weight in the sample to each of the 100 equiprobable strata. (Of course, 100 could be replaced with

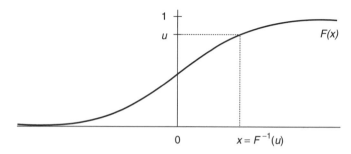

Figure 5.1 Illustration of the inverse transform method. The cumulative distribution function F takes values between 0 and 1, so its inverse F^{-1} is a function on the unit interval. When U is uniformly distributed over $(0, 1)$, $F^{-1}(U)$ has distribution F

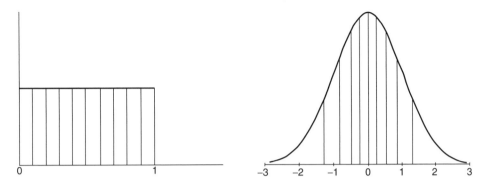

Figure 5.2 Applying the inverse normal to a stratified sample on the unit interval produces a stratified sample from the normal distribution. Subintervals of [0, 1] of equal width are mapped to intervals of equal probability but unequal width under the normal distribution

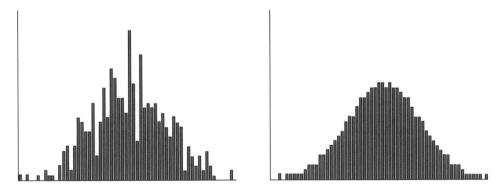

Figure 5.3 Comparison of random and stratified samples of 500 observations from the standard normal distribution

any other value in this example.) Figure 5.2 illustrates the transformation and Figure 5.3 compares histograms of 500 randomly sampled and stratified values. The price we pay for this additional regularity is the loss of independence among the Z_i in a stratified sample. This complicates statistical inference from simulation results, a point we return to later.

It would be much more difficult to generate a stratified sample using other methods for transforming uniform variates into standard normals. For similar reasons, the inverse transform method is also the best suited for use with *low discrepancy* sequences, the topic of Section 5.5.

We now turn to the problem of generating correlated random vectors. Financial simulations frequently require samples from a multivariate normal distribution $N(\mu, \Sigma)$ in which μ is an m-dimensional mean vector and Σ is an $m \times m$ covariance matrix. Suppose Σ has rank k. Given a vector $\mathbf{Z} = (Z_1, \ldots, Z_k)$ of independent standard normals, we generate such a random vector $\mathbf{X}$ by setting $\mathbf{X} = \mu + \mathbf{AZ}$, where $\mathbf{A}$ is any $m \times k$ matrix satisfying $\mathbf{AA'} = \Sigma$. Among all such matrices the one found by *Cholesky factorization* of Σ (for Σ of full rank) has the advantage that it is guaranteed to have all entries equal to zero in its upper triangular region; this saves computation in evaluating the product $\mathbf{AZ}$. Other choices of $\mathbf{A}$ have other advantages when combined with other methods; we return to this point in Section 5.4.2.

Once we go beyond the normal case, the distribution of a random vector is typically no longer determined by the mean vector and covariance matrix alone, and correlation may be a less meaningful measure of dependence among the components of a vector. An alternative specifies the marginal distributions of the components and their *rank* correlations.[4] Rank correlations are sometimes considered more robust than ordinary correlations and may well be appropriate in precisely the settings (such as Value-at-Risk calculations) where one is unwilling to assume that a normal distribution is adequate. There are potentially many joint distributions consistent with a specified set of marginal distributions and a rank correlation matrix; a specific algorithm for sampling from one such multivariate distribution is given in Stein (1987).

5.3.3 Basic Path Generation

We now proceed to the next layer of simulation in which random variables and vectors are transformed into paths of the underlying processes of the type discussed in Section 5.2. The key step in most cases is generating increments of the driving Wiener process. We use the fact that for a standard Wiener process W_t, we have $E[W_t] = 0$ and $Var[W_t] = t$. Moreover, for any $0 \le t_0 < t_1 < \cdots < t_m$, the increments $W_{t_i} - W_{t_{i-1}}$, $i = 1, \ldots, m$, are independent, the vector $(W_{t_0}, \ldots, W_{t_m})$ is multivariate normal with mean zero and covariance matrix determined by $Cov[W_{t_i}, W_{t_j}] = \min(t_i, t_j)$. Given independent standard normals $Z_0, Z_1, \ldots, Z_m$, we can generate these points along a Wiener path by setting $W_{t_0} = \sqrt{t_0} Z_0$ and

$$W_{t_i} = W_{t_{i-1}} + \sqrt{t_i - t_{i-1}} Z_i, \quad i = 1, \ldots, m \tag{14}$$

This turns out to be exactly the same as computing the Cholesky factorization of the covariance matrix and using it to multiply the column vector $(Z_0, Z_1, \ldots, Z_m)'$.

In light of (2), we can generate values at a fixed time t of an underlying asset described by (1) by setting

$$S_t = S_0 \exp \left(\left[\mu - \tfrac{1}{2}\sigma^2 \right] t + \sigma \sqrt{t} Z \right) \tag{15}$$

with Z a standard normal. To generate a (discrete) path of the underlying asset we can substitute (14) into (2) to get

$$S_{t_i} = S_{t_{i-1}} \exp \left(\left[\mu - \tfrac{1}{2}\sigma^2 \right] (t_i - t_{i-1}) + \sigma \sqrt{t_i - t_{i-1}} Z_i \right), \quad i = 1, \ldots, m \tag{16}$$

Suppose, next, that we want to generate values of multiple correlated assets, $S_t^{(1)}, \ldots, S_t^{(k)}$, each described by (1) with asset-specific drift and volatility parameters μ_i and σ_i and driving Wiener process $W_t^{(i)}$. Suppose the instantaneous returns on assets i and j have correlation ρ_{ij}, meaning more precisely that $E[W_t^{(i)} \cdot W_t^{(j)}] = \rho_{ij} t$. We now set

$$S_t^{(i)} = S_0^{(i)} \exp \left(\left[\mu_i - \tfrac{1}{2}\sigma_i^2 \right] t + \sqrt{t} X_i \right) \tag{17}$$

where $\mathbf{X} = (X_1, \ldots, X_k)$ is multivariate normal with mean zero and covariance matrix $\Sigma_{ij} = \sigma_i \sigma_j \rho_{ij}$. As discussed in Section 5.3.2, $\mathbf{X}$ can be generated through Cholesky factorization of $\mathbf{\Sigma}$. As in the single-asset case, the process can be repeated to obtain a discrete path of asset prices.

The GARCH equations (6)–(7) can be directly interpreted as a simulation algorithm. The only issue in implementation is the choice of driving sequence. The normal case is the most common and requires no further comment. Heavier tails can be produced by using a t-distribution instead, as in Engle and Rosenberg (1995). Methods for sampling from this distribution are discussed in Fishman (1996, pp. 207–208).

We noted in Section 5.2 that interest rates in the Vasicek model (8) are normally distributed; this makes simulation straightforward. To specify the right mean and variance, define

$$\mu(s, t) = \alpha \int_s^t e^{-\alpha(t-u)} b(u) \, du$$

and

$$\sigma^2(s, t) = \frac{\sigma^2}{2\alpha}(1 - e^{-\alpha(t-s)})$$

The discussion following (8) shows that given r_s, $s < t$, the interest rate at time t is normally distributed with mean $\exp(-\alpha(t - s))r_0 + \mu(s, t)$ and variance $\sigma^2(s, t)$. Thus, we generate a path $r_{t_1}, \ldots, r_{t_m}$ recursively by setting

$$r_{t_i} = e^{-\alpha(t-s)} r_{t_{i-1}} + \mu(t_{i-1}, t_i) + \sigma(t_{i-1}, t_i) Z_i, \tag{18}$$

where $Z_1, \ldots, Z_m$ are independent standard normals. In practice, the function b would be chosen to reproduce the initial term structure and $\mu(s, t)$ would be evaluated numerically.

The algorithms in (16), (17), and (18) have the feature that they produce paths with the *exact* distribution desired. This is made possible by the relative tractability of the lognormal and normal distributions. Some of this tractability extends to the CIR model (10), at least if b is constant. In this case the distribution of r_t given r_s, $s < t$, is non-central chi-square, so path generation reduces to sampling from this distribution. More precisely, Scott (1996) shows that we may set

$$r_{t_i} = r_{t_{i-1}} + 2c_i Y_i, \qquad c_i = \frac{2\alpha}{\sigma^2[1 - \exp(-\alpha(t_i - t_{i-1}))]} \tag{19}$$

where Y_i has the non-central chi-square distribution[5] with $v = 4\alpha b/\sigma^2$ degrees of freedom and non-centrality parameter $\lambda = 2c \exp(-\alpha(t_i - t_{i-1}))r_{t_{i-1}}$. He also discusses simulation of Y_i. If $v > 1$, then Y_i can be written as the sum of a central chi-square random variable having $v - 1$ degrees of freedom and $(Z + \lambda)^2$, with Z a standard normal. For $0 < v < 1$, Y_i can be obtained as a central chi-square random variable with N degrees of freedom, N a Poisson random variable with mean $\lambda/2$. Scott (1996) considers a multifactor CIR model as well and further shows how to sample from the distribution of $\int_s^t r_u \, du$ conditional on r_s and r_t. This is valuable in sampling discount factors accurately when the time increments $t_i - t_{i-1}$ are large.

Once we go beyond the simple models considered so far, the exact distribution of the underlying process is generally either unknown or too cumbersome to work with directly. At the next level of generality are models described by vector SDEs of the form

$$dX_t = \mu(X_t, t) \, dt + \sum_{j=1}^m \sigma_j(X_t, t) \, dW_t^{(j)} \tag{20}$$

The driving Wiener processes may be assumed independent without loss of generality. The key property in this representation is that randomness in the drift and volatility is limited to dependence on the current state of the process, making the process Markovian. This can frequently be achieved by augmenting the set of state variables. With the exception of the GARCH model (which is intrinsically a discrete-time process), all the examples in Section 5.2 can be viewed as models of this type.[6] Indeed, if a process cannot be modeled via (20), its dynamics must depend on past history in a complicated way, so simulation is likely to be difficult, if not impossible.

In the absence of a special structure, simulation of (20) entails discretization of the SDE. There is an extensive literature on discretization methods about which we can say only the barest minimum in this chapter. The most obvious and basic discretization method is the *Euler scheme*, which sets

$$X_{t_i} = X_{t_{i-1}} + \mu(X_{t_{i-1}}, t_{i-1})(t_i - t_{i-1}) + \sum_{j=1}^{m} \sigma_j(X_{t_{i-1}}, t_{i-1})\sqrt{t_i - t_{i-1}}Z_i^{(j)} \qquad (21)$$

with $Z_i^{(j)}$ independent standard normals. Even in the absence of statistical variability, this and all other schemes are subject to *discretization bias*. If, say, all $t_i - t_{i-1}$ are equal to a constant time increment h, then discretization bias error using the Euler scheme is $O(h)$, in a sense and under assumptions made precise in Kloeden and Platen (1992). More refined schemes use information about the derivatives of μ and the σ_j to make the bias $O(h^2)$ or even a higher power of h. These require more effort per path but the additional effort may be justified when very precise results are required. Duffie and Glynn (1996) analyze the trade-off between the number of paths generated and the effort expended per path.

5.3.4 Computing Payoffs

The next and often the final layer of a simulation is the computation of discounted payoffs from each path of underlying assets and rates.[7] Consider, first, the case in which discrete paths of the underlying processes can be generated exactly (as in (16)–(18)) and the payoff depends on the underlying only at a predetermined set of dates. An ordinary European call or put would be one example; a barrier option with a discretely monitored barrier would be another. In this case, one may generate the values of the underlying at the necessary dates (and only those dates) and then compute the discounted payoff.

Let $C_1, \ldots, C_n$ be the discounted payoffs computed from n independent paths. Under our assumption that all necessary values of the underlying are generated from the exact distribution, each C_i is an unbiased estimate of the expected discounted payoff. So, too, is the sample mean

$$\overline{C}_n = \frac{1}{n}\sum_{i=1}^{n}C_i$$

The precision of this estimator can be estimated through its (estimated) standard error $s/\sqrt{n}$, where

$$s = \sqrt{\frac{1}{n-1}\sum_{i=1}^{n}(C_i - \overline{C}_n)^2}$$

This can also be used to compute confidence intervals.

In this case, the only source of error is statistical variability, but this depends critically on our simplifying assumptions. If, for example, the distribution of the underlying cannot be sampled directly, then a discretization scheme must be used and this introduces discretization bias. Note, also, that even if the payoff depends on the value of the underlying at only a single date, a discretization scheme would require simulation of intermediate values as well if the bias is to be controlled. Discretization error can be introduced by the payoff as well as the underlying process. Consider, for example, the pricing of a continuously monitored barrier option on an underlying asset following geometric Brownian motion. Although we can simulate discrete paths with arbitrarily small increments, we cannot simulate a truly continuous path; the simulation implicitly underestimates the probability of a barrier crossing.[8] The two types of discretization error — in the process and in the payoff — can of course both occur in a single problem.

One further source of bias deserves mention. We describe it through a simple example — the pricing of a five-year European option on a 30-year bond in a state-variable (rather than HJM) model. To price the option, we simulate a path of the state variables for five years. At the end of the path we need to know the value of the bond to compute the payoff of the option. Unless our model is simple enough to provide a bond pricing formula, this means that we must simulate another 25 years to price the bond. But starting a single path from the end of the five years will not suffice: we must generate a large number of *subpaths* from the original path to obtain a reasonable estimate of the bond price. Even with a large number of subpaths there will be some variability in the estimated bond price. Jensen's inequality implies that options will be overvalued. The same type of "simulation within a simulation" problem arises in pricing American options and computing Value at Risk.

5.4 IMPROVED PATH GENERATION AND ESTIMATION

This section discusses some of the ways simulation can be made more effective through alternatives to the straightforward random sampling and estimation discussed in the previous section. The methods we describe attempt to reduce the variability in simulation estimates and thereby increase the precision that can be obtained from a fixed computational budget. The methods discussed in this section — antithetics, various forms of stratification, moment matching, and regression-adjusted controls — are all based on a statistical view of Monte Carlo. In contrast, the methods to be discussed in Section 5.5 are based on a deterministic, numerical-integration perspective.

5.4.1 Antithetics

In referring to improved path generation, we do not mean improving the way any one path is generated, but rather improving the statistical properties of a collection of simulated paths. The most basic property one would like to get right in a simulation is the mean trajectory of an underlying process. Simulating with antithetics accomplishes that when the process is symmetric about its mean.

Most of the applications we have in mind ultimately rely on simulating discrete approximations to paths of underlying Wiener processes. This can be accomplished using (14). In this context, simulating with antithetics means that each for each path $W = (W_{t_1} \ldots, W_{t_n})$ generated from a random sample $(Z_1, \ldots, Z_n)$ of independent standard normals we generate a second path $\tilde{W} = (\tilde{W}_{t_1}, \ldots, \tilde{W}_{t_n})$ using $(-Z_1, \ldots, -Z_n)$. When the paths are generated according to (14), $\tilde{W}$ is just the mirror image of W.

Generating paths this way does not alter the marginal distribution of any one path, but it clearly does affect the joint distribution of the paths; in particular, it makes the mean path identically zero. Thus, antithetic sampling is one way to get a sample of paths to reflect a property of the entire population of paths. We will encounter other methods shortly.

To estimate a price or similar quantity from m paths $W^{(1)}, \ldots, W^{(m)}$ and their mirror images $\tilde{W}^{(1)}, \ldots, \tilde{W}^{(m)}$, we average the values obtained from the $2m$ paths. However, to estimate the standard error of this estimate we cannot simply compute the sample standard deviation because the $2m$ observations are not independent. Instead, we must first average the value obtained from each $W^{(i)}$ with the value obtained from its antithetic mate $\tilde{W}^{(i)}$ and then compute the sample standard deviation of these m independent averages. Dividing by $\sqrt{m}$ then yields a valid (estimated) standard error. Here, as in subsequent examples, changing the way we generate paths requires some "batching" of results to estimate a standard error.

When is antithetic sampling effective? A few benchmarks help shed some light on this question:

- Simulating m antithetic pairs of paths results in a lower-variance estimate than simulating $2m$ independent paths if and only if the values computed from a path and its antithetic mate are negatively correlated.[9]

- If f is monotone in each argument, then antithetic sampling reduces variance in estimation of $E[f(Z_1, \ldots, Z_n)]$.

- If f is linear, then an antithetic estimate of $E[f(Z_1, \ldots, Z_n)]$ has zero error.

- If f is symmetric in the sense that $f(-Z_1, \ldots, -Z_n) = f(Z_1, \ldots Z_n)$, then an antithetic sample of size $2m$ has the same variance as an independent sample of size m.

The first two of these results provide no information on the magnitude of the variance reduction; it would in fact be more precise to say that antithetics are merely guaranteed not to increase variance under the stated conditions. The last two cases obviously never apply exactly, but they are helpful in building intuition: the more nearly linear the payoff (as a function of the underlying Z_i) the greater the benefit from antithetics; the more nearly symmetric the payoffs the smaller the benefit.

The role of approximate linearity is illustrated in Figure 5.4. The graphs plot the payoff on a standard call, as a function of the input normal random variable, for various parameter values. More precisely, they plot the function (see (15))

$$z \mapsto \max \left\{ 0, S_0 \exp \left([r - \tfrac{1}{2}\sigma^2] T + \sigma\sqrt{T}z \right) - K \right\}$$

Because antithetic sampling is applied to the input Z, it is the degree of linearity in Z, rather than S_T, that determines the effectiveness of the method.

The top three graphs correspond to options that are out-of-the-money, at-the-money, and in-the-money, respectively; the bottom three graphs correspond to low, intermediate, and high volatility for an at-the-money option. (The precise parameter values are given in the caption to the figure.) As one would expect, increasing moneyness and decreasing volatility both increase the degree of linearity. For the values indicated in the figure, we find numerically that antithetics reduce variance by 7 per cent, 42 per cent, and 80 per cent in the top three cases and by 64 per cent, 49 per cent, and 37 per cent in the bottom

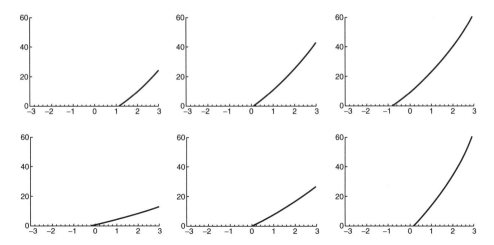

Figure 5.4 Illustration of payoffs for antithetic comparisons. The vertical axes give payoffs and the horizontal axes give values of z, the input standard normal. All cases have $r = 5$ per cent, $K = 50$, and $T = 0.5$. The top three cases have $\sigma = 0.30$ and $S_0 = 40$, 50, and 60; the second three cases have $S_0 = 50$ and $\sigma = 0.10$, 0.20, 0.30.

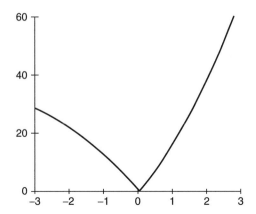

Figure 5.5 Payoff on a straddle as a function of input normal Z based on the parameters $S_0 = K = 50$, $\sigma = 0.30$, $T = 1$, and $r = 0.05$

three. The results are fully consistent with the intuition that greater linearity brings greater variance reduction.

Figure 5.5 illustrates the payoff $|S_T - K|$ on a straddle but as a function of the input Z rather than S_T. (The parameter values are given in the caption.) The graph shows a high degree of symmetry around zero, suggesting that antithetic sampling may not be very effective in this case. In fact, numerical results show that an estimate based on m antithetic pairs actually has higher variance than an estimate based on $2m$ independent samples.

These examples indicate that the effectiveness of antithetic sampling can vary widely, and that it is useful to understand the structure of the function being integrated by the simulation in anticipating the utility of the method. It is worth emphasizing that the clear intuition available in the simple examples above would be harder to apply in using antithetics with a more complicated process of the general type in (20) and (21).

5.4.2 Stratification

In Section 5.3.2 we showed how to generate a stratified sample from a univariate probability distribution, such as the standard normal. If, for example, we stratify the standard normal distribution into n bins and let $(Z_1, \ldots, Z_n)$ be a stratified sample obtained by using these bins, then these Z_i can be used in, for example, (15) to generate n (stratified) values from the terminal distribution of a lognormally distributed asset price. These, in turn, can be substituted into an option payoff function to obtain n payoffs and finally an estimate of the option price. This method is guaranteed to reduce variance: the variance from a random sample can be decomposed into contributions within strata and across strata; stratified sampling eliminates the second term.

Can the method be extended to multiple dimensions? In principle, the extension is straightforward. Just as in one dimension we started by partitioning the unit interval into equal-width subintervals, in k dimensions we start by partitioning the unit hypercube $[0, 1]^k$ into n^k equal-volume hypercubes having length $1/n$ along each dimension. By sampling uniformly from within each hypercube we obtain a stratified sample from $[0, 1]^k$, the points of which can then be transformed to an arbitrary k-variate distribution. The shapes of the resulting strata depend on the transformation used.

In practice, however, this method quickly becomes infeasible as the dimension k increases, unless n is made so small as to eliminate the effect on variance. The problem is that generating a full stratified sample in this way requires generating n^k points, and this is unlikely to be viable for k larger than 5 or 6, say. Using just the initial portion of the full set of n^k points would give very poor results as it leaves a large part of the unit hypercube completely unsampled. In view of these difficulties, we describe two alternatives to full stratification in high dimensions. The first method stratifies along a small number of dimensions and samples randomly from the others; the second method, called *Latin hypercube sampling*, samples n of the n^k full-stratification bins in a particularly effective way.

Suppose, then, that as an input to our simulation we need to generate a k-dimensional Gaussian vector with covariance matrix Σ. (The mean vector is less important because it can always be added at the end once a zero-mean vector has been generated; see Section 5.3.2.) This vector could, for example, represent k steps along the path of a standard Wiener process, but it could also represent the values of, say, m correlated Wiener processes at k/m points in time. Suppose that k is too large to allow full stratification in k dimensions and that instead we decide to stratify $k' < k$ dimensions, perhaps with $k' = 1$ or 2.

Let $\mathbf{A}$ be a matrix satisfying $\mathbf{AA'} = \Sigma$; $\mathbf{A}$ could be the Cholesky matrix discussed in Section 5.3.2, but in general it need not be. For random sampling we would set $\mathbf{X} = \mathbf{AZ}$ with $Z_i = \Phi^{-1}(U_i)$, $i = 1, \ldots, k$, with the U_i independently and uniformly distributed over $[0, 1]$. To stratify k' dimensions we could replace $(U_1, \ldots, U_k)$ with a vector $(\mathbf{V}, U_{k'+1}, \ldots, U_k)$, where $\mathbf{V} = (V_1, \ldots, V_{k'})$ is obtained by stratifying $[0, 1]^{k'}$ as described above. This has the effect of perfectly stratifying $(Z_1, \ldots, Z_{k'})$ and sampling the remaining entries of $\mathbf{Z}$ randomly. However, the matrix $\mathbf{A}$ rotates and stretches the vector $\mathbf{Z}$, so while the resulting vector $\mathbf{X}$ is stratified in k' directions, these directions do not ordinarily coincide with the marginals of $\mathbf{X}$. The question, then, is: How do we choose the matrix $\mathbf{A}$ so that the resulting k'-dimensional stratification is most effective? We discuss two specific choices.

For our first illustration, we restrict attention to the case of a discretely sampled one-dimensional Wiener process — i.e. $\Sigma_{ij} = \min\{t_i, t_j\}$. In this case, it is easy to see that Cholesky factorization does not provide a particularly effective choice of $\mathbf{A}$: stratifying the inputs in k' dimensions merely stratifies k' increments along the path. An alternative uses a *Brownian bridge* construction along the lines proposed by Caflisch and Moskowitz (1995) and Caflisch et al. (1997).[10] This construction generates a discrete Wiener path $(W_{t_1}, \ldots, W_{t_k})$ by sampling the terminal value first and then filling in the rest of the path recursively. Specifically, it sets $W_{t_k} = \sqrt{t_k} Z_1$ and then, once $0 = W_0, W_{t_1}, \ldots, W_{t_i}$ have been determined it sets

$$W_{t_{i+1}} = \left(\frac{t_k - t_{i+1}}{t_k - t_i} \right) W_{t_i} + \left(\frac{t_{i+1} - t_i}{t_k - t_i} \right) W_{t_k} + \sqrt{\frac{(t_{i+1} - t_i)(t_k - t_{i+1})}{(t_k - t_i)}} Z_{i+1}$$

This construction is based on the Brownian bridge property that conditional on W_{t_i} and W_{t_k}, the distribution of $W_{t_{i+1}}$ is normal with a mean that lies on the line segment connecting W_{t_i} and W_{t_k} and a standard deviation equal to the factor multiplying Z_{i+1} in the equation above. The construction is illustrated in Figure 5.6.

Using this construction, stratifying even just Z_1 (and sampling $Z_2, \ldots, Z_k$ randomly) yields a path $(W_{t_1}, \ldots, W_{t_k})$ with the desired joint distribution and a stratified terminal value (as illustrated in Figure 5.6). When applied in conjunction with, for example, (16) or (18), this results in a perfectly stratified terminal asset price or interest rate. This is attractive in pricing options that, though perhaps path dependent, are primarily sensitive to terminal values. Moreover, the method easily extends to $k' > 1$. For example, with $k' = 2$, we could stratify (Z_1, Z_2), use Z_1 to generate the terminal value and then Z_1 to generate the midpoint. The rest of the path could then be filled in recursively. This

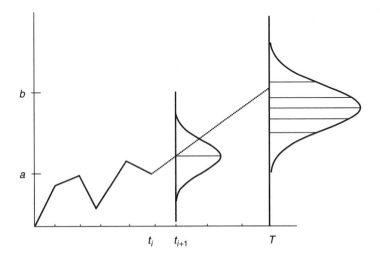

Figure 5.6 Conditional on $W_{t_i} = a$ and $W_T = b$, the distribution of $W_{t_{i+1}}$ is normal with a mean that lies on the line segment connecting (t_i, a) and (T, b) and a standard deviation that depends only on $T - t_{i+1}$ and $t_{i+1} - t_i$

construction and the one above correspond to an implicit choice of the matrix **A** which could also be specified explicitly; see Caflisch et al. (1997).

The objective of the Brownian bridge approach is to use the k' stratified coordinates to generate the most important points along a path — often, the most important value is the last one, the second most important is the midpoint, and so on. But can "importance" be made precise? Can this approach be extended to other Gaussian vectors for which "terminal value" may have no natural interpretation?[11] These questions can be addressed by using a principal components decomposition: factor the covariance matrix Σ into **VDV'**, where **D** is a diagonal matrix of eigenvalues of Σ arranged in decreasing order and the columns of **V** are the corresponding eigenvectors. The matrix $\mathbf{A} = \mathbf{VD}^{1/2}$ then satisfies the requirement $\mathbf{AA'} = \Sigma$, so we can set $\mathbf{X} = \mathbf{AZ}$. The magnitude of the ith eigenvalue is a precise measure of the variability in **X** attributable to Z_i; among all constructions, this one assigns maximal variability to the first k' coordinates of **Z**, for all $1 \le k' \le k$. In this sense, it makes optimal use of the k' stratified entries of **Z**. Moreover, it is directly applicable to any Gaussian vector. Acworth et al. (1997) proposed and evaluated this method for use with low discrepancy sequences (see Section 5.5). Though not directly comparable with the case of stratified sampling, the results reported there suggest that the construction can be very effective.

We now turn to a discussion of Latin hypercube sampling (LHS), an alternative approach to extending stratification to high dimensions. As in our discussion of stratification, we start by considering the problem of sampling from $[0, 1]^k$. Whereas full stratification would generate n^k points in dimension k, LHS generates just n points in dimension k, but these points are chosen so that all k marginal distributions are perfectly stratified. The distinction is illustrated in Figure 5.7. In both cases, each point generated is uniformly distributed within the cube from which it is selected, so the difference lies in the selection of the cubes. Stratified sampling selects all n^k, whereas LHS chooses n randomly subject to the contraint that each row and column contain exactly one selected cube.[12] The constraint ensures that each of the one-dimensional projections is stratified.

To make this procedure more explicit, let $U^i_j, j = 1, \dots, k, i = 1, \dots, n$, be independent and uniformly distributed over $[0, 1]$. Let $\pi_1, \dots, \pi_k$ be independent random

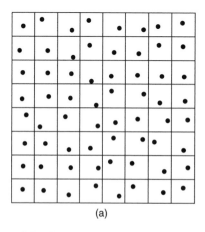

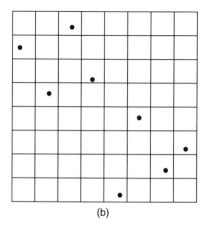

(a)

(b)

Figure 5.7   Comparison of (a) stratified sampling with (b) Latin hypercube sampling in dimension $k = 2$ with $n = 8$

permutations of $\{1, \ldots, n\}$ sampled uniformly from all $n!$ such permutations.[13] Now set

$$V_j^i = \frac{\pi_j(i) - 1 + U_j^i}{n}$$

Then the n points $V^1 = (V_1^1, \ldots, V_k^1), \ldots, V^n = (V_1^n, \ldots, V_k^n)$ constitute a Latin hypercube sample of size n in dimension k. Each of these vectors can then be transformed into, for example, vectors of normals as before.

This method was proposed by McKay et al. (1979). Stein (1987) analyzes the variance reduction achieved using this method and shows that LHS asymptotically eliminates the contribution to the variance due to the additive part of the function being integrated. Thus, the more closely an integrand over $[0, 1]^k$ can be approximated as the sum of k one-dimensional functions over $[0, 1]$, the greater the effectiveness of LHS. Stein (1987) also describes an extension of the method to generate vectors with a specified rank correlation matrix. Shaw (1995) gives an interesting application of this extension in computing Value at Risk.

One drawback of all the methods of stratification discussed in this section is that they do not provide a means of estimating a standard error to be used to form a confidence interval around a point estimate. In particular, the sample standard deviation obtained from a stratified sample is not informative because it ignores the very strong dependence induced by stratification. A compromise solution generates a set of independent stratified or LHS batches and estimates the standard error across batches. For example, if our computational budget allows for the generation of 10 000 points, we may choose to generate 100 independent batches of 100 stratified or LHS points, rather than a single batch of 10 000. By batching we lose some variance reduction but we recover the possibility of computing confidence intervals.

5.4.3 Matching the Underlying

A basic principle in the pricing of derivative securities is that a numerical method should be calibrated to market data before it is used to price less liquid instruments. A minimal requirement of this type is that the method should correctly reproduce the price of an underlying before it is used to price options on the underlying. In simulation, this condition is met if the paths of the underlying are generated under the risk-neutral measure — at least in the limit as the number of paths increases. The methods we describe next enforce correct pricing of the underlying even in finite samples. Specific approaches of this type are proposed in Barraquand (1995) and in Duan and Simonato (1995); various versions appear to be widely used in practice.

For simplicity, we begin by considering the simple lognormal diffusion model (1), and to be concrete we take $\mu = r$, the risk-free rate. Standard calculations show that, for any $t \geq 0$,

$$S_0 = e^{-rt} E[S_t] \qquad (22)$$

In other words, the price today is the expected present value of the price at any future date. If we simulate n paths $S_t^{(1)}, \ldots, S_t^{(n)}$ of this price process (e.g. using (16)), then we would find that

$$S_0 \approx e^{-rt} \bar{S}_t \equiv e^{-rt} \cdot \frac{1}{n} \sum_{i=1}^{n} S_t^{(i)}$$

but the approximate equality becomes exact equality only in the limit as n increases to infinity. *Moment matching* applies an adjustment to the paths that produces equality for finite n. If we set

$$\tilde{S}_t^{(i)} = S_t^{(i)} \frac{\mathrm{E}[S_t]}{\bar{S}_t} \tag{23}$$

then

$$\mathrm{e}^{-rt} \frac{1}{n} \sum_{i=1}^{n} \tilde{S}_t^{(i)} = \mathrm{e}^{-rt} \cdot \frac{1}{n} \sum_{i=1}^{n} S_t^{(i)} \frac{\mathrm{E}[S_t]}{\bar{S}_t} = \mathrm{e}^{-rt} \mathrm{E}[S_t]$$

exactly. If (23) is applied at all simulated t, then the effect is to adjust the collection of simulated paths so that their empirical mean exactly matches the population mean path.

This adjustment also has the effect of enforcing put–call parity:

$$\left(\mathrm{e}^{-rt} \frac{1}{n} \sum_{i=1}^{n} \max\{0, \tilde{S}_t^{(i)} - K\} \right) - \left(\mathrm{e}^{-rt} \frac{1}{n} \sum_{i=1}^{n} \max\{0, K - \tilde{S}_t^{(i)}\} \right) = \mathrm{e}^{-rt} \left(\frac{1}{n} \sum_{i=1}^{n} \tilde{S}_t^{(i)} - K \right)$$

$$= S_0 - \mathrm{e}^{-rt} K$$

Thus, adjusting the paths of the underlying can also be interpreted as enforcing a no-arbitrage condition in finite samples.

The adjustment in (23) is just one way to achieve this property. Another would be to make the additive adjustment

$$\tilde{S}_t^{(i)} = S_t^{(i)} + (\mathrm{E}[S_t] - \bar{S}_t) \tag{24}$$

However, this adjustment can produce negative asset prices. Moreover, since the lognormal model (1) is the continuous-time limit of the product of independent multiplicative returns, a multiplicative adjustment seems natural in this case. But in both (23) and (24) the $\tilde{S}_t^{(i)}$ fail to be lognormally distributed even if the $S_t^{(i)}$ are. A third alternative replaces (15) with

$$S_t^{(i)} = S_0 \exp\left(\left[r - \tfrac{1}{2}\sigma^2 \right] t + \sigma\sqrt{t}\tilde{Z}_i \right) \tag{25}$$

where

$$\tilde{Z}_i = Z_i - \frac{1}{n} \sum_{i=1}^{n} Z_i \tag{26}$$

and $Z_1, \ldots, Z_n$ are independent standard normals. Unlike the Z_i, the $\tilde{Z}_i$ have a sample mean of exactly 0, the population mean of the standard normal distribution. The adjustment in (25) has the effect of making the sample mean of $\log S_t^{(i)}$ match the population mean $\mathrm{E}[\log S_t^{(i)}]$. Though matching the logarithm of the underlying may look less attractive than matching the underlying itself, adjusting the Z_i extends the scope of the method to models (such as (3)) where $\mathrm{E}[S_t]$ is not available in closed form and to models with multiple state variables (such as (4)–(5)) where even if the means of the state variables are known, it may not be obvious how they should be simultaneously adjusted.

Similar mean adjustments appear to be popular in interest rate simulations. In the case of the Vasicek model (8), the noise terms $\mathrm{d}W_t$ enter additively so the most natural way to match the mean interest rate path makes the additive adjustment

$$r_t^{(i)} \to r_t^{(i)} - \frac{1}{n} \sum_{j=1}^{n} r_t^{(j)}$$

to independent paths $r_t^{(1)}, \ldots, r_t^{(n)}$. This adjustment is more easily implemented by applying the mean shift in (26) to the Zs used to generate an increment using (18).[14] In a CIR simulation based on (19), one could match the mean interest rate path by adjusting the non-central chi-square random variables Y_i. Because these must be non-negative, a multiplicative adjustment may be preferable to an additive one.

An alternative to matching the mean interest rate path adjusts the paths to match the prices of zero-coupon bonds. Let P_t denote the price today of a riskless bond paying one unit of account at time t, as determined either from a model or from market prices. In any model of the short rate r_t

$$P_t = \mathrm{E}\left[\exp\left(-\int_0^t r_s\, ds\right)\right]$$

under the risk-neutral measure. Now consider a simulation of the short rate at discrete times $0, \Delta t, 2\Delta t, \ldots$. Write r_j for $r_{j\Delta t}$ and let $r_j^{(1)}, \ldots, r_j^{(n)}, j = 1, 2, \ldots$, denote n independently simulated paths. The simulation estimate $\hat{P}_{N\Delta t}$ of the true price $P_{N\Delta t}$ is

$$\hat{P}_{N\Delta t} = \frac{1}{n} \sum_{i=1}^{n} \exp\left(-\Delta t \sum_{j=1}^{N} r_{j-1}^{(i)}\right)$$

To make the simulated and true price coincide, we adjust the interest rate path based on forward rates. Let

$$F_j = \frac{1}{\Delta t}[\log P_{(j-1)\Delta t} - \log P_{j\Delta t}]$$

be the true forward rate for the interval $[(j-1)\Delta t, j\Delta t]$ and

$$\hat{F}_j = \frac{1}{\Delta t}[\log \hat{P}_{(j-1)\Delta t} - \log \hat{P}_{j\Delta t}]$$

the simulated forwards. If we replace the original interest rate paths with the adjusted paths

$$r_j^{(i)} \to r_j^{(i)} - \hat{F}_j + F_j$$

then a simple calculation shows that the simulated bond price will then exactly match the true bond price at all maturities. Notice that this adjustment simultaneously accounts for statistical variability (the fact that only finitely many paths have been simulated) and discretization error (the fact that the integral defining the bond price is replaced with a sum in the simulation).

The examples above suggest that there can be some ambiguity in which features of the underlying should be matched and how the paths should be adjusted to enforce the match. In choosing among the alternatives and, more fundamentally, in using any such method, it is important to understand the strengths and weaknesses of the approach:

- A finite set of paths adjusted to match a set of means will produce exact prices for any instrument depending linearly and exclusively on the quantities whose means have been matched. For example, if zero-coupon bond prices are matched, then so are the prices of coupon bonds and swaps. Options are generally not priced exactly if the mean of the underlying is matched. The more nearly linear the payoff, the greater the error reduction that can be anticipated.

- All such methods produce *biased* estimates for non-linear payoffs (e.g. option prices) though the bias vanishes as the number of paths increases. For example, the adjustment in (26) gives each $\tilde{Z}_i$ a normal distribution with mean 0 but variance $(n + 1)/n$ rather than 1. Of course, in this case one could multiply by $\sqrt{n/(n + 1)}$ to restore the correct variance, but in general the adjustments applied above change the distributions of the underlying in ways that can be difficult to compensate for.

- Because the adjustments are applied across paths, they introduce dependence among what would otherwise be independent observations. This complicates confidence interval estimation. As with stratification, the only reliable way to estimate a standard error is to batch the paths, applying adjustments within batches but keeping the batches themselves independent of each other.

- The adjustments described above can all be viewed as ways of exploiting analytically available information about the underlying process. In the next subsection we will see that the same information can alternatively be exploited through control variates. As discussed in Boyle et al. (1997), this alternative is typically preferable in large samples. When very few paths are used, as is often the case in, for example, pricing mortgage-backed securities, the methods can be compared only through experimentation.

5.4.4 Control Variates

The methods we have discussed thus far — antithetics, various forms of stratification, and moment matching — all involve altering the way a set of paths is generated, with the intent of making a finite sample of paths more representative of the infinite population from which they are drawn. The last method we discuss in this section adjusts the *estimate* computed from a set of paths rather than the paths themselves. The adjustment is made based on analytically available information about the underlying or about prices of simpler instruments.

As a motivating example, consider the pricing of a path-dependent option on an underlying asset S_t modeled as the lognormal diffusion in (15) but with $\mu = r$, the risk-free rate. Let the discounted payoff on the option be denoted by $h(S_0, S_{t_1}, \ldots, S_{t_m})$; we assume the payoff depends on the value of the underlying only at the dates $t_1, \ldots, t_m$, as in the case of a discretely monitored barrier or Asian option. Let $S^{(i)} = (S_0, S_{t_1}^{(i)}, \ldots, S_{t_m}^{(i)})$, $i = 1, \ldots, n$, be n independently generated paths and let

$$V_i = h(S_0, S_{t_1}^{(i)}, \ldots, S_{t_m}^{(i)})$$

be the price estimate from the ith path. The standard Monte Carlo estimate of $V = E[V_i]$ is

$$\frac{1}{n} \sum_{i=1}^{n} V_i$$

Suppose now that on the same set of n paths we evaluate

$$C_i = g(S_0, S_{t_1}^{(i)}, \ldots, S_{t_m}^{(i)})$$

for some discounted payoff function g for which the theoretical price

$$C = \mathrm{E}[C_i] = \mathrm{E}[g(S_0, S_{t_1}^{(i)}, \ldots, S_{t_m}^{(i)})]$$

is known in closed form (or can easily be evaluated numerically). The method of *control variates* uses the known error

$$\frac{1}{n}\sum_{i=1}^{n} C_i - C$$

in the simpler instrument to reduce the unknown error

$$\frac{1}{n}\sum_{i=1}^{n} V_i - V$$

in the instrument of interest.

The controlled estimator has the form

$$\frac{1}{n}\sum_{i=1}^{n} V_i - \beta\left(\frac{1}{n}\sum_{i=1}^{n} C_i - C\right) \tag{27}$$

Since the term in parentheses has expectation zero, (27) provides an unbiased estimator of V so long as β is independent of the term it multiplies — in particular, if β is a constant. A standard calculation shows that among all such estimators the one with the smallest variance sets

$$\beta = \beta_* \equiv \frac{\mathrm{Cov}[V_i, C_i]}{\mathrm{Var}[C_i]}$$

If, say, the V_i and C_i are positively correlated, then (27) adjusts the simulation estimate of V downward when C has been overestimated and upward when C has been underestimated. Compared with the crude estimator ($\beta = 0$) this procedure reduces variance by a factor of $1 - \rho_{VC}^2$, where ρ_{VC} is the correlation between V_i and C_i.

Of course, in practice β_* is rarely known, but it is readily estimated using

$$\hat{\beta}_* = \frac{\displaystyle\sum_{i=1}^{n}(V_i - \overline{V})(C_i - \overline{C})}{\displaystyle\sum_{i=1}^{n}(C_i - \overline{C})^2}$$

where $\overline{V}$ and $\overline{C}$ are the sample means of the V_i and C_i, respectively. At least in large samples, using $\hat{\beta}_*$ is nearly as effective as using the true optimum β_*. Estimating $\hat{\beta}_*$ from the same set of paths used to price the option introduces some bias in the estimate (27), but this bias vanishes as the number of paths increases. It can be eliminated entirely by reserving a (relatively small) subset of paths for estimation of β_* and using the rest for pricing.

The key to the effectiveness of the method lies in finding easily computed quantities that are highly correlated with the object of interest. Standard calls and puts frequently provide a convenient source of control variates, and so does the underlying itself: in the discussion above, we could take $C_i = S_{t_m}^{(i)}$ and $C = S_0 \exp(rt_m)$. The most effective controls take advantage of special features. A well-known and highly effective example is the use of the (analytically tractable) option on a geometric mean as a control for estimating the price of an option on an arithmetic mean, as proposed by Kemna and Vorst (1990). Figure 5.8 compares the effectiveness of the underlying asset, a standard call, and

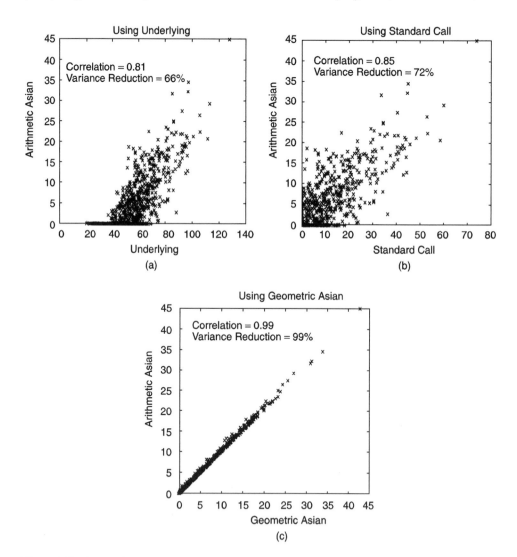

Figure 5.8 Comparison of correlation between payoff on arithmetic average rate option and (a) terminal value of underlying, (b) payoff on a standard call, and (c) payoff on geometric average rate option. The figures shows scatterplots of prices obtained from 1000 simulations. In all cases, $S_0 = K = 50$, $T = 1$, $\sigma = 0.30$, and $r = 0.05$; the arithmetic and geometric averages are computed from 20 evenly spaced times along a path

a call on the geometric mean. The results illustrate the dramatic potential for variance reduction but also suggest that the most effective controls are problem-dependent.

Though our discussion thus far has focused on the case of a single control variate, the method extends easily to the case of multiple controls. For example, since $E[S_{t_j}] = S_0 \exp(-rt_j)$, the estimator

$$\overline{V} - \beta_1 \left(\frac{1}{n} \sum_{i=1}^{n} S_{t_1}^{(i)} - S_0 e^{-rt_1} \right) - \cdots - \beta_m \left(\frac{1}{n} \sum_{i=1}^{n} S_{t_m}^{(i)} - S_0 e^{-rt_m} \right) \tag{28}$$

is unbiased for all $\beta_1, \ldots, \beta_m$. The optimal (variance-minimizing) β_js can be estimated by regressing the V_i against $(S_{t_1}^{(i)}, \ldots, S_{t_j}^{(i)})$.

Note that (28) exploits exactly the same information used in (23) to match the mean path of the underlying. Indeed, all of the mean adjustments discussed in Section 5.4.3 could alternatively be used to design control variates. In the interest rate setting, for example, it is natural to use bond prices as controls, subtracting

$$\beta \left(\frac{1}{n} \sum_{i=1}^{n} \exp \left(-\Delta t \sum_{j=1}^{N} r_{j-1}^{(i)} \right) - P_{N\Delta t} \right)$$

from the payoff of an interest rate derivative and estimating the optimal β as before. This alternative mechanism to reducing variance by exploiting the same information used in Section 5.4.3 motivates a comparison of the two methods:

- Both methods produce zero-variance estimators of quantities depending linearly on the known mean, whether the mean is used as a control or to adjust the paths. This property of mean adjustment was noted in Section 5.4.3. That it also holds for control variates is evident from, for example, (27): if V_i depends linearly on C_i, then $\hat{\beta}_*$ will be exactly the slope in this linear relation, so subtracting $\hat{\beta}_*(\overline{C} - C)$ exactly eliminates the error in $\overline{V}$.

- As noted in Section 5.4.3, adjusting paths introduces some bias; the control variate estimator can be made unbiased by separating the estimation of the coefficients from the estimation of prices.

- The extra degree of freedom provided by the flexibility to choose the βs suggests that the control variate method can make *optimal* use of information about a known mean, at least in large samples. A more precise argument in this direction is made in the appendix to Boyle et al. (1997). In small samples it is difficult to compare the methods on theoretical grounds without making more specific distributional assumptions. Experimentally, we have found that the two methods often give similar results.

- The need to estimate a separate coefficient for every instrument priced from a simulation could in some cases be viewed as a drawback of the control variate method. If, as in Section 5.4.3, the sample mean of the underlying is adjusted to match the theoretical mean, put–call parity holds exactly on the simulated paths. If the mean of the underlying is used as a control variate, with separate coefficients estimated for puts and calls, then put–call parity will not hold exactly. It would if the same coefficient were used for both.

- We noted in Section 5.4.3 that when paths are adjusted to match a mean, confidence intervals can be computed only through batching. Confidence intervals are easily estimated using control variates. With fixed coefficients, interval estimates can be computed from the standard error of the adjusted estimates. These remain asymptotically valid with estimated coefficients; small sample modifications based on the connection with regression are also easily incorporated.

5.5 QUASI MONTE CARLO

The improved methods of path generation discussed in Section 5.3 were based on a statistical view of Monte Carlo. Antithetics, stratification, and moment matching modify the random simulation input in order to generate improved paths. Control variate techniques generate improved estimators by adjusting simulation output. Quasi Monte Carlo (QMC) methods, also termed low discrepancy methods, can be viewed as an extreme form of input modification, where the inputs are completely deterministic instead of random. At an operational level, QMC involves replacing a (pseudo-) random number generator with another routine that generates a low discrepancy sequence.

Suppose our goal is to estimate $E[f(Z)]$, where Z is a standard normal random variable. Using the transformation $z = \Phi^{-1}(x)$ introduced in Section 5.3.2, we note that the expectation $E[f(Z)] = \int_{-\infty}^{\infty} f(z)\phi(z)\,dz$ (where $\phi(x)$ is the standard normal density function) can be written as $\int_0^1 f(\Phi^{-1}(x))\,dx$. The latter integral can be approximated by $(1/N)\sum_{n=1}^{N} f(\Phi^{-1}(x_n))$, where $\{x_n\}_{n=1,\dots,N}$ is a sequence of numbers in $[0, 1]$. QMC methods choose the points x_n deterministically to obtain a good approximation to the integral for a broad class of functions f.

We first describe a low discrepancy sequence in one dimension and then proceed to higher dimensions. To obtain the nth point x_n of the van der Corput sequence (with a base of 2), first write the integer n in base 2:

$$n = \sum_{i=0}^{I} a_i 2^i$$

Then transpose the digits a_i around the "decimal point" to get

$$x_n = \sum_{i=0}^{I} \frac{a_i}{2^{i+1}}$$

This sequence begins 1/2, 1/4, 3/4, 1/8, 5/8, 3/8, 7/8, ... The van der Corput sequence is contained in the interval $(0, 1)$ and it fills in the interval in a "nice" way. For example, every consecutive pair of points has one point in $(0, 1/2)$ and the other in $[1/2, 1)$; every consecutive quadruple of points has one point in $(0, 1/4)$, $[1/4, 1/2)$, $[1/2, 3/4)$, and $[3/4, 1)$, etc. After every $N = 2^n - 1$ points, the sequence is "maximally spread out", i.e. the longest interval $(a, b) \subseteq (0, 1)$ which does not contain any points from the sequence is as short as possible.[15]

The previous one-dimensional example illustrates the principal ideas behind quasi Monte Carlo. First, the problem of estimating an expectation is recast as one of numerical integration. Secondly, the integral is approximated using a well-chosen sequence of points. The quasi Monte Carlo approach often leads to better point estimates for a similar computational budget compared with standard Monte Carlo. However, error estimation which is straightforward in Monte Carlo, is not readily available with QMC.

Now suppose our goal is to estimate $E[f(Z_1, \ldots, Z_s)]$, where $(Z_1, \ldots, Z_s)$ follows a multivariate normal distribution. Proceeding as before, the expectation can be written as

$$\int_{-\infty}^{\infty} \cdots \int_{-\infty}^{\infty} f(z_1, \ldots, z_s)\phi(z_1, \ldots, z_s)\, dz_1 \ldots dz_s = \int_0^1 \cdots \int_0^1 f(g(x_1, \ldots, x_s))\, dx_1 \ldots dx_s$$

where the transformation $(z_1, \ldots, z_s) = g(x_1, \ldots, x_s)$ was described in Section 5.3.2. The latter integral can be approximated by $(1/N)\Sigma_{n=1}^N f(g(x_1^{(n)}, \ldots, x_s^{(n)}))$, where $\{(x_1^{(n)}, \ldots, x_s^{(n)})\}_{n=1,\ldots,N}$ is a sequence in the unit hypercube $[0, 1]^s$. Two keys to the successful use of QMC in higher dimensions are the construction of good sequences and the intelligent use of the sequences for path generation. Next we turn to the construction of higher-dimensional sequences.

Several high-dimensional sequences have been proposed for use in quasi Monte Carlo methods. We give a very brief introduction to the Halton, Faure, and Sobol sequences. Other important sequences include the Niederreiter and generalized Faure sequences (see Bratley et al. (1992) and Ninomiya and Tezuka (1996)). The Halton sequence is a general s-dimensional sequence in the unit hypercube $[0, 1]^s$. The first dimension of the Halton sequence is the van der Corput sequence using base 2 and the second dimension is the van der Corput sequence using base 3. Dimension s of the Halton sequence is the van der Corput sequence using the sth prime number as the base. The van der Corput sequence using base 3 begins 1/3, 2/3, 1/9, 4/9, 7/9, 2/9, 5/9, 8/9, 1/27, 10/27, 19/27, ... The two-dimensional Halton sequence is illustrated in Figure 5.9.

Problems with the Halton sequence are illustrated in (c) of Figure 5.9. Panel (c) of the figure shows the projection of coordinates 29 and 30 of the first thousand points of the thirty-dimensional Halton sequence. Since the base of the van der Corput sequence becomes larger as the dimension increases, it takes increasingly longer to fill the unit hypercube. (The 29th and 30th primes are 109 and 113, respectively.) The figure shows that points in successive dimensions are highly correlated and, in high dimensions, the initial points in the Halton sequence are clustered near zero. All of these problems can lead to poor integral estimates.

The Faure sequence is also a general s-dimensional sequence. Unlike the Halton sequence, all dimensions use the smallest prime p such that $p \geq s$ and $p \geq 2$ as the base. The first dimension of the Faure sequence is the van der Corput sequence in base p. Higher dimensions are permutations of the sequence in the first dimension. The three-dimensional Faure sequence begins (1/3, 1/3, 1/3), (2/3, 2/3, 2/3), (1/9, 4/9, 7/9), (4/9, 7/9, 1/9), (7/9, 1/9, 4/9), (2/9, 8/9, 5/9), (5/9, 2/9, 8/9), (8/9, 5/9, 2/9), (1/27, 16/27, 13/27), (10/27, 25/27, 22/27), (19/27, 7/27, 4/27), ... Details of the Faure sequence and an implementation are given in Fox (1986).

In the general s-dimensional Sobol' sequence, all dimensions use the prime number 2 as the base. The first dimension of the Sobol' sequence is the van der Corput sequence in base 2, and higher dimensions are permutations of the sequence in the first dimension. The permutations depend on a set of direction numbers, and the Sobol' sequence is not uniquely defined until all of these direction numbers are defined. A three-dimensional Sobol sequence begins (1/2, 1/2, 1/2), (1/4, 3/4, 1/4), (3/4, 1/4, 3/4), (3/8, 5/8, 1/8), (7/8, 1/8, 5/8), (1/8, 3/8, 3/8), (5/8, 7/8, 7/8), (5/16, 5/16, 11/16), (13/16, 13/16, 3/16), (1/16, 9/16, 15/16), (9/16, 1/16, 7/16), (3/16, 15/16, 9/16), (11/16, 7/16, 1/16), (7/16, 3/16, 13/16), (15/16, 11/16, 5/16), ... The Sobol sequence can be generated significantly faster

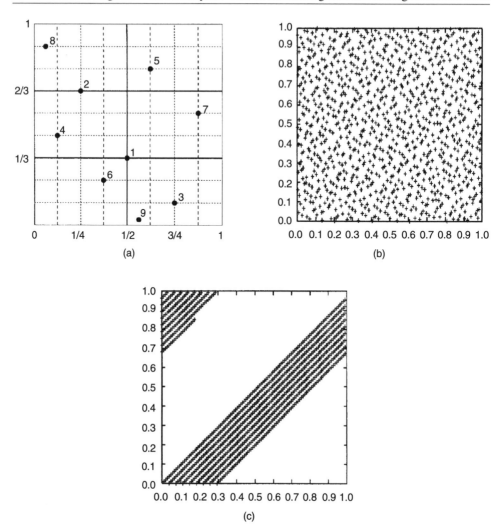

Figure 5.9   (a) The first nine points of the two-dimensional Halton sequence; (b) the first thousand points of the two-dimensional Halton sequence; (c) the first thousand points in dimensions 29 and 30 of the 30-dimensional Halton sequence

than the Faure sequence and faster than most pseudo-random number methods. Details are given in Bratley and Fox (1988).

A better understanding of the merits of various sequences can be gained through the concepts of (t, m, s)-nets and (t, s)-sequences. We give a brief introduction next; for more details see Niederreiter (1992). An elementary interval in base b in dimension s is a set of the form

$$\prod_{j=1}^{s} \left(\frac{a_j}{b^{k_j}}, \frac{a_j + 1}{b^{k_j}} \right) \tag{29}$$

with k_j, a_j non-negative integers and $a_j < b^{k_j}$. A (t, m, s)-net (with $0 \le t \le m$) is a set of b^m points in the s-dimensional hypercube such that every elementary interval of volume

b^{t-m} contains b^t points. That is, elementary intervals that "should" have b^t points do have b^t points, but elementary intervals that "should" have b^{t-1} points, b^{t-2} points, ..., or one point, may not. Smaller t is preferred since it implies greater uniformity. An infinite sequence forms a (t, s)-sequence if, for all $m \geq t$, certain finite subsequences of length b^m form (t, m, s)-nets in base b. Infinite (t, s)-sequences are useful, since if the first b^m points are not sufficient, then another b^m points will tend to fill in the gaps from the first set. A smaller base is preferable, since it implies that uniformity holds over shorter subsequences.

Faure points are $(0, s)$-sequences in prime bases not less than s and Sobol points are (t, s)-sequences in base 2. Thus, Faure points achieve the smallest value of t, but at the expense of a larger base. These properties are illustrated in Figure 5.10. Panel (a) of the figure shows $7^3 = 343$ Faure points in dimension 6, including zero as the first point of the sequence. Every box shown in (a) has volume $1/7^2$ and contains exactly $b = 7$ points. When counting the points, note that the left and bottom sides are included in each box, but the right and top sides are not, as specified by the definition in (29). Furthermore, closer inspection of panel (a) shows that every elementary interval with volume $1/7^3$ contains exactly one point. Panel (b) shows $2^8 = 256$ Sobol points in dimension 5, also including zero as the first point in the sequence. Every box in (b) has volume $1/2^6$ and contains exactly $2^2 = 4$ points. However, as the box on the lower left of (b) illustrates, not every elementary interval with volume $1/2^8$ contains exactly one point.

Figure 5.11 gives a comparison of one thousand uniform (i.e. pseudo-random), Halton, Faure, and Sobol points in the thirty-dimensional hypercube. Plots of the uniform points in any pair of dimensions yield qualitatively similar results. Any finite set of points from the other sequences suffers, to some degree, from problems of non-uniformity. As illustrated in Figure 5.11, the non-uniformity is quite pronounced for the Halton sequence, but is much less problematic for the Faure and Sobol sequences. The figure also illustrates that the initial coordinates have better uniformity properties than later coordinates.

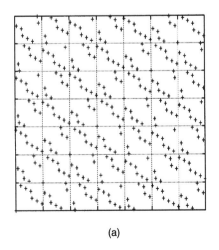

(a)

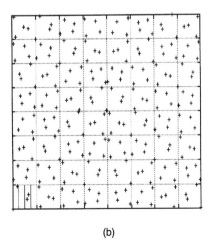

(b)

Figure 5.10 (a) $7^3 = 343$ Faure points in dimension 6. The base is $b = 7$ with dimension 2 vs. dimension 5 shown. (b) $2^8 = 256$ Sobol points in dimension 5. The base is $b = 2$ with dimension 4 vs. dimension 5 shown

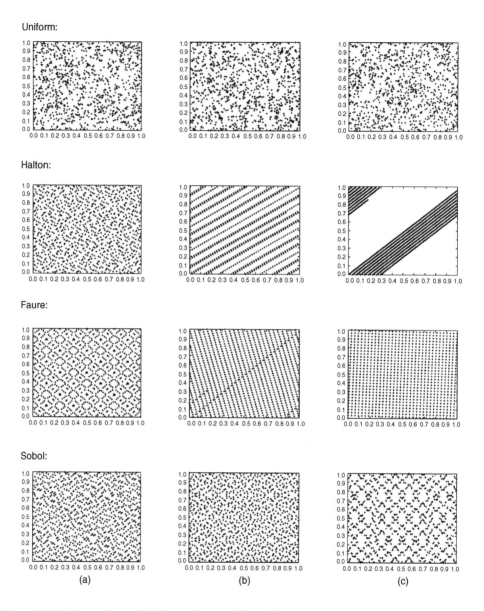

Figure 5.11   Comparison of uniform (i.e. pseudo-random), Halton, Faure, and Sobol sequences in thirty dimensions: (a) dimensions 1 and 2; (b) dimensions 14 and 19; (c) shows dimensions 29 and 30

The concepts of (t, m, s)-nets and (t, s)-sequences are related to the notion of discrepancy which, in turn, is related to the effectiveness of a sequence for numerical integration. Let $x_1, x_2, \ldots, x_N$ be a sequence in the s-dimensional unit hypercube $[0, 1]^s$. Let $J \subseteq [0, 1]^s$ and define

$$D(J; N) = \frac{\#\{n : x_n \in J\}}{N} - V(J)$$

where $V(J)$ is the volume of J. We would like $D(J;N)$ to be zero (or as small as possible) for all sets J, for this would mean that every set J that "should" contain $NV(J)$ points does contain that many points. Expressed another way, $D(J;N) = 0$ would mean that the sequence $\{x_n\}_{n=1,\dots,N}$ can integrate simple functions exactly: define the indicator function f by $f(x) = 1$ if $x \in J$, and $f = 0$ otherwise. Then $\int_{[0,1]^s} f(x)\,dx$ is the volume $V(f)$. The estimate of the integral $(1/N)\sum_{n=1}^{N} f(x_n)$ is $\#\{n : x_n \in J\}/N$. Hence, $D(J;N) = 0$ means that $(1/N)\sum_{n=1}^{N} f(x_n) = \int_{[0,1]^s} f(x)\,dx$.

Unfortunately, the definition of $D(J;N)$ is useless unless the set of subsets J is restricted to a "reasonable" class, for otherwise $D(J;N)$ could always be arbitrarily close to one. The *star discrepancy* of the sequence is

$$D_N^* = \sup_{J \in E^*} |D(J;N)|$$

where E^* is the set of all subrectangles of $[0,1]^s$ with a corner at 0. The importance of star discrepancy is contained in the Koksma–Hlawka inequality for integration error.

Define the integration error by

$$\varepsilon_N(f) = \frac{1}{N}\sum_{n=1}^{N} f(x_n) - \int_{[0,1]^s} f(x)\,dx$$

The Koksma–Hlawka inequality states that

$$|\varepsilon_N(f)| \le V(f)D_N^* \tag{30}$$

where $V(f)$ is the variation of f, i.e. a measure of the variability or non-linearity of f (see Niederreiter (1992) for a detailed definition). The first term on the right of (30) depends only on the function f; the second term depends only on the sequence $\{x_n\}$. An infinite sequence $\{x_n\}_{n=1,2,\dots}$ is a *low discrepancy (or quasi-random) sequence* if

$$D_N^* \le \frac{c(\log N)^k}{N}$$

where the constants c and k may depend on the dimension s. Hence, by the Koksma–Hlawka inequality, a low discrepancy sequence has integration error which converges as $O((\log N)^k/N)$ for functions of finite variation. The Halton, Faure, and Sobol sequences are all low discrepancy sequences.

The deterministic error measure $\varepsilon_N(f)$ defined above can be contrasted with the usual measure of Monte Carlo integration error. If the points $x_1, \dots, x_N$ are random and uniformly distributed on $[0,1]^s$, then

$$\sqrt{E[\varepsilon_N(f)^2]} = \sigma(f)\frac{1}{\sqrt{N}}$$

where

$$\sigma(f) = \sqrt{\left(\int_{[0,1]^s} (f(x) - \overline{f})^2\,dx\right)}$$

and $\overline{f} = \int_{[0,1]^s} f(x)\,dx$. The probabilistic integration error with standard Monte Carlo converges as $O(1/\sqrt{N})$. For N large enough, the (deterministic) integration error with quasi-random sequences will be smaller than the (probablistic) Monte Carlo error.

Although low discrepancy sequences will eventually dominate random sequences, which method dominates for a given set of functions f within a reasonable computational budget is largely an empirical issue. Some general results have emerged (see, for example, Boyle et al. (1997), Caflisch et al. (1997), and Paskov and Traub (1995)):

- For functions that typically arise in security pricing, many studies have found the performance of QMC methods to equal or exceed that of standard Monte Carlo (although the latter method can easily generate error estimates, whereas the former cannot).

- In low dimensions, the performance of some low discrepancy sequences is often dramatically better than Monte Carlo.

- The Halton sequence is dominated by the Faure and Sobol sequences.

- The relative advantage of QMC over standard MC decreases as the dimension of the problem increases.

- For some high-dimensional problems the relative advantage of QMC can be increased by judicious use of the sequences.

On the last point, note that problems with a high nominal dimension may have a much lower effective dimension. For example, the high dimensionality of integrals often arises from the number of points sampled on a low-dimensional process. In this case, the Brownian bridge or principal components constructions described in Section 5.4.2 can be used to lower the effective dimension of the problem (see Acworth et al. (1997) and Caflisch et al. (1997)). These ideas are particularly well suited to QMC, because of the property noted earlier that the early coordinates of low discrepancy sequences enjoy better uniformity properties than the later coordinates.

5.6 ESTIMATING VALUE AT RISK

Our discussion thus far has focused primarily on the use of Monte Carlo simulation for the pricing of derivatives. A related and growing area of application of simulation in risk management is the estimation of Value at Risk (VaR). In the simplest implementations, VaR calculation can be carried out without simulation; but as realism is added to the modeling of risk factors and complexity is added to the universe of instruments that must be incorporated in VaR, simulation becomes the method of choice. Whereas the underlying theory and methods for option pricing are fairly well developed — and the application of simulation well established — both the principles underlying risk measurement and their implementation are still emerging.

We begin with a standard definition: a portfolio's VaR for a time horizon T and a probability α is the magnitude of loss that will be exceeded with probability α. Thus,

$$\text{Pr (Loss} > \text{VaR)} = \alpha \qquad (31)$$

where "Loss" is the difference between the portfolio's current value and its value at time T. Essentially all approaches to VaR calculation are based on specifying (if only implicitly) a set of risk factors and market rates $X_1, \ldots, X_n$ to which a portfolio is exposed, and a valuation function $f(X_1, \ldots, X_n)$ giving the change in the value of the portfolio for each outcome of the underlying factors and rates at the end of the horizon T. We may therefore re-express (31) as

$$\Pr(f(X_1, \ldots, X_n) > \text{VaR}) = \alpha \qquad (32)$$

Viewed from the general perspective of Monte Carlo simulation, the calculation of VaR is thus a problem of quantile estimation. Two particular features distinguish it from the generic problem: (i) the joint distribution of $X_1, \ldots, X_n$ may be poorly understood and difficult to model reliably; and (ii) the function f may be inordinately burdensome to evaluate. Several issues contribute to these features:

- The number of relevant factors may be large. For a relatively simple portfolio — one consisting solely of foreign exchange positions, say — a limited set of factors may suffice to determine the portfolio value. But for a complex portfolio combining positions in individual equities, bonds, mortgage-backed securities, and options the number of factors can easily become unmanageable.

- The distributions of the factors are frequently heavy-tailed and sometimes skewed. As a result, the simplifying assumption of normality is often inappropriate.

- The dependence among factors can be difficult to model; in particular, correlation can be of limited value in describing complex interactions. For example, the dependence between two factors that usually move independently but occasionally make large moves together is not easily captured through correlation.

- For portfolios containing options or mortgage-backed securities, each evaluation of the function f (i.e. each revaluation of the portfolio) may entail execution of multiple, complex pricing routines. The computational burden is multiplied by the fact that the portfolio must be revalued many times (for different outcomes of the factors) in order to form a distribution of changes in portfolio value from which VaR can be estimated.

With these points in mind, it is useful to categorize approaches to VaR according to (i) how they specify the distribution of the underlying factors and (ii) how they revalue a portfolio in each factor scenario. For (i), there are two main approaches — parametric (including normal) and non-parametric. The principal methods used for (ii) are linear approximation, full revaluation, and some combinations of these methods. We now briefly describe some of the most notable combinations of these methods.

5.6.1 Covariance Solution

This method, popularized by J.P. Morgan's RiskMetrics^{TM}, assumes that changes in the underlying factors are multivariate normal and that all instruments in the portfolio depend linearly on the factors. Because linear combinations of normal random variables are normal, these assumptions imply that changes in portfolio value are normally distributed. As a consequence, calculation of VaR reduces to calculation of the portfolio standard deviation. This standard deviation is easily obtained from the covariance matrix of the factors and the sensitivities of the instruments to these factors. The covariance matrix is typically estimated from historical data. No simulation is required for this method. Its primary attraction is its simplicity; but its key assumptions of normality and linearity are very restrictive.

5.6.2 Historical Simulation

This method takes the actual changes in market prices and rates over a specified lookback period (e.g. 40 days or 1 year) as the total population of factor changes. A portfolio is walked through the historical movements and revalued after each movement to create a distribution from which VaR can be calculated. In principle, each revaluation can require major calculations; in practice, simplifications are usually made to keep the method feasible. Historical simulation is not simulation in the sense that the term was used earlier in the chapter because it does not involve sampling from distributions. In using only historical data, the method is completely non-parametric and makes no explicit assumptions about distributions; a shortcoming of the approach is that small samples of historical data inevitably leave unrealistic gaps in the distributions of factor changes and tend to underrepresent the tails. For further discussion of this method, see Chapters 3 and 4 in this volume

5.6.3 Monte Carlo Simulation with Full Revaluation

The main alternative to assuming factor movements are normally distributed or using only historical movements fits a parametric distribution to historical data. For the marginal distributions a heavy-tailed distribution like the Student's t or Pareto is often suggested. The four-parameter family of Ramberg et al. (1979) (RDTM) provides enough flexibility to match a wide range of values of skew and kurtosis. To model dependence among the factors, rank correlation may be more convenient than ordinary correlation for non-normal distributions. Shaw (1995) advocates a combination of the RDTM family and Stein's (1987) rank correlation method as a way of balancing the advantages of historical data and standard distributions.

Once we move away from the normal assumption, the analytical calculation of VaR generally becomes intractable even for simple portfolios — for example, even when all instruments depend linearly on the factors. Monte Carlo simulation becomes the method of choice. We generate a set of factor scenarios from the fitted distribution and for each scenario we revalue the portfolio. We then estimate VaR from the distribution of changes in value.

The bottleneck in this procedure is not the sampling of scenarios (which can usually be done very quickly) but rather the revaluation of a portfolio in each scenario. If the portfolio contains mortgage-backed securities or path-dependent options, then each revaluation may itself require many replications of a Monte Carlo algorithm, so we are forced to run simulations within simulations. The computational burden of this approach generally renders it infeasible, though in the absence of computational constraints this method would produce the most credible VaR estimates.

5.6.4 Monte Carlo Simulation with Interpolation

This method balances the realism of the full Monte Carlo procedure just described with the constraints imposed by computing resources. Rather than revalue the portfolio in every factor scenario, this method revalues at a prespecified grid of combinations of factor levels. The grid points are chosen to be representative of a wide but realistic set of factor levels. Then, for each randomly generated factor scenario, an approximate portfolio value is computed by interpolating between grid points. Using, say, 100 grid points and 10 000 factor scenarios, a distribution of 10 000 changes in portfolio value can be evaluated for little more than the cost of 100 portfolio revaluations. Specific versions of this general idea have been proposed by Jamshidian and Zhu (1997) and Shaw (1995). In some cases, the portfolio revaluations can be supplemented with estimates of sensitivities to underlying factors with modest additional computing, and these are potentially useful for interpolation; Broadie and Glasserman (1996) present efficient methods for estimating price sensitivities by simulation.

The grid method is particularly attractive when the number of relevant factors is large but each instrument in the portfolio is sensitive to few factors. As an extreme case, suppose each instrument is sensitive to just one factor. This could be the case in a portfolio of FX options if each option is assumed to be sensitive to just a single exchange rate. In this case, we can write

$$ f(X_1, \ldots, X_n) = f_1(X_1) + \cdots + f_n(X_n) $$

where f_i gives the value of all instruments sensitive to the ith factor. Now suppose that in designing a grid we choose k levels for each factor, corresponding to a range of positive and negative movements. By carrying out k evaluations of each f_i, $i = 1, \ldots, n$ (at a total computational cost roughly proportional to nk) we obtain k^n grid points (corresponding to the number of combinations of the k values of the f_i) at which the portfolio is valued exactly and from which we can interpolate. For $n = 7$ and $k = 4$ this corresponds to 16 384 grid points for the cost of 28 evaluations of the f_i.

An additional feature of this approach, relevant for computing VaR over longer horizons, is that the grids can, to some extent, be computed in advance. Consider, for example, the estimation of a two-week VaR carried out every two weeks. Until the end of a two-week period, we do not know the levels of market rates from which VaR should be estimated; however, we may have a good idea of their likely range, and this is sufficient to choose grid points. The computational cost of building a grid can therefore be spread over two weeks, at least if the portfolio composition is stable. At the end of the two weeks, factor scenarios can be generated starting from current market levels and the changes in portfolio value interpolated from the precomputed grid.

5.7 ENDNOTES

1. In this and all subsequent examples, the choice of drift depends on the application, even once the security is fixed. For option pricing, one would typically simulate the underlying asset under the risk-neutral probability measure, in which the drift would be the risk-free interest rate less any dividend yield. To calculate value at risk and related risk measures, one would simulate the real-world dynamics of asset prices using some estimate of the actual drift parameter.
2. Nelson (1990) shows, however, that they have precise interpretations as approximations to continuous-time processes.
3. The operation $a \pmod{b}$ returns the remainder of a after division by b.
4. From a vector X determine the vector of ranks of the entries of X. For example, the rank vector for $(0.25, -1.34, 0.12, 0.44)$ is $(2, 4, 3, 1)$. The rank correlation matrix of X is the correlation matrix of its rank vector.
5. For background on this distribution, see Johnson et al. (1995).
6. To view (12) as a special case (20) we need to interpret "vector" broadly enough to include a forward curve defined by a continuum of rates. In practice, one would ordinarily simulate only finitely many points along the curve.
7. There are at least two settings in which yet another layer of simulation could be imposed. In computing a price *sensitivity* one might price at two or more different initial values of an underlying and then take differences. In computing Value at Risk, one might repeatedly price

at various randomly generated initial values to get a distribution of prices and then a quantile of the distribution.

8. In some cases this bias can be eliminated; see Andersen and Brotherton-Ratcliffe (1996) and Beaglehole et al. (1997). In other cases, Richardson extrapolation, as in Kloeden and Platen (1992, p. 285), can be used to reduce discretization bias.

9. This is easily verified; see, for example, Boyle et al. (1997). We compare the variance from m antithetic pairs with the variance from $2m$ independent samples in order to compare results that can be obtained with roughly the same computational effort.

10. These authors used the construction with quasi Monte Carlo sequences but it can also be applied with stratified sampling.

11. Consider, for example, an option on k correlated underlying assets simulated via (17). In this case, the relevant Gaussian vector is the X_i in (17), whose components are associated with different assets rather than different times.

12. This is the Latin square property.

13. To generate a random permutation of $\{1, \ldots, n\}$, select an element of this set randomly, then select one of the remaining elements randomly, and so on.

14. The adjustment would be made across paths to all Zs used to generate an increment from some fixed t_j to t_{j+1}, not to the Zs used along a single path to generate increments at different times.

15. For a given N, the set of points which is "maximally spread out" in $(0, 1)$ is $y_n = (2n - 1)/2N$. However, increasing N by one leads to a completely disjoint set of points, which is not a useful property for computational purposes.

5.8 REFERENCES

Acworth, P., Broadie, M. and Glasserman, P. (1997) "A comparison of some Monte Carlo and quasi Monte Carlo methods for option pricing", in H. Niederreiter, P. Hellekalek, G. Larcher and P. Zinterhof (eds), *Monte Carlo and Quasi-Monte Carlo Methods*. New York: Springer-Verlag.

Andersen, L. and Brotherton-Ratcliffe, R. (1996) "Exact exotics". *Risk*, **9**, 85–89.

Barraquand, J. (1995) "Numerical valuation of high dimensional multivariate European securities". *Management Science*, **41**, 1882–1891.

Beaglehole, D.R., Dybvig, P.H. and Zhou, G. (1997) "Going to extremes: Correcting simulation bias in exotic option valuation". *Financial Analysts Journal*, **53**, 62–68.

Boyle, P., Broadie, M. and Glasserman, P. (1997) "Monte Carlo methods for security pricing". *Journal of Economic Dynamics and Control*, **21**, 1267–1321.

Bratley, P. and Fox, B.L. (1988) "ALGORITHM 659: Implementing Sobol's quasirandom sequence generator". *ACM Transactions on Mathematical Software*, **14**, 88–100.

Bratley, P., Fox, B.L. and Niederreiter, H. (1992) "Implementation and tests of low-discrepancy sequences". *ACM Transactions on Modelling and Computer Simulation*, **2**, 195–213.

Bratley, P., Fox, B.L. and Schrage, L. (1987) *A Guide to Simulation*. New York: Springer-Verlag.

Broadie, M. and Glasserman, P. (1996) "Estimating security price derivatives by simulation". *Management Science*, **42**, 269–285.

Caflisch, R.E., Morokoff, W. and Owen, A. (1997) "Valuation of mortgage backed securities using Brownian bridges to reduce effective dimension". *Journal of Computational Finance*, **1**, 27–46.

Caflisch, R.E. and Moskowitz, B. (1995) "Modified Monte Carlo methods using quasi-random sequences", in H. Niederreiter and P.J.-S. Shiue (eds), *Monte Carlo and Quasi-Monte Carlo Methods in Scientific Computing*. New York: Springer-Verlag.

Cox, J., Ingersoll, J.E. and Ross, S.A. (1985) "A theory of the term structure of interest rates". *Econometrica*, **53**, 385–407.

Devroye, L. (1986) *Non-Uniform Random Variate Generation*. New York: Springer-Verlag.

Duan, J.-C. and Simonato, J.-G. (1995) "Empirical martingale simulation for asset prices". Working paper, Faculty of Management, McGill University, Montreal, Canada.

Duffie, D. and Glynn, P.W. (1996), "Efficient Monte Carlo simulation of security prices". *Annals of Applied Probability*, **5**, 897–905.

Dupire, B. (1994) "Pricing with a smile". *Risk*, **7**, 18–20.

Engle, R.F. and Rosenberg, J.V. (1995) "GARCH gamma". *Journal of Derivatives*, **Summer**, 47–59.

Fishman, G.S. (1996) *Monte Carlo: Concepts, Algorithms, and Applications*. New York: Springer-Verlag.

Fishman, G.S. and Moore, L.S., III (1986) "An exhaustive analysis of multiplicative congruential random number generators with modulus $2^{31} - 1$, *SIAM Journal on Statistical Computing*, **7**, 24–45.

Fong, H.G. and Vasicek, O. (1992) "Interest rate volatility as a stochastic factor". Working paper, Gifford Fong and Associates.

Fox, B.L. (1986) "ALGORITHM 647: Implementation and relative efficiency of quasi-random sequence generators". *ACM Transactions on Mathematical Software*, **12**, 362–376.

Heath, D., Jarrow, R. and Morton, A. (1992) "Bond pricing and the term structure of interest rates: A new methodology for contingent claims valuation". *Econometrica*, **60**, 77–105.

Hellekalek, P. (1995) "Inversive Pseudorandom Number Generators: Concepts, Results, and Links". *Proceedings of the Winter Simulation Conference*. San Diego: IEEE Press, pp. 255–262. (See also `http://random.mat.sbg.ac.at.`)

Hull, J. and White, A. (1987) "The pricing of options on assets with stochastic volatilities". *Journal of Finance*, **42**, 281–300.

Jamshidian, F. and Zhu, Y. (1997) "Scenario simulation: Theory and methodology". *Finance and Stochastics*, **1**, 43–67.

Johnson, N.L., Kotz, S. and Balakrishnan, N. (1995) *Continuous Univariate Distributions*, Vol. 2, 2nd edn. New York: Wiley–Interscience.

Kemna, A. and Vorst, T. (1990) "A pricing method for options based on average asset values". *Journal of Banking and Finance*, **14**, 113–129.

Kloeden, P.E. and Platen, E. (1992) *Numerical Solution of Stochastic Differential Equations*. New York: Springer-Verlag.

L'Ecuyer, P. (1994) "Uniform random number generation". *Annals of Operation Research*, **53**, 77–120.

Longstaff, F.A. and Schwartz, E.S. (1992) "Interest rate volatility and the term structure: A two-factor general equilibrium model". *Journal of Finance*, **47**, 1259–1282.

Marsaglia, G. and Zaman, A. (1991) "A new class of random number generators". *Annals of Applied Probability*, **1**, 462–480.

Marsaglia, G., Zaman, A. and Marsaglia, J. (1994) "Rapid evaluation of the inverse of the normal distribution function". *Statistics and Probability Letters*, **19**, 259–266.

McKay, M.D., Conover, W.J. and Beckman, R.J. (1979) "A comparison of three methods for selecting input variables in the analysis of output from a computer code". *Technometrics*, **21**, 239–245.

Moro, B. (1995) "The Full Monte". *RISK*, **8**, 57–58.

Nelson, D.B. (1990) "ARCH models as diffusion approximations". *Journal of Econometrics*, **45**, 7–38.

Niederreiter, H. (1992) *Random Number Generation and Quasi-Monte Carlo Methods*, CBMS-NSF, Vol. 63. Philadelphia: SIAM.

Ninomiya, S. and Tezuka, S. (1996) "Toward real-time pricing of complex financial derivatives". *Applied Mathematical Finance*, **3**, 1–20.

Paskov, S. and Traub, J. (1995) "Faster valuation of financial derivatives". *Journal of Portfolio Management*, **22**, 113–120.

Ramberg, J.S., Dudewicz, E.J., Tadikamalla, P. and Mykytka, E.F. (1979) "A probability distribution and its uses in fitting data". *Technometrics*, **21**, 201–214.

Scott, L.O. (1996) "Simulating a multi-factor term structure model over relatively long discrete time periods", in *IAFE First Annual Computational Finance Conference*. Stanford University, Graduate School of Business.

Shaw, J. (1995) "Beyond VaR and stress testing", Working paper, Global Market Risk Management Division, BZW, London.

Stein, M. (1987) "Large sample properties of simulations using Latin hypercube sampling". *Technometrics*, **29**, 143–151.

Vasicek, O.A. (1977) "An equilibrium characterization of the term structure". *Journal of Financial Economics*, **5**, 177–188.

6
An Introduction to the Technology of Risk

NIGEL WEBB

6.1 INTRODUCTION

The risk technology industry has logged only perhaps 10 years of history. During this time the nature of the systems required to manage risk have changed beyond recognition. Undoubtedly, some of this change has been led by the major advances in technology that the period has seen. Perhaps the greater force for change, though, has been the increased sophistication of the user requirement, and the demands for better systems support made by regulators and industry bodies.

In this chapter we offer an introduction to the technology required to manage risk, and describe the organizational context in which such technology should be deployed. We also cast an eye over the software industry that has grow up around the risk management imperative. This business is itself a fast-changing one, in which major mergers can seem as frequent as the arrival of new niche suppliers. This chapter attempts to peer into the mists to predict the direction that the software industry will take.

Before reading on, it is worthwhile reflecting that by the time this chapter is published, at least some of its contents will have been rendered obsolete, and some of its speculative comments will have been shown to be incorrect. Indeed, few areas of the financial markets change quite so rapidly, or as unpredictably, as risk. This starts right down at the level of the functional requirements associated with a risk management system.

6.2 FUNCTIONAL REQUIREMENTS

What should a risk system do? This apparently simple question lies at the root of many failed risk Information Technology (IT) projects. Risk itself means many things to many people. These different definitions frequently lead to contradictory or undeliverable systems requirements. Before looking at the technology itself, we look at the different risk functionality needed by modern financial institutions. Only once this is clearly understood can technology be applied to the problem with any hope of success. The reader familiar with the different families of risk measure and the distinctions between risk control and risk management may wish to go directly to Section 6.3, Designing Risk Systems.

It is conventional for textbooks to break risk into two major categories: market risk and credit risk. Market risk is usually defined as an exposure to an adverse movement in either prices, rates or volatilities, whilst credit risk is described as exposure to default or a credit event affecting a counterparty or instrument issuer.

These definitions have been so central to the industry's understanding of risk that a second, arguably more important, categorization has been almost completely eclipsed. Risk measurement requirements vary according to who the intended user is.

The way in which users wish to have risk represented to them, and the frequency with which they wish to be updated is very much a function of their role within an institution. Whereas a trader may genuinely need to see the sensitivities of his options book continuously updated at his desk, it is doubtful that this information would be of much practical use to his board of directors. And yet, the board has (increasingly) a legal requirement to understand the nature of the risk being taken by their organization.

For the purposes of this chapter we propose a model with a second axis by which risk can be categorized, namely the role of the intended information-user. The broad divisions proposed are front office, middle office and senior management. Figure 6.1 summarizes the resultant universe of risk.

6.2.1 The Front Office Requirement

In most institutions traders are organized into groups responsible for trading specific types of financial instrument. Perhaps only in the case of proprietary trading does this

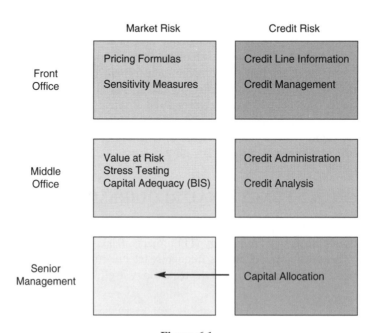

Figure 6.1

delineation start to break down. Each of these instrument types is rich with its own terminology, trading practices and market risk measures.

Whilst the jargon varies, these risk measures are usually indicators of the sensitivity of an instrument's value to a movement in one or more external rates or prices. As such, they are strongly oriented towards providing the trader with information on the hedging required to immunize a specific position against specific market risks. Some examples of the risk measures in common use are given in Table 6.1.

From a trader's perspective, the IT system he uses should be capable of capturing and displaying the transactions that he enters into, as well as being able to re-price those transactions as market conditions change. The risk information required by the trader is typically limited to the ability to see the appropriate sensitivities for his positions, calculated in real time. For more complex markets, the trader may also require the ability to perform "what if?" style operations, predicting the effect of hypothetical transactions, or market movements, on his risk sensitivities. Finally, since trading limits are frequently expressed in terms of sensitivities, traders also need the ability to view their limits and the effect of each trade on that limit.

From the credit risk perspective, the traditional view has been that the trader simply needs to be able to determine his limit utilization on a trade-by-trade basis. Until recently, credit limits have also tended to be expressed in terms of either nominal values or sensitivities, so that the same information that was appropriate for market risk had a role in the measurement of credit risk too. In more recent times this position has started to change. The sophistication and efficiency of many traded markets has taken a significant toll on the profits that are available from trading pure market exposure. As a result, financial institutions have increasingly turned to trading in markets with much poorer liquidity, using instruments whose expected future value has as much to do with the creditworthiness of the issuer or counterparty, as it has to do with more classical market movements. Such developments have led to the requirement for significantly more sophisticated credit risk quantification, much of which is finding its way through to the trader in the form of more complex limits structures. These newer structures are frequently not based on measures of risk that are specific to the instrument being traded. Rather, measures such as Credit Value at Risk (CVaR) are designed intentionally to be instrument-independent, permitting risks to be summated across many different product areas.

Not only does this give rise to the urgent need to retrain traders unfamiliar with such risk measures, it also gives rise to a very different technology requirement. Whereas the front office of the past could consist of many different systems serving the disparate

Table 6.1   Risk measures in common use

Instrument Type	Market Risk Measure
Bonds	Convexity
	Modified Duration
	PVBP
Options	Delta
	Gamma
	Vega
	Theta
Equities	Beta

and specialized requirements of each product area, the new *additional* requirement is for systems capable of calculating consistent risk measures that span the entire institution.

6.2.2 The Middle Office Requirement

This product-independent form of risk measure is much more the speciality of the middle office. A relatively new term, middle office covers a poorly defined collection of departments that normally includes:

- Risk Control
- Internal Audit
- Accounting
- Finance
- Product Control

At this juncture it is important to define two terms on which much of the rest of this chapter will depend, namely *risk management* and *risk control.*

A number of states including, most notably, Germany in its "minimum requirements" regulations, have provided strong legal definitions for the two risk departments. Over the course of the next few years, many other countries will certainly follow. The intended distinction being made between risk control and risk management can be summarized as follows.

Risk management operates within, and reports to, the front office. Risk management is responsible for pro-actively working with desk or portfolio level sensitivity information in order to ensure that during the course of the day, trading is conducted in accordance with the risk guidelines defined in each business unit's stated goals. This typically entails that risks are being hedged to an appropriate degree, and that (for example) arbitrage desks are really arbitraging, and not entering into directional speculation. Risk management groups are typically attached to each business unit, and may in reality consist of a committee formed of the head trader of the unit, assisted by other trading or quantitative resources drawn from within the team. This possibility is not regarded as problematic since risk management groups are not expected to be independent from the trading teams they work with. Such an approach also reflects the need for specialist instrument knowledge, if risk management is to be performed adequately.

Risk control, by contrast, operates within the middle office, and is required in most jurisdictions to be independent from the front office, both in terms of staff and reporting lines. The primary role of risk control is to re-actively monitor the risk profile of the entire institution, ensuring that both regulatory and internal limits on risk-taking are being adhered to. To perform this task, the risk control function should potentially be capable of re-valuing all of the positions the institution enters into, on an independent basis, permitting in turn the calculation of objective measures of the risk that each business area is running. The enterprise-wide scope of risk control gives rise to two significant differences in the information requirements of such a unit. First, the logistic and technical issues associated with consolidating all of the trades that an institution enters into means that the risk control function rarely acts upon a real-time view of risk. Secondly, the firm-wide nature of the risk measures employed by the middle office is such that real-time re-calculation, even were it possible, would be of limited additional value.

The interaction between risk control and risk management is a crucial one. Whereas risk control is expected to identify situations in which the institution's risk profile is undesirable, it is not expected to recommend a specific solution. Rather, risk control is expected to localize the issue to one or more business areas and to inform the appropriate risk management groups. These groups, with their product-specific knowledge, are then expected to map a path in trader-specific terms by which the risk situation can be normalized. This chain of command plays a key role by permitting the separation of risk control from the directing of the specific positions taken by the front office. This separation ensures that risk control do not themselves become moral or actual owners of a position that subjects the institution to risk.

This definition of risk control and risk management gives rise to quite specific IT requirements for the middle office. Compared with the real-time, product-specific requirements of the front office, the middle office requires product-independent measures, which are not necessarily calculated in real time. At first glance the lack of real-time requirement may seem odd. However, given the requirement for risk control to oversee the entire organization, the frequency with which genuine firm-wide risk-oriented decisions will realistically be taken is likely to be perhaps twice daily at the most. As we will see in due course, the lessening need for real-time data at the middle office level is a welcome factor in the design of risk systems.

Whereas the risk measures used by the front office were heavily influenced by the product being traded, the middle office has long required a measure that provided a view of risk that was independent from the product mix concerned. This need has been addressed by one of the major risk phenomena of the 1990s, namely Value at Risk (VaR). Together with stress-testing and back-testing, these are the key risk information requirements for the middle office.

VaR is more than adequately addressed elsewhere in this book. For systems purposes, though, VaR can be seen as a measure that provides the user with an indication of the maximum probable loss that a portfolio (or by extension, an institution) can be subjected to, over a given period, and with a given degree of confidence. Within reason, a VaR number can be calculated for a portfolio containing any number of different types of asset. The obvious fit of the VaR concept to the needs of the middle office has not been lost on the various banking regulators. Recommendations issued by the Basle Group (BIS) and now embodied in legal frameworks such as the European Capital Adequacy Directive (CAD2) are starting to permit financial institutions to measure their regulatory capital requirements in terms of VaR. As VaR grows in acceptability, so the functional requirements of the middle office are expanding in turn to encompass regulatory reporting, based on the same risk information required for internal risk control.

Many different techniques exist to calculate VaR and each presents a slightly different set of challenges to the underlying technology. In turn, each form of VaR can be criticized for certain methodological weaknesses. Generically, though, the biggest single weakness in VaR as a middle office risk measure is its inability to indicate the degree of loss possible in the event of a market move that falls outside the model's designed degree of confidence.

For this reason, industry bodies such as the Basle Group require middle offices using VaR for capital calculations to use other additional forms of risk measure. In addition to VaR, the institution must be able to perform so-called "stress testing", in which the entire institution's positions are re-valued under the assumption of various prescribed large-scale price and rate movements. The resultant changes in overall profit and loss are another input that risk control must be able to monitor through their IT systems.

Finally, the middle office systems must also be capable of performing retrospective analysis of the actual profits and losses encountered by an institution, and contrasting them with the VaR predicted loss patterns. Such "back-testing" is a continuous task, aimed at ensuring that the VaR models being used by the institution are providing a valid view of the risks actually inherent in the market. Poor back-testing results will ultimately disqualify a model from use for regulatory purposes, as well as providing a warning to the risk controllers about the safety of their decision making.

6.2.3 The Back Office Requirement

Whilst the failure of financial institutions is always a complex matter, the poor quality of information available to senior management is frequently cited as one of the causal factors. The recent focusing by regulators on risk has further intensified the appetite amongst boards of directors for risk-related management information. This said, there is considerable confusion as to what type of information management should be provided with, and with what frequency it is required.

One approach to this problem is to think in terms of capital. The board of directors and their immediate reports are, amongst other things, responsible for determining the level of returns that a company's shareholders will see on their investments. By making this decision, the directors are also implicitly determining the level of risk that their institution is prepared to tolerate. In an institution comprising several different business units, the problem becomes one of how to allocate economic capital between the different units. In a well-diversified institution, this presents a analogous problem to that of a private investor invited to allocate his funds between a variety of high-risk/high-return and low-risk/low-return investment opportunities.

To make such an allocation, the board needs to know not only the return characteristics of each business unit, but also to understand the risks that each unit runs. This concept is captured in a family of measures known as Risk Adjusted Performance Measures (RAPMs). Conventionally, it is assumed that performance can be measured by relating the return made by a business unit to the capital that it employs in making that return. However, such a performance measure does not take into account the degree of risk taken by the unit to realize the return, giving no basis for direct unit-to-unit comparison. In essence RAPMs work by biasing either the apparent return made, or the amount of economic capital employed, to reflect the risk involved in the business unit. The effect of this biasing is to risk-normalize the performance measures of each unit, allowing a direct comparison to be made. A board of directors can then allocate capital more efficiently between units in pursuance of a specific defined risk profile.

For such an approach to be valid, the measure of risk used to create such an RAPM must be consistent with the view of risk being taken in the middle office. As a result, the middle office finds itself in the position of inheriting one further functional requirement, namely the production of performance data for senior management.

Summarizing the preceding requirements, a number of key points emerge. Each of these points has a profound impact on the design of risk systems. Table 6.2 presents such a summary.

Table 6.2

Organizational Level	Risk Measures	Timeliness	Scope	Examples
Front office	Instrument-specific	Real time	Portfolio-wide, Desk-wide	Delta Convexity Duration
Middle office	Instrument-independent	Daily	Firm-wide	VaR, CVaR Stress-testing Back-testing
Back office	Performance-related	Monthly?	Group-wide	RAROC RORAC

6.2.4 Key Design Considerations

1. The requirement for real-time data is largely restricted to the front office.

2. The risk data required by the front office are widely varying and highly specific to the nature of the products being traded.

3. The risk-related conclusions being drawn by the middle office must be demonstrably independent from the front office.

4. The requirements of risk management and risk control are very different, but the conclusions drawn by each must be reconcilable.

5. Credit risk and market risk become more closely linked the higher up the organizational structure one goes. At the risk control level, they are virtually inseparable.

6.2.5 A Final Note on Organizational Structure

Before moving on to the nature of the technology required to service these functional requirements, it is worthwhile making one last comment on the nature of real financial institutions. Whilst the model that we have unveiled over the course of the last few pages implies a single risk control function, operating alongside a number of risk management teams, in fact this is likely to be an oversimplification. The distributed nature of many institutions and the global nature of the traded markets frequently forces the creation of local risk control functions to service each major trading centre. This has the effect of creating an additional tier to the model, in which local risk management are overseen by local risk control, who in turn report to a central risk control function. Such a real-world structure has the effect of introducing another level of risk consolidation at the local risk control level, prior to the overall consolidation of risk, performed by central risk control. The effect of this pre-consolidation, compounded with the delays inherent in operating across multiple time zones, further underlines the non-real-time nature of the data acted upon by central risk control.

6.3 DESIGNING RISK SYSTEMS

Having established that an institution's risk management requirements at the desk level are fundamentally different from its risk control requirements at the firm-wide level, it follows that risk is not a problem resolved by a single system. This is not an original observation.

However, during the 1980s and early 1990s the tendency to think in terms of a market risk and credit risk division resulted in systems designers splitting the technology along these lines, rather than along the organizational lines described earlier in this chapter. Whilst there are still many commercially available products that fit this early characterization, most modern risk management systems now aspire either to the enterprise-wide role required by the risk control function, or to the product-specific speciality role appropriate to the risk management function.

6.3.1 The Risk Management System

Assuming the definitions of risk management offered earlier, the concept of a risk management system is something of a misnomer. Rather, risk management functionality should be a fundamental part of any trading system. This view is borne out strongly by the growth in risk-related functionality in many of the most popular trading systems. A good example of this is Summit Systems' "Summit" product which, whilst being predominantly aimed at traders of over-the-counter interest rate derivatives, also provides all of the functionality necessary to hedge and report on the risk being run, tick by tick. Similar functionality is provided in Reuters' "Kondor+" product which, whilst it is aimed at a different product area, draws considerable attention to its support for basic hedging and risk management functionality in a real-time environment.

The screen shot shown in Figure 6.2 demonstrates the class of risk management functionality increasingly prevalent amongst front office systems. Whilst such risk functionality is becoming more common, it is also evident that at a more basic level many products in this class remain solidly rooted in one particular class of financial instrument. Support for other instruments is frequently implemented as an add-on in response to specific client demand, rather than as a core element of the software. This approach to front office systems design reflects the large number of niche providers that populate the market, frequently started by former traders, and intended to exploit specific knowledge of a particular market sector.

The fragmented nature of the market has also impacted on the nature of financial institutions' use of front office technology. Since the front office is the primary profit centre in most institutions, traders have frequently been able to select their own front office systems, largely unfettered by the constraints of any IT strategy. Whilst this has permitted them to select systems that closely fit their requirements, it has also left their host institutions with a disparate collection of systems, each with its own data formats, hardware platforms and support requirements. This difficult situation is further worsened by the frequency with which trading staff circulate between institutions, taking their technological preferences with them.

The result of this picture is that whilst risk management functionality is typically well covered by the trading systems in each business unit, risk control is either seriously neglected or suffers from late and variable-quality information. As the importance increases of optimizing traders' return on capital, this situation is becoming less tenable, and risk management becomes less able to operate.

6.3.2 Risk Control Systems

Against this backdrop, the major problem facing the risk control systems designer is obtaining and aggregating data. A typical large institution may operate more than 100

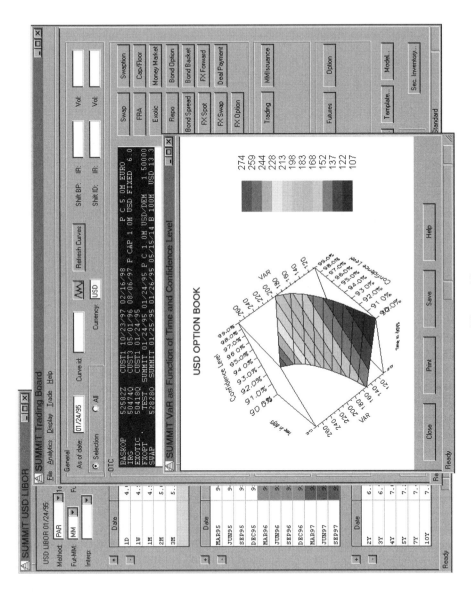

Figure 6.2

different front office systems, each of which holds its own private pool of data. Such systems are frequently referred to by technologists as "islands of information".

For risk control purposes, we need to understand three generic types of information stored in such islands. These are Transactions, Valuation Parameters, and Standing Data (Figure 6.3).

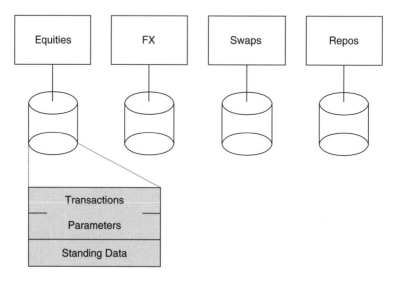

Figure 6.3

- *Transactions.*   Every time a trader performs a trade, one or more transaction records are typically recorded by his front office system. These transaction records will often contain information such as the deal date, the settlement date, the instrument type concerned, the price at which the deal was entered and any expiry, maturity or delivery date concerned.

- *Valuation Parameters.*   To be able to price a transaction, most front office systems also store such structures as yield curves, volatility surfaces and price histories.

- *Standing Data.*   Standing Data is typically divided into two elements. First, most front office systems will have a mechanism for storing details relating to the counterparties with which transactions are performed. These details may include such information as names and addresses, as well as trading limits and standard settlement instructions. The second type of Standing Data normally found on such systems consists of master instrument definitions, defining the structure, terms and re-valuation rules associated with each of the key instrument and contract types.

Having defined the problem in these terms, the role of the risk control system is to act as a focal point for the collection of sufficient data so as to be able to re-create the risk characteristics of every transaction contained in each of the front office systems. This brings us to the architecture of a risk control system.

Risk control systems can be seen as comprising three key elements: a data warehouse, a middleware layer, and an analytics facility. These are defined as follows:

A *data warehouse* is a term used to refer to a piece of software capable of storing and organizing large quantities of data. Data warehouses are normally based on commercial database management systems (the terms are frequently used interchangeably), with the added implication that a warehouse is focused towards storing data related to a particular set of business objectives. In the context of a risk control system, the data warehouse is primarily intended to store information relating to the transactions that were originally captured in each of the individual front office systems. Also stored will typically be instrument and counterparty master definitions.

To capture information from each of the front office systems within an institution, the data warehouse will normally be wrapped in a software layer often referred to as *middleware*. The objective of middleware is to present the data warehouse with the impression that all the data stored on the various front office systems has a consistent format. Well-designed middleware should therefore be capable of accepting many and various data formats from each of the source systems, mapping each one into a common format for insertion into the warehouse. By the same token, the middleware layer is also responsible for ensuring that should the data format of the warehouse change, the front office systems should be able to continue contributing data without modification. The middleware should be capable of re-mapping the data to the revised format without significant modification. A commercial middleware product frequently consists of many components, ranging from software to assist with the physical extraction of data from systems, through to rules-based mapping functionality, permitting the transformation of data from one format to another through the repeated application of a series of rules.

Having successfully consolidated the relevant details of an institution's trading data into a warehouse, the final component of the risk control system is the *analytics facility*. This describes the combination of mathematical routines, report generation facilities, and graphical displays which converts the underlying data into information for use by risk controllers to make decisions. The varied nature of the risk requirements noted earlier in this chapter means that many different suites of analytics may well be employed on the same data warehouse. Typical uses for the different suites may be internal risk control, regulatory reporting, and performance reporting to senior management.

This theoretical architecture is represented in Figure 6.4.

So far we have avoided stating explicitly the exact nature of the data stored within the data warehouse. We have simply indicated that it needs to be sufficient to re-create the risk inherent in each of the institution's positions. Two schools of thought exist as to how to achieve this goal.

In an ideal world, each transaction captured on each front office system would be transported, via middleware, into the central data warehouse. This data warehouse would have the analytic capability to re-value each transaction, and to determine its risk sensitivities. These sensitivities would then be used to produce VaR style measures, whilst the re-valuation capability would be employed to implement stress-testing. Whilst the vast majority of commercial risk control software vendors have embraced this model, it suffers from a number of significant drawbacks. The three most commonly cited are:

1. For most institutions, warehousing every transaction in a single logical warehouse would generate technically unmanageable quantities of data.

2. Despite their sophistication, there is currently no single commercially available product capable of re-valuing every transaction that an institution can generate.

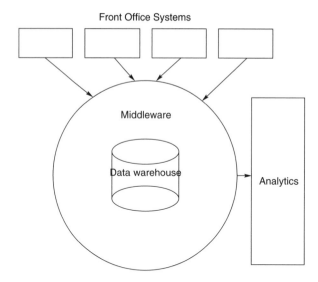

Figure 6.4

3. The re-valuation of some transactions will require local specialized judgement which
    it is difficult to embody in a single central system.

As a result of these limitations, it is doubtful that any major institution is controlling risk
using a full transaction-based data warehouse that encompasses all of its product lines
across all geographies. Instead, many institutions have succeeded only on an individual
country or product-line basis.

Many institutions aiming for genuine global risk control have adopted a different
approach. They reason that in the front office at least, each of the specialized trading
systems in use must be capable of re-pricing its positions, and generating risk sensitivities. This was, after all, a requirement for front office risk management (see above).
In preference to capturing each transaction, the central database acts as a repository for
pre-calculated risk sensitivities, each position being decomposed into a series of sensitivities to underlying risk factors. This means that rather than representing a book, or
the positions of a trading desk as a series of transactions, they are instead represented as
a series of sensitivities. This immediately solves the three problems listed above. Data
volumes decrease markedly, and the diversity and complexity of the institution's transactions are dealt with at the front office, where the specialist knowledge and systems already
exist. The calculation of VaR, given a data warehouse of sensitivities is a straightforward
matter, consisting of little more than applying either historic scenarios, or pre-calculated
risk data (such as that provided by J.P. Morgan under their Riskmetrics[TM] program) to
the assembled sensitivities.

Although this approach to risk control systems seems very appealing, it also comes at
the cost of a number of disadvantages:

1. Unless the sensitivities are produced and warehoused at a low level of granularity,
    vital credit-related information, such as the counterparty associated with a transaction,

will be lost. Such a loss of data will prevent the risk control system from expanding to deal with credit risk.

2. Relying on front office systems to pre-calculate the sensitivities used by risk control gives rise to data quality concerns. Specifically, how can one guarantee the consistency of mathematical and market assumptions inherent in the sensitivities received centrally? Equally, if the sensitivities are calculated on front office systems, the overseeing role of local risk controllers becomes even more critical if the possibility of fraud or inadvertent error is to be minimized.

3. For many instruments, their price sensitivity to an underlying risk factor will be constant with respect to that factor. The owner of a foreign equity has linear sensitivity to the rate of exchange between his own currency and that of the equity. However, for other instruments the impact of a risk factor is not linear, so that relying on a single sensitivity measure will only be valid for small movements in that factor. The sensitivity of an option's price to movement in the price of the underlying instrument (delta) is a good example of a non-linear sensitivity. Capturing the non-linearity of the sensitivity will in fact be a prerequisite for stress-testing which relies on the ability to predict the effect of large market movements on a position. The resultant requirement for each front office system to calculate a matrix of sensitivities for each position places a burden on those systems, as well as eroding the warehouse manageability gains made through this sensitivity-based approach.

It will be clear from the discussion above that neither the transaction, nor the sensitivity approach, is a clear winner in the design of a risk warehouse. For reasons of pure practicality, the first generation of such warehouses being built now are almost always based around the sensitivity approach. It remains to be seen whether the emerging technology to build genuine global transaction-based warehouses proves persuasive enough to be the backbone of the second generation.

6.4 THE RISK TECHNOLOGY INDUSTRY

Risk is a world that sells software. It will come as no surprise to find that there are many diverse organizations willing to sell systems that claim to support risk in one form or another. Increasingly, though, the industry has been marked by heavy merger activity and the rise of a few large software houses. This final section reviews the trends underlying these mergers, and looks ahead to the future of the industry.

6.4.1 The Two Types of Software Vendor

Genuine vendors of risk-related systems tend to fall into one of two groups. Either they address the real-time, front-end risk management requirement, or they seek to address the firm-wide risk component. Under the definitions suggested earlier, the former class are properly described as risk management systems, whilst the latter are risk control systems.

One of the best known vendors of risk control systems is Infinity, now part of the Sungard group of companies. Infinity was formed in the late 1980s and sought to provide a trading and pricing system, primarily aimed at sophisticated interest rate derivatives trading desks. Making liberal use of object-oriented design concepts, Infinity produced a product capable of supporting the valuation and risk analysis of heavily customized financial structures. To accomplish this degree of flexibility, Infinity was based around a comprehensive and extensible data model and database, intended to provide the capability to represent transactions which could not even be captured by more conventional trading systems. As risk has become more potent as a selling message, it has been the flexibility of this database that has permitted Infinity to modify its marketing strategy over the course of the 1990s, such that at the time of writing, Infinity positions itself with the following words:

> Infinity Financial Technology, Inc. develops and markets enterprise software solutions for financial risk management [*sic*]. These solutions address the rigorous business requirements of global organisations that manage complex financial assets, including banks, fund managers, and corporate and government treasuries.

This re-positioning has served Infinity well, permitting it to sell risk systems to some of the largest financial institutions in the developed markets. In 1997, the transformation of Infinity was completed by a series of announcements indicating that it was predominantly licensing front-end applications from third-party vendors, whilst it focused on the continued development of the underlying data model and infrastructure.

By contrast, a good example of a vendor whose product supports "risk management" functionality is Summit Systems Inc. Summit was formed in 1990 and its product of the same name was originally conceived as a trading system primarily targeted at dealers in over-the-counter interest rate derivative products. The richness of the system's functionality has found it many customers, to the extent that the breadth of instrument support found within Summit has grown dramatically. Whilst Summit supports extensive risk *management* functionality, it cannot properly be described as a firm-wide risk *control* system, since its analytics are still heavily targeted at the front office user, rather than the middle office consolidator. Summit appears to recognize this and in complete contrast to Infinity, their development direction continues to be to add further instruments to the trading systems capability, rather than to develop deeper enterprise-wide risk measures.

In the case of both Infinity and Summit, their respective risk control and risk management capabilities have effectively emerged as a side-benefit of creating a trading system. Whereas Summit has chosen to continue along the trading systems route, Infinity has mutated visibly over a short space of time. This process of convergence of risk is common in the industry, with very few companies having set out specifically to produce risk systems.

6.4.2 The Way Forward for the Technology Vendors

As this chapter has sought to demonstrate, the technical challenges involved in producing a firm-wide risk control system are considerable. The challenges relate less to the analytics than to the provision of a robust, reliable warehouse and surrounding infrastructure. A client buying such a solution will rightly expect it to underpin every single trading system in his organization. He will expect that the solution will perform appropriately despite the volumes of data involved and he will also expect support for the solution across all applicable time zones.

The size of this undertaking is infeasible for anything less than a well-resourced global firm. Whilst firms like Infinity survived their transformation to global risk vendor by way of close co-operation with established global systems integrators like IBM and Andersen

Consulting, this can only ever provide a part of the solution. The result in Infinity's case has been its incorporation into the tremendously successful Sungard group, where it expects to benefit from the global presence and increased manpower available from that group's stable of similar software houses.

At the opposite end of the scale, the prerequisites for success as a vendor of niche trading and risk management analytics systems seem as far removed from Infinity as it is possible to get. The trading and analytics systems industry is crammed full of small companies, many operating with less than 50 employees, in geographical locations far removed from the major financial centres. Companies of this type sell their products directly to the relevant parts of their clients' front offices, and expect their relatively lower price tags to be balanced by a higher number of sales.

Looking forward, it seems almost inevitable that the true firm-wide risk market will continue to be dominated by a small number of truly global firms. The mergers that have marked the late 1990s give some strong indications as to who these firms will be. We should expect to find these *megavendors* focusing increasingly on the infrastructure required for true risk control, and less on the specific analytics and functionality required for trade capture and upstream risk management.

Vendors of trading, risk management and analytics systems will continue to flourish during the coming years, although some familiar names are also likely to leave the market as the client base itself starts to undergo a period of consolidation. The route to growth for these smaller vendors will be more likely to follow the Summit model of extending the software's product coverage, rather than in migrating towards risk control infrastructure development. The Infinity route of trading system becoming risk control system is an increasingly difficult one to copy as the height of the functional hurdle is raised with each new regulatory pronouncement.

Mark-to-Future™: A Consistent Firm-Wide Paradigm for Measuring Risk and Return

RON S. DEMBO

7.1 INTRODUCTION

The typical bank today measures risk in many different ways. It computes measures at the desk level that are inconsistent with those used at the enterprise-wide level. It calculates trading limits that bear little relation to the bank's overall financial goals. It does regulatory reporting with one system and risk control with another. The incentive structures implied by the risk control function are inconsistent with the risk-adjusted return goal of the firm. Trader compensation incentives are based on risk measures that are often inconsistent with the firm's desire for maximizing risk-adjusted return. Economically efficient management of capital is hindered, if not made impossible, by the lack of a firm-wide, consistent risk measure.

This situation is partly a result of the rapid growth of the derivatives business and the massive changes in complexity experienced in capital markets. It is primarily the result of the lack of availability of a consistent, easy-to-describe framework that covers all aspects of a bank's trading risks. Most risk measures currently used in financial institutions are "backward-looking", for example measures such as volatility, and Value-at-Risk standards such as RiskMetrics™ base their inputs solely on history or point forecasts. Since risk is the result of an uncertain future, we expect a successful risk measure to focus on future events. A new, forward-looking, consistent risk paradigm is needed.

In this chapter we describe a risk measurement framework that covers all aspects of risk, from risk measured at the trading level, to risk at the enterprise level, to measures that are useful for capital allocation purposes. It is also a simple paradigm for linking different sources of correlated risk, such as credit, market and liquidity risk. It has been used successfully for over nine years in enterprise-wide risk management software developed by Algorithmics.

Risk Management and Analysis. Vol. 1: Measuring and Modelling Financial Risk.
Edited by Carol Alexander © 1998 John Wiley & Sons Ltd

7.2 A PARADIGM FOR MEASURING RISK

Risk is the result of an uncertain future. Measures of risk should therefore be forward-looking, not backward-looking. To the extent that history plays a role in risk measures it is in defining reasonable scenarios for future events. Mostly, our future follows smoothly from our past. It is not often, although it does occur, that tomorrow's environment will be radically different from today's. Typically, one day follows from the next with incremental changes in the environment. Thus, in all but totally chaotic systems, the past can be a good guide to the typical or most likely future. The farther out in time we go the more likely it is that we will find larger and larger deviations from past events. Occasionally there is a shock to our system; a market crash, an unexpected earthquake, chaos in the financial system, etc. Risk management is about being able to deal with both the typical and unusual events.

By definition, unusual events will be difficult to predict using information exclusively derived from the past. Proper measures of risk should account for both typical and atypical situations. But how atypical should the events we consider be? Should we consider the possibility of the market going to zero value? Should we assume that it is possible for three earthquakes a day to hit Tokyo for the next 10 days? Where do we draw the line between atypical and believable? What some might find believable others might dismiss.

A paradigm for risk measurement must be able to accommodate a diversity of opinions about the future. It must be able to deal with the past as a guide to the typical. It must include subjective assessments as a guide to the atypical. It must be sufficiently general to handle a multitude of risks. It must be able to present many different measures of risk, each of which might be suitable for different situations. Moreover, for financial institutions, there is a need for a single risk measure that integrates market, credit, operational, liquidity and other risks in a single framework. The risk capital that is allocated to self-insure a portfolio should cover all relevant risks. Since they are all inter-linked, a single, extensible paradigm that can accommodate such disparate but correlated sources of risk is essential.

To define such a paradigm we start with a definition of financial risk.

Financial risk is a measure of the potential changes in a portfolio as a result of changes in the environment between now and some future point in time.

A precursor to risk measurement is the ability to determine the value of one's position today. If you are unable to value your holdings today, then you are unable to measure the change from today's value that the future will bring. As a consequence, you will be unable to measure your risk. In finance this is known as mark-to-market^{TM}.

Both upward and downward movements in value generate risk. A holder of a bond profits as the fixed coupon payment becomes more valuable. But, at the same time, the issuer of the bond is paying more than expected, and is less likely to be able to pay this value. This means that just when the market risk has disappeared, credit risk to the bondholder has increased.

These observations lead to the first rule of risk measurement.

Rule 1: *Know the value of your holdings today (mark-to-market^{TM}).*

Since the risk we assume will depend on how far in the future we wish to look, choosing the horizon over which risk is to be measured is essential in order to compute a value for risk. Different situations will lead to different horizons. For example, a pension plan manager has a need to control risks over much longer periods than a trader. This motivates the second rule of risk measurement.

Rule 2: *Choose an appropriate future time horizon or time horizons.*

Risk will depend on the possible events we describe for the future. These should accommodate many types of forecasts, estimates based on history, subjective estimates and those based on models.

Probably the most general way of describing risk is scenarios. Each scenario is a realization of the future value of all the parameters that are likely to affect the portfolio under consideration. The collection of scenarios captures the likely variation in these parameters that could occur between now and the horizon. Scenarios are general in nature and can capture all the richness we will need. They are the essence of risk measurement. It is scenarios that bind the disparate sources of risk and enable measures to be developed that include all sources of risk. For example, a scenario could be the combination of a series of changes in the interest rates in different currencies, a series of credit downgrades and upgrades in various sovereign and corporate debt, simultaneous movement in the forward exchange rate curves between the ten major currencies, an increase in equity index volatility, and an operational event causing trading losses. For, as we will see, once scenarios have been determined, all that is left are calculations that are mechanical in nature. Omitting important possible events will lead to poor risk measures. Placing too heavy an emphasis on extremes may also lead to erroneous conclusions.

Choosing appropriate scenarios is the art of risk management. There are many quantitative techniques that guide the choice of scenarios. These methods are usually good at generating the more typical events. Scenarios are easy for non-technical managers to define. It is a straightforward task for an expert to understand whether or not a scenario "makes sense" or is "reasonable".

As inputs to a risk measure scenarios are preferable to data such as a covariance matrix, a commonly used input to Value-at-Risk models. A set of scenarios will generate a covariance matrix if it is required. Whereas the contents of a covariance matrix are numbers that are difficult to link precisely to one's market intuition, scenarios are easy to understand for anyone involved in the market.

At the very least, however, it is essential to know the scenarios that are being used to calculate the risk measure of choice. Many popular industry-standard risk methodologies, such as RiskMetrics™, hide the scenario choice. Scenario choice and the statistical risk measure are combined. Without explicit knowledge of the scenarios that are being used in the risk measure it is impossible to assess whether or not the risk measure is adequate.

This leads us to the third rule of risk measurement.

Rule 3: *Choose a wide range of scenarios to describe possible future events; include extremes and scenarios that contradict popular opinion; if necessary, assign a probability to each scenario. Make the scenario choice explicit!*

We are now in a position to quantify risk.

Rule 4: *Value the aged portfolio at the horizon under each and every future scenario (mark-to-future™).*

Mark-to-market™ results in a unique number because there is no uncertainty in the number. A *mark-to-future™* is a vector of numbers, one for each scenario at the horizon. The possible measures of variation in the values that are obtained are the way in which we express risk. Different measures are applicable to the many consumers of financial risk information. A fund manager might require statistics that are different than those required by a bank regulator. Yet one remarkable aspect of risk measurement is that *the raw numbers that go into these different risk measures are always the same!* They are always obtained from a valuation of your portfolio under all scenarios. The measures come in many disguises, but at the end of the day they are all derived after Rule 4 is applied either implicitly or explicitly.

In most situations risk is not an absolute measure. It is invariably the risk of one action versus another. Or, it is the risk of one portfolio as compared with another. For example, the risk might have to do with buying an additional stock versus keeping one's portfolio unchanged. It is important in such a case to measure the risk not only of holding the stock alone but also of holding the stock plus the original portfolio versus holding the original portfolio. In this case the original portfolio is the benchmark. This is important because the original portfolio as well as the stock will depend on the chosen scenarios. The incremental risk of holding the stock in addition to your portfolio will be different from holding the stock alone.

For comparative risk measures, therefore, benchmarking is essential. When benchmarking is required, the mark-to-future™ is computed on a portfolio, which consists of a long position in the original portfolio and a short position in the benchmark (see Figure 7.1).

In this paradigm all risk measures are computed from the same underlying information. That is, the values of the portfolio at the horizon under all possible scenarios. The risk measures themselves become simply different statistics computed on the mark-to-future™. For example, a Value-at-Risk number is one statistical measure that describes the lower tail of the distribution of outcomes at the horizon. The standard deviation, or volatility as it is sometimes called, is another. Regret is a third. Downside risk is a fourth. The best case and worst case ignore probabilities but are still simple statistics on the distribution of outcomes. Without doubt other new measures will be proposed in the future. The importance of the paradigm is that it separates the basic information required. *The choice of scenarios is separate from the choice of methodology for valuation, which is in turn separate from the particular choice of risk measure that is used.* By understanding this paradigm, it is easy to compare risk measures. It is easy to know when a particular risk measure is relevant.

Today, it is often the case that the scenario generation method and methodology for computing a risk statistic are intertwined; take, for example, the standards introduced by J.P. Morgan (1994, 1997) for market and credit risk measurement: RiskMetrics™ and

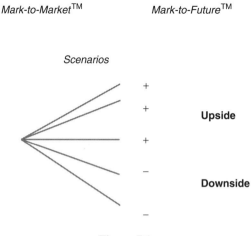

Figure 7.1

CreditMetrics®. One cannot take a RiskMetrics™ value and add it to a CreditMetrics® value and obtain a risk statistic that combines credit and market risk. That is because the methodologies for generating scenarios might not be compatible. By separating out the scenario generation method from the numbers that are computed for each scenario, one is able to calculate complex risk measures that are consistent. For example, if one chooses complex scenarios that incorporate both credit and market risk factors, then the resulting outcomes at the horizon will be values affected by both credit and market parameters. The risk statistic used will reflect both the credit and market exposures.

It is an appropriate choice of scenarios, and a pricing engine that computes the mark-to-future™ value correctly, that enables one to compute risk measures which link market and credit risk. In the same way one can link market, credit, operational, legal and liquidity risks. The only prerequisite is that, given an event involving changes in all of these variables, one can compute the effect on future portfolio value. With this machinery and a choice of scenarios one has all that is needed to get a risk measure that links all of these complex variables in a correlated fashion. The correlation matrix is a by-product of the scenario choice. The primary inputs to a mark-to-future™ are the scenarios and a benchmark. The remaining calculations are mechanical. This means that a non-technical person can understand the relevant information in a risk measure by understanding the scenarios that are used. Since scenarios are expressed in market terms, anyone with an understanding of markets can understand the input data. It is not some obscure correlation matrix that is difficult to decipher.

7.3 MARK-TO-FUTURE™

The mark-to-future™ calculations are seldom done correctly in risk management systems. For example, in RiskMetrics™ a 10-day Value-at-Risk is computed by multiplying a one day value-at-risk (VaR) by the square root of 10. This will typically give a very different answer than if the portfolio were marked-to-future™ 10 days from now. In the latter case, every instrument in the portfolio is path-dependent and its terminal value will depend on the events that affected it over those 10 days.

To see this, consider a bond that pays a coupon in nine days time. The RiskMetrics™ VaR does not take the coupon payment into account since a one-day VaR is computed and scaled by the square root of 10. A mark-to-future™ will account for the fact that the bond in 10 days' time has one less coupon and will be valued taking this into account. The two methods will give very different answers. This is the case for the simplest of instruments, namely a bond. For a slightly more complex security, such as an option on a bond future, the situation gets worse. The value of such an instrument will depend on the cheapest-to-deliver bond. The cheapest-to-deliver bond is itself scenario dependent. So it is possible that for each scenario a different cheapest-to-deliver bond would have to be used to get the correct value for the underlying. In the RiskMetrics™ case a VaR value for the option on a bond future would be computed using a single cheapest-to-deliver bond, namely the current spot cheapest-to-deliver. The VaR value would then be scaled by the square root of 10. The error in such a case could be well over 100 per cent!

It is disconcerting that an industry standard benchmark could be so inaccurate a measure, even in the case of simple instruments. Provided the path dependence of the instruments is taken into account in marking-to-future™, it will always yield the correct result. What appear to be minor approximations, as we have shown above, can lead to substantial errors in valuation.

Another important observation is that the mark-to-future™ values, together with the probabilities assigned to the scenarios, provide all the necessary input to compute *any* risk statistic. For example, VaR, volatility, and downside risk are all simple statistics on the mark-to-future™ distribution. There is no need therefore to be restricted to VaR, volatility, downside risk or any other single risk measures. The entire loss distribution is known. Useful risk measures are also available even if scenario probabilities are not. For example, the scenario with the largest loss, all scenarios with losses greater than $50 million, etc. are independent of the probability choice. They are particularly useful if these probabilities are controversial (see Figures 7.2, 7.3 and 7.4).

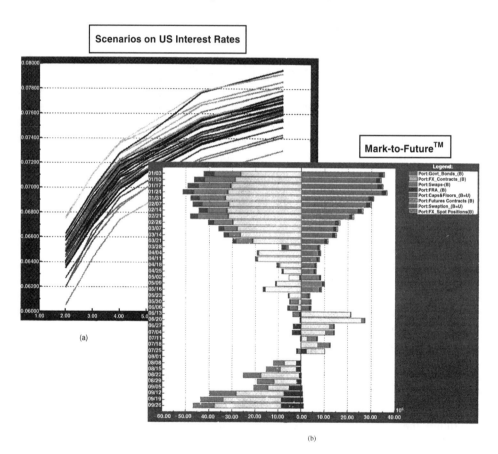

Figure 7.2   Mark-to-future™: a bank's US portfolio. Graph (a) shows US yield-curves for 1994, sampled weekly. Graph (b) shows how the Bank's portfolio might change in value under each scenario. The scenarios are generated by perturbing spot rates to match the 1994 weekly movements in yields. Each horizontal bar corresponds to one week in 1994. Bars to the left of the centreline are losses. Those to the right of the line are gains. The losses and gains are shaded by portfolio type. Whereas these views are easy to interpret with some practice, computing them requires a mark-to-future™ engine that properly accounts for the effects of ageing at the chosen horizon. This, in turn, requires tracking detailed cash accounting and settlement across all portfolios in all jurisdictions and all currencies

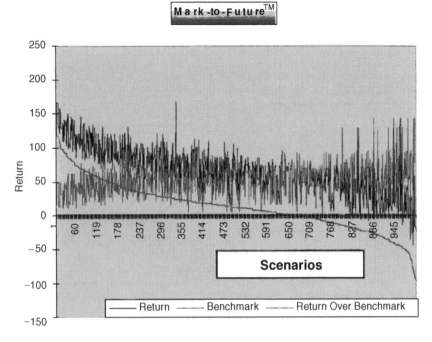

Figure 7.3 Mark-to-future™: an equity portfolio. This graph shows the performance of a portfolio relative to a benchmark for 1000 different scenarios. The solid line indicates this difference. The scenarios are ordered from best to worst. The best case (scenario 1) shows the portfolio outperforming the benchmark by over 150 basis points. The worst case (scenario 1000) occurs when the portfolio underperforms the benchmark by over 100 basis points. In approximately 670 scenarios the portfolio outperforms the benchmark and in approximately 330 cases it underperforms the benchmark. If all scenarios were equally weighted, then this would indicate a 67% chance that the portfolio will outperform the benchmark at the horizon

7.4 REGRET: AN IDEAL MEASURE OF RISK

Once the values for the portfolio under different scenarios have been computed (the end values in the scenario tree) almost any desired risk measure can be calculated.

For many years we have proposed the use of regret as an appropriate risk measure for portfolio risk. Regret is the absolute loss under each scenario. It is positive when, if the scenario in question were to occur, one would regret having invested in one's portfolio. To compute regret:

1. Compute the aged portfolio value at the horizon for each and every scenario (i.e. mark the portfolio to future).
2. Regret is zero whenever this number is positive (one makes money = no regrets).
3. Regret is the absolute value of this number when it is negative (when one loses money).

Regret is what an insurer would have to pay you if she insured the downside on your portfolio. To see this, note that the insurer pays nothing in scenarios in which you make

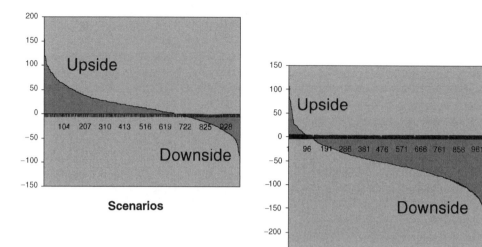

Figure 7.4   Mark-to-future™: best vs. worst trading desk. Simple forward-looking risk views like these allow one to rank trading desks in terms of their risk and return relative to a benchmark. The first trading desk clearly outperforms the second since its ratio of upside to downside is much higher. That is, it has far more likelihood of outperforming the benchmark than the second and consequently much less downside. The measure of risk-adjusted return we propose is the difference between the upside and downside. For scenarios with equal weights, this corresponds to subtracting the area covered by the downside from the area covered by the upside

money. The insurer pays you exactly your loss in the scenarios where a loss occurs. For the reader familiar with options, regret is the payoff of a put option on the downside risk, with maturity equal to the horizon and strike equal to the mark-to-market™ value. The price of such an option is also the mark-to-market™ value of regret. In turn, this is an excellent measure of the true value of risk.

> *The value we should associate with a given risk is the cost of insuring the downside or the mark-to-market™ value of regret.*

Regret also makes no assumptions about symmetry, the method of scenario generation or the methods used to mark-to-market™ or mark-to-future™.

When risk measures are to be used for comparative purposes, such as in the allocation of capital, portfolio regret should be computed relative to a benchmark. This is done by first computing the mark-to-future™ of a benchmark-adjusted portfolio consisting of a long position in the original portfolio and a short position in the benchmark. The regret of this benchmark-adjusted portfolio is the cost of insuring losses relative to the benchmark.

Since regret and insurance are synonymous, it is an appropriate measure for determining the allocation of capital. Allocating more capital than regret would be inefficient since for the price of regret one could eliminate all risk. Allocating less capital than regret would leave one exposed. For these reasons regret may be considered as a "perfect" measure of risk. The mark-to-market™ of regret is an appropriate way to compute a "Value-at-Risk".

7.5 ACCOUNTING FOR THE UPSIDE

Whereas regret is a good measure of risk, for risk management purposes we are also concerned with the trade-off between risk and return. That is, our decisions on the management of portfolio risk will need to take into account the upside as well. All decisions involving risk are resolved based not only on the potential downside (regret) but on the potential upside as well. Fortunately, in the paradigm that has been described the values for the portfolio and benchmark under different scenarios are available (the mark-to-future™) and we know exactly which scenarios have upside and which have downside.

The upside is the complement of regret. In all scenarios where the exposure is positive (the portfolio makes money) there is positive upside. In all scenarios where there is regret the upside is zero. Just as regret was shown to be equivalent to the payoff of a put option on the downside, with a strike equal to the mark-to-market™ value and a maturity equal to the horizon, the upside has the same payoff as a call option with the same strike and maturity. The upside, when properly priced, is the most the portfolio is worth today.

Thus, by pricing the mark-to-future™ values, one can separate the true value of the upside and the true value of regret. This brings us to our next topic, risk-adjusted valuation.

7.6 RISK-ADJUSTED VALUATION

The *risk-adjusted value* of a portfolio is the upside (U) − regret (R), which is the value of the portfolio minus the cost of insuring the downside. So if a portfolio has more upside value than the cost of insuring its downside, then we say it has positive risk-adjusted value. It is a good deal. If we could purchase the downside insurance, then we would be in a position to lock in a possibility of profit with no chance of loss (that is, provided the insurer does not default). A positive risk-adjusted return is different from arbitrage because it does not guarantee risk-free money. It just says that the profit in the deal is worth more than the potential loss.

In some situations we might wish to weigh the downside more heavily (charge more for risk) to reflect the fact that "we do not want to take any chances", another way of saying that we are "risk-averse". We may have different aversion to risk at different stages in our lives. It is also true that we might want to treat various parts of our portfolio differently when it comes to taking risk.

To accommodate this we add a *risk-aversion weight*, λ, to the equation for risk-adjusted return: risk-adjusted value $= U - \lambda R$. The larger λ, the more risk-averse the decision-maker since she is paying a higher price to self-insure her risk. People who exaggerate the downside when making a deal essentially have very high λs. Typically, λ is greater than 1, since otherwise we are in effect paying less than the cost of insurance to cover the risk and we will not be adequately covered. On the other hand, when a decision is largely based on the upside, the decision-maker discounts risk with a very small λ. Such people are referred to as risk seekers. We might take a small part of our portfolio and use a low λ since we can afford to lose the amount invested. In other words, we can absorb the regret.

Valuing an investment on a risk-adjusted basis is quite different from the usual way we value things. It is a powerful guide to decision-making.

Value the upside and subtract the cost of insuring the downside. If the result is positive, then you have a good deal. If it is negative, then you had better have some other good reason for wanting to do it.

Sometimes, as is the case in trading, we can get take more risk and get more return. This trade-off is what finance is all about. Risk-adjusted valuation tells us when to stop looking for more return or when there is too much risk for a given level of return. The true value, that is the price you should be prepared to pay today for a portfolio is the upside − regret $(U - R)$, that is the price of the call on the deal minus the price of the put. Using put/call parity, this value is the price of a forward on the deal. This value differs from the expected value of the deal because to get the expected value we discount the mark-to-future™ values using the scenario probabilities, and to get the forward value we discount using risk-neutral probabilities (Dembo (1989)).

7.7 TRADING-OFF RISK AND RETURN

When deciding on a risky venture we are often able to trade extra return for more risk. Just what is the optimal mixture of risk and return?

Upside (or return) and regret are related. The more upside you require from a deal the more regret you will have to assume. Upside is also limited. In any given situation, no matter how much regret you are willing to bear, there is a finite limit to the upside that can be achieved. The instruments that are available in the market will determine this limit.

The curve shown in Figure 7.5 is a curve of minimal regret for various levels of upside. To compute this curve one solves the parametric optimization problem (Dembo (1989)). Find the portfolio x that solves:

$$\min R(x) \text{ (regret)}$$

$$\text{s.t. } U(x) \text{ (upside)} = K$$

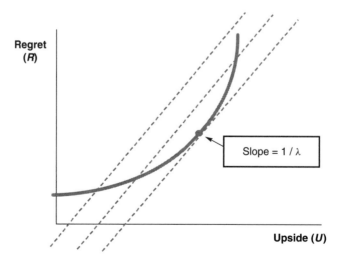

Figure 7.5

for various levels of K. The constant K is the desired upside over the horizon (an input to the model). A point on the curve is then the portfolio whose downside risk can be insured for less than any other portfolio with the same upside. In other words, any point on the curve corresponds to a portfolio that has the highest risk-adjusted return $(U - \lambda R)$ for the assumed level of the upside. This is a consequence of the fact that the model fixes U and finds R that is minimal, thereby maximizing the quantity $(U - \lambda R)$ for fixed U. Following Markowitz (1952), we refer to such portfolios as *efficient portfolios*. There are portfolios that have more regret at the same level of upside and these are called *inefficient portfolios*. They are points on the graph above the curve. We refer to this curve as the *minimal regret frontier*.

The above risk/return framework is significantly different from that proposed by Markowitz. For one thing, Markowitz relies heavily on the symmetry or linearity of the portfolio. The above model does not require symmetry, linearity or normality. Also, the above model is forward-looking in the sense that the distribution of returns of the portfolio is a function of the portfolio that is calculated explicitly by the model and is not assumed as input data. Details of the mathematics involved are available in Dembo (1989).

The point on the curve where the tangent has a slope of $1/\lambda$ is the point at which $(U - \lambda R)$ is maximized, that is, the portfolio of *maximal risk-adjusted return*. This is the portfolio that has the largest value for $(U - \lambda R)$, regardless of the level of upside. As λ increases, the optimal portfolio, represented by a dot on the curve, rolls down towards the vertical axis. That is, the more risk-averse one is the more marginal upside one needs to justify an additional unit of regret.

This same framework can be used to derive a capital allocation model for the firm and to quantify the amount of capital required to support liquidity risk. Details are given in Dembo (1989).

7.8 CONCLUSION

This chapter describes a framework for financial risk measurement and a definition of risk-adjusted value that is consistent across the firm and permits comparison of the risk of various trading units across markets and instrument types. The framework also makes it possible to link multiple risk sources such as market, credit and operational risk. Different tiers of risk capital and different risk preferences are accounted for by a risk-aversion parameter.

The key to this framework, or risk paradigm, is the de-coupling of the mark-to-market™, scenario generation, mark-to-future™ and statistical calculations that are required implicitly or explicitly by all risk measurement methods. By separating these components, it becomes possible to explain the risk measures to a non-technical audience. The consumers of risk information need only know which scenarios and benchmarks have been used to understand all aspects of a risk measure. Since these items do not require a technical background they are accessible to non-technical managers.

This paradigm allows senior management to focus on the control parameters they should monitor, namely the scenarios that describe the benchmark against which results are to be measured. All the remaining aspects are mechanical (non-trivial, however) and can be delegated to sufficiently expert quantitative analysts. Knowledge of the scenarios empowers management to control trading risk in a way that is consistent across the firm. It also makes it feasible for management to compare risks across the enterprise and within trading units in a uniform manner. It links these risk measures with the risk-adjusted return measures required for limits management and provides a consistent, theoretically sound framework for the allocation of capital. A mathematical model for optimal capital allocation, using this paradigm, is described in Dembo (1989).

In a mark-to-future™ paradigm any risk measures, such as market, credit and operational risk, can be linked easily. One key to doing so is the scenario choice, which accommodates multiple sources of risk. The other is an engine that can price forward in time and value portfolios as a function of all of these factors.

Scenarios and benchmark portfolios are easily described and understood by non-technical senior managers. This enables them to understand and control the financial risk of a firm. The mark-to-future™ paradigm eliminates the need for arcane formulas and risk measurement methods that nobody without a Ph.D. in Nuclear Physics could understand. There is no need to fly blind anymore!

7.9 NOTES

This paper has been abstracted from Dembo (1997). A less technical presentation, with many examples drawn from the day-to-day financial decisions, is presented in Dembo and Freeman (1998).

7.10 REFERENCES

Dembo, R.S. (1989) *Optimal Portfolio Replication*. Toronto: Algorithmics Inc.
Dembo, R.S. (1997) *Risk, Regret and Return*. Toronto: Algorithmics Inc.
Dembo, R.S. and Freeman, A. (1998) *Seeing Tomorrow*. Chichester: John Wiley & Sons.
J.P. Morgan (1994) *RiskMetrics*, Technical Document. New York: J.P. Morgan & Co., Inc.
J.P. Morgan (1997) *CreditMetrics*, Technical Document. New York: J.P. Morgan & Co., Inc.
Markowitz, H.M. (1952) "Portfolio selection", *Journal of Finance*, **7**, no. 1, 77–91.

8
Credit Risk
ROBERT JARROW AND STUART TURNBULL

8.1 INTRODUCTION

We consider two facets of credit risk. First, the pricing of derivatives written on assets subject to default risk. An example is the pricing of derivatives written on corporate bonds, where there is a positive probability that default may occur on the part of the issuer of the bonds. Second is the pricing of derivatives where the writer of the derivative might default. Consider an over-the-counter option written on a Treasury bond. There is no default risk arising from the underlying asset — the Treasury bond. However, there is default risk arising from the fact that the writer of the option may not be able to honour the obligation if the option is exercised. This form of risk is referred to as *counterparty risk*. In the over-the-counter market counterparty risk is a major concern to financial institutions and regulatory bodies. We will describe a simple approach to the pricing and hedging of both forms of credit risk. We will give a number of examples: the pricing of options on credit risky bonds, the pricing of over-the-counter caps, and the pricing of credit default swaps.

8.2 PRICING CREDIT RISKY BONDS

Firms are allocated to particular risk classes AAA, AA, etc. on the basis of their current creditworthiness. A typical set of term structures is shown in Figure 8.1. A firm in credit class AAA is assumed to have the least credit risk among corporate firms. Firms of lower credit than AAA, such as those in credit class AA, trade at a lower price and are thus higher yield.

Suppose we want to price a derivative written on a zero coupon bond issued by a firm with credit rating ABC. We must price this derivative in such a way that it is (i) consistent with the absence of arbitrage; (ii) consistent with the relevant initial term structures of interest rates; and (iii) consistent with a positive probability of default. We do this by first constructing a lattice of one-period interest rates to model the term structure of default-free Treasury bills. This is described in Jarrow and Turnbull (1995). Next we consider zero coupon bonds for the firm belonging to the particular risk class, ABC.

Risk Management and Analysis. Vol. 1: Measuring and Modelling Financial Risk.
Edited by Carol Alexander © 1998 John Wiley & Sons Ltd

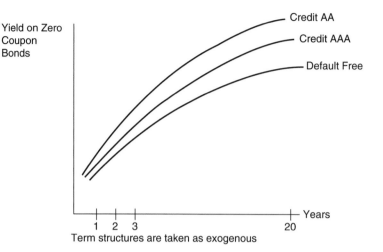

Figure 8.1   Term structures

8.2.1 Lattice of Default-free Interest Rates

The prices of default-free zero coupon bonds are given in Table 8.1. Following Black et al. (1991), it is assumed that spot interest rates are log-normally distributed. The lattice is shown in Figure 8.2. The value of the one-year default-free bond, face value 100, is

$$B_F(0, 1) = 100 \exp(-0.047175) = 95.3921$$

The value of the two-year default-free zero coupon bond, face value 100, at year one is

$$B_F(1, 2) = 100 \exp(-0.053810) = 94.7612$$

if the spot rate is 5.3810 per cent, and

$$B_F(1, 2) = 100 \exp(-0.048689) = 95.2477$$

if the spot rate is 4.8689 per cent.

We know from Black et al. (1991) that normalized prices are a martingale under the martingale probabilities. It is assumed that the martingale probability of the spot interest in an up-state is 0.5. Therefore,

$$B_F(0, 2) = \exp(-0.047175)(0.5 \times 94.7612 + 0.5 \times 95.2477)$$

$$= 90.6267$$

Table 8.1   Prices of zero coupon bonds

Maturity (Years) T	Default-Free $B_F(0, T)$	Credit Class ABC $v(0, t; \overline{D})$
1	95.3921	95.0486
2	90.6264	89.7056
3	85.7820	84.1008

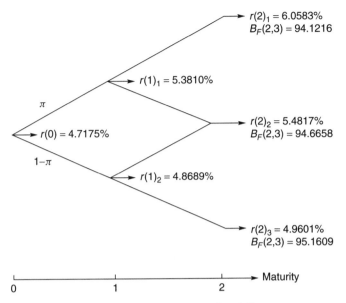

$r(2)_1 = 6.0583\%$
$B_F(2,3) = 94.1216$

$r(1)_1 = 5.3810\%$

π

$r(0) = 4.7175\%$

$r(2)_2 = 5.4817\%$
$B_F(2,3) = 94.6658$

$1-\pi$

$r(1)_2 = 4.8689\%$

$r(2)_3 = 4.9601\%$
$B_F(2,3) = 95.1609$

Maturity

0   1   2

π is the martingale probability of an up-state ($\pi = 0.5$).
$1-\pi$ is the martingale probability of a down-state ($1-\pi = 0.5$).
Volatility is 5 per cent.

Figure 8.2   Default-free spot interest rates

which equals the number in Table 8.1, ignoring a small round-off error. Extending this analysis gives $B_F(0, 3) = 85.7820$.

8.2.2 Risky Debt

We want to value a zero coupon bond for a firm belonging to the credit class ABC. Let $v(t, T; DS_t)$ denote the value at date t of a zero coupon bond issued by the firm. The debt matures at time T and the bondholders are promised the face value of the bond at maturity. Let the face value be USD 100. There is a positive probability that the firm might default over the life of the bond. If default occurs, the bondholders will receive less than the promised amount. The symbol DS_t is used to denote the default status of the bond at date t:

$$DS_t \equiv \begin{cases} \overline{D}; & \text{default has not occurred at date } t \\ D; & \text{default has occurred at or before date } t \end{cases}$$

As the symbol DS_t indicates, there are two possibilities. One, default does not occur before or at date t, denoted $\overline{D}$; and two, default does occur before or at date t, denoted D.

We can always view the pricing of credit risky bonds in terms of a foreign currency analogy. Imagine a hypothetical currency, called ABCs. In terms of this currency, we can view the debt issued by the firm as default-free. Indeed, at maturity, the bondholder is issued the face value of debt in ABCs. But, this currency is useless to the bondholder, so we need to define an exchange rate which converts this hypothetical currency to dollars. After all, the bondholders are interested in the dollar value of their ABCs. If default has not occurred before or at date t, then the exchange rate is unity. If default did occur, it is assumed that we get some fraction, δ, of a dollar for each ABC. This is the same as being paid the fraction δ of the face amount of the debt. The fraction δ is also called the *pay-off ratio* or *recovery rate*. Defining $e(t)$ as the date t exchange rate per ABCs, we have:

$$e(t) \equiv \begin{cases} 1; \text{ with probability } 1 - \mu(t)h \text{ if } DS_t = \overline{D} \\ \delta; \text{ with probability } \mu(t)h \text{ if } DS_t = D \end{cases} \tag{1}$$

where $0 \le \delta < 1$; h denotes the time interval and $\mu(t)h$ is the martingale probability of default occurring, conditional upon no default at or before date $t - h$. We are interested in the martingale probabilities of default because we want to develop pricing formulae which are arbitrage-free.[1] If default has occurred at or before date $t - h$, then it is assumed that the bond remains in default and the pay-off ratio constant at δ dollars,

$$e(t) \equiv \delta \tag{2}$$

The conditional martingale probabilities of default can be estimated using the observed term structures of interest rates. We will discuss how to do this below.

To simplify the analysis, we are going to assume that the default process is independent of the level of the default-free rate of interest. This implies that if interest rates are "high" or "low" this has no effect on the probability of default. It is a useful first approximation, and its relaxation is discussed in Jarrow and Turnbull (1995b).

8.2.3 Credit Risky Debt

In Table 8.1 we are given two sets of prices for zero coupon bonds. The first is for default-free bonds and the second is for bonds belonging to credit class ABC. The default-free bonds at each maturity are seen to be more valuable than the equivalent maturity bond issued by the firm in credit class ABC. This difference reflects the likelihood of default. We want to estimate these implicit martingale probabilities of default.

Before we can do this, however, we must first specify the pay-off ratio δ in the event of default. This value comes from our credit risk analysts, who estimate that given the nature of the debt, we expect to receive USD 0.40 on the dollar in the event of default.[2]

Consider first the one-year bond. For simplicity, we take the interval in the lattice to be one year. At maturity, the credit risky bond's value is:

$$v(1, 1, DS) = 100 \begin{cases} 1; \text{ probability } 1 - \mu(0)h \text{ if } DS_1 = \overline{D} \text{ (no default)} \\ \delta; \text{ probability } \mu(0)h \text{ if } DS_1 = D \text{ (default)} \end{cases} \tag{3}$$

where $h = 1$ and $\delta = 0.40$. The face value of the bond is 100.

The default process is shown in Figure 8.3. Given that default has not occurred at date $t = 0$, the conditional (martingale) probability that default occurs at $t = 1$ is denoted by $\mu(0) \times h$, where h is the time interval. In this example $h = 1$. The conditional (martingale) probability that default does not occur is $1 - \mu(0)h$. We can use the term structures of interest rates for default-free bonds and for credit class ABC bonds to infer the value of $\mu(0)$.

The expected value of the pay-off is

$$100\{1 \times [1 - \mu(0)] + \delta \times \mu(0)\}$$

and discounting at the risk-free rate gives, using Table 8.1

$$v(0, 1, \overline{D}) = 0.9539 \times 100\{1 \times [1 - \mu(0)] + \delta \times \mu(0)\} \tag{4}$$

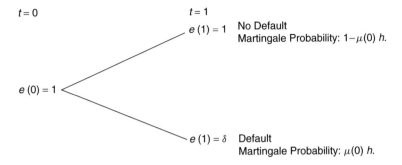

$\mu(0).h$ is the martingale probability that default occurs at date $t = 1$, conditional that default has not occurred at date $t = 0$.

Figure 8.3   One-period credit risky debt default process

From Table 8.1, we know that $v(0, 1, \overline{D}) = 95.0401$. Therefore

$$95.0486 = 0.9539 \times 100\{[1 - \mu(0)] + 0.40\mu(0)\} \qquad (5)$$

Solving for martingale probability of default gives

$$(1 - 0.40) \times \mu(0) = 1 - (95.0486/0.9539)/100$$

or

$$\mu(0) = 0.006$$

The pricing of the two-period zero coupon bond is slightly more complicated because at the end of the first period both interest rates and the default status of the firm are uncertain. The default process is shown in Figure 8.4. If default has occurred at date $t = 1$, then the bond is assumed to remain in default. If default has not occurred at date $t = 1$, then one period later at date $t = 2$ either default occurs or it does not. The martingale probability of default occurring at date $t = 2$ conditional upon the fact that default has not occurred at date $t = 1$ is $\mu(1)h$. The conditional (martingale) probability that default does not occur at date $t = 2$ is $1 - \mu(1)h$. Figure 8.4 is combined with Figure 8.2 and the possible states are shown in Figure 8.5. The same argument is used to determine the conditional martingale probability of default $\mu(1)$.

Let us start at State A, at date $t = 1$. The value of a default-free bond, face value of 1, that matures at $t = 2$ is

$$B(1, 2)_d = \exp(-0.0487)$$

The subscript "d" refers to the "down" state for the default-free spot rate of interest.
Default has occurred at date $t = 1$, so the pay-off to the bond at date $t = 2$ is

$$v(2, 2; D) = 100\delta$$

The value in State A at date $t = 1$ is

$$v_A(1, 2; D) = \exp(-0.0487)(100\delta)$$

$$= B(1, 2)_d(100\delta)$$

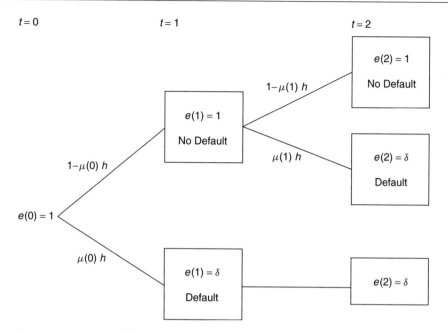

Figure 8.4 Two-period credit risky debt default process

A similar argument applies if State B occurs:

$$v_B(1, 2, D) = \exp(-0.0538)(100\delta)$$

$$= B(1, 2)_u(100\delta)$$

where $B(1, 2)_u$ is the value at date $t = 1$ of a one-period default-free bond and is equal to

$$B(1, 2)_u = \exp(-0.0538)$$

The subscript "u" refers to the "up" state for the default-free spot rate of interest.

If State C occurs, then the argument is more interesting. In State C default has not occurred, so that one period later, at maturity, one of two possible states can occur:

$$v(2, 2, DS) = 100 \begin{cases} 1; \text{ probability } 1 - \mu(1) \text{ if } DS_2 = \overline{D} \text{ (no default)} \\ \delta; \text{ probability } \mu(1) \text{ if } DS_2 = D \text{ (default)} \end{cases}$$

Therefore, in State C the value of the bond is

$$v_C(1, 2, \overline{D}) = B(1, 2)_d 100\{[1 - \mu(1)] + \delta\mu(1)\}$$

In State D a similar argument applies:

$$v_D(1, 2, \overline{D}) = B(1, 2)_u 100\{[1 - \mu(1)] + \delta\mu(1)\}$$

The value of the credit risky bond today, $v(0, 2, \overline{D})$, is determined by calculating the expected value of the bond at date $t = 1$ using the martingale probabilities and discounting at the risk-free rate of interest. Referring to Figure 8.5, there are four possible states.

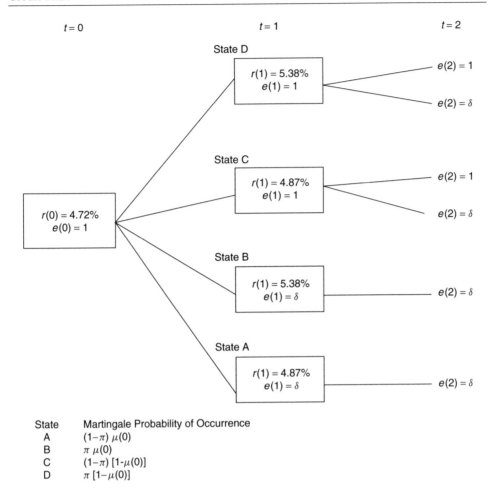

State	Martingale Probability of Occurrence
A	$(1-\pi)\,\mu(0)$
B	$\pi\,\mu(0)$
C	$(1-\pi)\,[1-\mu(0)]$
D	$\pi\,[1-\mu(0)]$

Figure 8.5 Two-period credit risky debt: determining the implied probabilities

Therefore

$$v(0, 2; \overline{D}) = 0.9539 \times [(1 - \pi)\mu(0)v_A(1, 2; D) + \pi\mu(0)v_B(1, 2, D)$$
$$+ (1 - \pi)[1 - \mu(0)]v_C(1, 2, \overline{D}) + \pi[1 - \mu(0)]v_D(1, 2, \overline{D})]$$

Substituting the values of the bond in the four different states gives

$$v(0, 2; \overline{D}) = 0.9539 \times [(1 - \pi)\exp(-0.0487) + \pi\exp(-0.0538)]\mu(0)(100\delta)$$
$$+ 0.9539 \times [(1 - \pi)\exp(-0.0487) + \pi\exp(-0.0538)]$$
$$\times [1 - \mu(0)]100\{[1 - \mu(1)] + \mu(1)\delta\}$$

The above calculation can be simplified by considering the pricing of a two-period default-free zero coupon bond. Consider the value of the default-free bond at $t = 1$:

$$B(1, 2) = \begin{cases} \exp(-0.0538); & \text{martingale probability } \pi \\ \exp(-0.0487); & \text{martingale probability } 1 - \pi \end{cases}$$

and the value of the default-free bond today at $t = 0$ is

$$B(0, 2) = 0.9539 \times [(1 - \pi) \exp(-0.0487) + \pi \exp(-0.0538)]$$

Therefore

$$v(0, 2; \overline{D}) = B(0, 2)[\mu(0)(100\delta) + [1 - \mu(0)]100\{[1 - \mu(1)] + \mu(1)\delta\}] \tag{6}$$

From Table 8.1 we have $B_F(0, 2) = 90.6264$, $v(0, 2, \overline{D}) = 89.7056$ and $\delta = 0.40$. We have estimated $\mu(0) = 0.006$. Therefore, substituting these values into equation (6) and solving for $\mu(1)$ gives

$$\mu(1) = 0.011$$

The martingale probability of default at time 1, as implied by the bond prices, is almost twice that of default at time 0. Given $\mu(0) = 0.006$ and $\mu(1) = 0.011$, the pricing of the two-period credit risky debt is summarized in Figure 8.6.

Repeating this argument for the three-year zero coupon bond gives

$$\mu(2) = 0.016$$

Equation (5) can be written in the form

$$v(0, 1, \overline{D}) = B_F(0, 1)E_0^Q[e(1)] \tag{7}$$

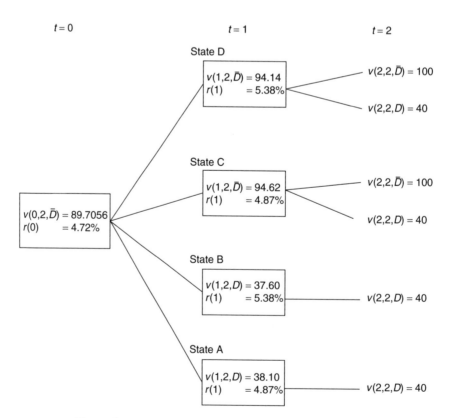

Figure 8.6 Two-period credit risky debt: summary of results

where the expected pay-off is

$$E_0^Q[e(1)] = 1 - \mu(0) + \delta\mu(0)$$
$$= 0.9964$$

Hence

$$B_F(0, 1)E_0^Q[e(1)] = 95.3921 \times 0.9964$$
$$= 95.0486$$

which agrees with Table 8.1.
  Equation (6) can be written in the form

$$v(0, 2, \overline{D}) = B_F(0, 2)E_0^Q[e(2)] \tag{8}$$

where the expected pay-off is

$$E_0^Q[e(2)] = [1 - \mu(0)][1 - \mu(1) + \delta\mu(1)] + \delta\mu(0)$$
$$= 0.989840$$

Hence

$$B_F(0, 2)E_0^Q[e(2)] = 90.6264 \times 0.989840$$
$$= 89.7056$$

which agrees with Table 8.1.
  In general one can write

$$v(0, T; \overline{D}) = B_F(0, T)E_0^Q[e(T)|\overline{D}] \tag{9}$$

Equation (9) gives the value of the zero coupon bond if the firm is not in default. Equation (9) is an important and intuitive result. It is important because (i) it provides a practical way of computing the martingale probabilities of default using market data, and (ii) it can be used for pricing derivatives on credit risky cash flows. It is intuitive because the second term in equation (9), $E_0^Q[e(T)|\overline{D}]$, can be interpreted as the date 0 present value of the promised pay-off at date T. We can rewrite equation (9) in the form

$$E_0^Q[e(T)|\overline{D}] = v(0, T, \overline{D})/B_F(0, T) \tag{10}$$

where the right-hand side can be interpreted as a credit spread.

8.3 PRICING OPTIONS ON CREDIT RISKY BONDS

Consider a put option written on debt issued by the ABC company. The maturity of the option is one year. At maturity the option allows you to sell, for a strike price of 94, a two-year bond with a coupon of USD 3 paid annually and face value of USD 100, issued by the ABC firm. To price this option, we start by considering the value of the option at its maturity date. For simplicity of exposition, we maintain our assumption that the length of the lattice interval is one year, so that we can use all the results summarized in Figure 8.6. In practice, one would use intervals of shorter length than a year.

At the maturity of the option, at date $t = 1$, there are four possible values of the underlying bond depending on interest rates and whether default has occurred or not. If default has not occurred, then the value of the coupon bond is

$$v_c(1; \bar{D}) \equiv 3B(1, 2)E_1^Q[e(2)|\bar{D}] + (3 + 100)B(1, 3)E_1^Q[e(3)|\bar{D}]$$

using equation (9), where $B(1, T)$ denotes the value at date 1 of receiving one dollar for sure at date T. If default has occurred, then the value of the coupon bond is

$$v_c(1; D) \equiv 3B(1, 2)E_1^Q[e(2)|D] + (3 + 100)B(1, 3)E_1^Q[e(3)|D]$$

Relevant values are shown in Figure 8.7.

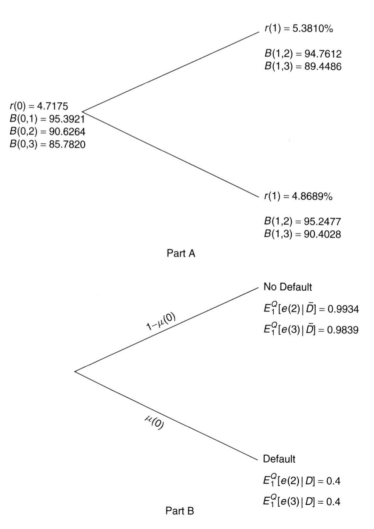

Part A

Part B

Figure 8.7   Part A: default-free term structure, Part B: default/no default states

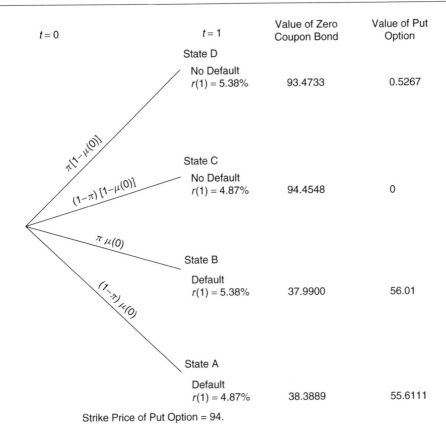

Strike Price of Put Option = 94.

Figure 8.8   Pricing a put option written on credit risky debt

The values of the coupon bond in the four possible states are shown in Figure 8.8, along with the values of the put option. To determine the option value today, we must calculate the expected value of the option at date $t = 1$ and discount back at the risk-free rate of interest.

In States A and B default has occurred on the underlying ABC zero coupon bond. The value of the option varies over these two states because the value of the underlying asset varies due to the interest rate risk. In States C and D the underlying asset at $t = 1$ is not in default. The value of the option today is

$$p(0) = 0.9539 \times \{[1 - \mu(0)][\pi 0.5267 + (1 - \pi)0]$$
$$+ \mu(0)[\pi 56.01 + (1 - \pi)55.6111]\} \qquad (11)$$

Given that $\pi = 0.5$ and $\mu(0) = 0.006$ then

$$p(0) = 0.9539 \times \{[1 - \mu(0)]0.2634 + \mu(0)55.8105\}$$
$$= 0.5692$$

This methodology can easily be extended to price American options on credit risky bonds.

8.4 PRICING VULNERABLE DERIVATIVES

This section studies the pricing of vulnerable derivatives. *Vulnerable derivatives* are derivative securities subject to the additional risk that the writer of the derivative might default. Consider an example of an over-the-counter (OTC) option written on a Treasury bill. There is no default risk associated with the underlying asset — the Treasury bill. However, the writer of the option is a financial institution which may default, so that there is the risk that if the option is exercised the writer may be unable to fulfil the obligation to make the required payment to the option owner. The methodology that we have developed can handle this problem. A simple example is used to illustrate the procedure.

First, let us assume there is no risk of the writer defaulting. Consider a call option written on a Treasury bill. The maturity is one year, and at expiration the option holder can purchase a one-year Treasury bill at a strike price of 92. The option is valued using the information summarized in Figure 8.9. The lattice of interest rates comes from Figure 8.8. The date 0 value of the call option is

$$c(0) = 0.9539[0.5 \times 2.76 + 0.5 \times 3.40]$$

$$= 2.94$$

Now assume that the financial institution that wrote the option belongs to the ABC risk class. When the option matures there are four possible states depending on whether interest rates go up or down and whether the writer defaults. The four states are shown in Figure 8.10. This figure is similar in nature to Figure 8.8. In States A and B the writer defaults. By assumption, claim holders receive as a pay-off ratio 40 per cent of the value of their option.

The value of the vulnerable option today is

$$c_V(0) = 0.9539 \times \{[1 - \mu(0)][\pi 2.76 + (1 - \pi)3.40]$$
$$+ \mu(0)[\pi 2.76 + (1 - \pi)3.40] \times 0.40\}$$

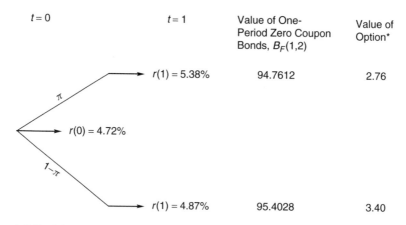

$t = 0$	$t = 1$	Value of One-Period Zero Coupon Bonds, $B_F(1,2)$	Value of Option*
	$r(1) = 5.38\%$	94.7612	2.76
$r(0) = 4.72\%$			
	$r(1) = 4.87\%$	95.4028	3.40

* Strike Price is 92 where $\pi = 0.5$ represents the martingale probability of an up-state.

Figure 8.9 Pricing a default-free Treasury bill call option

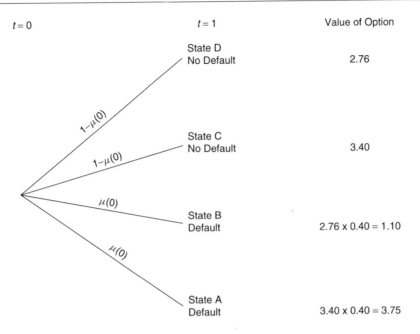

Where $\mu(0) = 0.006$ represents the martingale probability of default occurring at date $t = 1$, conditional upon not being in default at date $t = 0$.

Figure 8.10 Pricing a vulnerable call option

Given that $\pi = 0.5$ and $\mu(0) = 0.006$, then
$$c_V(0) = [1 - \mu(0)]2.94 + \mu(0)2.94 \times 0.40$$
$$= 2.93 \tag{12}$$

The difference in the option prices is small, only 1 cent, which is to be expected given that the martingale probability of default is small.

8.4.1 Formalization

This section formalizes the analysis in the previous example. This involves little more than replacing numerical values with symbols. Let $c(1)$ represent the value of the option at date $t = 1$ in the absence of default on the part of the writer, and $c_V(1)$ the value of the vulnerable option. At maturity the pay-off to the option holder is

$$c_V(1) = \begin{cases} c(1); & \text{no default} \\ \delta c(1); & \text{default} \end{cases}$$

where δ represents the pay-off fraction of the option the holder receives if default occurs. The date 0 value of the option in the absence of default is $c(0)$ and the value of the vulnerable option is, using equation (12),

$$c_V(0) = [1 - \mu(0)]c(0) + \mu(0)\delta c(0)$$
$$= E_0^Q[e(1)]c(0) \tag{13}$$

because $E_0^Q[e(1)] = (1 - \mu(0)) + \mu(0)\delta$.

This result has an important implication. Given that there is a positive probability of default, then

$$E_0^Q[e(1)] < 1$$

which implies that a vulnerable option must always be worth less than a non-vulnerable option,

$$c_V(0) < c(0) \tag{14}$$

Equation (14) generalizes in a natural way for a European option that matures at date T:

$$c_V(0) = E_0^Q[e(T)]c(0) \tag{15}$$

Using equation (9) this can be written in the form

$$c_V(0) = [v(0, T; \overline{D})/B_F(0, T)]c(0) \tag{16}$$

Table 8.2   Pricing a vulnerable cap

Part A: Term structure data

Maturity (Years)	Default-Free	Credit Class A	Credit Class B	Credit Class C
0.5	97.7098	97.4460	97.4069	97.2334
1.0	95.3513	94.8364	94.7542	94.4131
1.5	92.9414	92.1883	92.0598	91.5571
2.0	90.4954	89.5169	89.3397	88.6816
2.5	88.0269	86.8356	86.6079	85.8011
3.0	85.5478	84.1563	83.8770	82.9279
3.5	83.0689	81.4894	81.1579	80.0733
4.0	80.5994	78.8440	78.4602	77.2466
4.5	78.1475	76.2278	75.7919	74.4562

Part B: Pricing the caplets

Maturity (Years)	Value of Caplet*	Credit Class A	Credit Class B	Credit Class C
0.5	70	69.81	69.78	69.66
1.0	1092	1086.10	1085.16	1081.26
1.5	3212	3185.97	3181.53	3164.16
2.0	5877	5813.45	5801.95	5759.21
2.5	8709	8591.14	8515.19	8488.79
3.0	11 484	11 297.20	11 259.71	11 132.30
3.5	14 094	13 826.01	13 769.77	13 585.75
4.0	16 472	16 113.25	16 034.81	15 786.79
4.5	18 593	18 136.26	18 032.55	17 714.76
Total	79 603	78 119.19	77 750.45	76 782.60
Difference		1483.81	1852.55	2820.32
		1.86%	2.33%	3.54%

*Volatility	1.2 per cent
Volatility Reduction Factor	0.15
Cap Rate	7.00 per cent
Principal	USD 10 million

This form of the expression is useful in practice because it involves pricing a vulnerable option in terms of a credit risk spread for the writer, and the price of a non-vulnerable option.

8.4.2 Example

A firm wants to buy a five-year interest rate cap on the six-month default-free interest rate. Three institutions offer to sell the firm a cap. The institutions, however, have different credit ratings. Institution A belongs to credit class A, institution B belongs to credit class B, and institution C belongs to credit class C. Credit class A has a lower risk of default than credit class B and credit class B has a lower risk of default than credit class C.

The term structure details are given in Table 8.2, Part A, for default-free interest rates and the three credit classes. The value of the caplets, assuming no counterparty risk, is calculated using the Heath et al. (1991) model, assuming interest rates are normally distributed. The prices of the caplets are given in Table 8.2, Part B.

To incorporate the effects of counterparty risk, equation (16) is used. Consider the last caplet. The value in the absence of counterparty risk is USD 18 593. For institution A, belonging to credit class A, using the figures from the last row of Table 8.2, Part A:

$$v_A(0, 4.5, \overline{D})/B_F(0, 4.5) = 76.2278/78.1475$$

$$= 0.9754$$

Therefore using equation (16) the value of the caplet is

$$\text{USD } 18\,593 \times 0.9754 = \text{USD } 18\,136.26$$

as shown in Table 8.2, Part B. The values of the other caplets are calculated in a similar way. For institution A, its credit risk lowers the value of the cap by approximately 1.86 per cent; for institution B, 2.33 per cent; and for institution C, 3.54 per cent.

8.5 CREDIT DEFAULT SWAP

We now examine the pricing of a simple credit default swap. Consider a one-year credit default swap referenced to two credits. The basic structure is shown in Figure 8.11. The bank is buying protection from the counterparty on the first of two credits to experience a default. The counterparty has a liability to pay the bank in the event that one of the two reference credits defaults. The counterparty's exposure is to two names or reference

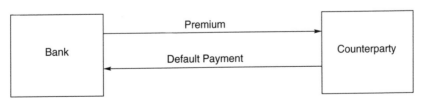

Nominal Principal: $60 million
Default Payment: Nominal Principal × (1 – Recovery Rate)
Recovery Rate: 30 per cent

Figure 8.11   A simple credit default swap

credits and the exposure is limited to the first name to default. After the first default, any exposure to subsequent defaults is terminated. In the event of a default by one of the two names, the counterparty pays a fixed amount to the bank. In return for this default insurance, the bank pays a premium to the counterparty.

To illustrate how to price this form of swap, the data in Table 8.2 will be used. It is assumed that the counterparty belongs to credit class A and the two reference credits belong to credit class C. Conditional on no defaults by the two reference credits at date $t - 1$, payment by the counterparty at date t is described by one of four mutually exclusive and exhaustive events:

1. First credit defaults, second credit does not default.
2. First credit does not default, second credit defaults.
3. First credit defaults, second credit defaults.
4. First credit does not default, second credit does not default.

If one of the first three events occurs, then the counterparty makes a fixed payment, F, to the bank. If event four occurs, then no payment occurs. The probability that first (second) credit does not default at date t, conditional upon no default at date $t - 1$ is $[1 - \mu_c(t - 1)h]$, where $\mu_c(t - 1)$ is the (martingale) conditional probability of default occurring at date t for a firm in credit class C, conditional upon no default at date $t - 1$, and h is the length of the interval between dates $t - 1$ and t. Assuming independence between the event of default for the first credit and the second credit, the conditional probability of event four occurring is $[1 - \mu_c(t - 1)h]^2$.

To summarize the payment by the counterparty to the bank, it will prove useful to define the following indicator function. Conditional upon no default at date $t - 1$,

$$e_1(t) \equiv \begin{cases} 0; \text{ probability } [1 - \mu_c(t - 1)h]^2 \\ 1; \text{ probability } 1 - [1 - \mu_c(t - 1)h]^2 \end{cases} \qquad (17)$$

If $e_1(t) = 0$ at date t, then this implies event four has occurred and no payment is made by the counterparty to the bank; if $e_1(t) = 1$ at date t, then this implies that either event one, two, or three has occurred and the counterparty makes a payment, F, to the bank. If a default has occurred at or prior to date $t - 1$, then define

$$e_1(t) \equiv 0 \qquad (18)$$

implying that the counterparty's exposure is terminated. In this example the credit swap has maturity of one year. For the sake of simplicity, we have divided the one year into two half year intervals. In practice, shorter intervals would be used. The default payment process over the two intervals is shown in Figure 8.12.

Referring to Figure 8.12, if no defaults have occurred at date $t = 1$, then the value of the swap is

$$V(1; \overline{D}) \equiv B(1, 2)[0 \times q_1 + F \times (1 - q_1)] \qquad (19)$$

where $B(1, 2)$ is the value at date $t = 1$ of a default-free zero coupon bond that pays one dollar at date 2. If one or more defaults occur at date $t = 1$, then

$$V(1; D) \equiv F \qquad (20)$$

Today the value of the swap is

$$V(0; \overline{D}) = B(0, 2)q_0[0 \times q_1 + F \times (1 - q_1)] + B(0, 1)(1 - q_0)F \qquad (21)$$

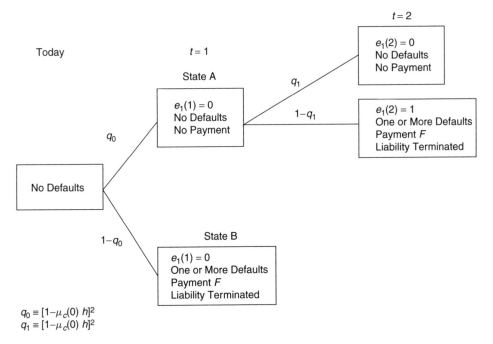

$q_0 \equiv [1-\mu_c(0)\ h]^2$
$q_1 \equiv [1-\mu_c(0)\ h]^2$

Figure 8.12   Default payment process

Table 8.3 Implies martingale conditional probabilities of default

Maturity (Years)	Credit Class A	Credit Class C
0.5	0.01	0.0143
1.0	0.01	0.0147

$q_0 = (1 - 0.0143 \times 0.5)^2 = 0.9858$
$q_1 = (1 - 0.0147 \times 0.5)^2 = 0.9854$

Using the values in Tables 8.2 and 8.3

$$V(0; \overline{D}) = F\{0.9049 \times 0.9858 \times (1 - 0.9854)\} + F\{0.9535 \times (1 - 0.9858)\}$$

$$= F0.0266$$

This analysis implicitly assumes that the counterparty does not default. This assumption can be relaxed using the analysis given in Section 8.4.

8.6 SUMMARY

We take as exogenous the term structure of zero coupon corporate bonds for firms within a given risk class and the term structure of zero coupon default-free bonds. Using standard arguments, we show how to extract the conditional martingale probabilities of default.

Given these probabilities we show how to price options on credit risky bonds, how to price vulnerable options, and how to price credit default swaps.

We have made the simplifying assumption that the martingale default probabilities are independent of the martingale probabilities for the default-free spot interest rates. This assumption can be relaxed and generalized in numerous ways. Jarrow et al. (1994) let the default probabilities for firm ABC be dependent on a current credit rating given by an external agency, such as Standard & Poors, Inc. or Moody's. This creates a Markov chain in credit ratings, in which historical default frequency data can be utilized. Lando (1994) allows the default probability to be dependent on the level of spot interest rates. This last modification appears promising in the area of Eurodollar contracts (see Jarrow et al. (1995)).

8.7 ENDNOTES

1. The existence and uniqueness of these martingale probabilities of default is discussed in Jarrow and Turnbull (1995).
2. For different types of bonds, average recovery rates are given in Moody's Special Report (1992).

8.8 REFERENCES

Black, F., Derman, E. and Toy, W. (1990) "A one factor model of interest rates and its application to Treasury bond options". *Financial Analyst Journal*, **46**, 33–39.

Heath, D., Jarrow, R.A. and Morton, A. (1992) "Bond pricing and the term structure of interest rates: A new methodology for contingent claims valuations". *Econometrica*, **60**, 77–105.

Jarrow, R.A., Lando, D. and Turnbull, S.M. (1993) "A Markov model for the term structure of credit risk spreads". Unpublished manuscript, Cornell University (Forthcoming, *Review of Financial Studies*).

Jarrow, R.A., Lando, D. and Turnbull, S.M. (1995) "The pricing of Eurodollar contracts". Work in progress.

Jarrow, R.A. and Turnbull, S.M. (1995) "Pricing options on derivative securities subject to credit risk". *Journal of Finance*, **50**, 53–85.

Lando, D. (1994) "Three essays on contingent claims pricing". Ph.D. thesis, Cornell University.

9

Credit Enhancement

LEE WAKEMAN*

9.1 INTRODUCTION

At the birth of the derivatives market in the early 1980s, credit officers quite often took the extremely conservative view that a swap was as risky as a loan. As the derivatives market grew, the pendulum swung toward the opposite view that the credit exposure on derivatives products was generally so much smaller than on loans, and often so well balanced by counterparty, that it could safely be ignored for both pricing and credit risk management purposes. More recently, defaults in the derivatives markets (especially that of the Borough of Hammersmith and Fulham) have convinced most observers that, although the potential default loss of a single swap is considerably less than that of a loan, default losses can be substantial for a portfolio of derivatives.

This reassessment of the default risks involved, combined with on-going, significant increases in the number, average size and maturity of derivative deals outstanding, has led credit officers to consider techniques for mitigating these risks. Each of these techniques is already in use in either the banking industry or on the organized exchanges, but generally they have been used separately. This chapter describes a "credit enhancement" approach, currently in use in the derivatives industry, which uses several of these techniques in combination, in a manner which explicitly models their interactions. Although this approach cannot guarantee the abolition of credit risk, its proper implementation can alleviate the fear of long-dated derivatives, reduce both expected and "stressed case" credit losses, and free up credit lines to be used elsewhere.

In order to discuss techniques for mitigating credit risk, we must first discuss the methods used to measure credit risk. This chapter therefore starts, in Section 9.2, with a brief overview of the process used by credit officers to model potential credit losses. The next four sections then discuss how each of the main elements of such a credit model can be modified to incorporate the various techniques which reduce potential credit losses. Several examples of the efficacy of such techniques are provided in Section 9.7, and the

* I am indebted to Tom Francois, Douglas Lucas, Charles Smithson and Stuart Turnbull, who have considerably enhanced my understanding of credit management techniques.

trade-off between the benefits and the costs of implementing these credit enhancement techniques is outlined in Section 9.8. The chapter concludes with a discussion of the changes in the roles of both marketers and credit officers that are engendered by the adoption of this credit enhancement approach.

9.2 THE BASIC CREDIT MODEL

The standard approach to measuring the potential credit loss of a portfolio of derivatives contracts is based on the models of potential credit loss used in the banking industry. These models generally have three main elements: calculating the potential credit exposure profile of a loan until it matures, assessing the probability that the borrower will default whilst the loan is outstanding, and estimating how much of the loan can be recovered if the borrower does default.

A general model of potential credit loss would incorporate the correlations between these three main elements into a joint distribution function. This approach would model, for example, the fact that a slowing economy could increase both credit exposure and default probability, and that the probability of default and the recovery rate can both be affected by a change in a counterparty's credit rating.[1] However, there are serious data deficiencies involved in estimating this multivariate probability distribution of potential losses. Most models implemented in the banking and derivatives industries therefore concentrate their firepower on analysing these three main elements independently.

Given these three elements, credit enhancement techniques can be simply viewed as efforts to reduce both credit exposures and default probabilities and to increase recovery rates.

9.3 CREDIT EXPOSURE MODIFIERS

Before detailing the techniques used to reduce the credit exposure to a counterparty, we need to discuss the alternative techniques currently used in the derivatives industry for measuring counterparty credit exposure.

9.3.1 Modelling Credit Exposure

Although the concepts of default probabilities and recovery rates translate reasonably well from the banking industry to the derivatives industry, the concept of credit exposure does not. Why not? Because the paradigm underlying credit exposure in the banking industry is inappropriate for the derivatives industry.

The credit exposure for a given loan is normally stable over time, varying only slightly around the amount of the loan, and is always significantly positive. Another loan or line of credit to the same counterparty can only add to the exposure. In these circumstances, using the sum of the projected loan balances to estimate a potential credit exposure profile is both simple and relatively accurate. By contrast, derivatives transactions generally have exposures which are a small proportion of the notional amount, may be negative as well as positive, and can be quite unstable over time.

For example, consider a USD 250 million notional ten-year interest rate swap in which we receive a fixed rate of 7.1 per cent and pay the semi-annual London Interbank Offering Rate (Libor), and assume that the Libor term structure of interest rates is rising from its

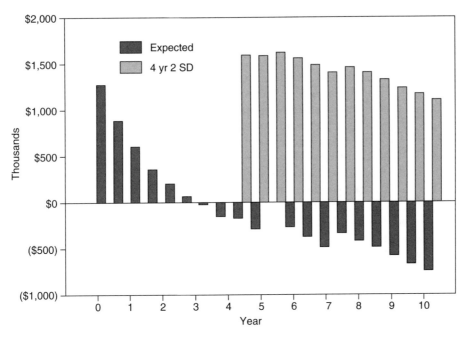

Figure 9.1   Receive fixed net cash flows: expected and four-year 2 SD

current 6.0 per cent. The 20 semi-annual expected cash flows associated with this swap
are set out in Figure 9.1. If this swap is initiated at the current market rate, it would
first be marked-to-market at zero and would therefore have no current credit exposure.
After we receive the first payment of approximately USD 1.3 million in six months' time,
the expected present value of the remaining cash flows becomes negative, and the swap
therefore has negative credit exposure. Only if interest rates fall does the swap become an
asset and create credit exposure to the counterparty. To illustrate this point, assume that
the Libor curve falls two standard deviations per year for the next four years. We would
then expect to receive the 12 semi-annual cash flows which start in year 4 in Figure 9.1,
creating a credit exposure exceeding USD 10 million at year 4.

Currently, the most widely used approach to measuring counterparty credit risk in the
derivatives industry is the Bank for International Settlements (BIS) model, which is used
to assess the capital required to be held by OECD banks against their derivative portfolios.
Credit exposure in this model is calculated as the sum of a deal's mark-to-market and
its potential exposure — a measure of how much the deal's value can change over its
remaining life.

For simplicity, potential exposure is calculated in the BIS model as a percentage of the
deal's notional principal outstanding, ranging from 0 per cent to 15 per cent, depending
on the type of deal and its remaining maturity. Unfortunately, the gain in simplicity
is more than offset by the loss in accuracy. Take, for example, a long-dated fixed rate
currency swap — in which the counterparties agree to exchange, at maturity, principal
amounts which reflect the current exchange rate. Unless the forward exchange rate equals
the current exchange rate, there will be a considerable one-way expected exposure at
maturity (approximately equal to the swap's notional amount times the difference between

the swap's fixed rate times the swap's maturity), depending on which currency is expected to strengthen over the life of the deal. Yet the BIS model assigns exactly the same potential exposure, regardless of whether the counterparty is paying the strengthening currency or the weakening currency.

For a counterparty with several deals outstanding, the BIS model now applies a netting factor, based on the netting effect of current exposures, to the sum of the deals' potential exposures. But netted potential exposures can vary considerably from netted current exposures, and it is therefore relatively easy for the BIS model to greatly overstate the potential exposure to such a counterparty.

Given the inability of the BIS model to reflect the nuances of all but the simplest of derivatives portfolios, most dealers have turned to estimating the distribution of potential exposures directly. The general approach taken is quite simple: identify the risk variables affecting the value of a derivatives portfolio, model the distribution of these variables and then map from this distribution to a distribution of values for the portfolio.

Because a counterparty's credit exposure profile is a function of the potential mark-to-market values of the deals currently outstanding with that counterparty, it depends in large part on exactly the same variables that impact the market risk of a derivatives portfolio: interest rate, equity and commodity yield and volatility curves, foreign exchange rates, and the correlations between these variables.

If there are only a few relevant risk variables, negligible correlations, and the value of the deals are computed from the underlying risk variables using simple, monotonic formulae, scenario analysis is sufficient to model the potential exposure. Take, for example, a portfolio of swaps, caps and floors executed in one currency. The "stressed case" potential exposure (defined for this example as the 95 per cent 2 tail confidence interval) at any future time, t, can be modelled by first valuing the deals in the counterparty's portfolio with an "upward shift" forward interest rate curve in which each expected forward rate from t onwards is increased by 2 times the volatility appropriate for that maturity. If netting is appropriate, the deals' values are summed to create the portfolio's value at time t under this scenario. If netting is inappropriate, all negative deal values are first set to zero, and then the deals' values are summed. The process is then repeated with a similarly constructed "downward shift" curve. The higher of these two portfolio values is then taken as the potential exposure of the portfolio at time t. Repeating this procedure over the remaining life of the portfolio of derivatives creates a potential exposure profile for a counterparty. This scenario analysis is remarkably simple to implement, is generally adequate for most single currency derivative portfolios and can be adapted to portfolios containing derivatives denominated in two currencies which are correlated.

This stressed case approach becomes increasingly inaccurate whenever the assumption of a monotonic link between risk variables and deal value becomes tenuous. For example, if a portfolio consists of range forward notes, the stressed case exposure will not occur on either of the upward or downward interest rate shift paths, but on some "interior" interest rate path. This particular problem can be successfully addressed by using the same binomial or trinomial lattice framework that prices such "exotics" to model credit exposure,[2] but even lattice pricing becomes increasingly burdensome when correlated variables are involved.

As the number of relevant risk variables increases, the importance of modelling the correlation between those variables increases, and the simplified approaches discussed above give way to a Monte Carlo simulation approach. This approach first models the joint distribution of movements in the term structures of interest rates, foreign exchange rates and equity indices. The value of the portfolio is then calculated at every time point in each simulation. Finally, the stressed case criteria are applied to the simulated distribution of portfolio values for each time point to create the potential exposure profile.[3]

Given that a potential exposure profile has been created for a counterparty, we now turn to the techniques that can be used to reduce this profile — collateralization and recouponing.

9.3.2 Collateral Arrangements

In order to trade on a futures exchange, an investor has to put up initial margin. The amount required is an estimate of what the investor would lose if there were a serious adverse move in the underlying price the next day. In addition, on days when the investor loses money, the margin account has to be "topped up" by the payment of variation margin (which is returned on days when the investor gains). This concept of the marking-to-market of a position on a regular basis, together with the related posting and return of collateral, has been adapted to the derivatives markets, albeit with several small changes.

The first change is that, for derivatives trades, dealers rarely require posting of initial margin if the deal's value is close to zero, and normally agree to require the posting of variation margin only if the mark-to-market exceeds a predetermined exposure limit. Agreeing on the appropriate exposure limits for two counterparties can involve some interesting discussions, especially when their assessments of a counterparty's creditworthiness differ. One solution to this problem is for the counterparties to agree on exposure limits which are a function of published credit ratings. They might, for example, agree to post margin if current exposure exceeds USD 20 million for an AAA counterparty, USD 15 million for an AA+ counterparty, etc.

The second change is that, rather than marking-to-market the position on a daily basis, the counterparties can agree on a longer period, such as a month or a quarter, between remarkings. The trade-off is that, although the operational costs are reduced by lengthening the remarking period, the probability of exceeding the exposure ceiling at the next remarking increases. This probability is explicitly recognized by many derivatives dealers, who set the counterparty's exposure ceiling equal to the contracted ceiling plus an amount reflecting how much that counterparty's portfolio could move between remarkings.

The third change is that, although an individual investor is normally required to post cash as margin, counterparties to exposure ceiling agreements often agree to post securities as collateral, with the amount posted increasing with increasing market and credit risk. For example, an agreement may specify a "haircut" of 100 per cent for cash, 101 per cent for short-term governments, 103 per cent for medium-term governments and 108 per cent for longer-term governments and shorter-term, AA or higher rated corporate debt.

The impact of this exposure limitation technique can be quite powerful. For example, consider a USD 100 million ten year interest rate swap in which we receive the floating rate. If, after one year, the yield curve drops 100 basis points (b.p.) we expect to receive an additional USD 1 million a year for nine years, creating an additional credit exposure of approximately USD 7 million. If interest rates drop a further 100 b.p. in the next year, the annuity rises to USD 2 million a year for eight years, creating a credit exposure of approximately USD 12 million. If yields continue to drop, the annuity continues to rise, but, at some point, the decrease in the remaining life outweighs this annuity effect,

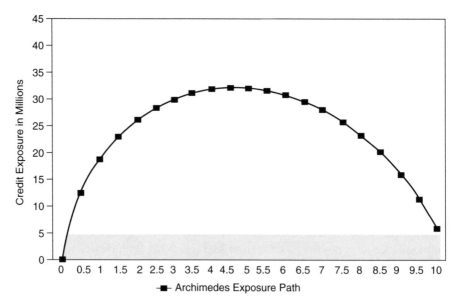

Figure 9.2   USD 100 million ten-year interest rate swap

and the credit exposure begins to drop. This 2 standard deviation potential exposure, or "Archimedes",[4] profile is illustrated in Figure 9.2, which shows the stressed case exposure for an uncollateralized deal reaching USD 30 million in year 4. Now assume that the counterparty agrees to post collateral if, at the end of any day, the mark-to-market exceeds USD 5 million. Then, although the new Archimedes exposure path rises to USD 5 million in the first year, it remains constant at USD 5 million thereafter, and therefore reduces the maximum potential exposure to the counterparty by a factor of 6.

Although collateral arrangements are used in short-dated interest rate swaps only for counterparties with poor credit ratings, they are increasingly used, even by counterparties with high credit ratings, for longer-dated interest rate swaps, commodity swaps (with their higher volatilities) and currency swaps which have an exchange of principal at maturity.

9.3.3 Recouponing

An alternative to providing collateral is to recoupon. The main similarity between the two methods is that, after a remarking, cash is exchanged. The main difference is that the deal's interest and/or exchange rates are reset at that time so that the value of the deal is either brought within an agreed range, or more commonly, reset to zero. Although this approach can cause some liquidity problems (in that it may require the sale of securities at short notice to provide the cash required), it is gaining popularity, especially in jurisdictions where there is uncertainty as to the rights afforded holders of collateral in bankruptcy (the motto for recouponing could be "Better to have a small, uncollateralized exposure than a large, collateralized one") and among counterparties which have restrictions on pledging assets. Given the certainty that cash will be exchanged at each remarking under this system, the remarking periods chosen are usually longer, and it is common for them to be set quarterly.

9.3.4 Netting

Although netting is generally not considered as a specific credit enhancement technique, it can be a very powerful tool for reducing potential exposure. Its impact on current exposure is illustrated by the survey of US intermediaries active in the derivatives market published in *Swaps Monitor* on 18 May 1992. The gross mark-to-market on the USD 1920 billion in notional principal booked by these intermediaries was USD 64 billion. Netting reduced this value to USD 27 billion — a 58 per cent reduction.

The impact on a counterparty's potential exposure profile can be even more dramatic. Consider first a counterparty that is paying floating on a USD 100 million, ten-year interest rate swap. As illustrated in Figure 9.2, its potential exposure profile rises to more than USD 30 million in year 4. Now assume that the same counterparty pays fixed on another USD 100 million for a similar maturity. Its Archimedes profile will collapse to almost zero. Why? As noted in Section 9.3.2, a 100 b.p. one-year drop in the yield curve will increase the credit exposure of the first swap by approximately USD 7 million. But that same 100 b.p. one-year drop in the yield curve will decrease the credit exposure of the second swap by an offsetting USD 7 million. More reasonably, assume that the counterparty pays fixed on a USD 100 million, seven-year swap. Then, although the two swaps have considerably different maturities, the portfolio's Archimedes exposure at year 1 will still be significantly reduced, since the credit exposure of the swap with six years remaining decreases by approximately USD 5 million. This offset will decrease over time as the second swap runs off, but, as can be seen in Figure 9.3, the portfolio's potential exposure will decrease for every year until the maturity of the shorter swap.

In general, the larger the number of deals outstanding with a given counterparty, the closer their maturities, and the more evenly balanced the portfolio between receiving and paying in each currency, the larger the reduction in potential exposure to that counterparty created by netting.

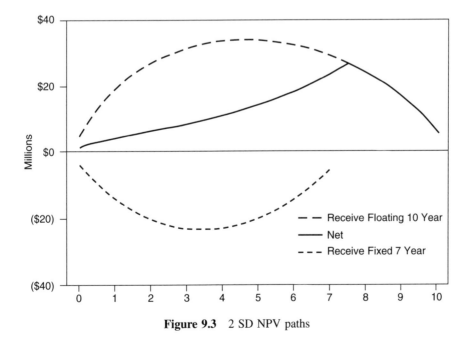

Figure 9.3   2 SD NPV paths

As discussed at the beginning of Section 9.3, the BIS exposure model does a rather simplistic job of modelling netting, and usually underestimates its impact on potential exposure significantly. Both scenario and simulation analysis can analyse the impact of netting on a counterparty's potential exposure profile quite accurately, and therefore are preferred to the BIS model by sophisticated derivatives credit officers.

9.4 DEFAULT MODIFIERS

In order to calculate the distribution of credit losses that would be suffered if a counterparty defaulted, the probability that the counterparty will default before the outstanding deals mature must be assessed.

Traditionally, in the absence of any external data on defaults, bank credit officers have had to rely on internal credit models to assess the probability that a counterparty will become insolvent whilst a deal is outstanding. Recently, both Moody's and Standard & Poor's have published studies of the history of bond defaults in the US in the last 25 years, and have classified their results by the senior, unsecured bond rating of the defaulting company.[5] For example, although no corporation has defaulted whilst it had a triple A rating, there are cases of defaulted companies which at some earlier point in their histories had a triple A rating, and these cases have been used to calculate cumulative probabilities of default over time for a company whose senior unsecured bond is currently rated triple A. The cumulative default rates for companies with Moody's ratings over the period 1970–1994 are graphed in Figure 9.4,[6] and they show that, apart from a slight

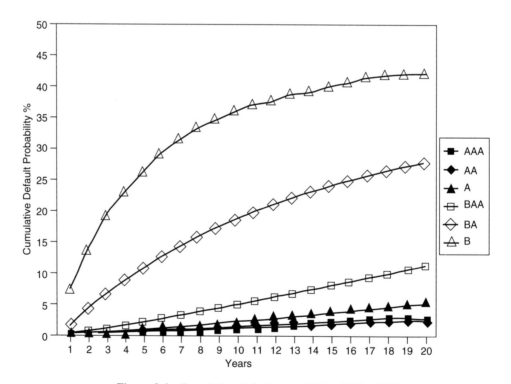

Figure 9.4 Cumulative default probabilities 1970–1994

inconsistency beyond 15 years (where the samples are quite small) for the AAA and AA rating groups, there is a strong correlation between Moody's ratings and default rates.

If you believe that the results drawn from the samples used by Moody's and Standard & Poor's are valid for your counterparties, then you can use these studies to estimate the probability that a rated counterparty will default in each of the next T years. First, break down the published cumulative probabilities (which are presented by year) into the appropriate marginal annual probabilities using:

$$\text{prob(default)}_t = \sum \text{prob(default)}_{t+1} - \sum \text{prob(default)}_t$$

Then, modify (using artistic licence) the relatively coarse rating class groupings used in these studies to reflect the finer gradations currently used by the rating agencies. An example of this approach is set out in Table 9.1.[7] Several points are of interest in this table. First, the first year default probabilities approximately double each time you move from AAA (0.009 per cent) to AA2 (0.022 per cent) to A2 (0.06 per cent) to BAA2 (0.16 per cent), but then tentuple as you move out of the investment grades to BA2 (1.79 per cent). Second, the marginal annual default probabilities for the higher ratings classes increase with time, rising, for example, for an AA1 rated company from 0.015 per cent in year 1 to 0.15 per cent in year 10. The explanation for this phenomena is quite simple. It is remarkably rare for a highly-rated company to be downgraded more than once in a given year, and therefore the 0.015 per cent reflects the probability of defaulting in the next year given that the company starts the year with an AA1 rating. On the other hand, the 0.15 per cent reflects the probability that a company will default in the next year, given that it had an AA1 rating nine years ago. There is a tendency for the ratings of highly-rated companies to drift downwards, rather than upwards, over time, so that the average rating of a group of companies initially rated AA1 will erode over the nine years to approximately a BAA2 rating, with a consequently higher marginal probability of defaulting in year 10. Conversely, the marginal default probabilities decrease with time for the lowest rating classes, falling, for example, for a B2 rated company from 8.31 per cent

Table 9.1   Marginal default probabilities

Years	1	2	3	4	5	6	7	8	9	10
AAA	0.01%	0.02%	0.03%	0.03%	0.07%	0.07%	0.11%	0.12%	0.14%	0.15%
AA1	0.02%	0.05%	0.07%	0.08%	0.10%	0.10%	0.11%	0.12%	0.13%	0.15%
AA2	0.02%	0.08%	0.12%	0.12%	0.14%	0.12%	0.11%	0.11%	0.13%	0.15%
AA3	0.03%	0.08%	0.13%	0.14%	0.17%	0.15%	0.12%	0.16%	0.19%	0.22%
A1	0.05%	0.09%	0.14%	0.16%	0.21%	0.18%	0.14%	0.20%	0.24%	0.28%
A2	0.06%	0.09%	0.15%	0.18%	0.24%	0.20%	0.15%	0.24%	0.30%	0.35%
A3	0.09%	0.18%	0.23%	0.30%	0.33%	0.30%	0.31%	0.38%	0.42%	0.42%
BAA1	0.13%	0.27%	0.31%	0.43%	0.42%	0.40%	0.47%	0.51%	0.53%	0.50%
BAA2	0.16%	0.36%	0.40%	0.55%	0.51%	0.49%	0.63%	0.64%	0.65%	0.57%
BAA3	0.70%	1.11%	1.11%	1.19%	1.15%	0.98%	0.93%	0.91%	0.90%	0.84%
BA1	1.25%	1.85%	1.82%	1.84%	1.80%	1.47%	1.22%	1.17%	1.15%	1.11%
BA2	1.79%	2.59%	2.53%	2.48%	2.44%	1.96%	1.51%	1.44%	1.40%	1.39%
BA3	3.96%	3.90%	3.53%	3.12%	2.71%	2.60%	1.81%	1.75%	1.50%	1.47%
B1	6.14%	5.21%	4.54%	3.75%	2.98%	3.25%	2.11%	2.05%	1.60%	1.55%
B2	8.31%	6.52%	5.54%	4.39%	3.24%	3.90%	2.41%	2.35%	1.70%	1.64%
B3	15.08%	6.82%	5.21%	3.80%	3.14%	4.43%	2.58%	1.69%	2.54%	2.01%

Source: Extrapolated from Moody's data.

in year 1 to 1.64 per cent in year 10. This suggests that a "survivorship bias" is present in that, although some companies initially rated B2 will struggle and default, others will flourish, be upgraded, and default thereafter with significantly lower frequency, so that the average rating of a group of companies initially rated B2 will improve over the nine years to approximately a BA2 rating.

These data are not complete — they cover only US corporations and a relatively short time period — but they are the best currently publicly available, and can serve as the basis for a credit rating system which can then be "tweaked" by the credit department. Several companies use a ratings based system, but modify a company's rating to reflect additional information. For example, it is common practice to raise the ratings of US municipalities (even after the Orange County debacle) to reflect a perceived lower rate of defaults.

Several academics have published studies showing that discriminant analysis, using up to three years of prior profit and loss statements and balance sheets, can successfully predict bankruptcy several years beforehand.[8] For example, Altman's study scans a series of financial ratios, such as the current and the debt/equity ratios, for matched samples of 50 bankrupt and 50 non-bankrupt firms, in order to find ratios that differentiate between companies that subsequently default and companies that do not. Discriminant analysis, by first choosing appropriate weights for each of these ratios and then summing these weighted ratios, constructs a formula which maximizes the difference between the formula values for the bankrupt sample and the non-bankrupt sample. Altman's model is generally regarded as being successful in that, using this formula, it correctly predicts 80 per cent of both the bankrupt and the non-bankrupt firms in a "hold out" sample of 50 bankrupt and 50 non-bankrupt firms.

But such a model could present problems when applied to companies that are well rated. Given the numbers presented in Table 9.1, a random sample of 10 000 companies rated A2 or above would include no more than ten that would default in the next two years. If the discriminant model's prediction accuracy was maintained, it would correctly predict eight of these bankruptcies, but would also incorrectly predict that 1998 of the healthy companies would default. Unless the costs of rejecting 1998 healthy counterparties are less than the costs of accepting ten counterparties that will default, using this model will provide results which are inferior to those provided by a model which extends credit to any counterparty rated A2 or above.[9] This implies that the ratings of more widely known and generally higher-rated credits (where the rating agencies have access to the best quality credit information available) should generally be accepted and that credit evaluation resources should be concentrated on lower-rated companies (especially if there is only one rating) and on companies that lack ratings.

An alternative approach to estimating default probabilities is to "unwind" them from the prices of a company's securities trading in the markets. Several examples of this approach are presented in a recent paper by Jarrow and Turnbull,[10] presented as Chapter 8 in this book. In this paper they describe a model which, in its simplest form, adds a series of independent coin tosses, to model default, at each node in a binomial or trinomial term structure model. Although this approach is conceptually rigorous, it requires as many instruments as there are nodes. It is therefore difficult to implement for a particular company because of the relative paucity of traded instruments issued by that company. This deficiency should not, however, limit the use of the model to estimate default probabilities for a ratings class.

9.4.1 Credit Guarantees

The simplest way to reduce the probability of default for a counterparty is to have a guarantee from another company. To the extent that these companies are entirely independent, such a guarantee can reduce the probability of default dramatically. For example, the cumulative default probability over five years for a company rated BA by Moody's is 11.1 per cent. If its performance is guaranteed by an entirely independent A rated company, with a cumulative default probability of 0.6 per cent, the joint probability of default is reduced to 0.07 per cent — less than the 0.1 per cent probability for an AAA company. There are cases where the independence assumption appears justified — an American energy company posting collateral in the form of lines of credit from a European bank, for instance — but generally guarantees are provided by parent organizations to subsidiaries. In these cases, it is usual to replace the subsidiary's rating with the parent's (higher) rating in the calculation of potential losses.

9.4.2 Credit Triggers

ISDA Master Agreements for longer-term derivative transactions now frequently contain a ratings downgrade clause, which permits a party to terminate all outstanding transactions (on the basis of "market quotation" and "full two way" payments) if the credit rating of the other party falls below a specified level. Typically these termination rights are referenced to the lowest of the ratings assigned by the rating agencies, and failure to maintain a rating gives rise to a termination event.

Ratings downgrade triggers can significantly reduce counterparty default probabilities. For example, if all outstanding transactions can be immediately terminated when a counterparty's rating falls below A3, the exposure to that counterparty becomes a function of the probability that the counterparty will default whilst rated A3 or higher. Default probabilities should therefore be adjusted downward in situations where such downgrade triggers exist.

To quantify this reduction, single stage Markov chain analysis can be used to create a rating transition matrix. One-year transition matrices have been published by both Moody's and Standard & Poor's,[11] and can be used for the purpose of calculating the impact on default probabilities of alternative downgrade triggers.[12] Table 9.2 illustrates this analysis. The rows beginning with a single rating (AAA, AA, etc.) report the cumulative default probabilities over time for that rating which are implied by Standard & Poor's one-year transition matrix. The rows beginning with a double rating (AAA/A, AAA/B, etc.) report the cumulative default probabilities assuming that, at the end of any year in which a counterparty finally "drifted" from the first rating to the second rating, all transactions are terminated and the drift process stops. The "% Reduction" rows show that the cumulative default probabilities are reduced substantially, with the percentage reduction being greater the higher the ratings trigger.[13]

For example, an AA rated counterparty has a cumulative default probability over ten years of 0.81 per cent. Given that the counterparty agrees to terminate the derivatives contract if, at the end of any year, its rating falls to BB or below, the cumulative default probability falls 72 per cent to 0.23 per cent. As the table shows, a higher downgrade trigger reduces the default probability even further. But there is a trade-off, since the higher downgrade trigger also increases the probability that a deal that would have otherwise run to its planned maturity will be prematurely terminated.

Two further caveats, in addition to those raised concerning the quality of the data underlying the rating agencies' analyses, should be mentioned. The first is that it is quite

Table 9.2 Impact of ratings downgrade triggers on cumulative default probabilitites

Years	1	3	5	10	15	20	25
AAA	0.00%	0.01%	0.04%	0.27%	0.73%	1.37%	2.13%
AAA/A	0.00%	0.00%	0.00%	0.00%	0.00%	0.00%	0.00%
% Reduction	0.00%	100.00%	100.00%	100.00%	100.00%	100.00%	100.00%
AAA/BBB	0.00%	0.00%	0.01%	0.04%	0.09%	0.14%	0.20%
% Reduction	0.00%	100.00%	82.94%	85.47%	87.70%	89.47%	90.78%
AAA/BB	0.00%	0.00%	0.01%	0.07%	0.17%	0.30%	0.43%
% Reduction	0.00%	100.00%	74.27%	75.03%	76.64%	78.35%	79.83%
AA	0.00%	0.06%	0.19%	0.81%	1.73%	2.77%	3.80%
AA/A	0.00%	0.00%	0.00%	0.00%	0.00%	0.00%	0.00%
% Reduction	0.00%	100.00%	100.00%	100.00%	100.00%	100.00%	100.00%
AA/BBB	0.00%	0.01%	0.04%	0.12%	0.21%	0.27%	0.32%
% Reduction	0.00%	76.47%	79.23%	84.67%	88.06%	90.15%	91.48%
AA/BB	0.00%	0.02%	0.06%	0.23%	0.42%	0.60%	0.75%
% Reduction	0.00%	66.27%	67.68%	72.16%	75.84%	78.43%	80.21%
A	0.07%	0.31%	0.69%	2.07%	3.65%	5.08%	6.27%
A/BBB	0.07%	0.19%	0.28%	0.43%	0.51%	0.56%	0.60%
% Reduction	0.00%	40.43%	60.21%	79.44%	85.94%	88.89%	90.46%
A/BB	0.07%	0.22%	0.38%	0.73%	0.99%	1.18%	1.32%
% Reduction	0.00%	28.27%	45.18%	64.86%	72.76%	76.69%	78.90%
BBB	0.25%	1.09%	2.21%	5.19%	7.55%	9.16%	10.24%
BBB/BB	0.25%	0.63%	0.90%	1.30%	1.51%	1.63%	1.71%
% Reduction	0.00%	41.98%	59.23%	74.92%	80.00%	82.20%	83.31%

Rating to right of slash is rating at which termination can be elected.
Methodology: Markov analysis applied to S&P's average one-year transition matrix from May 1995 study.

difficult to reproduce a rating agency's table of cumulative defaults by rating at different maturities using that agency's one-year transition matrix. The second, related caveat is that the assumption underlying single stage Markov chain analysis—that the probabilities of a company transitioning from its current state (rating) in the next period are independent of its state in the previous period—appears to be suspect. Recent research[14] at Moody's suggests that, for corporations with a BAA or lower rating, the probability of a downgrade in the next year is a function not only of the current rating, but also of last year's rating. For example, the marginal probability of being downgraded in the next year from BAA is 6.3 per cent (including a 0.1 per cent probability of defaulting). But the probability of being downgraded from BAA, given that the company was upgraded to BAA this year, is only 3.2 per cent, and the probability of being downgraded from BAA, given that the company was downgraded to BAA this year, is 11.5 per cent. Given this evidence, it may be necessary to expand the analysis to two stage Markov chain analysis if downgrade triggers are implemented at the lower ratings.

9.5 MUTUAL TERMINATION OPTIONS

One credit enhancement technique which combines potential exposure reduction with default probability reduction is the mutual termination option, or time put. This clause

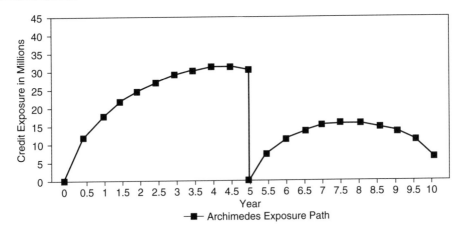

Figure 9.5 Termination option at 5 years

permits either counterparty to terminate unconditionally each of the derivative transactions covered by the ISDA Master Agreement on one or more dates before its maturity, using a pre-agreed formula to value the transaction at these times. For example, an agreement could permit termination of each transaction on its fifth anniversary and on each subsequent deal anniversary until maturity. This early termination option reduces the possibility that a company will have to stand by helplessly as a counterparty's credit standing deteriorates, and can possibly lessen the maximum potential exposure to a counterparty.

Apart from the problems of agreeing on the "pre-agreed formula" (which often includes an "Olympic" system of throwing away the high and the low "mid-market" quotes and averaging the remaining quotes), and worrying about the costs of finding a new, acceptable, and accepting counterparty, mutual termination options create conceptual problems for reserving unless there is a clear policy regarding exercise. If, for example, we state that we will always exercise this option at the first exercise date, the potential exposure profile is truncated at that date. If, however, we agree to recoupon the swap to zero at the mutual termination option date, the potential exposure profile begins again at zero on the option date. Figure 9.5 illustrates the impact on the potential exposure profile of a ten-year interest rate swap of an option either to terminate, or to continue with recouponing to zero, after five years.

More reasonably, the decision to terminate on an option date will be a function of the counterparty's rating and the effect of the deal's mark-to-market on the counterparty's current exposure at that time, and is best handled by simulation.

9.6 RECOVERY RATES

The third element in estimating the potential losses in a derivatives transaction is the recovery rate. It has been common practice in the past to ignore this element of potential loss, which implicitly assumes that there will be no recovery of sums owed in the event of a default by the counterparty. Whilst this may be a reasonable assumption for terminating triple A structured derivatives product companies, it appears rather inappropriate for ongoing companies which can wait the estimated two years to recover some of the moneys owed.

Both of the rating agencies have studied recovery rates, from differing viewpoints, and have come to similar conclusions regarding the factors affecting the distribution of recovery rates. The main conclusion, as stated in the S&P study of recovery rates for defaulted bonds, published in the 20 July 1992 edition of *Creditweek* is that "loss experience, on average, varied according to the obligation's rank". Derivative claims generally rank equally with senior unsecured debt obligations in insolvency, and therefore can be treated as such for the purposes of modelling recovery rates. Although the least conservative measure of the losses on the 78 senior unsecured debt issues, "L1" (which measures the loss of principal only), implied a mean recovery rate of 79 per cent, the most conservative measure, "L3" (which also includes the foregone compounded interest), implied a mean recovery rate of 45 per cent.

The Moody's study of corporate bond defaults (referenced in Section 9.4) produces remarkably similar results. Using the market prices of these bonds one month after default, it finds that "the 246 senior unsecured bonds sold for $44.62 on average". But this study raises some interesting points. The first is that Chart 9 in the study, "Distribution of Defaulted Senior Unsecured Bond Prices", shows a distribution that is not concentrated around the mean, but is quite uniformly distributed between 0 per cent and 90 per cent. The second, and probably related point, is that the study's Table 1, "Recoveries for Senior Unsecured Bonds by Rating before Default", shows that the recovery rate is not uniform across rating classes. For defaulted bonds that were rated CAA one year before default, the recovery rate was less than USD 31, while the recovery rate for bonds rated BAA one year before default was over USD 71. These points suggest, specifically, that modelling of downgrade triggers should link the recovery rate to the downgrade trigger and, generally, that joint simulations of interest rates, exchange rates and default probabilities should keep track of prior rating for simulations that end in default.

9.7 EXAMPLES

To illustrate the usefulness of these techniques, first assume that we operate with two limits:

- the "Archimedes" limit, which constrains a counterparty's Archimedes exposure (the maximum recovery-adjusted potential exposure to that counterparty), and is set as a function of the counterparty's rating, and
- the "PASCAL" limit, which constrains a counterparty's PASCAL exposure (the Probability Adjusted Stressed Case Anticipated Loss, which equals the stressed case replacement cost at time k times the marginal default probability at time k times $(1 - \text{recovery rate})$, present valued and summed over k), and is set at a single level for all counterparties,

and then assume that we hold two reserves:

- the Credit reserve, calculated as the expected replacement cost at time k times the marginal default probability at time k times $(1 - \text{recovery rate})$, present valued and summed over k, for each counterparty, and
- the Equity reserve, calculated as a return on the equity that needs to be held to cover the difference at each point in time between the credit reserve and the PASCAL exposure to a counterparty.

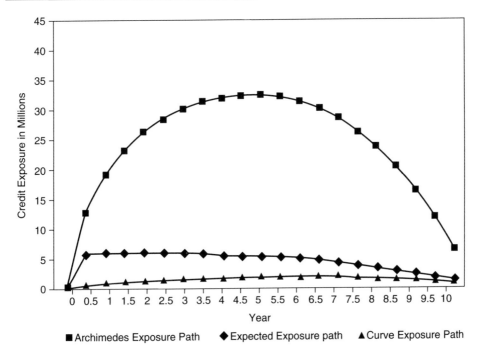

Figure 9.6 USD 100 million ten-year interest rate swap: TMG receives floating with five year recouponing to zero MTM

Then consider a USD 100 million interest rate swap in which the counterparty pays fixed for ten years. Figure 9.6 illustrates the three exposure paths usually considered:

- the curve exposure path, which calculates the value of the swap assuming that the forward rates remain at their expected level,
- the expected exposure path, used to calculate the credit reserve, and
- the Archimedes (stressed case) exposure path, used to calculate the PASCAL exposure.

Table 9.3 illustrates the impact on the limits and on the reserves of using exposure limits ("Credit Caps"), mutual termination options ("Time Puts"), and downgrade triggers ("Termination below A3") both separately and jointly, assuming a constant recovery rate of 40 per cent. Let us first examine the results for an AA2 rated counterparty.

The credit cap affects the credit reserve only slightly, since it is set at USD 5 million, which is only slightly exceeded by the expected exposure, but reduces the equity reserve considerably, since, by limiting the stressed case potential exposure (Archimedes drops from USD 19 430 to USD 3000), it lowers the PASCAL exposure from USD 121 200 to USD 23 600.

The time put at five years does not reduce the Archimedes exposure, since it does not occur before the point of maximum potential exposure, but since, for this example, we assume that the time put is exercised, the exposure paths all drop to zero at year 5, and therefore the credit reserve is significantly reduced, from USD 20 800 to USD 13 000. Although the credit reserve and the PASCAL exposure have been reduced by similar

Table 9.3   USD 100 million ten-year swap — TMG receives floating (numbers in thousands of dollars)

AA2 Rating				
Enhancement	Archimedes	Pascal	Default Reserve	Equity Reserve
None	19 430.1	121.2	20.8	4.5
Credit Cap*	3000.0	23.6	19.5	0.4
Time Put**	19 430.1	72.3	13.0	6.1
Both	3000.0	12.7	11.8	0.3
With Termination				
Below A3	19 430.1	56.9	10.7	2.0
With the Works	3000.0	7.3	7.1	0.1

A2 Rating				
Enhancement	Archimedes	Pascal	Default Reserve	Equity Reserve
None	19 430.1	202.5	33.9	7.6
Credit Cap*	3000.0	40.9	32.1	0.8
Time Put**	19 430.1	108.2	19.5	9.7
Both	3000.0	18.9	17.7	0.4
With Termination				
Below A3	19 430.1	70.4	13.7	2.3
With the Works	3000.0	9.3	8.9	0.1

*USD 5 million.
**At five years.

amounts, the credit reserve now runs off proportionally faster, and therefore the equity reserve has to increase slightly, from USD 4500 to USD 6100, although the total reserves still decrease, from USD 25 300 to USD 19 100.

The downgrade trigger set below A3 only affects default probabilities in this example, so the Archimedes exposure remains unchanged. But the reduction in default probabilities does reduce the PASCAL exposure and both the credit and equity reserves, which now total USD 12 700.

The combination of the three credit enhancement techniques ("With the Works") is quite powerful. The Archimedes and PASCAL exposures are reduced by 85 per cent and 90 per cent respectively, and the total reserves are reduced by 70 per cent to USD 7200.

Now consider a counterparty with an A2 rating. As one would expect, the impact on the Archimedes exposure is the same as for the AA2 counterparty. The credit cap and the time put still reduce the PASCAL exposure and the total reserves, but a more major role is now played by the downgrade trigger, which is now considerably closer to the initial rating, and therefore exerts a proportionally stronger downward influence on the probability of default. The combination of the three credit enhancement techniques reduces the PASCAL exposure by 95 per cent and the total reserves by almost 80 per cent, from USD 41 500 to USD 9000.

9.8 IMPLEMENTATION

The examples described in Section 9.7 illustrate that these credit enhancement techniques can significantly reduce the potential credit losses from derivatives transactions. There are, however, two considerations which must be addressed when considering the use of such techniques: are they legally enforceable, and do their potential benefits outweigh the costs of implementing them?

9.8.1 Legal Considerations

The techniques that raise the fewest legal warning flags are time puts, recouponings and credit downgrade triggers. Time puts are generally considered to be a normal part of contract law, and few questions, if any, have been raised concerning the recapture of sums paid when a time put is exercised if one of the counterparties subsequently goes into receivership. The treatment of recouponing payments is less well researched, but the conclusions are similar. Downgrade triggers are conceptually akin to the covenants included in traditional commercial lending, such as minimum net worth and coverage ratios, and are generally accorded the same legal standing.

The situation becomes more cloudy when one turns to collateral arrangements. For simplicity, assume that a counterparty who has posted collateral to us becomes insolvent. In an "ideal" situation, this insolvency would not affect the enforceability of the collateral arrangement. The receiver would recognize that we had a first priority perfected security interest in the collateral, and would not attempt either to avoid or to stay the liquidation of that collateral for our benefit. Assuming that the "haircut" was sufficient to cover the liquidation costs (an inaccurate assumption in the case of the 1994 insolvency of Askin Capital Management's portfolio of principal-only strips and inverse floaters, which were liquidated at prices substantially below their "fair economic value"[15]), our claim would be fully enforced, and in a timely manner.

The jurisdiction that comes closest to this ideal state is the US, where amendments made to the Bankruptcy Code in 1990 place swaps counterparties in a better position than ordinary secured creditors in that swap participants now enjoy an exemption from the automatic stay and preferential transfer clauses of the Code. The situation in other jurisdictions is less clear, and both Moody's and Standard & Poor's have raised concerns about the enforceability of collateral agreements in insolvency.[16]

These rating agencies have also raised questions about the ability of netting agreements to withstand the desire of a trustee or debtor in possession to "cherry pick" among contracts, and at present consider close-out netting provisions to be unambiguously enforceable only in Australia, the UK and the US. At this point, rather than continuing to pontificate on matters which are well beyond my competence, it seems appropriate simply to state that it is important, when contemplating the use of these credit enhancement techniques, to obtain legal advice on the laws governing insolvency in the counterparty's country of incorporation.

9.8.2 Economic Considerations

The resources required to monitor time put and downgrade trigger clauses are minimal, and therefore the decision to use them should be quite simple. But concerns have been raised about the potential adverse impacts that could be triggered by the exercise of such clauses. For example, if a 17-year aircraft lease-related swap is terminated after five years, there is no assurance that a substitute 12-year swap will be available in the market at a price close to the "mid-market" valuation agreed to by the counterparties. The main worry, however, is that the downgrading of a counterparty could create a "domino" effect on a counterparty's liquidity, and thereby cause that company to become insolvent. To illustrate this point, consider the case of a company, with derivatives trades outstanding to several counterparties, whose downgrade triggers a termination event. Those counterparties owed money will generally exercise their option to terminate their deals and demand payment. Unless the downgrade trigger requires the termination of all transactions (which is not customary), it is not clear that counterparties who owe money will exercise the option to terminate (although a counterparty may decide to make the payment in order to ensure that it is not owed money by the downgraded company at a later date). In these circumstances, there could be a serious cash drain on the downgraded company. (This drain is exacerbated if the downgrade trigger clause applies on a deal-by-deal basis, rather than on a master agreement basis, since a counterparty can then "cherry pick" and only terminate those trades which are "in-the-money".)

Although these concerns are recognized in the derivatives industry, the current consensus is that the potential benefits of time put and downgrade trigger clauses outweigh their potential costs.

Considerably more resources are required to implement recouponing and collateral arrangements. Not only must the value of the portfolio of deals outstanding with a given counterparty be calculated and compared with the appropriate limit on a frequent basis, but transfer costs may be involved. For recouponing agreements requiring the transfer of cash on an infrequent basis (for example, quarterly), these costs are generally small (although concerns have been raised about selling relatively illiquid assets to provide the cash). But collateral arrangements which involve both frequent (for example, daily) valuations and tight exposure limits can engender a considerable number of transfers of collateral. Furthermore, the required form of the posted collateral can create costs. For example, if a collateral agreement requires the posting of government securities as collateral, interest will be forgone by any counterparty that usually invests in securities which offer a higher return.

There is therefore an interesting trade-off between the costs and the potential benefits in a collateral agreement. Increasing the valuation frequency and decreasing the exposure limit raise the monitoring and potential transfer costs involved, but at the same time decrease the potential exposure at the next valuation date. Complete models for this decision have yet to be published, but will, in addition to the parameters discussed above, incorporate both the volatility of the value of the portfolio of derivative transactions outstanding with a given counterparty and the probability of default of that counterparty.

9.9 CONCLUSION

Traditionally, after the initial enquiries to the credit officers from the marketers as to whether or not the proposed counterparty is acceptable have been satisfactorily answered, there has been little interaction over time between them. Only if a counterparty's credit exposure exceeds limits and necessitates remedial action will marketers consider the dynamic nature of the credit, and thus capital, costs imposed on the company.

This wilful ignoring of the inter-relationships between the credit exposure profiles of deals in a counterparty's portfolio, and the widespread tendency to think in terms of a deal's current, static exposure rather than in terms of the impact of dynamic markets on a portfolio's potential credit exposure, can lead to significant errors in estimating the potential losses involved with derivatives transactions. Take, for example, a simple "off-market" asset swap involving a four-year bond issued with a detachable equity warrant and a low coupon of approximately 2 per cent. In order to compensate us for receiving the under-market fixed rate of 2 per cent and paying the current on-market floating rate, we would expect to receive a terminal payment of approximately 15 per cent of the deal's notional amount. Although the initial mark-to-market, and therefore the current exposure, of the swap will be approximately zero, the present value of the deal will undoubtedly increase over the next four years to approximately 15 per cent of its notional amount. Paying fixed and receiving fixed on such an asset swap should therefore have very different associated credit reserves, yet the BIS methodology currently used by many participants in the derivatives industry assigns the same 0.5 per cent of the notional amount as potential exposure to both sides of this swap.

But despite the potential for errors, the move toward an integrated, dynamically based approach to credit risk management has been quite slow.

One deterrent to the acceptance of such a credit system is the accounting policy most widely used in the derivatives industry until quite recently — the practice of creating profit and loss statements by marking derivatives deals to mid-market without taking specific reserves against future credit, hedging and operating costs. Specifically, this policy books to the profit and loss statement the present value of the future gross revenues whilst ignoring the future costs involved in running the derivatives portfolio until the deals mature. This policy is justified by assuming that the annual interest "earned" as the future revenues come a year closer will be sufficient to cover that year's costs. This assumption is becoming increasingly dubious for "vanilla" derivatives as gross profit margins are being squeezed whilst operating costs are steadily rising.

9.9.1 Incentives for Marketers

The most obvious impact of this accounting policy is on the marketing area, where it provided the incentive to assume that the difference between the transaction price and the mark-to-mid-market value is the "profit", rather than only the present value of the future revenues, of a deal. This non-recognition of expected future costs led to the obvious mind-set among marketers that, once a deal was done, it could be forgotten. This mentality could normally prevail for extended periods, until some deals, whose overlooked future risks were at least commensurate with the large "profits" booked, defaulted or, more usually, generated current credit exposures which were sufficiently high to preclude further trades with those counterparties.

Furthermore, only the first deal with a new counterparty will definitely invoke potential credit losses. Thereafter a prospective deal can incur either positive or negative expected future credit costs, depending on whether or not it reduces an existing counterparty's credit exposure. If an accounting policy ignores a prospective derivative deal's impact on a counterparty's potential credit loss, it increases the probability that the net profit contribution of that deal will be seriously misestimated.

More recently, as noted in the 1994 ISDA survey, many derivatives dealers are changing their accounting policies to hold explicit reserves against potential credit losses, and some are incorporating credit enhancement techniques into their credit management processes. If a system incorporating these points is put in place, the incentives provided to the marketers change quite dramatically, in that they are encouraged to work with the credit officers to correctly price the potential credit losses (positive or negative) involved in a prospective deal and motivated to work with the counterparty to minimize total credit management costs over time.

9.9.2 Role of the Credit Officer

The adoption of a credit system incorporating explicit credit reserves and modelling the impact of credit enhancement techniques will lead to a difference in the way that the credit management function is performed. Credit officers will shift their focus from the static calculation of current exposures to the dynamic nature of counterparty credit over time, mapping a counterparty's expected and "stressed case" exposures over the remaining life of the deals currently outstanding and incorporating explicit default probability and recovery rate assumptions into their credit management model to create that counterparty's potential credit loss profile over time.

Given this modelling capability, they will then not just passively respond to marketers' credit enquiries, but will keep them informed not only of a counterparty's current exposure, but also of future "orange" and "red" light potential credit loss situations. This modelling capability will further allow the credit officers both to guide the marketers to seek new deals, or negotiate credit enhancements to current deals that will reduce these potential losses, and to provide estimates of the reduction of reserves that can be attained thereby.

If the marketers and credit officers do interact in this manner, the growth of credit reserves can be seriously constrained, increasing both profits and bonuses.

9.10 ENDNOTES/REFERENCES

1. For a discussion of such a general model, see Mark, R.M. (1995) "Integrated Risk Management", Chapter 8, pp. 109–139, in *Derivative Credit Risk: Advances in Measurement and Management*. Risk Publications.
2. To implement this approach, first iterate backwards through the lattice, setting any negative value at a node to zero. Then, for any time *t*, collate the node values and their attendant probabilities into a probability mass function and identify the appropriate stressed case exposure value in the right tail.
3. For a more extended treatment of these points, see Rowe, D.M. (1995) "Aggregating Credit Exposures: The Primary Risk Source Approach", Chapter 1, pp. 13–31, and Lawrence, D. (1995) "Aggregating Credit Exposures: The Simulation Approach", Chapter 2, pp. 23–31, in *Derivative Credit Risk: Advances in Measurement and Management*. Risk Publications.
4. When we were implementing our first derivatives credit system at Chemical Bank in 1985, our concerned credit officers noted that, whilst our system calculated probability adjusted losses, the bank's credit committee would be far more interested in "how much of a bath we could take" if a counterparty did default. Hence "Archimedes".
5. Brand, L., Kitto T.C. and Bahar, R. (1994) "Corporate Default, Rating Transition Study Results", Standard & Poor's, and Carty, L.V., Lieberman D. and Fons, J.S. (1995) "Corporate Bond Defaults and Default Rates, 1970–1994", Moody's Investors Service.
6. This graph was prepared from data presented in Carty, L.V., Lieberman D. and Fons, J.S. (1995) *op. cit.*
7. This table was prepared by D. Lucas when he was the credit officer for TMG Financial Products. A more complete description is set out in Lucas, D. (1995) "Measuring Credit

Risk and Required Capital", Chapter 7, pp. 99–108, in *Derivative Credit Risk: Advances in Measurement and Management*. Risk Publications.

8. See, for example, Altman, E.I. et al. (1993) "Credit Scoring Applications", in *Application of Classification Techniques in Business, Banking and Finance*. JAI Press.

9. Using Bayes' theorem, we can write the probability of bankruptcy, given bankruptcy is forecast, as:

$$p(B|FB) = \frac{p(FB|B)p(B)}{p(FB|B)p(B) + p(FB|B')p(B')}$$

If the model predicts with 80 per cent accuracy, then $p(FB|B) = 0.8$ and $p(FB|B') = 0.2$. For a matched sample, $p(B) = p(B') = 0.5$. Then

$$p(B|FB) = (0.8)(0.5)/\{(0.8)(0.5) + (0.2)(0.5)\} = 0.8$$

i.e. 80 per cent of the companies forecast to go bankrupt will go bankrupt. For the A2 sample, $p(B) = 0.001$ and $p(B') = 0.999$. Then

$$p(B|FB) = (0.8)(0.001)/\{(0.8)(0.001) + (0.2)(0.999)\} = 0.004$$

i.e. 99.6 per cent of the companies forecast to go bankrupt will remain solvent.

10. Jarrow, R.A. and Turnbull, S.M. (1995) "Pricing derivatives on financial securities subject to credit risk". *Journal of Finance*, **50**, no. 1, 53–85.

11. Moody's matrix is published in Carty, L.V. and Fons, J.S. (1993) "Measuring Changes in Corporate Credit Quality", Moody's Investors Service. Standard & Poor's matrix is published in its 1995 "Special Report on Corporate Defaults".

12. These matrices include a "Withdrawn Rating" column. It is common practice to redistribute a probability in this column proportionally over the other columns, but since rating withdrawals are associated with debt retirements and exchange offers and not with defaults, it would be better either to reapportion this probability over the non-default probabilities or explicitly to model "Withdrawn Rating" as a non-defaulting "sink" state.

13. The one-year default probabilities show no decrease because of the one-year "transition step" used in the transition matrix. Experiments with one-month transition matrices produce, as one would expect, greater reductions in default probabilities.

14. Fons, J.S. and Carty, L.V. (1995) "Probability of Default: A Derivatives Perspective", Chapter 3, pp. 36–47, in *Derivative Credit Risk: Advances in Measurement and Management*. Risk Publications.

15. See Smithson, C.W. *Managing Financial Risk: 1995 Yearbook*. Chase Manhattan Bank, pp. 15–16.

16. Bahar, R. and Gold, M. "Structuring Derivative Product Companies: Risks and Safeguards", Chapter 11, pp. 173–188, and Curry, D.A., Gluck, J.A., May W.L. and Backman, A.C. "Evaluating Derivative Product Companies", Chapter 12, pp. 189–203, in *Derivative Credit Risk: Advances in Measurement and Management*. Risk Publications.

Index

Absolute risk, 48–53
AGARCH, 135, 138
Analytics systems, 219–20
Antithetic sampling, 183–6
Approximate distribution methods, 87–8
Arbitrage
    Pricing Theory, 44
    relationships, 75–6
ARCH models, 56, 58, 100, 134, 136, 144
Archimedes
    exposure path, 267, 269
    limit, 268
    profile, 260
Asset–Normal method, 81–2, 118
Assets to capital multiple, 3
Asymmetric GARCH, *See* AGARCH

Backpropagation, 161
Backtesting, 15–16
Bank for International Settlements (BIS), 2,
    257, 258
    current exposure method, 114
    market risk proposal 1995, 7–17
    methodology, 18–19, 273
    potential exposure add-ons, 114
Bank of Tokyo–Mitsubishi, 9
Bankers Trust, 6
Bankruptcy Code, 271
Basis risk, 24
Basle Accord, 2–7
Basle Committee 63, 65, 101
Basle Group, 213
BEKK model, 146–8
Benchmark role, 48–50
Biased estimates for non-linear payoffs, 192
Black–Scholes, 92, 112, 132, 148–50, 155
Box–Muller transform, 177
Brownian bridge, 187, 188
Brownian motion, 76
Building block approach, 101–3

CAD2, 213
Capital adequacy, 62–3, 65
Capital allocation, 152–4
Capital Asset Pricing Model (CAPM), 10,
    41–2, 151
Capital at Risk (CaR), 61 (*see also* Value at
    Risk)
Capital charge, 19–24, 27–34
Capital
    for options according to simplified approach,
        22
    ratio, 14–15
    requirements, 14–15
Carry costs, 165
Cholesky factorization, 179, 180, 187
CIR model (Cox et al.), 175, 181, 191
Cointegration, 162–5
Collateral arrangements, 259–60
Commodities risk, 24–5
Commodity Futures Exchange Commission
    (CFTC), 63
Commodity price risk, 10–11
Components GARCH, 135, 139–40
Conditional distribution, 134
Continuous-time asset price, 175
Control variates, 192–6
Convexity risk, 11, 22
Cooke ratio, 3–4, 6–7
Core capital, 7
Corporate bond defaults, 262, 268
Correlation, 125–71
    credit defaults, 108–12
    EWMA, 129–32
    forecast evaluation, 159
    GARCH, 145–8
    historic, 127–9
    implied, 150–1
Counterparty
    credit exposure profile, 256
    credit rating, 256
    default, 115, 262–4

Counterparty (*continued*)
  events modelling, 107–8
  risk, 12, 237
Covariance, 41, 125–6, 145–8, 151–4,
  203
Credit
  default modifiers, 262–6
  default process, 240–2
  default swap, 251–3
  enhancement techniques, 255–75
  equivalent for off-balance-sheet
    exposures, 4–6
  events, 106, 108, 111–13
  exposure, 113, 256–62
  guarantees, 265
  migrations, 116–17
  officers, 274
  portfolio sensitivities, 114–18
  reserve, 268
  risk, 8, 12, 103–7, 210–12, 237–54
  risky bonds, 237–47
  risky debt, 239–45
  spread, 106–7
  state, 116
  Suisse Group, 104
  triggers, 265
  VaR, 103–21, 211
  worthiness, 237
CreditMetrics®, 12, 103, 112, 115,
  119–20, 229
CreditPortfolio View, 112, 115, 117, 120
CreditRisk+, 120
Credit risk capital 8, 210
Cross currency portfolio, 27
Cumulative
  default probability, 120, 262, 265–6
  distribution function, 178
Currency risk, 40, 55–7
Current exposure (CE), 113
Cyclical default behaviour, 111–12

Daily Earnings at Risk (DEaR), 61
Data warehousing, 218–21
Debt crisis, 16
Default
  correlations modelling, 108–11
  free interest rates, 238–9
  modifiers, 262–6
  no-default approach, 120
  prediction model, 110
  rate correlations, 108–11
  risk, 12
Delta 9, 72, 155
  hedge, 73
  risk, 11, 70
  gamma approximation, 98
  gamma methods, 71, 72, 85–92

Normal methods, 70, 82–4
  plus approach, 22–3
Derivatives Policy Group (DPG), 63
Diagonal risk factors, 90 (*see also* Principal
  Components Analysis)
Discretization, 182, 183
Diversification principle, 40–1, 53–7
Dollars at Risk (DaR), 61
Downside risk, 161–2, 228
Duration method, 18

Efficient
  frontier, 153
  portfolios, 235
EGARCH, 135, 139
Empirical simulation methods, 92–4
Equally weighted moving averages, 128–9,
  159 (*see also* 'Historic' volatility and
  correlation)
Equity risk, 10, 23
Equity reserve, 268
ERM crisis, 16, 76
Error correction model, 164
Euler scheme, 182
European Economic Union, 53
European Monetary System (EMS), 55
Exact distribution approach, 86–7
Exchange rate
  correlations, 55–7
  risk, 10
Expected losses, 104, 105
Expected maximum loss, 162
Expected potential exposure, 114
Exponential GARCH, 138–9 (*see also*
  EGARCH)
Exponentially weighted moving averages
  (EWMA), 129–32, 151, 152, 153, 159
Extreme value methods, 100–1

Factor ARCH and GARCH, 135, 140
Factor models, 42–4, 45–6, 151–2
Factor push stress testing method, 90, 96–9,
  114
Fat-tails, 74–5, 100, 126, 159–61 (*see also*
  Leptokurtosis)
Faure sequences, 197, 199
Financial risk, definition, 226
Finite difference approximations, 155
Finite dimensional state variable models, 175
Foreign exchange risk, 23–4
Forward rate agreement (FRA), 71
Forwards, 5–6
Futures, 164

Gamma, 9, 70–2, 155
  capital charge, 22
  risk, 11, 22, 101–2

GARCH models, 48, 75, 126, 133–48, 151,
    154–5, 159, 161, 174–5, 180, 182
  correlations, 146
  estimating methods and results, 141–4
  survey, 136–40
  techniques, 85
  types, 135
  volatility term structure forecasts, 140–1
    (*see also* Specific models)
Garman–Kohlhagen formula, 92–3
General market risk, 18–22, 30, 31, 32, 33
Genetic learning algorithms, 107
Geometric Brownian Motion (GBM), 95, 96,
    112, 154–5, 174
Ghost features, 128, 129
Gold price risk, 23–4
Granger causality, 164
Greeks, 9, 11, 72
Group of Ten (G-10) countries, 3
Group of Thirty (G-30) countries, 63

Halton sequence, 197–202
Hedging, 154–5 (*see also* Delta, Gamma,
    Greeks, Vega)
Heteroscedasticity, 133 (*see also* GARCH)
Historic volatility and correlation forecasting
    methods, 127–9, 158–9
Historical simulation, 85, 92, 204
Horizontal disallowance, 19, 22

IGARCH model, 130, 135
Illiquid exposures 116–17
Inefficient portfolios, 235
Information Technology (IT) projects, 209, 211
In-sample predictive tests, 159
Integrated GARCH, 138 (*see also* IGARCH)
Integrated risk systems, 158
Integration
  error, 201
  versus segmentation, 53–5
Interest rate
  curve, 29 (*see also* Yield curve)
  risk, 10, 17, 24
  default-free, 238–9
Internal models approach, 8–17, 25–34
Inverse transform method, 177–8
ISDA
  LIBA Joint Models Task Force, 16
  Master Agreement, 265, 267

Joint stationarity, 126

KMV modelling approach, 119–20
Koksma–Hlawka inequality, 201
Kuhn–Tucker multiplier, 89

Latin hypercube sampling (LHS), 186, 188,
    189
Leptokurtosis, 74

Leverage effect, 149
Linear congruential generators, 177
Liquid positions, 114–16
Loan equivalent exposure, 113, 114
Local
  currency correlations, 55
  risk measures, 72–3
Lognormal diffusion model, 189
London Interbank Offering Rate (LIBOR), 18,
    256
Long-term risk models, 52–3
Loss distributions for illiquid assets, 117
Low discrepancy sequences, 179, 201–2

Macroeconomic
  cycles, 110
  factor models, 47
Marginal
  default probability, 263
  probability, 117
Mark-to-future™, 225–36
Mark-to-market, 226–8
Market
  crashes, 16
  model, 12
  rate distribution assumptions, 73–6
  risk, 7–22, 24, 30–1, 33, 106–7, 151–8,
    210–11
  VaR, 69, 103 (*see also* Value at Risk)
Market risk capital, 8, 14, 210
Markov chain analysis, 265, 266
Markovian process, 182
Markowitz, H., 40, 57–8
Martingale probability of default, 240–5
Matching underlying, 189–92
Maturity
  bands, 18, 19
  ladder, 18, 25
Maximal risk-adjusted return, 235
Maximum potential exposure, 114
Mean reverting
  spread, 165
  stochastic volatility, 175
Mean–variance analysis, 152
Megavendors, 223
Middleware, 218, 219
Migration approach, 114–17
Minimal regret frontier, 235
Model risks, 73, 76–8
Moment matching, 190
Money at Risk (MaR), 61 (*see also* Value
    at Risk)
Monte Carlo techniques, 11, 85, 92, 94–6,
    114, 154–5, 157, 201, 204–5, 258 (*see also*
    Quasi Monte Carlo (QMC) methods)
Moving averages, 127–32
Multiple controls, 195

Multiple factor models, 44–8, 108–9
Multivariate GARCH, 145–7
Mutual termination options, 266–7

Net replacement ratio (NPR), 6
Netting, 6, 261–2
Neural networks, 107
Nikkei 225 index, 49
Non-linear risks, 11
Non-linear sensitivity, 221
Normal distribution, 76, 160, 178, 179
Numerical search methods, 99–100

OECD, 18, 257
Off-balance-sheet exposures, 4
Oil shocks, 16
Operational risk measures, 104
Optimization techniques, 88–90
Option pricing, 23, 154–5
  credit risky bonds, 245–7
  simulation techniques, 173–207
Options, 5–6, 22–3, 266–7
Ordinary least squares (OLS) regression, 151
Ornstein–Uhlenbeck process, 175
Orthogonal GARCH, 147–8
Out-of-sample predictive tests, 159
Outright price risk, 24
Over-the-counter (OTC)
  derivatives, 106
  markets, 63, 150
  option, 248
  trading, 12

PASCAL exposure, 268–70
Path generation, 176–96
Payoff, 182–3, 185, 194, 240
Percentile-preserving property, 178
Performance measurement, 63–4
Piecewise linear approximation, 91
Portfolio
  effect, 28
  diversification, 53–7
  selection (risk–return), 40
  sensitivity, 69–73, 112
Position sensitivities, 70
Potential credit loss, 255
Potential exposure, 113–14
Pre-commitment approach, 25–7
Price sensitivity, 221
Pricing
  credit risky bonds, 237–45
  options on credit risky bonds, 245–7
  vulnerable derivatives, 248–51
Probability distribution, 69
Procter and Gamble, 4, 6
Pseudo-analytic methods, 11
Put-call parity, 190

Quasi Monte Carlo (QMC) methods, 196–202
Quasi-random sequences, 96, 199–201

Random
  number generation, 176–7
  variables, 177–9
  vectors, 179–80
Recouponing, 260
Recovery rate, 240, 267–8
Regret, 162, 228, 231–3
Regulator's building block approach, 101–3
Regulatory framework for capital adequacy,
  1–37
Relative risk, 48–53
Residual risk, 41–4, 51 (see also Specific risk)
Retail loss rate portfolios, 117–18
Return On Risk-Adjusted Capital (RORAC), 62
Risk
  Adjusted Performance Measures
    (RAPMs), 64, 67, 68, 214
  Adjusted Return on Capital (RAROC), 64,
    66, 68
  adjusted valuation, 233–4
  analysis, 39, 40–4
  aversion weight, 233
  based capital ratio. See Cooke ratio
  capital, 3–4, 67, 69
  characterization, 40
  comparability, 62, 67
  control, 39, 212–15, 216–21
  diversification, 53
  factor coverage, 70
  forecasting, 48
  management, 9, 67, 173–207, 212–13,
    215–16, 220–1
  measurement, 39–60, 210, 225–36
  position weights, 70
  return trade-off, 234–5
  segmentation, 43
  technology, 209–23
RiskMetrics™, 70, 82, 92, 101, 130–2, 160,
  203, 220, 225, 227, 228
RiskWatch™, 158
Risky debt, 239–40
Root mean square errors, 159
R-squared, 110, 111

Scenario matrix approach, 23
Scenarios, 227–9
Securities Exchange Commission (SEC), 63
Segmentation versus integration, 53–5
Semi-variance, 161
Sharpe, W., 41–4
Short-term
  currency risk forecasting, 57
  hedging, 161
  risk models, 53

Simulation techniques, 173–207
    underlying stochastic processes, 173–6 (see
        also) Monte Carlo techniques
Single factor models, 42–4
Smiles, 149, 174
Smoothing constant, 129
Sobol
    points, 199
    sequence, 197
Software vendors, 221–2
Specific risk, 12–13, 17–18 (see also Residual
    risk)
Spot prices, 164
Square root of time rule, 132
Stable relationships, 75
Standard
    deviation, 228
    models, key parameters, 76
    normal distribution, 178, 179
Standardized approach to Risk Capital, 8, 12,
    17–34
Star discrepancy, 201
Statistical models, 47–8
Stochastic
    differential equation (SDE), 174, 181, 182
    volatility models, 174
Stratified sampling, 178, 179, 186–9
Stress-testing, 16–17, 219
Supplementary capital, 7
Swaps, 5–6
    credit default, 251–3
Swiss Bank Corporation, 104
Syndicated Eurodollar loans, 16
Systematic risk, 41–4

Taylor series expansion, 23, 72, 92, 98
Time series properties of credit events,
    111–12
Time spread risk, 24
Time-varying parameters, 151, 152
Tracking error, 50–2
Trading-off risk and return, 234–5
Transactions, 218–21

Unconditional distribution, 134
Underlying matching, 189–92
Upside, 232, 233

Value at Risk (VaR), 11, 49, 58, 61–124,
    155–8, 220, 227–30
    as operational risk limits, 64
    as risk-controlling tool, 67
    credit portfolio measurement, 66
    criticisms of calculation methods, 77
    estimation, 202–5
    exposure, 33
    impact, 62–4
    incentives, 68
    interpretation, 63
    models, 8, 10, 16, 27, 126, 152, 155–8,
        213–14, 227
    preconditions for impact, 65–8
    systems, 68
    trading example, 66
    uses, 62–8 (see also Credit VaR; Market
        VaR)
van der Corput sequence, 196, 197
Vanilla GARCH, 136–8, 144
Variances, 125, 126, 151, 152
Vasicek model, 175, 181, 190
Vega, 9, 72
Vega risk, 102
Vertical disallowance, 19, 22, 101–2
Volatility, 125–71, 228
    cones, 150
    definition, 125
    EWMA, 129–32
    forecast evaluation, 158–9
    GARCH, 140–1
    historic 127–9
    implied, 148–51
    risk, 11 (see also Vega)
    smile, 149
Vulnerable derivatives, 248–51

Weiner process, 154, 174, 176, 180, 181, 183,
    186, 187
Worst-case market scenario, 102

Yield curve, 20, 157

Zero-coupon curves, 29
Zeta models, 107
Z-score, 107